HOUSEHOLDS

ALSO BY WILLIAM JAMES BOOTH

Interpreting the World:
Kant's Philosophy of History and Politics (1986)

HOUSEHOLDS

ON THE
MORAL ARCHITECTURE
OF THE ECONOMY

WILLIAM JAMES BOOTH

CORNELL UNIVERSITY PRESS

ITHACA AND LONDON

First published 1993 by Cornell University Press.

International Standard Book Number 0-8014-2791-6 (cloth)
Library of Congress Catalog Card Number 92-25141
Printed in the United States of America
Librarians: Library of Congress cataloging information
appears on the last page of the book.

♾ The paper in this book meets the minimum requirements of
the American National Standard for Information Sciences—
Permanence of Paper for Printed Library Materials, ANSI Z39.48-1984.

FOR JANE

CONTENTS

ACKNOWLEDGMENTS

Many debts are incurred in a project such as this, and one of the sources of pleasure in its coming to fruition is the opportunity to acknowledge them. Colleagues at Duke University, and especially those involved in an informal faculty seminar on politics and economics, Robert Bates, Joseph Grieco, Herbert Kitschelt, Peter Lange, George Tsebelis, and Michael Gillespie, offered valuable criticisms of parts of this book while they were still in their formative stages. Martha Nussbaum has encouraged me in this project, and she pointed me to a relationship between Aristotle and Marx on the one side and Kant on the other which contributed much to the analysis set out in Parts One and Three. At McGill University, Hudson Meadwell and Patrick James have been very generous interlocutors. It is also a pleasure to thank the students of a McGill undergraduate seminar on philosophy, politics, and economics who put questions to me for which I had no adequate answer and, in so doing, forced me to rethink my arguments. And finally, I could not have wished for a better editor and adviser than Roger Haydon.

I am also grateful to the National Humanities Center for the year-long fellowship (1987–88) that provided me the time to begin the research toward this book, and at least as important, for the company of its other Fellows with whom to discuss that research as well as their own. The Social Sciences and Humanities Research Council kindly gave me funds to purchase a computer that enormously facilitated the revising of this manuscript.

As this book was going to press, I learned of the death of Judith Shklar.

It was my good fortune to have been a student of hers at Harvard in the late 1970s, to have read Kant and Rousseau with her and to have been in her marvelous seminar on Enlightenment political thought. I hope that her influence is apparent in the pages that follow.

This book is dedicated to my wife, Jane Easdown, with whom I started building a household just as my writing about it was coming to an end.

Elements of Part Three are adapted from these works: "Gone Fishing: Making Sense of Marx's Concept of Communism," *Political Theory* 17 (1989): 205–22 (© 1989. Reprinted by permission of Sage Publications, Inc.). "Rejoinder to Tierney," *Political Theory* 19 (1991): 656–61; "Economies of Time: On the Idea of Time in Marx's Political Economy," *Political Theory* 19 (1991): 7–27 (both © 1991 by Sage Publications, Inc. Reprinted by permission of Sage Publications, Inc.). "The New Household Economy," *American Political Science Review* 85 (1991): 59–75 (© 1991 by the American Political Science Association. Reprinted by permission). "Households, Markets, and Firms," in George McCarthy, ed., *Marx and Aristotle: Nineteenth-Century German Social Theory and Classical Antiquity* (Rowman & Littlefield, 1992. Reprinted by permission of the publisher).

W. J. B.

HOUSEHOLDS

But even so, what I want and all my days I pine for is to go back to my house and see my day of homecoming. And if some god batters me far out on the wine-blue water, I will endure it, keeping a stubborn spirit inside me, for already I have suffered much and done much hard work on the waves and in the fighting. So let this adventure follow.

Odysseus, speaking to Kalypso. Homer, *Odyssey* 5.215–25

INTRODUCTION

A story has been passed down to us from some two millennia ago of a conversation between a wealthy Athenian estate owner, Ischomachos, and his nameless bride. Bringing her into his *oikos,* Ischomachos says to his new wife, "This household is what is common [*koinos*] to us." And truly it is common, this most familiar of human institutions—so much a part of our shared memory that even when we read Homer's ancient story of homes and homecoming, Penelope's household in Ithaka awakens in us an immediate recognition, suggesting that her home is not really that distant. This book too is about households, about communities of persons, the purposes that bind individuals in their association and that define the moral location of their community in a wider array of goods. It is, to speak more exactly, about the household viewed under one of its aspects: that mesh of human relations, the norms and ends of their conduct, within which they conduct their necessary interchange with nature. In a word, it is taken up with the household as a way of thinking about the moral economy. "In a word": but the word tells us much, still more by its origins, and I do not only mean that we learn of the history of the word/idea. For the *oikos,* the root of our economy, was an association of persons united in a certain purpose and mutuality (*philia*), in relations of domination and subordination, and striving for those ends that composed the good life as they understood it. It is precisely this way of thinking about the economy, as a household, a "vast *oikos,*" though of many types, which I want to draw upon here. My motivation for this reappropriation of the *oikos* is not antiquarian or philological, and it is certainly not a romantic longing for a recovery of that world. No reader, I imagine, of classical Greek texts on the household could derive from them any particularly sentimental notions about that institution. And indeed these pages ought to serve, in part, as a warning against the seductiveness of the idea of the household. The value, then, of this ancient reflection on the economy and the reason for going back to it are to be found rather in its ability, at the most general level, to call our attention to those human relations that permeate the economy (narrowly understood) and in which the latter is in turn implicated, whether as means to an end or as itself the governing end. The directness of the Greeks in this regard, a simplicity that makes them immortal teachers, is their great virtue. For they invite us to remove those very modern blinders that cause us to see the economy as a discrete set of phenomena with theoretically distinct borders, and so invite us to think through the question of its moral location. Lest it be thought that the object of that last remark are those economists who subscribe, in Amartya Sen's phrase, to the engineering approach to their subject matter, allow me to add that it might with equal justice be made about those political philosophers who are cramped in their vision by the very same blinders, who appear to have forgotten Aristotle's statement that the human being is a *zōion oikonomikon:* "man is by nature a pairing creature [*sunduastikon*] even more than he is a political creature inasmuch as the household is an earlier and more necessary institution than the polis" (*Nicomachean Ethics* 1162a16ff.).

The idea of the household is made up of a conceptual tapestry, any strand of which might have provided a valuable theoretical starting point. I have chosen to focus here on its economic dimension, the normative content of the production of human sustenance, and, within that still-too-open a topic, on the problem of freedom and the economy. Thus the position of the economy in the fabric of human relations, its internal moral structure, and its relation to other goods are considered along a single governing line of analysis, that of freedom and the social organization of the human interchange with nature. The importance of this issue requires no demonstration, and even less so given the debate over whether markets are the sole or the principal economic mechanism consistent with freedom, a dispute all the more pressing in light of the collapse of marxist regimes in these waning years of the twentieth century. I thus concentrate in the following pages on one cluster of concepts among the many that compose the idea of the household. That is to say, I focus on the ideas of freedom, the manner of coordinating the economy, and the purposes served by that institution. I could have considered the household from the point of view of its members' motivations and the forms of exchange between them, as a locus of (perhaps incomplete) altruism and of reciprocity in exchange. This type of exchange might then be contrasted with its market counterpart. I could as well have studied the household as a form of community: (said to be) less individualistic, less dominated by the optimizing rationality at work beyond its boundaries, and more affective and unspoken in its bonds than the market. Another possible line of approach would have been to take up these themes and ground them in the idea of gender. Here we would see how power, motivation, and ties between persons are shaped by gender relations within the household, and attempt to read out from there the nature of relations in the enveloping society. Or perhaps, forsaking altogether those arguments that draw a boundary line between the household and the market, we might, with Gary Becker, see in the household a market complete with (shadow) prices, production functions for children, and so on.[1] Most of these issues do enter into the analyses laid out in this book. But because, as Martin Heidegger tells us, every inquiry is guided beforehand by what is sought, and because what I was seeking was the heart of the debate between household and market models and for the consequences of that debate, these concerns remain the quieter voices in the chorus—and tasks for future reflection.

In this book, I look at three households: the ancient *oikos,* the liberal household and economy, and Marx's socialist household economy. I outline in the following pages the arguments of the three parts that deal with each of them. Before doing that, however, I want to remark further on the overarching purpose and structure of the book. First, the ordering of the parts mirrors that of the historical appearance of these grand, antagonistic views of the good economy; and a selective intellectual history is, to be sure, one of my tasks. So likewise is there a history within each of its three parts: there are, for example, discussions of Marx's use of the idea of class in the analysis of premodern societies and of the relationship between Lockean and Rousseauian political economy. But in each of its parts, and in the book as a unity, this history is in the service of a project the overriding purpose of which is to learn from these magnificent antagonists, from their failures as well as their achievements, about how we might think about the moral location of the economy. It is that end which determines the whole of this work and its parts. Second, marxism oc-

---

[1] Gary Becker, *The Economic Approach to Human Behavior* (Chicago: University of Chicago Press, 1976).

cupies a special place in this work, and that focus too requires comment. Its particular visibility has in part been forced upon it, the result of circumstances external to the writing of the book. Rarely does a writer have the good fortune to watch from his study as the world beyond his pen and paper appears to unfold as if in reflection of the words on the sheet of paper before him. Such has been the luck of this author; and fortune it most certainly is, not prescience. For as I sought to think through the arguments of the two most formidable critics of markets, Aristotle and Marx, one of this century's great experiments in nonmarket, relatively advanced economies came to its end. Whatever the fate of the peoples of Eastern Europe and the now defunct Soviet Union as they attempt to remake the political and economic structures of their societies, we can say with virtual certainty that the communist experiment in command-type economies and polities is over. The moral and technical failures of those ventures are now so well known that these experiments have lost their intellectual grip on what followers they still had, as they had long ago lost their hold on our hopes. I say "had long ago lost" here only to call attention to the fact that the crises of marxism are hardly new. We need only call to mind some of the more celebrated names—Victor Serge, Silone, Orwell, Koestler, Spender, and Solzhenitsyn—to see for how long the diagnosis of Soviet society and of its imitators has been with us. The present collapse, dramatic and rapid as it was, simply made evident to the eye what was already known: the sweeping failure of these regimes. What is not clear is the meaning of these developments for marxism, for proponents of nonmarxian socialism, and for the defenders of market society—more generally, for those who wish to situate the economy, in theory or elsewhere, on the broad canvas of human goods.

These massive failures, at all levels, brought on by the attempt to shift the location of the economy away from markets and to subordinate it to the plan pose anew, and perhaps more vividly than before, the challenge before marxian and other socialists: to present a superior and feasible alternative to markets, if that is what they think must be replaced, whole or in part. Less plain, I suspect, but just as important is the recognition that the collapse of communism by no means demonstrates that the day has been won, once and for all, by advocates of the market. This victory is clouded by the fact that the cluster of values which marxism draws upon (though they are by no means its exclusive property) is so deeply held that we should fully expect elements of those values, in some altered form perhaps, to survive. Whether in currents of feminism, in the green movements, or in a combination of these with more traditional redistributive political parties, the rejection of market society (I use the term loosely; nothing like the pure model exists now, if indeed it ever did) will endure, and Marx will continue to provide a part of its critical apparatus.[2]

My concern with marxism is, however, not at all with its political prospects, or for that matter with those of kindred movements. Rather, it is with the Marx on whose theoretical terrain the claims of the *oikos* and the liberal market models contest, a battle that ends with (I argue) a false reconciliation—an attempt as breathtaking in its intellectual grandeur and ambitions as it was disastrous in practice. The struggle I consider in the first two parts reaches its conceptual zenith in his works, and it is for that philosophical reason, rather than because of the shifting fortunes of our times, that Marx is central to this book. He is also central because his arguments, for all of their profound and probably insuperable difficulties, discourage a theoretically facile assumption of the unblemished superiority of the market model. Therefore, in Part Three, I attempt to defend the claim that central elements of Marx's critique of capitalism ought to give us occasion to pause and reflect before pronouncing an encomium for the market. That much can now be said in the silence of the passions, even by those who recognize no political kinship with him. I further maintain that other, and no less central, elements of Marx's project were ill supported, untenable, and ultimately catastrophic in their consequences, once the decision was made to see in practice how well they fit the world, or how well the world might be made to fit them. This latter observation, as plain I think as daylight, ought to disturb the faith of those who imagine that some variety of marxism can be resurrected whole from the present debris. Marx, in short, emerges as a better critic than prophet or artificer of worlds-to-come.

Third, I said that the convergence of events and ideas was, from my perspective, much more *fortuna* than foresight. That is because, as I suggested, this book was conceived not as an inquiry into the political collapse of marxism or into marxism as such. It began in (and remains) an effort to think through changing conceptions of the location of the economy. Allow me to probe somewhat further this language of "location." By location I mean, at a first cut, this: the place of the economy within an overarching set of goods, to some of which the economy is related as means to an end and others of which inform relations within

---

[2] Alain Lipietz discusses the place of marxism in relation to some of the new critical-social movements. See his "Les crises du marxisme: De la théorie sociale au principe d'espérance," in Jacques Bidet and Jacques Texier, eds., *Fin du communisme? Actualité du marxisme?* (Paris: Presses Universitaires de France, 1991).

the economy. In this, as I remarked, I take my bearings from Aristotle and from Marx's observation in *Capital,* vol. 1, that the economy is a relation among persons, which may, under specific historical conditions, assume the appearance of a relation between persons and the things they make and consume. This observation suggests that the economy is embedded in a mesh of moral conceptions, of political/legal and various other social institutions, embedded in some cases to the point of being theoretically indistinct though by no means invisible, and in other cases sufficiently distinct to allow of a separate phenomenology of its own. The language I make use of here, that of location and embeddedness, is adapted from Karl Polanyi, who used the concept behind that last term to make the case that the idea of the economy is, in a certain sense, a product of modern market society and thus not applicable to the theoretical/moral universes of the non- or precapitalist worlds. That argument, and its corollaries, I reject, and so though his language is congenial to the purposes of this study, the concepts with which I frame it are rather to be found in Aristotle and Marx. This line of thought, the idea that the economy is embedded in a moral/political foundation, drives us to reject, on the one side, Hannah Arendt's argument to the effect that the economy has until the modern period remained invisible, in the shadow of the public space—a silent place of oppression and of *animal laborans*—and, on the other side, to dispute the claim of those economists who would banish ethics and politics entirely from their domain.[3] Because the economy is an ensemble of human relations, saturated by their moral and other norms; because, in various ways, it serves their many ends—for those reasons reflection on the moral location of the economy is vital to the understanding both of that institution/activity and of the human condition more generally.

The normative debate over the proper location of the economy was, in the Western tradition, first mapped out by Aristotle in a manner yet to be transcended, and I use his account to set the basic structure of this book. That framework consists essentially of a contrast between what he called the "natural" economy of the household, the *oikos,* and the world of the market. In the comparative valuation of those two economies, Aristotle is concerned not with efficiencies in production but with their relation to the good life, freedom, and community. What his argument yields, then, is a critical assessment of these formations in the light of their impact on

---

[3] See Amartya Sen's call for an ethics-related economics and his rejection of the "self-consciously 'non-ethical' character of modern economics" in Sen, *On Ethics and Economics* (Oxford: Basil Blackwell, 1987), p. 2.

other human goods. The method Aristotle employs in this project plays on the twofold sense of nature in his writings: the natural history, the genealogy, of the economy and the economy according to its realized or perfected nature, the good economy. It is especially in that second aspect of his analysis, the question of the good to be served by the economy, that this book is indebted to Aristotle and so as well to one of his greatest modern students, Karl Marx: not to their answers to that question, but rather to their ways of thinking it through.

Aristotle's idea of the household economy and its partial analogue in the city economy can be read as a statement of the fundamental orientation toward the economy outlined above: as immersed in a nexus of relations among persons, permeated by their moral and political norms, and subject in greater or lesser measure to their purposiveness. Clearly this approach tends to rob the economy of sharply defined boundaries, to situate it in the moral architecture of the *oikos*. In other words, it is one way of directing us toward the study of the economy in its context. But the idea of the household was for Aristotle more than a methodological prescription. It also stood as the natural economy, in the teleological sense, the perfected economy, and as such was contrasted to the market and the life of unlimited acquisition. It is my treatment of those topics that I now sketch.

In Part One, I explore classical (and much more briefly, archaic) Greek reflection on the economy. I do this in the presence of a substantial body of literature which maintains that there was no such systematic reflection on the economy in the ancient world (Karl Polanyi, Hannah Arendt, and, occasionally, Moses I. Finley are important contributors to this school of analysis) or that, if there was, it was of such a primitive character as to be without value (Joseph Schumpeter).[4] Both of these arguments rest on the idea that in ancient Greek (and premarket) theorizing there is an absence of a sharp boundary line demarcating economic phenomena. The reason for this is the persistent conflation of status, politics, and ethics with economic matters. And that results in a failure to so much as venture an independent, law-like account of the economy. What emerges is a political or moral philosophy, perhaps, but no economic theory. I argue the contrary, and in Part One I seek to recover from that tradition its reflection on the economy—the purpose of that exercise being, again, the reinstating of ideas from which we may still expect to profit. This reappropriation

----

[4] Joseph Schumpeter, *History of Economic Analysis*, ed. Elizabeth Brady Schumpeter (Oxford: Oxford University Press, 1954), pp. 53–54.

of ancient economic thought is grounded in precisely the same claim that leads Schumpeter and others to reject its possibility, the claim that the Greeks tended to blur the boundary lines between the moral and political on the one side and the economic on the other. They knew of the economy, in other words, but as a moment of the *oikos,* in its service and informed by its values. And it is just this idea that the economy is fully intelligible only as an ethical domain which is to be counted among the most significant of their contributions.

We thus find Aristotle, with his characteristic theoretical acuity, setting up a conceptual dichotomy that, under different guises, remains with us today. The household is understood as an institution (the principal one) in which the human interchange with nature is conducted, in which that interchange is organized according to what is appropriate for the persons involved and for ends determined within the community of the *oikos.* That is still too skeletal a portrait, however. The existence of the household illuminates the limits of our self-sufficiency in relation to nature, those inherent in our being as *zōion oikonomikon.* The household is the institution in which we labor to provision ourselves in the things necessary for life; but it is also where we seek to emancipate ourselves, as far as we are able, from the drudgery that is our estate. The *oikos,* in its struggle for autarky, is the locus of our efforts to free ourselves from another, related, sort of limitation: the dependency on others which flows from poverty. The household, then, is the means by which we secure such freedom as is possible from the poverty of our condition and in which we avoid a freedom-robbing dependence on others. Autarky and leisure, two overlapping forms of freedom, are the principal goods of the household to which its productive activities are subordinated. We can speak of this subordination as the moral embedding of the economy, the governance of the economy by the ends of the household members. And the purpose of that embedding is to contain the impact of the economy on its non-economic activities (praxis).

The economy is embedded in a second sense as well: in the affective and hierarchical internal relations of the *oikos.* The intimate, intensely personal rank-ordering of the household assigns to individuals their respective functions—master, wife, servant, and slave—and it determines the source of command and of the purposes to be served by the community. The *oikos* model of the good economy is then contrasted to the world of market trade: dominated by the acquisitive life, unfree, consumed by the pursuit of unlimited wealth, and disruptive of the proper (natural hierarchical) order of the household. The household thus serves a dual purpose in the Aristotelian version: as a framework that brings into view the essential normative permeation of the human economy and as one specification of the good economy. The first, more methodological, aspect guides this book (as I have said) and constitutes a refrain of each of its parts. The second facet demarcates one set of substantive claims about the proper location of the economy around which the subsequent debate revolves, that is, the household as subordinated to the purposes of the *oikos* master, purposes that are noneconomic in character and that require the transfer of economic activity to other, servile, persons. This properly ordered economy is, then, tied to a certain conception of freedom and the good life. Conversely, the life of the trader or of the individual driven by greed, or *pleonexia,* is unlikely to be autarkic or leisured and is therefore unsuitable for the free person pursuing the best of lives. The choice between the *oikos* model of the economy and its market counterpart rests on issues of freedom and the good life for both the individual and the community.

In Part Two, I move from the despotic, *oikos* model of the embedded and contained economy to the liberal household, its changed relations, and the theory of the moral economy related to it. Essentially this watershed transformation, the negative element of which is the critique of the patriarchal household, involves these revolutions in thinking about the family and other relationships: the move from status to contract as the foundation of relations of power among persons, whether husband and wife, master and servant, or ruler and ruled; the shift of preferences from the commanding *kurios,* or master, to all persons indiscriminately; the transition from the idea of the *oikos* and the polis to the idea of the community as an equal and voluntary association, which is composed of individuals alike in their freedom and rights-claims, and which is thought of as existing for the sake of the maintenance of those attributes. The continued genuflections to the "natural" superiority of the husband, or to his de facto rule, should not blind us to this fundamental shift in the conceptualization of the household, or to the revolution in moral economic thought with which it is allied. The contractarian (liberal) household is set on radically new foundations, expressed variously as equality, consent, and autonomy. The household economy is thus morally relocated from one embedded in a hierarchical community, under the master's command and oriented principally toward his purposes, to one in which persons are self-owners (or Kantian autonomous agents), pursuers of their own abilities, and individuals over whom control can be exercised, or exchanges effected, only through their consent.

In this manner, a deep transformation is wrought: the setting of virtually all human relations, including economic ones, on a contractlike footing. The economy is thus disembedded from the *oikos* and starts to resemble, at the level of the social economy, something like the market. In examining this, I pay special attention to the place of labor. The reason for this emphasis is, I think, evident. One does not have to subscribe to the labor theory of value or to the concept of exploitation based on it (I accept neither, as it happens) to be able to see that the purchase and sale of labor, a commodity inseparable from its human owner, her will, time, and so forth, raises central normative questions. Here I unfold the concepts of the person and of autonomy which underpin the market in labor, and I give that institution a liberal moral gloss: for this shift, although it can be conceptualized in the language of "commodification" or alienation, may also be seen from the standpoint of self-owners who can, within certain limits and as a function of that ownership, alienate their activity and time. My key interest in this part is to analyze the liberal debate with the *oikos* model of the economy and its attempt to provide a new moral economy, both within the household and in the surrounding society. In so doing, I attribute no particular genius of foresight to the founders of liberal political thought. I do not, for example, assume that they were able to foretell the emergence of a full-blown market society, much less explain its workings or institutions. Rather, I read them as engaged in a battle with the *oikos,* an encounter that yields (under certain plausible empirical assumptions) a picture of the market as that coordinating mechanism most consistent with liberal desiderata.

In the third and last part of the book, I consider marxism. The beginning point is once more the idea of the household: of Marx's account of the dissolution of the patriarchal family and of the grander social institutions that were its counterparts. This part of Marx's story is, in its broad outlines, adapted from the classical liberal self-portrait, which, in important respects, Marx accepts. He also adopts, I argue, central liberal desiderata, especially the ideal of individual autonomy. Marx's debate with liberalism then centers on the question of whether contract and markets do not, under the conditions characteristic of capitalism, rebound upon that promised freedom in ways that substantially void it of content. Marx's claim, I suggest, is not that liberalism is a fraud, in either the political or economic sphere, but that one of its core emancipatory institutions, the market, generates perverse effects, foremost among them the creation of new sources of unfreedom. Marx seeks to show that the shift of the economy from the despotic *oikos* type of structure to its new location in the capitalist market has both largely put an end to the restrictions on autonomy found in the premodern world (as it claimed to have done) and introduced novel ones in their place.

That is the critical dimension of Marx and, shorn of its antiquated elements, it raises far-reaching challenges to markets. For those questions we remain in his debt. But that is not the whole of Marx's project. The perverse effects he identifies in capitalism led him to the conclusion that only the abolition of markets would allow individuals and society to control their affairs, that is, to be autonomous. For that latter purpose, as well as in key elements of his critique of market society, Marx turned to Aristotle—sometimes with results that have enriched our thinking about these matters, in other areas, catastrophically. The most fertile results of Aristotle's and Marx's encounters in opposition to markets are to be found, at the highest order of abstraction, in their ways of thinking about the economy, in an understanding of autonomy and its limits deeper than that offered in contractarian liberalism, and in certain of the critiques of market society based on that understanding. Disastrous, theoretically and practically, was Marx's return to the *oikos* model as the solution to the problems he had identified in capitalism. The reembedding (and containing) of the economy in Marx's new household economy was plainly meant to reintroduce a use-value, needs-oriented economy coordinated (*ex ante*) by the community, that is, to relocate the human interchange with nature and among themselves away from the market, with its uncontrolled, naturelike properties, and toward one in which individual and collective purposes would guide production and distribution. Marx thought that this new household economy could be erected without the despotism (the command function) of the ancient *oikos*. He asserts this claim in the face of the historical evidence he himself employed, evidence that strongly suggests that where markets are absent (as in the internal organization of the firm, in the premodern patriarchal household, and so forth), coordination is effected through forms of command-type, hierarchical organization. Marx offers no theory of how his (and liberalism's) normative desiderata could be wedded to an economy relocated under *ex ante* planning—no theory, only an unsatisfactory coupling of each side of the equation: "free association" with "conscious control."

Three remarks need to be made about what we may still hope to learn from Marx. The first is that, in key respects, he remains the most forceful critic of market society. In that role, Marx pursues several related lines of argument: alienation, exploitation, inequality, and so forth. Here I have followed him down one of his argumentative paths, the principal and I think the most fertile one: markets, freedom, and compulsion. The questions that emerge from this critical engagement with classical liberalism are sufficiently fundamental and acute that they map, if only roughly and incompletely, the limits of market society and put an end to any easy thought that we have come across the final and most perfected form of freedom. Second, I take Marx's failure to develop an adequate theory of the new household economy—to marry, that is, a liberal ethic with the (antimarket) household model of society—to be not a shortcoming of his but a problem in the logic of the antimarket employment of the family/household model. This model seems to have driven with considerable consistency toward a view of the community, the individuals who compose it, and their economy which is, at its roots, in conflict with the norms of liberalism and above all with its notion of autonomy. Marx's twentieth-century followers, those who attempted to set walking in the full light of day that dream which, as Marx wrote, humans had long possessed, saw this probably irreconcilable tension more clearly than did the founder himself. In their practice they chose against freedom, and the retreat of their successors as well as of allied parties in Western Europe and elsewhere from the goal of communism, and in that sense from Marx as well, puts a practical seal on the theoretical problem.

And so, third, inasmuch as the failure of this central part of Marx's project is, in the same moment, a dilemma for a class of alternatives to liberal (market, contractarian) society—those that draw, in their various ways, on the idea of the (nonmarket) household—we are reminded of the need to be skeptical about claims that norms such as autonomy may easily be reconciled with a society made in the image of the household: of its thick (noncontractual) bonds, of its reciprocity, its altruism and intimacy, of the subordination of its internal economy to the needs of its members. Or, if we are presented with what I suspect is the more philosophically coherent argument (I leave to one side the question of its attractiveness), that such freedoms as are offered in classical liberalism are not the only, or even the most important, goods to be secured and that their loss or diminution is outweighed by other gains—at least, then, we stand on clear ground and can weigh the claims of liberalism against those being proffered to us, rather than being seduced by a childlike world in which all is said to be possible.

When in this book I analyze Marx's failure to set out a theory of the vast new *oikos*, I do not thereby mean to dismiss as a mere illusion the idea of the household and the location of the economy therein as a starting point to the critique of markets, as an unfortunate bit of *schwär-*

merei which seized people's minds and guided their practice. Just the contrary: that idea, in the varied forms it has assumed, consistently serves to remind us of the limits of markets, contracts, the rationality associated with them, and the bonds they create, even if, in the end, it is unable to put forward a superior and feasible alternative. The longevity and resilience of the household model also point out how deeply embedded it is, how its norms remain a part of us, relatively impervious it seems to the market and to the normative discourse of that world. Consider this microlevel illustration. On the one side, efforts to "legalize" the family, to transform it into a mesh of rights and contracts among equals, have a powerful appeal because of the underlying drift of such measures: the recognition of the autonomy and equality of persons in the household. The "de-legalized" family seems, from that perspective, a residue of the premodern world, with its hierarchical and unfree institutions: a trap, especially for women.[5] To make family relations more like those to be found in the market appears, by contrast, as an emancipatory project. Simply to phrase the issue in that manner is, however, to draw the contrary view: that the family is a shelter from the market, a refuge from the predatory, impersonal aspects of that latter sphere. For to refashion the family in the image of the market is (or so it is urged) to destroy one of the last sanctuaries of altruism, reciprocity, and community. Yet I think it the case that just as we might be concerned if the motivations and relations typical of the market were fully to absorb those of the family, so too would we have reason to fear the refashioning of society according to the idea of the household. The enduring quality of that ideal, what it tells us about the values and institutions we consider to be constitutive of what we are and about the limits of other types of communities, and, as well, what we now know about attempts to write it large in the world—it is for these reasons, among others, that we are called to think about the household, and about the place of the economy within its moral architecture.

[5] See Frances E. Olsen, "The Family and the Market: A Study of Ideology and Legal Reform," *Harvard Law Review* 96 (1983): 1497–1578, especially pp. 1509–13, 1521–23, for an analysis of the legal/theoretical aspect of this issue and its impact on strategies for reform.

THE *OIKOS*: BEAUTY, DOMINATION, SCARCITY

Homère, dieu pluriel, avait oeuvré sans ratures, en amont et en aval à la fois, nous donnant à voir l'entier Pays de l'homme et des dieux.

—René Char

Achilles' shield, lovingly described by the poet in the eighteenth song of the *Iliad*, presents us with an image of the Homeric world and its elements: nature, work, leisure, and war.[1] On the outermost rim of the shield, Hephaistos, the lame god of craftsmen, had made an image of the river Oceanus. And on its inner folds were portrayed a "great vineyard heavy with clusters" and a "soft field," "wide and triple-ploughed"; the earth, sky, the sun, moon, and the "constellations that festoon the heavens" found their place at the center of the cosmos of Achilles' shield. Surrounding this center, Hephaistos wrought an image of the cities of man "in all their beauty," the city of peace and the city of war, of dancers and disputants in the agora and the "forces of armed men." On the shield's next fold, the god made a scene of plowmen at work in the fields, of laborers reaping, of children gathering the "cut swathes," and of herds-

---

[1] Archaeological evidence, as well as the work of such historians as Sir Moses Finley, has served to remind us that the Homeric poems are just that, poems. While I make free use of such phrases as "the Homeric world" as described by the Poet, they are meant to suggest the world represented to us in the poems and nothing more, nor less. Chester G. Starr's *Economic and Social Growth of Early Greece, 800–500 B.C.* (New York: Oxford University Press, 1977) contains valuable cautionary notes on the use of Homer and Hesiod as historical sources.

men attending their flocks. And lastly, Hephaistos made an image of dancers, acrobats, and a "great multitude" watching these golden youths.

The poet provides us a universe in which nature and the changing seasons stand at the center, for it is they that determine the cycles of human activity and the wealth of the fields and vineyards. It is also a world at war, for that activity too is a way of procuring the necessities of human life: "For one side counsel was divided whether to storm and sack, or share between both sides the property and all the possessions the lovely citadel held hard within it."[2] Work and leisure, plowing, dancing, and wine drinking are other ways in which the persons of the Homeric world are shown spending their hours. This is a world in which the political community of the city is largely absent. To be sure, Homer in his description of the shield does tell us about cities, counsels, and kings, but sovereignty, rulership, and justice of the public sort are missing here. It is this absence of the city as an overarching political community that (among other things) sharply distinguishes the society Homer portrayed from the classical period of Greek antiquity.[3] This city is understood as a collection of households in which there are many kings, or heads of large households, and among whom the ruler is the head of the most powerful household.[4] There is little public activity of any kind in the *Odyssey,* and disputes there are often settled privately. Indeed, we are led to believe that in the twenty years of Odysseus' absence from Ithaka there was not a single piece of public business to be considered.[5] War itself appears not so much as an affair between cities as between households, and while councils are held rather more often in the *Iliad* than in the *Odyssey,* they are typically forums for personal confrontation, as that between Agamemnon and Achilles, or for the consideration of tactical matters.

[2] Homer, *The Iliad,* trans. Richmond Lattimore (Chicago: University of Chicago Press, 1951), 18.510ff.

[3] See Homer, *The Odyssey,* trans. Richmond Lattimore (New York: Harper and Row, 1965), 1.394ff. M. M. Willcock's edition of the *Iliad,* 2 vols. (New York: St. Martin's Press, 1978, 1984), and the Loeb bilingual edition of the *Odyssey* are readily accessible Greek-language texts. Hesiod, *Hesiod: Works and Days,* edited with a Prolegomena and Commentary by M. L. West (Oxford: Oxford University Press, 1978), contains the Greek text of *Works and Days.* In subsequent references to West's commentary, I cite it as West, *Prolegomena and Commentary* in order to distinguish it from Hesiod's *Works and Days.* On the relative unimportance of the city in the Homeric world see p. 151.

[4] Philippe Gauthier, *Symbola: Les étrangers et la justice dans les cités grecques* (Nancy: Annales de l'Est, 1972), p. 19.

[5] See Moses I. Finley, *The World of Odysseus* (London: Penguin, 1979), p. 80. Aristotle does, however, speak of Homer's "constitutions"; see *Nicomachean Ethics,* trans. H. Rackham (London: Loeb Classical Library, 1982), 1113a7ff.

The virtual invisibility of the public world serves to illuminate the centrality of the *oikos* or household. That community, and not the city, is the heart of Homeric society.[6] If the absence of the political distinguishes the Homeric from the later Greek world, his picture of the household— its relationships and its functions—endures into the classical age even if its ideal of autarky is later judged unrealizable and is replaced by that of the (greatest attainable) self-sufficiency of the city. In brief, these poems present us with the vision of household autarky in its purest form. We turn then to the study of the Homeric view of the household in part because of the lasting quality of that portrait but more important because it provides us with an understanding of a conception of community, hierarchy, and economy which will, in turn, serve as an introduction to the theoretical discussions of the household economy set out in Athenian literature of the classical period.

1. Odysseus' Household

1.1   The *Kurios*

The *Odyssey* is above all a poem about the household, about being at home and a member of one's community as a central moment of the human condition. Odysseus' wanderings through the supra- and subhuman worlds serve only to focus our gaze on the importance of his return home. This return is not the tale of Odysseus rejoining his family, in the modern sense of that term. For the Greek *oikos* is not a narrow grouping of blood relations.[7] Rather, it is a community composed of free, slave, and servile members and of the household's inanimate property. At the core of that community stand two principles: hierarchy and *philia,* a word that carries the meaning both of friendship or affection and of belonging, of what is one's own.

When we say that the household was characterized by hierarchy, we mean that an important part of what bound it together as a community

[6] See Pierre Vidal-Naquet, "Economie et société dans la Grèce ancienne: L'oeuvre de Moses I. Finley," *Archives européennes de sociologie* 6 (1965): 124, and S. C. Humphreys, *The Family, Women, and Death* (London: Routledge & Kegan Paul, 1983), p. 22. Cf. Georges C. Vlachos, *Les sociétés politiques homériques* (Paris: Presses Universitaires de France, 1974), p. 258.

[7] See Pierre Vidal-Naquet, *Le chasseur noir* (Paris: Maspero, 1983), p. 47, and Moses I. Finley, *The Ancient Economy* (Berkeley: University of California Press, 1973), p. 18.

was the presence at its center of a ruling element, the *kurios,* or lord. Indeed, the physical center of the *oikos* was the master's dwelling, and within those dwellings the *megaron,* the large room with its hearth at which were received new members of the household, a wife, and slaves.[8] The *Odyssey* displays before us the crucial importance of this element of rule within the community. The poem contains the story of the hero's wanderings far from his home and of the disorder of the household in his absence; it is, in other words, the story of the lord's adventures and of a community that has lost its *kurios* and hence its proper order. For Odysseus is the lawgiver of his household, and without him there can be only anarchy and disorder. The crimes of the suitors, offenses against the ethos of *xenia* (which prescribes the fitting conduct of strangers and guests)—consuming another man's substance, courting his wife, and other acts "beyond all decency,"[9] in short, crimes against the order of the household—flow directly from the fact that the *kurios* is missing. To this we might add that the uncertainty over Odysseus' fate renders even weaker the already shaken household hierarchy, inasmuch as Telemachos' position as the new lord ("For mine is the power in the household") must remain questionable as long as the possibility exists of Odysseus' returning. Telemachos' dream that his father might return, a dream fulfilled in the poem's climax, shows once again the centrality of the master: "how he might come back and all throughout the house might cause the suitors to scatter, and hold his rightful place and be lord of his own possessions."

To be such a lord meant to rule not only over possessions but as well over the persons, free and unfree, of the household. While the absence of Odysseus obscures (till the end of the poem) this ruling function, we can discern it in other episodes. In relation to the wife, this sovereign element is apparent in the manner in which she addresses her husband (or in which her husband is described), that is, as her lord. Marriage itself was seen as the giving of the woman by one lord, her father, to another, her husband: here, as in the Athens of the classical period, the woman was the passive object of the marriage, something exchanged between her two lords. Indirectly, we also see glimpses of this relationship in Telemachos'

[8] See Gisela Wickert-Micknat, *Unfreiheit im Zeitalter der homerischen Epen* (Wiesbaden: Franz Steiner Verlag, 1983), p. 186; W. K. Lacey, *The Family in Classical Greece* (Ithaca: Cornell University Press, 1968), pp. 21–22; and Edouard Will, *Le monde grec et l'orient,* vol. 1 (Paris: Presses Universitaires de France, 1972), p. 564.

[9] Homer, *Odyssey* 2.62–64. The idea of *xenia* is extensively discussed in Gauthier, *Symbola,* and in Karl Latte, "Der Rechtsgedanke im archaischen Griechentum," in Latte, *Kleine Schriften* (Munich: C. H. Beck, 1968).

behavior toward Penelope, for example, in his ordering her to return to work. Were Odysseus known to be dead, Telemachos could give his mother away in marriage.[10] Of the power of the master's wife we read relatively little in the poem, though it would include the authority belonging to the manager of domestic affairs, the overseeing of the household's indoor servants and of the mistress's own attending women.

The centrality of rule within the household is also apparent in the relations between lord and slave. Odysseus, without mercy, puts to death twelve of the servants who had shared his household. Those unfree servants or slaves are property. They are bought by their masters (Eurykleia and Eumaios), brought from abroad as prizes of war (Eurymedousa, Nausikaa's servant), and they are passed from one member of the family to the other. Penelope is given Dolios by her father when she marries Odysseus. Though they were considered as property—to be given away, for example, as a prize for winning a race[11]—it would be wrong to think that they were therefore considered as mere things, radically inferior in their person to the free household members. As tempting as that latter reading may be, particularly in light of the later Aristotelian theory of natural slavery, it misrepresents this world in which slaves were viewed as persons who had fallen into their condition often through war and conquest—a fate that, given the existence of slaves with aristocratic backgrounds, must have been seen as one possibly awaiting all members of that society.[12] This, to us so paradoxical, combination of the treatment of slaves as property and the recognition of them as persons is also signaled by the absence in the poems of the pejorative terms designating slaves as animals to be found in later Greek writings. Still more startling is the coexistence within the household of affective relations among all its varied ranks, of a type of friendship, of mutuality or *philia*.

[10] Homer, *Odyssey* 1.293, 21.350–51, and Lacey, *The Family in Classical Greece,* p. 44. Classical and pre-classical Greek marriages are analyzed in Raphael Sealey, *Women and Law in Classical Greece* (Chapel Hill: University of North Carolina Press, 1990); on the treatment of women as objects of the marriage contract see pp. 25, 33. And for an argument suggesting Penelope's relative freedom of choice (compared to that of women in classical Athens) in choosing her new husband see Sealey, pp. 122–24. In *Pandora's Daughters: The Role and Status of Women in Greek and Roman Antiquity*, trans. Maureen B. Fant (Baltimore: Johns Hopkins University Press, 1987), pp. 24–33, Eva Cantarella challenges the distinction between the allegedly more benign Homeric and the classical treatment of women.

[11] Homer, *Iliad* 23.262.

[12] See Elisabeth Charlotte Welskopf, "Gedanken und politische Entscheidungen der Zeitgenossen der Krisenperiode Athens über Charakter und Entwicklung der Sklaverei," in Welskopf, ed., *Hellenische Poleis* (Berlin: Akademie Verlag, 1974), pp. 47, 68, and Homer, *Iliad* 21.75ff., 22.45–46, 62ff.

1.2   *Philia*

That the sovereign or lord is the organizing principle, the core of the *oikos,* should not lead us to see the community as one resting on power alone. There is rather, as we observed above, a *philia* that binds this community and that flourishes together with the presence of lordship and hierarchy. This *philia* is evident in Penelope's long wait for her husband's return. It is also to be seen in Andromache's mourning for Hektor, whose death outside of Troy's walls, and outside of his *oikos,* meant that he "did not die in bed, and stretch your arms to me, nor tell me some last intimate word that I could remember always, all the nights and days of my weeping for you."[13] It is perhaps still more visible in the risks and humiliation that Priam incurs to recover his son's body. Even more strikingly, it is evident in the testimony of the *Odyssey* that there are substantial bonds of affection between master and servant. Eurykleia, a slave, was Odysseus' wet nurse and addresses him not only as "my lord" but also as "dear child." Eumaios, a male slave, is described by Athene as a friend of Telemachos' and Penelope's, and he was raised by Odysseus' mother alongside Ktimene, Odysseus' sister, and by his own account Eumaios was only slightly less favored than Ktimene. Not only did Odysseus' mother treat Eumaios with almost as much devotion as she did her daughter, but Odysseus is also said by Eumaios to have "cared greatly for me." These bonds of (one might almost say) friendship are particularly evident in the relations between Eumaios and Odysseus, and they carry with them the idea of belonging to one another as part of the community of the household. Read against this background, the suitors' liberties with the female servants, as well as other lesser offenses against the servants, such as allowing them only young, unfattened pigs to eat, are also crimes against the community of which Odysseus is lord, and it is there that we find the source of the suitors' final and bloody downfall.[14]

To be a member of a household, then, is to be enmeshed in a *philia,* to belong to and to recognize this community as one's own and to have a place in the *oikos* hierarchy. The absence of community, homelessness, is one of the central themes of the *Odyssey,* and the fear of that condition pervades both poems and provides yet another dimension to our understanding of the power of the *oikos* theme in the Homeric cosmos. The world outside of the household, if it is not governed by *xenia,* the rules of

---

[13] Homer, *Iliad* 24.742ff.
[14] See Wickert-Micknat, *Unfreiheit,* pp. 158, 189.

host and guest behavior, is that of the Cyclopes, violent and without order.[15] More specifically, to be rendered homeless is to lose the protection of the community and to lose one's position within it. Odysseus' journey has left his servants, in a sense, homeless and so subject to the severe indecencies of the suitors. Their circumstances are not far removed from those the Trojan women foresee for themselves after the killing of Hektor. Andromache understands that she and her child will soon have to go away in "the hollow ships . . . and there do much hard work for a hard master."[16] And Hektor's mother, Hekabe, knows that Achilles had previously sold some of her sons into slavery. It is hardly surprising therefore that one of the recurring themes of the *Iliad* is the need to fight off the "day of slavery" on behalf of the wives and children. To be rendered homeless was in effect to be made a slave, a thought that, as we shall see below, adds another nuance to the position of the slave within his new household.

1.3   The Livelihood of Odysseus' Household

The second circle of Achilles' shield, the portrait of plowing, harvesting, and grape-growing, points to a further crucial aspect of the *oikos*: that it is the center of production and consumption. Or, in other words, the household is conceived of as autarkic, as materially self-sufficient and hence independent.[17] The image from Achilles' shield also suggests the pervasive presence of necessity as the background of production. Humans must interact with nature—plant seeds and reap "Demeter's grain"; there is toil, and even the gods (e.g., Hephaistos) sweat when they work. Thus Hesiod writes that before doing anything else a man must store the season's harvest and that toil is required to get the earth to yield that harvest.[18] In the shield's city at war, that city which forms the core of the

[15] See Gauthier, *Symbola,* p. 20.

[16] Homer, *Iliad* 24.732ff. Euripides, *The Trojan Women,* trans. Richmond Lattimore, in David Grene and Lattimore, eds., *Greek Tragedies* (Chicago: University of Chicago Press, 1960), vol. 2, displays magnificently the lives that await these women who have lost the protection of their households.

[17] See M. M. Austin and Pierre Vidal-Naquet, *Economic and Social History of Ancient Greece,* trans. and rev. M. M. Austin (Berkeley: University of California Press, 1977), p. 41; Vlachos, *Les sociétés politiques homériques,* p. 98; Will, *Le monde grec,* vol. 1, p. 632.

[18] Hesiod, *Works and Days,* in *Hesiod,* trans. A. N. Athanassakis (Baltimore: Johns Hopkins University Press, 1983), 31–32; and see Elisabeth C. Welskopf, *Probleme der Musse im alten Hellas* (Berlin: Rütten & Loening, 1962), p. 62.

Iliad, nature, the seasons, and the soil are largely absent; there it is rather the agonal spirit of the heroes which draws the poet's sightless gaze. The life of the city at peace is, however, intimately bound up with reaping and planting, with nature and with the cycle of the seasons, and it is that which Hesiod paints for us in his *Works and Days:* the world of necessity, nature and labor. But it is also, as was suggested above, production for the sake of autarky, for the independence and self-sufficiency of the household. Production, the exchange of human labor for Demeter's grain, was subordinated to a purpose: survival, of course, in the first instance but beyond that—whether we speak of the great households of Odysseus, Priam, or Alkinoos or of Hesiod's more modest establishment—an independent life and some modicum of leisure.[19] In sum, this is a portrait of a need-driven, semiautarkic economy carrying out its productive activities against the background of a necessity-imposing nature. We now must move from this overarching concept of the *oikos* community as a hierarchical group, bound at its core by a *philia* and aiming at autarky within the limits set by nature and the necessity of labor, to an analysis of the *oikos* as a specific form of economy.

1.3.1   Labor

The importance of labor to one aspect of the household's existence makes it the natural starting point for an analysis of the household economy, and because much of this labor is servile in character we shall focus on that type in particular. Labor in the Homeric world was not considered a disgrace, and the presence or absence of laboring activity is not the dividing line between masters and servants.[20] Penelope and Andromache are represented by the poet working at their distaffs, accompanied by servants engaged in the other tasks of weaving. Arete, queen of the Phaiakians, is shown "sitting by the fireside with her attendant women, turning sea-purple yarn on a distaff." Her daughter, Nausikaa, shares the washing of clothes with her maids. The act of bathing and anointing visitors seems to

---

[19] Hesiod, *Works and Days* 300ff.; Welskopf, *Probleme der Musse,* p. 52, citing Homer, *Odyssey* 1.183–85, 8.162–64; Homer, *Iliad* 7.467–80; Will, *Le monde grec,* vol. 1, p. 646.

[20] See William L. Westermann, *The Slave Systems of Greek and Roman Antiquity* (Philadelphia: American Philosophical Society, 1955 [vol. 40]), p. 3; Robert Schlaifer, "Greek Theories of Slavery from Homer to Aristotle," *Harvard Studies in Classical Philology* 47 (1936): 165; Wickert-Micknat, *Unfreiheit,* p. 194. André Aymard, "Hiérarchie du travail et autarcie individuelle dans la Grèce archaïque," *Revue d'histoire de la philosophie et d'histoire générale de la civilisation* 2 (1943): 124–46, offers an excellent overview of pre-classical discriminations among various types of labor; see especially pp. 130–33, 140–41.

be shared equally by the mistress of the house and her servants. Among the gods there are those who work, Hephaistos the divine smith and Athene who teaches Pandora the *erga gunaikōn,* here the female craft of weaving, and whose own "elaborate dress . . . she herself had wrought with her hands' patience."[21] Of the work of the male servants we hear much less, testimony to the indoor character of the Ithaka-portrait in the *Odyssey.* Two male servants in Odysseus' household whom we know to be slaves, Eumaios and Mesaulios (Eumaios' slave), are responsible for attending to the lord's outdoor properties, his herds and crops. The noble-born males in the *Odyssey* we never see at work, but in *Works and Days* the master (undoubtedly much poorer than Odysseus, but nevertheless a slave owner) is advised to till the fields side by side with his slaves.[22] A very clear suggestion that Odysseus did not disdain physical labor is to be found in his exchange (when he is disguised as a beggar) with the suitor Eurymachos. Odysseus taunts Eurymachos, offering to compete with him in field labor, in driving oxen or in plowing. We may reasonably infer from this incident that Odysseus is not inexperienced in these matters and does not believe that his aristocratic adversary would be unfamiliar with them. This inference receives further confirmation from a scene near the end of the poem, in which Odysseus meets his father: Laertes is said to have spent much labor on his estate, and when Odysseus finds him he is digging in his orchard.

We can say, then, that Homer and Hesiod do not distinguish between slaves and free persons according to whether or not they engage in labor. Rather, the slave is typically made known to us through an account of his or her origins, that is, a description of the act of enslavement or the moment of purchase. More surprisingly still, the distinction between slaves and the noble-born is also not immediately apparent in the nature of their work. Penelope and her servants (and the other noblewomen and servants of the *Odyssey*) share, for example, the activity of weaving, and indeed Penelope's servants remonstrate with her for undoing her weaving. Although Nausikaa rides to the stream to do the washing (her servants

[21] See Homer, *Iliad* 1.570ff., 5.733ff.; Hesiod, *Works and Days* 65ff.; Ja. Lencman, *Die Sklaverei im mykenischen und homerischen Griechenland,* trans. from Russian by Maria Braeuer-Pospelova (Wiesbaden: Franz Steiner Verlag, 1966), pp. 294, 296. On the inferior position of the laboring gods see Austin and Vidal-Naquet, *Economic and Social History of Ancient Greece,* p. 13; Jean-Pierre Vernant, *Mythe et pensée chez les Grecs* (Paris: Maspero, 1969), p. 209n.

[22] Hesiod, *Works and Days* 466ff., and for commentary see West, *Prolegomena and Commentary,* p. 54. Clearly incorrect is Hannah Arendt, *The Human Condition* (Chicago: University of Chicago Press, 1958), pp. 19n.19, 83n.8.

walk), she is to be found with them by the side of the stream stooped over
the smooth washing stones. The Homeric evidence is not as extensive for
male labor, perhaps because the most noteworthy activity of noblemen is
to be found in the *Iliad* (i.e., in the heroic deeds of war) and not in the
domestic affairs of the household. However that may be, there is no
evidence in the *Odyssey* of disdain for labor, and there is, in *Works and
Days,* positive support for the conjecture that the line between the free
person and the slave is not likely to have been one of not-laboring versus
laboring.

In her splendid commentary on the place of labor in Homeric society,
Gisela Wickert-Micknat suggests that the division of labor in Odysseus'
household is horizontal rather than vertical.[23] She means by this that
work is not something allocated according to (vertical) status-position
within the *oikos,* to the noble/free or to the servant/slave, but rather is
divided along gender lines. Indoor work is the business of the household's
females (Penelope, her free servants, and slaves alike), who are therefore
sometimes described in the poem and in pictorial art as "white armed."[24]
The work of men is outdoors, and accordingly they are painted in dark
tones. The accuracy of this interpretation depends on the unstated premise that the similarity of activities across noble/free–servant/slave lines
makes that status distinction of little value in the examination of the issue
of labor and servitude in the Homeric *oikos.* It is this premise that requires modification. Everyone in Odysseus' household works or knows
how to do so. Penelope weaves as do her servants. But under what conditions? She has been weaving Laertes' shroud for three years and undoing
her day's work each evening. The fact that it is a shroud for a man not yet
dead, that she is (in her story to the suitors) weaving it so as not to lose
honor with the Achaian women, and that her efforts of three years are
deliberately for naught (viewed from the perspective of the household's
material needs) suggest that Penelope's weaving is more a pastime, or in

[23] Wickert-Micknat, *Unfreiheit,* pp. 151–54. On Homeric women see also Cantarella,
Pandora's Daughters, pp. 24–33; Sealey, *Women and Law in Classical Greece,* pp. 110–50.
[24] See Lacey, *The Family in Classical Greece,* p. 47, and the abundant references in the
poems to the paleness and white arms of women, divine and mortal. On the artistic conventions governing the portrayal of women's flesh see John Boardman, *Athenian Black Figure
Vases* (London: Thames and Hudson, 1974), pp. 197–98, and for social background to the
representations of females on Greek vase art see Claude Bérard, "The Order of Women," in
Bérard et al., *A City of Images: Iconography and Society in Ancient Greece,* trans. Deborah
Lyons (Princeton: Princeton University Press, 1989), pp. 89–108. On weaving as the female
craft, see Eva C. Keuls, "Attic Vase-Painting and the Home Textile Industry," in Warren G.
Moon, ed., *Ancient Greek Art and Iconography* (Madison: University of Wisconsin Press,
1983), pp. 209–30.

any case not labor under compulsion, either that of the household's needs or of a master.[25]

Finley notes that "Odysseus was not required to plow in order to live. [T]hough he knew how to till and herd . . . he rarely did any work on his estate except in sport. That was the great dividing line, between those who were compelled to labor and those who were not."[26] Consider again the description near the end of the poem of Laertes digging in his orchard. But of Laertes' slaves, the poet says that they "worked at his pleasure under compulsion." Even in doing the same work the nobles and their slaves did not do it in the same way. Compulsion over the labor of the latter distinguished it sharply from the activities of the nobles. Understood in this manner, there is a vertical division of labor within the household, a division corresponding to the free or servile statuses of the various groups comprising the home's order. In the Homeric world the free plow and reap but as a sport, a demonstration of prowess, and perhaps here, as in the later Greek world, as a preparation for war. The servile, on the other hand, labor to produce, and they do so under the compulsion of a master. And within that ordering there is a further status differentiation: that between male and female. Free men and free women have different activities appropriate to their gender, as do their servile counterparts.

1.3.2 The Purposes of the *Oikos* Economy

Toil is something given to humans, a necessity. Once, Hesiod writes, there was a race of men who "knew no constraints," who "did as they pleased," for they lived in a time when a day's labor would yield enough for a year. Under such conditions one could, so Hesiod concludes, "live without a thought for the work of oxen" and, we might add, without the need for slaves, because production, the struggle with nature for daily sustenance, would not take place. But Zeus, angry with Prometheus, designed sorrows and above all the sorrow of "grim poverty"[27] and the need to toil—and he had Pandora release these evils from her jar so that they might spread among humankind. Previously humans were free from necessity, economic necessity, that is, the need to toil: they "knew no

---

[25] See Finley, *The World of Odysseus,* p. 73. Finley notes the uselessness of Penelope's weaving and suggests that her role is managerial. The preceding lines draw on his analysis.

[26] Finley, *The World of Odysseus,* p. 71.

[27] Hesiod, *Works and Days* 43ff., 118, 638, and for a gloss on the first two passages see West, *Prolegomena and Commentary,* p. 180.

constraint." Now that is no longer possible. Yet this necessity can be contained as far as possible by the use of servile labor; in other words, by the greatest restriction of economic necessity to the unfree persons within the household.

The dancing scene on Achilles' shield, the merrymaking of Penelope's suitors, in short, the leisure necessary to the good life, is a substantial part of what the *oikos* economy was intended to yield. Even the more modest household described by Hesiod, which is not able to liberate its master from labor in the way that Odysseus' or Priam's might, nevertheless allows its free members those precious moments without constraint during which they may enjoy "a shady ledge . . . choice wine . . . [and] Zephyr's breeze as it blows from mountain peaks." In this economy wealth is, to be sure, measured by possessions—the lavish, fantastically so, homes of the great kings of the Homeric poems attest to that—but it is also (and perhaps most important) measured by the absencĕ of necessary labor or, in more positive terms, by the presence of leisure. The toil of slaves takes place so as to make that possible.[28]

We might, then, describe the Homeric household economy as one crucially concerned with time: of the seasons binding humans to a cycle of material reproduction, and of leisure, time free from production.[29] This is an economic conception of time not as of abstract units measuring the output of goods but in the sense of a search for the greatest achievable space for unbound activities, for dancing, reveling, or merely for feeling Zephyr's cooling breezes on one's face. The structure of the *oikos,* the rank ordering of its members, is fully comprehensible only against the background of that economy of time. For the hierarchy of the household, the pervasive and abiding relations of rulers and ruled, is a central part of the function or purpose of its economy, the latter embracing the *oikos's* self-sufficiency for the daily needs of life, the possession and display of beautiful objects, and the leisure of its free members. The most obvious way of understanding this idea of hierarchy and economy is to say that in wealthier households the lower members of the community carry virtually the entire burden of production. However, this arrangement also suggests to us that they carry that burden precisely so that the economy, the material reproduction of the household, will be contained, that is, assigned to its servile members and kept at the greatest possible distance

[28] Hesiod, *Works and Days* 585ff. For further commentary on these ideas see Austin and Vidal-Naquet, *Economic and Social History of Ancient Greece,* p. 16; Welskopf, *Probleme der Musse,* pp. 46–47; Lencman, *Sklaverei,* p. 294, citing Homer, *Odyssey* 20.118.

[29] On time and nature see Hesiod, *Works and Days* 641; and see West, *Prolegomena and Commentary,* pp. 376–77; Vidal-Naquet, *Le chasseur noir,* p. 73.

from the free persons of the *oikos*. And that idea in turn brings to light one central moment in the governing purpose of the *oikos:* the unconstrained life, the leisure of the free.

This economy aimed at autarky, which is to say at the satisfaction of the household's material needs from its own resources and, beyond that, at the freedom from constraint of the household's nonservile members, that is, the containment of the necessitous struggle for livelihood. Wealth meant freedom from the constraints of toil and, in poorer households where that goal was attainable only in the most modest proportions (as in the *oikos* of *Works and Days*), freedom from dependence on others. Such a subordination of production to the end of autarky would clearly not place any great premium on surplus for its own sake. This conception of the economy and of the place of surplus within it underpins, and is revealed by, the Homeric/Hesiodic understanding of labor. Labor is conceived either as agricultural production or in its artisan form as the creation of beautiful things. To work hard enough, or (better) to have sufficient slaves, to supply the household's needs is important because, failing that, beggary and dependence await one.[30] Beyond that, the object of work is to create a space in the world for beauty and leisure. The Homeric poems abound in descriptions of singing and dancing and of the intricacy and fineness of Hephaistos' creations, of Achilles' armor and shield and of Athene's dress. Nowhere is attention devoted to the intrinsic value of producing more. Here, as in classical Greece, technological innovation was usually connected not with increases in productivity but with military purposes, beauty, or religion. What is more, insofar as the social division of labor, one of the principal techniques for improving productivity, might reduce the autarky of the household (by forcing it into a market and hence into reliance on other households and cities) it was likely considered suspect. To be sure, new wealth was acquired in the Homeric world not, as Finley notes, through enterprise but typically by means of war, and this wealth usually consisted of new slaves, the ransom for them, or their sale price (e.g., the hundred oxen that Achilles received for Priam's son, Lykaon) or trophies, symbols of victory in battle.[31] Not only were trade and commerce not the appropriate ways of acquiring wealth, but they were viewed with suspicion and contempt. Hesiod grudgingly allows that

[30] See West, *Prolegomena and Commentary,* p. 47.

[31] Homer, *Iliad* 21.79ff. See also M. I. Finley, "Technical Innovation and Economic Progress in the Ancient World," in Finley, *Economy and Society in Ancient Greece* (New York: Viking, 1982), p. 188. For commentary on the preceding points see Henry Hodges, *Technology in the Ancient World* (New York: Knopf, 1970), p. 216; Vidal-Naquet, *Le chasseur noir,* p. 32; and Will, *Le monde grec,* vol. 1, p. 632.

one may sail "the stormy seas" in pursuit of trade but this activity is clearly seen only as a supplement to the fitting life, namely agriculture. Trade, to make up for shortfalls in household production, is an unavoidable evil; trade for gain and the division of labor threatens the autarky of the household economy. Commerce is left to foreigners as an occupation held in contempt and at odds with the independence of the *oikos.*[32]

The consigning of commerce to foreigners and, wherever possible, of necessary labor to slaves or other servile persons tells us something both about their position in the community and, relatedly, about the location of the economy in that society. These persons are both part and not part of the community: resident foreigners and slaves share the same physical space with the community (both are in a literal, though not historical, sense *met-oikoi,* those who live with us[33]), but the former remain *xenoi,* outsiders, and the latter are members of the *oikos,* though, as we shall see, in a special sense. Similarly, the economy, necessary production, is most certainly a recognized part of the Homeric and Hesiodic world—the plowing and reaping of Achilles' shield, the grim poverty of Hesiod's farmer—but it is something to be kept at a distance, to be subordinated as much as possible to the proper purposes of the household. I now wish to explore further this theme of the embedded and contained economy such as it appears in the Homeric world.

1.3.3   The Place of the Economy within the Household

Here again, the best avenue of approach for this part of our inquiry is to turn once more to the slave's position in the household. The household, as we saw, is a community embracing all of its members in varied relations of ruling and being ruled and providing them among other

[32] Homer, *Odyssey* 8.162–64, and see Hesiod, *Works and Days* 618–94, and West's analysis, *Prolegomena and Commentary,* p. 313; Johannes Hasebroek, *Trade and Politics in Ancient Greece,* trans. L. M. Fraser and D. C. Macgregor (London: G. Bell, 1933), pp. 18, 22; Austin and Vidal-Naquet, *Economic and Social History of Ancient Greece,* pp. 43, 46; Aymard, "Hiérarchie du travail et autarcie individuelle dans la Grèce archaïque," pp. 134–37. Starr's *Economic and Social Growth of Early Greece* is valuable as a balance to the "trade-less" view of pre-classical society; see particularly its discussion of the importance of commerce in the Homeric world. On the ancient contempt for traders see Adam Smith, *Lectures on Jurisprudence,* ed. R. L. Meek et al. (Indianapolis: Liberty Classics, 1982; reprint of vol. 5 of the Glasgow edition), p. 527: "In the Odyssey, Ulysses is sometimes asked, by way of affront, whether he be a pirate or a merchant. At that time a merchant was reckoned odious and despicable." More analysis can be found in Will, *Le monde grec,* vol. 1, p. 646, and in Paul Cartledge, "'Trade and Politics' Revisited: Archaic Greece," in Peter Garnsey et al., eds., *Trade in the Ancient Economy* (Berkeley: University of California Press, 1983), p. 9.

[33] See David Whitehead, *The Ideology of the Athenian Metic* (Cambridge: Cambridge Philological Society, 1977), suppl. vol. 4, pp. 6–10.

things peace and security under the rule of the *kurios.* The importance of belonging to an *oikos* is evident in the fear of the Trojan women after the death of Hektor, as it is also in the offense given in calling a person hearthless or a refugee. Slaves, though considered as property and compelled to labor, are members of the household, and the suitors' crimes against them in the *Odyssey* are a grave violation of the duties of a stranger, if not perhaps on the same level as Paris' seduction of Helen.[34] The importance for the slave's position of this condition of belonging to the household can be seen in Achilles' conversation with Odysseus in Hades. Achilles says, "I would rather follow the plow as a thrall to another man, one with no land allotted him and not much to live on, than be a king over all the perished dead." Although for a modern reader the condition of the *thēs* (a free laborer, someone who sold his labor, for a time, to the household) however impoverished it might have been, would most likely be preferred to that of the slave, in Odysseus' world Achilles, when naming the worst possible condition on earth to contrast with the best condition in Hades, selects that of the *thēs* and not the condition of slavery. The idea of a life given over to the temporary sale of labor is judged inferior by the poet to a life of slavery. Why should this be so? A definitive answer is impossible to give, but the most compelling explanation is that the *thēs* is without an *oikos.*[35] Better, in short, to be a subordinate member of a household than a person without community altogether.

We should now examine the special sense in which the slave, unlike the *thēs,* belongs to the *oikos* community. He is, to be sure, a full member of the household, but the later Greek practice of welcoming slaves (and wives) into the house with showers of nuts and figs, and the bringing of them to the household's hearth, signifying the beginning of a new life, indicate that the new slave had once been a member of another community.[36] It is this fact, that the slave belongs by compulsion to the household and that this membership is coterminous with the loss of freedom, that in part distinguishes the slave's position within the household. He is, one might say, at home and yet not at home.

Odysseus, disguised as a beggar, invites the slave Eumaios to recount

---

[34] See Homer, *Iliad* 3.354, 6.56ff.; Gauthier, *Symbola,* pp. 19–20; West, *Prolegomena and Commentary,* p. 199.

[35] For an account of the *thēs*/slave distinction in later Greek society see Welskopf, "Gedanken und politische Entscheidungen," pp. 81–82. The reading presented here draws on Finley, *The World of Odysseus,* pp. 57–58. An opposed analysis is to be found at Lencman, *Sklaverei,* p. 278, and Austin and Vidal-Naquet, *Economic and Social History of Ancient Greece,* pp. 44–45.

[36] See Mark Golden, "*Pais,* 'Child' and 'Slave,'" *L'antiquité classique* 54 (1985): 99n, and Will, *Le monde grec,* vol. 1, p. 564.

the history of his origins, saying to him, "You must have been very little, O swineherd Eumaios, when you wandered away from your own country and your parents." Eumaios' history is that he was son of a king, and that he had been kidnapped by a Phoenician slave anxious to escape servitude in his father's house. He was taken to a Phoenician ship and finally sold to Laertes in Ithaka. While Eumaios had earlier expressed (to the beggar) his devotion to the missing *kurios,* Odysseus, it is also plain that, as Odysseus himself recognizes, loss of home is a part of the slave's condition. Eumaios acknowledges the goodness of his master, but the remembrance of his own household is clearly evident in the tale of his enslavement and in his comment to Odysseus that his "longing is to behold them [his parents] with these eyes and in my own country."[37]

These words of Eumaios' tell us much about the slave's position in the master's household. Greek slavery, in both the Homeric and later periods, was for the most part an institution that used foreigners as slaves. Eumaios belongs to a community, his new home, through an original act of force. That act of compulsion removed him from a home where he would likely himself have become the lord. All possibility of autonomy was lost once he left his original community, and he became subject to the vagaries of the will of his master. To be protected against this condition meant to belong to one's original community and for that community itself to remain independent. A part of what the word *eleutheros* (freedom) conveyed was, as Wickert-Micknat writes, "belonging to one and the same people."[38] Eumaios' fate, however, shows how the two moments, the individual and the community are united: he is without protection against his new masters (the suitors) because the community (both the household and Ithaka) are not his; hence his only resort is to hope for the return of Odysseus.

The theme of homelessness is present throughout the *Odyssey.* It stands behind the havoc wrought on Odysseus' household by the suitors; it is at the core of Odysseus' many travails on his return to Ithaka. It is also at the center of Eumaios' history, something which may help to account for the sympathy between the beggar and the swineherd, and indeed between

[37] Homer, *Odyssey* 14.142–43, 15.485–90.

[38] Wickert-Micknat, *Unfreiheit,* pp. 127–29; see also Walter Beringer, "Freedom, Family, and Citizenship in Early Greece," in John W. Eadie and Josiah Ober, eds., *The Craft of the Ancient Historian: Essays in Honor of Chester G. Starr* (Lanham, Md.: University Press of America, 1985), esp. pp. 46–53. On slavery and foreignness see Wickert-Micknat, *Unfreiheit,* pp. 128–29. I have allowed myself something of a conflation here: in the only embryonically political world of the Homeric poems, the outsider was not contrasted with the citizen but with members of the *oikos* or of the "country." See Gauthier, *Symbola,* p. 19.

the man behind the beggar, Odysseus, and his uprooted slave. Both have known homelessness, that worst of fates.[39] Odysseus returns and restores his community, his household, and in so doing he again assumes power over his possessions, human and inanimate alike. Eumaios, as a member of that household, is also as it were restored to his position; he need no longer fear the new masters. Yet he is, as we have seen, a different member of the *oikos,* a special sort of *xenos,* a slave-foreigner, who has started a new life there. His presence in Odysseus' home came about through force, and though he was raised from a young age in the house of Laertes and is evidently fond of Odysseus, it is equally plain that the sense of at once being a part of the community of the household and yet homeless has not left him even in old age.

The preceding paragraphs set out the ambiguous position of the slave within the household in light of the origins of his presence there. But the explanation of his position requires more than a genealogy, for it is also a consequence of the location of the economy or production. The economy, as we observed, is an inescapable feature of human existence as it is presented in the Homeric poems. That *kosmos* contains, as we can see on the hero's shield, land and labor. Labor is also something necessitous, toil and drudgery under the constraint of nature and the cycle of her seasons, and for the slave necessitous under the master's coercion. Its necessity arises not just from the fact that it is something given (Pandora, the poisoned gift and gift-giver of the gods) but from this consideration too: that it can make possible the good life, the enjoyment of one's "choice wine," of Zephyr's breezes, of dancing and revelry, to say nothing of the great demonstrations of virtue in war of the heroes of the *Iliad.* For these latter, free, activities—the life "without constraint" which was once the whole of the human condition—to be available, production is now necessary, but also it has necessarily to be the labor of others, of the strangers within the *oikos.*

The Homeric household is a production/consumption unit, the means by which the ruling members' material needs are secured. As Max Weber writes, "Its dominant motive is . . . the lord's organized want satisfaction."[40] But it aims at something more than the satisfaction of material wants: its object is also to preserve, as far as is possible, the household's *philia,* the common bond and purpose of its free members, against the

[39] Homer, *Odyssey* 15.343–44, and see Gilbert Rose, "The Swineherd and the Beggar," *Phoenix* 34 (1980): 289.

[40] Max Weber, *Economy and Society,* ed. Guenther Roth and Claus Wittich, trans. Ephraim Fischoff et al. (Berkeley: University of California Press, 1978), vol. 1, p. 381.

intrusions of constraint and necessity which are an essential part of the reproduction of human livelihood. The *oikos* achieves this goal, autarky now taken as the self-rule of the master family within the *oikos* community, through its governing and containing of the economy. In blunter language, hierarchy, the presence of slaves, is the instrument by which the *oikos* frees others from the slavelike constraint of the necessity to produce. The slave and the productive activity that consumes his life are central moments of the household community and yet isolated within it. The subordination of the laborer and the suppression, or containment, of the economy are thus intimately bound one to the other.

It would be a wild distortion to write as if the Homeric poems were meant to convey an idea, even a naive and pretheoretical one, of the place of the economy in that society. What these two poems, and Hesiod's *Works and Days,* do allow us access to, however, is the story of several households: the grand, lordly ones of the Homeric tales and the modest establishment of the *Works and Days.* And it is in that collection of portraits that the poems' value for this book is to be found. These households are both ordered, hierarchical communities and production/consumption units, that is, associations engaged among other things in the securing of the livelihood of the households' free members. We have initially, then, a cluster of thoughts to consider: community, hierarchy, and economy. The center of Achilles' shield suggests a further dimension, one set out much more vividly by Hesiod: scarcity, nature, the cycle of the seasons, and the world of toil which is bound to them. What we have sought to draw from this bundle of images, and they can scarcely be counted as more than that, is the purpose of the economy, its occupants (producers and masters) and their status and function within the *oikos.*

Production is at once central to that world and suppressed or contained within it. Its centrality is displayed in the portraits of plowing and reaping on the hero's shield and throughout the *Works and Days.* In that latter poem, work, the interchange with nature required to produce human livelihood, is spoken of as a necessity, something that humans are compelled to do, that consumes their hours but that nevertheless is an abiding feature of their existence because Zeus gave them grim poverty as their eternal affliction. That grim poverty we may call scarcity in the sense that human needs and nature's miserliness demand that they expend their labor and so in greater or lesser measure give up what once was theirs, leisure and a world without painful toil. Humans are not, however, helpless in the face of this necessity of production; they are not powerless to resist the compulsion of toil. The *oikos* is one way of controlling, as far as

is possible, this human exchange with nature and of organizing the satisfaction of the community's wants. One dominant purpose of that organization we also see on Achilles' shield: dancing, the life apart from toil, in
short, the substance of the free household's *philia* which can only fully
emerge in those moments saved from necessity.

The *oikos* is accordingly a production/consumption unit governed by a
set of purposes, those of its ruling members. The satisfaction of wants,
which is the core goal of its economic functions, must be understood, in
the first place, as material: the sustenance of human beings. Beyond that,
the household seeks those goods that in their artistry and beauty display
the status of the lord. The poems also invite us to take this idea in an
extended, nonmaterial sense, that is, to look to freedom from compulsion, that space in which the free *oikos* members may enjoy their "choice
wine" or Zephyr's cooling breezes or in which they can demonstrate their
virtue in war and sport. It is just this freedom from "hard work" and a
"hard master," the loss of which is most feared by the Trojan women and
lamented by Hesiod, which constitutes one central moment of the community and its *philia*.

The containment of the economy, or in other words the safeguarding of
that space free from drudgery, is a crucial part of the explanation of the
hierarchical organization of the household, and especially of the place of
slave and hired laborers within it. For it is they who become the bearers of
production, who shoulder the compulsion and necessity, the toil associated with the provision of daily needs. And what is more, slaves are, like
the economy they populate, at once part of the household and distinct
from it. They are a part of the *oikos* inasmuch as they are a vital moment
of its function and because they come under the lord's authority. They are
strangers to the household in the most transparent sense because they
once had another home and by force or sale were brought into their new
one. More than that, however, the servile are strangers to the governing
philia of the household, however intimate they may be with the master
family. They are foreign to the bonds uniting the household's free persons
not simply because of their origins but also as a consequence of their
activity and its place within the *oikos* world. The economy and its characteristic activities—whether those are performed by legally free persons,
for example, the *thēs* or the trader, or by slaves—are to be contained,
kept at the greatest possible distance from the *kurios* and his wife and
children. Subsistence, display, leisure, and autarky, the latter understood
in the more modest *oikos* simply as freedom from dependence on others
and beyond that, in households well equipped with slaves, as freedom

from toil: these were the governing purposes of the household community.

2. The Political Economy of the Ancient Household

With Aristotle's *Politics*, Book 1, and other lesser works on economics,
we have opened before us a window on the ancient understanding of the
pursuit of human livelihood. Here again, the *oikos* figures prominently
both as that association or community most directly occupied with the
satisfaction of life's daily wants and as an analogue in a number of ways
for the broader community of which it is a part. But what a different
world this is from that one recounted in the poems of Homer and Hesiod!
The *agora* of Aristotle's Athens was no longer the meeting place of Odysseus' Ithaka but a market populated by traders, cheeky greengrocers, for
example—if we accept Aristophanes' testimony—selling among other
things expensive bass, anchovies, and leeks.[41] And down from the city
was Piraeus, a trading port into which flowed grain for the no longer (if
ever fully) autarkic Athens. Gone was the household of the Homeric
world which had appeared to be virtually self-sufficient and in relation to
which foreign trade and domestic markets seemed to play at most a
marginal role. The Athens of Aristotle is, of course, also distinguished
from the society portrayed in the Homeric poems by the dominating
presence of the political community, by the substitution of the polis for
the kingly *oikos* of a Priam or an Odysseus.[42] And last, with Aristotle we
move from a nontheoretical cluster of representations of the household to
a full-scale philosophical analysis of that community, of its order and
purposes and of its relationship to the polis. Yet for all of these by no
means trivial differences, much of what we might loosely and with important reservations (to be discussed below) call the economic thought of
classical Athens, with Aristotle's writings at its center, takes its bearings
from the natural or household economy. It deepens our understanding of
that community, of its relations of dominance and freedom and of its
guiding purposes, and it extends the idea of the *oikos* by seeking its

[41] See Aristophanes, *Wasps* 490ff., in *Aristophanes*, vol. 1, trans. B. B. Rogers (London:
William Heinemann, 1967).
[42] Suggested in Thucydides, *The Peloponnesian War*, trans. Richard Crawley (New York:
Modern Library, 1951), bk. 1, chap. 1.

proper place, and with it that of human livelihood, in the political association of which it is such an essential part.

2.1   The Community of the Household

It is customary, when one reads Aristotle's *Politics,* to concentrate on the proposition that humans are by nature political animals, to unpack that by referring to their capacity for speech and to the uniquely human ability to distinguish the good from the bad, the just from the unjust.[43] This focus, as crucial as it is for understanding the centrality of the political community, immediately encounters an exegetical difficulty that in turn reveals an important philosophical problem. That difficulty is that the better part of Book 1 of the *Politics,* the gateway to Aristotle's analysis of the polis, is taken up by a discussion of *oikonomikē,* of the art of household management. Attempts to dispel this difficulty by the suggestion that Book 1 and its study of *oikonomikē* properly belong to a "separate course,"[44] presumably a nonpolitical one, reflect a modern distinction between political and economic thought more than they do Aristotle's meaning. In the end, we must recognize that for Aristotle and much of ancient Greek thinking on these matters man is a *zōion oikonomikon* as well as a political animal: "man is by nature a pairing creature [or wedded, *sunduastikon*] even more than he is a political creature inasmuch as the household is an earlier and more necessary institution than the polis."[45] We might more accurately say that the human is not merely a household being "as well as" a political one but that those two aspects of what is distinctively human are deeply intertwined one with the other. Our analysis of this proceeds as follows: (1) an examination of what it means to say that humans are household beings; (2) how that status is related to membership in another community, that of the city; (3) the primacy of the political association over the household. We then turn to a more detailed examination of the *oikos* economy and from there to a discussion of whether one may speak of a concept of the public economy in the ancient world.

[43] Aristotle, *The Politics,* trans. Carnes Lord (Chicago: University of Chicago Press, 1984), 1253a1ff.

[44] See Ernest Barker's comment in his edition of Aristotle's *Politics* (Oxford: Oxford University Press, 1946), p. 38.

[45] Aristotle, *Nicomachean Ethics* 1162a16ff., translation slightly modified, and Finley, *The Ancient Economy,* p. 152.

The household is a *koinōnia,* a community, and, like every community, it is an association in something and to some end. The *oikos,* according to Aristotle, is composed of two principal relationships, that between man and woman and that between master and slave. The binding of male and female is not a matter of deliberate choice (*proairesis*), but is rather the outcome of the natural necessity of generation, for the sake of which they first unite.[46] The second relationship, that of master and natural slave, I discuss in greater detail below; for the present I say of it simply that it is for the sake of preservation or security (*sōtēria*). The household that results from the combining of these two relationships is, however, something quite different from, and superior to, its parts. Male and female humans may indeed unite in order to propagate the species and in that respect they differ not at all from animals. But the union of man and woman in the household aims at more than begetting; it seeks to provide for the needs of life and as such presumably establishes the foundation of an enduring community rather than being the human analogue to the transient sexual communion of animal reproduction. Or, in different words, if their sexual union is something necessary and not the object of choice, their union in marriage, in the household, *is* chosen, a decision to live together in *philia.* Household management, Aristotle writes, does not exist among animals; which is to say that the proposition that man is a *zōion oikonomikon* is intended not to display what he has in common with the subhuman world of the production and reproduction of life but rather to point to the specifically human nature of the *oikos* as an association dedicated to the securing of human livelihood.[47]

A range of related characteristics of the household serve to distinguish it from lower types of association and to unite it with other human communities. One, which we have just seen, is *philia,* the friendship or mutuality of its members, and the other a certain partnership (*koinōnia*) in a perception of the good and bad, the just and unjust.[48] These qualities, it should be observed, apply almost exclusively to relations between the free persons of the *oikos,* the husband and wife and their children: there can be virtually no *philia* between the free person and the slave, and if there is justice toward one's own property (i.e., slaves) it is of the most tenuous sort. Yet it is not these two characteristics that concerned Aristotle in his discussion of the common ground of community shared by the household and the city. Rather, the line of argument he develops is di-

[46] Aristotle, *Politics* 1252a26ff.
[47] Aristotle, *Politics* 1264b5, 1280b38ff.
[48] Aristotle, *Nicomachean Ethics* 1162a24; Aristotle, *Politics* 1253a17ff., 1280a34–35.

rected toward the idea of autarky, a central notion that is at the heart of Aristotelian and ancient Greek thinking about the individual and the community.[49] We might say that autarky means the greatest possible independence from external forces: a way of life or a city which can stand largely on its own and which has little need of a supporting chorus.

Man outside of a community is not self-sufficient, and the household is an association that is a partial remedy for that inability; it is partial, Aristotle argues, because alone it cannot provide the same level of self-sufficiency as can a union of households or, at a still higher level, the city. The city is that community which assures the greatest achievable measure of autarky, and in that sense it is the end or completion of what the household can only partially be. This analysis suggests that however much political rule may differ from that exercised within the household, the two forms of community are united in that they represent ways in which human beings combine to secure for themselves a measure of material self-sufficiency—an answer, in other words, to the scarcity, the grim poverty, which is such a central part of the human condition.

The city provides one forum in which material autarky, the secured livelihood of a combination of households, can be put to its proper use, that is, for the pursuit of the most authoritative good of all.[50] Politics, we might say, is the art of securing the means for and the making use of material self-sufficiency. That is what Aristotle intends when he writes that the city exists *not only* for the sake of living but of living well, a thought nicely captured in the (pseudo) Aristotelian *Economics:* "The city is a collection of households, of land and riches, which is self-sufficient for the good life [*pros to eu zēn*]."[51] The securing of livelihood is a central part of what the city is as a community, and the proper use of the equipment thereby provided, the ends it is to serve, is its particular function: the former quality draws the polis toward the household, the latter distinguishes it and its science as having mastery over the lower type of association—mastery in the sense of using and knowing how to use what is necessarily provided for it by the household.

Thus far we have considered the question of man as a *zōion oikonomikon* only in the most general terms, that is, the relationship between humans as household beings and as political beings. We now turn to a more detailed analysis of the household, to a consideration of the

[49] See Will, *Le monde grec,* vol. 1, pp. 202, 632.

[50] Aristotle, *Politics* 1252a5.

[51] (pseudo) Aristotle, *Economique,* trans. André Wartelle (Paris: Société d'Edition "Les Belles-Lettres," 1968), 1343a10ff.

place of the search for human livelihood, as a complement to the poetic sketch of the *oikos* set out in my earlier comments on Homer and Hesiod.

2.2   *Philia* and Hierarchy in the Household

Ischomachos, the wealthy farmer of Xenophon's *Oeconomicus,* says to Socrates that, upon marrying his wife, he told her: "this household is what is common to us."[52] The household is a community as well as a totality of possessions, animate and inanimate, and it is a community, above all, of its free members. When Ischomachos said to his new wife that the household was their community we may assume that he meant a number of things: that it was the something-in-common that is the pre-requisite of all associations, that they were united by a certain *philia* or mutuality in their actions over this common something, and that their community had a purpose.[53] The idea of the *oikos* community also car-ries with it, as we have seen, a strong sense of a hierarchical order. Let us briefly examine these concepts. The suggestion that the household must rest on a something-in-common, some tangible and almost material bond, we find expressed by Aristotle in these words: "To have nothing in common is impossible, for the city is a community,"[54] and he concludes, therefore, that a necessary condition of the political community is a place, a space-in-common. So too with a household: just as we can imagine a group of persons sharing a geographical location without forming a polis but cannot conceive of a city that does not have a shared physical space, so we can imagine individuals living together who do not form a house-hold, but we cannot think of a household whose members share in noth-ing, including not having a common dwelling place. While Aristotle's statement shows the necessity of this shared dwelling place, it also sug-gests that the idea of sharing involves more than community in some tangible property. Living together makes persons neither citizens nor members of a household, though it is a requirement of both. What is needed, over and above that minimum, is *philia,* a mutuality in something greater than that of a shared location—in virtue, for example, or a per-

[52] Xenophon, *Oeconomicus,* trans. Carnes Lord, in Leo Strauss, *Xenophon's Socratic Discourse* (Ithaca: Cornell University Press, 1970), 7.12/13. On occasion I have preferred Pierre Chantraine's translation in his *Xénophon: Economique* (Paris: Société d'Edition "Les Belles-Lettres," 1949).

[53] See M. I. Finley, "Aristotle and Economic Analysis," in Finley, ed., *Studies in Ancient Society* (London: Routledge and Kegan Paul, 1974), p. 32.

[54] Aristotle, *Politics* 1260b39–40.

ception of justice; in pleasure or, in its lowest form, in utility. *Philia* also carries with it the idea of a chosen bond, that this mutuality uniting free persons in a household is the result of "intentional choice," an aspect of *philia* that applies to marriage but that also finds a resonance in political friendship, not in the sense that citizens choose to live together—they are born into their city—but that they deliberate over and choose the nature of their bonds to one another, that is, the form of their regime.[55]

The household, like all communities, has a purpose, some good to which it is directed. The purpose governing the *oikos* is, in fact, twofold in the texts we are considering: securing and increasing the wealth of the household and the proper use of the wealth thereby created. That latter idea, which forms the core of the ancient conception of the household, we shall turn to shortly. The first purpose I have already alluded to in saying, with Aristotle, that the household exists for the satisfaction of recurrent needs, that it is an association of persons for the sake of production and consumption. That formulation provides us with a surer grasp of what was understood by wealth in this context. If *oikonomikē* aims at wealth, at the growth of the household, this wealth is understood as what is needed by and benefits the household. The *oikos* is not conceived of as a wealth-creating association in the same sense that, say, a group of traders plying the seas might be. Its wealth is seen rather as measured by the satisfaction of the consumption needs, broadly construed, of its members and, in addition, by its capacity for autarky, which, in its *ideal* form (recognized as unrealizable), implies the household's detachment from markets.[56]

The *oikos* is a community of persons living together, bound by a *philia* and sharing a common purpose, wealth creation within the framework of need-satisfaction and autarky. Giving this community its distinctive form, however, is its order, both human and inanimate:[57] everyone and everything has its proper place. Ischomachos, speaking to Socrates, tells him of the beauty of a finely ordered house, one with each room being built for the greatest possible advantage, cool in summer and warm in the winter.[58] And likewise with the household's persons: there is an order of

[55] Aristotle, *Nicomachean Ethics* 1156a6ff., 1159b25ff., 1161a23–25, 1161b12; Aristotle, *Politics* 1280b39. See also Vernant, *Mythe et pensée chez les Grecs*, pp. 208–9.

[56] Xenophon, *Oeconomicus* 9.12; Aristotle, *Nicomachean Ethics* 1094a10. Commentary can be found in S. C. Humphreys, "Economy and Society in Classical Athens," in Humphreys, *Anthropology and the Greeks* (London: Routledge and Kegan Paul, 1978), pp. 143–44; Weber, *Economy and Society*, vol. 1, p. 381.

[57] See Chantraine, Préface to *Xénophon: Economique*, p. 11.

[58] Xenophon, *Oeconomicus* 8.20; 9.2, 4.

authority and of appropriate functions among them. The master oversees the *oikos'* outdoor work and the wife is the guardian of its indoor functions; a good steward manages the work of the household's servants and slaves. The master, the wife, and the servile laborers—these are the elements that compose the *oikos* hierarchy, and rulership is essential to that composition. Indeed, it is precisely the proper ranking of rulers over ruled that raises a composite, whether the soul, the household, or the city, above the level of a mere heap, an aggregate, and transforms it into an ordered whole. To be sure, one does not want to collapse the distinction made by Aristotle (against Plato) between household rule and some types of political rule, but nor would one wish to miss the fact that even for Aristotle the polis and the household belong to the same "genus," that of human communities and of other composites characterized by rule and subjection. With that said, we can also see how the emphasis on the *oikos* is meant to stand in contrast to the democratic city and, for the same reason, to the market. Both of those latter institutions make equal (the one through the common coin of citizenship, the other through the medium of money) what is unequal and accordingly violate proportional equality, the proper order of things and persons.[59]

[59] Aristotle, *Nicomachean Ethics* 1254a20ff, and Xenophon, *Oeconomicus* 21.2; Aristotle, *Politics* 1254a21ff. with 1252a6ff., 1255b15ff.; (pseudo) Aristotle, *Economique* 1343a4, and Glenn R. Morrow, *Plato's Law of Slavery in Its Relation to Greek Law* (Urbana: University of Illinois Press, 1939), pp. 32n, 42. This inclusion of hierarchy captures the Greek attitude toward the community, household or political, more accurately than does an unqualified emphasis on *isonomia* and *isēgoria.* An undiscriminating focus on these equalities (respectively, that before the law and of the freedom to have a voice in the making of laws), which were to become the expressive phrases of democracy in Athens, conceals both the ready acceptance of hierarchy even within the democratic community and, just as important, the debate over who ought to be counted as equal and who, therefore, should be given a voice by being admitted to the public space. Paul Veyne, *Le pain et le cirque* (Paris: Editions du Seuil, 1976), pp. 201–10, and Moses Finley's *Politics in the Ancient World* (Cambridge: Cambridge University Press, 1983), pp. 27–28, 70–84, 139–41, provide a balanced assessment of these characteristics of the ancient community. See also Pierre Lévêque and Pierre Vidal-Naquet, *Clisthène l'athénien: Essai sur la représentation de l'espace et du temps dans la pensée politique grecque de la fin du VIᵉ siècle à la mort de Platon* (Besançon: Annales littéraires de l'Université de Besançon, 1964), p. 31. Victor Ehrenberg, "Origins of Democracy," *Historia* 1 (1950): 515–47, suggests that *isonomia* had an aristocratic, antityrannical origin. This reading is questioned in Gregory Vlastos, "Isonomia," *American Journal of Philology* 74 (1953): 337–66. The parallel between the market and the democratic city is noted by Humphreys in *The Family, Women, and Death,* p. 11. I discuss the relationship between the *oikos* and the political realm in my "Politics and the Household: A Commentary on Aristotle's *Politics,* Book One," *History of Political Thought* 2 (1981): 203–26. Josiah Ober, *Mass and Elite in Democratic Athens* (Princeton: Princeton University Press, 1989), pp. 262–63, 272, 277, discusses the democratic Athenian conception of its polity as "well-born" in its entirety as well as other residues of the (hierarchical) aristocratic ethos to which the demos clung despite the prevailing egalitarian ideology.

2.3   The Household's Purposes

We remarked above that the household was thought of as a community the purpose of which was the securing of wealth or, more modestly, the securing of life's daily needs, that is, sustenance. We must now push more deeply into the meaning of that purpose. It would be well to begin by noting the inadequacy of the word "wealth" for capturing the sense of the term *chrēmata*. That latter word is one of a number of terms whose root is *chreia*, "need," and not, as it is frequently rendered and modernized, "demand." This connection between wealth and use can be seen in the following passage from the *Nicomachean Ethics:* "Now riches are articles of use; but articles of use can be used either well or ill."[60] When we say that the purpose of the household is to acquire wealth, we must keep before us the thought that wealth, need, and use are closely related, not only etymologically but analytically as well. Wealth, the specific object of the household's activities, is something useful, "beneficial for life" in both senses—things necessary for sustenance and things valuable for ends beyond that of life alone.[61] This distinction suggests that in the view of Aristotle and Xenophon wealth is an instrument or tool (*organon*), a thing to be used to sustain life and to provide for the good life. Thus when Socrates, in the *Oeconomicus,* tells Kritoboulos that he is without wealth, he says, "For I myself have never possessed the instrument—wealth [*organa chrēmata*]," and Aristotle too speaks of "wealth . . . and instruments generally" and again of property as "tools for the purpose of life."[62]

Like all instruments, wealth is not an end in itself but a means to something else. What that something else is varies, but Xenophon's Kritoboulos and Ischomachos give us a part of the picture: autarky, the freedom from necessary toil and from restraint by others, and their close relative, leisure, with the space it creates for joining with friends or in the affairs of the city. True wealth, in this sense, is freedom from the necessity of labor. Other fitting uses we may classify with Aristotle as liberality in giving, either privately or to the public; for example, Ischomachos says to Socrates that he is concerned with riches because it is a pleasant thing to

[60] Aristotle, *Nicomachean Ethics* 1120a4–6. See M. I. Finley, review of Pierre Chantraine, *Xénophon: Economique, Classical Philology* 46 (1951): 253, and "Aristotle and Economic Analysis," pp. 33, 41; Odd Langholm, *Price and Value in the Aristotelian Tradition* (Bergen: Universitetsforlaget, 1979), p. 16.

[61] Xenophon, *Oeconomicus* 1.7, 8; 6.4; Aristotle, *Politics* 1253b24–25, 1256b29–30; Aristotle, *Nicomachean Ethics* 1096a6ff.

[62] Xenophon, *Oeconomicus* 2.13; Aristotle, *Nicomachean Ethics* 1097a28; Aristotle, *Politics* 1253b31–32.

"honor the gods magnificently, to aid friends and to see that the city is never unadorned."[63] In Lysias' orations we also see testimony of that latter employment of wealth in the adorning of the city and the honor that it brought to the giver: "while I am frugal in the private use of my means, I delight in the discharge of my public duties [i.e., liturgies] . . . [I spent] my patrimony upon you in the pursuit of honour. . . . " And again in Oration VII: "For I have performed all the duties laid upon me with greater zeal than the city required: alike in equipping a warship, in contributing to war funds."[64] These passages make plain that one should treat with caution the view that the *oikos* was an association for the acquisition of wealth simply, a view that too easily leads us to see in a work such as Xenophon's *Oeconomicus* a text, if perhaps a primitive one, in economics not much different except in its simplicity from its modern counterparts—as a treatise on how to become rich or to increase output.[65] That dialogue is, to be sure, about wealth and how to get it— through the use of a good wife and hard-working stewards—but it understands wealth in the light of its good and appropriate use, and that use is creating not more wealth but leisure and autarky, assisting friends and adorning the city. Xenophon (and even less, Aristotle) gives no evidence of having considered wealth as anything but an instrument in the service of the good life and as embedded within the hierarchical household, its order and its purposes.

2.3.1   The Ancient Economy of Time

Central among those purposes is leisure (*scholē*), a way of life closely allied to freedom. For, as Aelian wrote, "Socrates said that leisure is the

---

[63] Xenophon, *Oeconomicus* 11.9 and also 6.9; Aristotle, *Nicomachean Ethics* 1107b9ff., 1120b1ff., 1122b19ff.

[64] Lysias, *Orations*, trans. W. R. M. Lamb (London: William Heinemann, Loeb Classical Library, 1930), 21.16, 22, and 7.31. For an analysis of the turn from private exhibitions of wealth to public/political displays see S. C. Humphreys, "The Work of Karl Polanyi," in Humphreys, *Anthropology and the Greeks*, p. 39; P. J. Rhodes, *A Commentary on the Aristotelian Athenaion Politeia* (Oxford: Clarendon Press, 1981), p. 339; Finley, *The Ancient Economy*, p. 151.

[65] See S. Todd Lowry, "Recent Literature on Ancient Greek Economic Thought," *Journal of Economic Literature* 17 (1979): 74–75; Louis Gernet, *L'approvisionnement d'Athènes en blé au V et IVᵉ siècle* (reprint; New York: Arno Press, 1979), p. 330. Claude Mossé comes close to this reading but then qualifies it; see Mossé, "Le IVᵉ siècle," in Edouard Will et al., *Le monde grec et l'orient* (Paris: Presses Universitaires de France, 1972), vol. 2, p. 108, and Mossé, "Xénophon économiste," in Jean Bingen, Guy Cambier, and Georges Nachtergael, eds., *Le monde grec: Hommages à Claire Préaux* (Brussels: Editions de l'Université de Bruxelles, 1975), p. 170.

sister of freedom."[66] Leisure, time free from necessary activities, is also intimately related to the possession of wealth, for it is to be found only in the absence of occupation. When Socrates asks Ischomachos if their conversation is not keeping him from going about his affairs, Ischomachos answers that no it is not, because he has a steward (*epitropos*) to take care of these matters. Time free for such conversations, for horsemanship, or for attending to political responsibilities is made possible for Ischomachos by his wealth. We see here a three-cornered relationship bound up with the household economy: freedom from constraint by others, the possession of sufficient wealth, and leisure. The condition of a free man, Aristotle wrote, is that he does not live under the constraint of others,[67] for to be in the employ of someone or to be his slave robs the person of the capacity to dispose of his time as he wishes and denies him the possibility of leisure. This statement, as we shall see further on, amounts to the assertion that freedom, including leisure, is possible only in the absence of economic compulsion and therefore only in the presence of sufficient wealth. And finally, where material autarky is not possible, neither is leisure—because in the extreme case the person is forced to sell his labor and time to another or because, like Hesiod's farmer, his relative penury forces him into a life of toil, of time usurped as it were by nature.[68] The household economy is thus a wealth-creating community in which one of the principal uses of wealth is to ensure some of its members' autarky, and thereby their freedom and, relatedly, to open free time for their activities.

The centrality of the role of leisure in Aristotle's analysis of both the good regime and the good life, and the connection of this role to his account of the household economy, requires further analysis. This analysis is especially necessary because it is through a discussion of leisure that we will arrive at an understanding of what Aristotle means when he writes that the household exists for the sake of the satisfaction of life's needs. That statement unnecessarily restricts the purpose of the household, which is, of course, in the first instance the satisfaction of material

[66] Aelian, *Varia Historia*, ed. M. R. Dilts (Leipzig: Teubner Verlagsgesellschaft, 1974), 10.14. Aelian uses the word *argia* meaning literally "without function or job" and not *scholē*. See also Aristotle, *Nicomachean Ethics* 1124b24.

[67] Aristotle, *Rhetoric*, in *The Complete Works of Aristotle*, ed. Jonathan Barnes (Princeton: Princeton University Press, 1984), vol. 2, p. 1367a32.

[68] This three-cornered relationship is discussed indirectly by Elisabeth C. Welskopf, "Loisir et esclavage dans la Grèce antique," in *Actes du colloque 1973 sur l'esclavage* (Paris: Les Belles Lettres, 1976), p. 163, and Yvon Garlan, "Le travail libre en Grèce ancienne," in Peter Garnsey, ed., *Non-Slave Labour in the Greco-Roman World* (Cambridge: Cambridge Philological Society, 1980), suppl. vol. 6, p. 17.

wants but beyond that the use that can be made of the goods thereby provided. Principal among those goods are not produced things but the praxis or free activity of the master. When Aristotle writes that the slave is an instrument not of production but of praxis, he is saying that the end of the household extends beyond its material needs to the possibility of the unconstrained actions of its free members. And action, Aristotle writes, is of two kinds: one directed toward the necessary and the other toward the beautiful or noble. The latter are to be found only where there is freedom from toil and thus, while the use to which free time is to be put is a central question both of the *Nicomachean Ethics* and of the concluding books of the *Politics,* the analysis of the negative conditions of praxis—that detachment from economic necessity which is an important part of what the idea of *scholē* conveys—is also vital: the house steward "ministers leisure to his lord, so that he, undistracted by the care of daily necessities, may not be debarred from any of those noble actions which befit him."[69]

Leisure, time free for noble actions, is the proper goal of life, and it is for the sake of leisure, "the beginning point of everything," that we must sometimes be unleisured. The household master occupies himself in wealth gathering not as an end in itself—that is, neither with the view that wealth making as an activity belongs among *ta kala,* among beautiful and noble actions, nor under the assumption that wealth has an intrinsic value, but rather because that wealth may be employed to allow him time free for praxis. All productive activity in the household aims principally at that end, the master's leisure.[70] The relationship between wealth and leisure also points, as we observed above, to that between wealth and freedom, for freedom, meaning the capacity to legislate for one's self, to be autonomous, requires, among its material preconditions, independence from constraining toil, whether that constraint comes from subjection to nature or from subordination to another person. Constraint or unfreedom meant, in short, the necessity to engage in economic activity, imposed on a person through poverty or slavery. Conversely, wealth is understood as the means by which one is freed from the "burden of earning one's living," as Finley puts it,[71] and thereby permitted a leisured

[69] Aristotle, *Magna Moralia,* trans. G. Cyril Armstrong (Cambridge: Harvard University Press, 1935), 1198b12ff.; Aristotle, *Politics* 1255b35–37.

[70] Aristotle, *Nicomachean Ethics* 1177b4ff.; Aristotle, *Politics* 1273a36–37, 1334a18ff., 1337b30ff. See Welskopf, *Probleme der Musse,* pp. 215–16, and "Loisir et esclavage," p. 162. On *ta kala* see Martha C. Nussbaum, *The Fragility of Goodness* (Cambridge: Cambridge University Press, 1986), p. 178.

[71] Moses I. Finley, "Land, Debt, and the Man of Property in Classical Athens," in Finley, *Economy and Society in Ancient Greece,* p. 72.

life. The activities that should fill those free hours (and whose best ranking is a central concern of Aristotle's) was a matter of philosophical
dispute, and one may doubt that the Athenian wealthy were much occupied with this ranking. More certain is that relatively few Athenians
had sufficient wealth to lead an entirely idle life.[72] Yet we can also be
confident that the ideal of a life free from economic activity was not a
peculiar vision of the philosophers alone, or of the wealthy few. The ethos
of the leisured, noneconomic life is cited as a substantial part of the
explanation for the absence of productive investment in Athens: profits
were more typically used to finance the rentier's life of ease and to win
honor through liturgies rather than to expand an enterprise. Once a level
of wealth had been achieved which would make possible such a life of
leisure or political activity, the goal seems to have been to withdraw from
the economy rather than to reinvest. This is not to deny, it must be
underlined, that Athenians sought wealth. As Finley has written, they
most certainly did pursue wealth and that quite without embarrassment;
but wealth for them had a function that was not to produce, without end,
more of its own kind. Rather, the fitting use of wealth "was to liberate its
owner from economic activity and concern."[73]

Leisure as the background condition of praxis, the world of *ta kala*, is
one central object of the *oikos* community. Intimately linked to one understanding of freedom, freedom from constraining necessity, it is also
bound up with the possibility of *philia* and therefore with the idea of
community as well. To see this relation, we must consider the following
passage from the *Nicomachean Ethics:* "some friends drink or throw dice
together, others practice gymnastics and hunt or philosophize together;
each sort spending their time together in the activity they love best of
everything in life." These activities, hunting, philosophizing (and, for
Aristotle, philosophy especially), and so forth are, we might surmise,

[72] See Garlan, "Le travail libre en Grèce ancienne," p. 10; Claude Mossé, *La fin de la
démocratie athénienne* (Paris: Presses Universitaires de France, 1962), p. 42; Mossé, "Le IVᵉ
siècle," p. 126.
[73] Finley, "Land, Debt, and the Man of Property," p. 72. See also Philippe Gauthier, *Un
commentaire historique des Poroi de Xénophon* (Paris: Librairie Minard, 1976), p. 249;
Humphreys, "Economy and Society in Classical Athens," pp. 149, 153; Paul Millett, "Maritime Loans and the Structure of Credit in Fourth-Century Athens," in Peter Garnsey et al.,
eds., *Trade in the Ancient Economy* (Berkeley: University of California Press, 1983), p. 47;
Mossé, *Fin de la démocratie athénienne*, pp. 57, 60, 66, 102. For some important qualifications see Xenophon, *The Politeia of the Spartans*, in *Aristotle and Xenophon on Democracy
and Oligarchy*, trans. J. M. Moore (Berkeley: University of California Press, 1975), 7.1ff.;
Aristotle, *Politics* 1267b1ff.; Mossé, "Le IVᵉ siècle," p. 108; Vidal-Naquet, "Economie et
société dans la Grèce ancienne," p. 133.

pastimes desirable in themselves and consequently are not chosen for some further end. For they are *ta kala,* the noble praxis that is the common something that forms the bond of the best types of friendships.[74] Such noble actions are possible, as we have seen, only in leisure, the forum for praxis. And the *philia* that unites those who wish to live together in their activity must also have leisure as its condition. The individuals depicted in the passage quoted above are passing their days together in what they love most of life. If their time were constrained, such *philia* would not be possible; they would either simply not pass their days together as friends do, or if they found themselves together, out of necessity, the activities they would then share would not be chosen pastimes but rather a constrained way of life—the sort of association to be found among slaves, in a ceramics atelier, or among traders.[75]

Friendship, in short, requires leisure, and thus in the *Oeconomicus* Socrates says to Kritoboulos that the life of the gentleman farmer is to be preferred because, among other reasons, it "seemed least of all to cause any lack of leisure for joining in the concerns of friends and cities" ("the concerns of friends and cities": leisure is necessary for both the private *philia* of persons hunting or philosophizing and also for the friendship of the larger community, that of the city).[76] Here, as in the case of private *philia,* there is a plain meaning to this proposition about leisure and political community and a more extended sense. Let us look first at the evident meaning of the statement that leisure is necessary for a good regime. Friends may share in pastimes—fishing, dice playing, or reflection; citizens share not in pastimes but in the securing of life and of the good life. More precisely, citizens share in making decisions and in holding office. The virtue of a citizen, consisting in the excellence with which he performs these activities, can be fully achieved only under such regimes as equip him with sufficient leisure to attend to public affairs which, in a nonrepresentative system of rule, means literally to attend the public deliberative body: "In classical Athens the claims upon [the citizen's] time by the *ekklesia,* jury court service . . . were of proportions which no other differentiated culture in history has ever experienced before or after."[77]

---

[74] Aristotle, *Nicomachean Ethics* 1172a3–5. "Spending time together" would be more accurately translated as "passing the day together" (*sunēmereuontes*). See also *Nicomachean Ethics* 1156b8ff., 1176b5ff.

[75] See Aristotle, *Politics* 1256b5ff.

[76] Xenophon, *Oeconomicus* 6.9. For further analysis see Welskopf, *Probleme der Musse,* pp. 247, 252, and "Charakter und Entwicklung der Sklaverei," p. 80.

[77] Weber, *Economy and Society,* vol. 2, p. 1361, and see Aristotle, *Politics* 1278a8–11, 1326b30–33.

Persons without leisure must of necessity be ruled because they cannot themselves assume any public deliberative function, and thus tyrants, Aristotle writes, often seek ways in which citizens may be kept busy and without leisure.[78] In sum, leisure is required for political praxis and excellence, just as it is for the virtues of private friendships, those of the *Nicomachean Ethics'* hunters and philosophers.

There is, as we indicated, a second meaning to this relationship between leisure and the political community. The friendship of citizens is, in part, that of utility and need derived from the fact that persons isolated are not self-sufficient, even in the minimal sense of the ability to provide the necessities of existence for themselves. Need is part of the cement of their community,[79] as it is too of private friendships of utility. But beyond the demands of material autarky and the ties of need they create, there is also the possibility of a mutuality in the good life, whether that life is understood as political praxis or as activity apart from that sphere. In either case, leisure is a prerequisite, for without it citizens could no more share in the praxis of political life than they could in passing their days in hunting or dice throwing. The *philia* and praxis of the political sphere demand leisure. And more than that, a central part of the political art is to educate citizens in the uses of their leisure. For a city victorious in war or masterful in commerce but whose citizens are unable to use their free time in the cultivation of excellence has failed in what is most important, namely sharing in the good life—such as it can be achieved politically— that is, the end of living well together in the city.[80]

2.3.2 The Limits of Acquisition

In this idea of leisure, of time saved from necessary toil and production, and of the possibility of the actions that fill that free time, we have before us one of the central purposes of the household as a wealth-creating community. The purposes of the *oikos* community, above all that of making possible the virtue and praxis of its master and derivatively of his

---

[78] Aristotle, *Politics* 1313b21ff., and Aristotle, *The Constitution of Athens*, in *Aristotle and Xenophon on Democracy and Oligarchy*, sec. 16.3.

[79] Aristotle, *Nicomachean Ethics* 1132b32–1133a2, 1133a17ff.

[80] Aristotle, *Politics* 1269a34–37, 1134a3ff. I have not discussed the issue of which is superior, the contemplative or the practical life, because the outcome of that debate does not bear directly on the question of the household's economic function. For the same reason, I have not sought to resolve the apparent tension between Aristotle's statement in the *Politics* that leisure is a prerequisite of the better regimes and his statement in the *Nicomachean Ethics* (1177b6–20) that political activity itself is unleisured.

family, make it clear that wealth is considered an instrument and that the principal art of household management consists in knowing its proper use, its contribution to the realization of the household's ends. Permit me to consider each of these. External goods, Aristotle writes, "like any instrument" have a limit because everything useful (i.e., every tool or instrument) is useful for something, for achieving some purpose. The possessions of a household are those things useful and necessary for living and living well. The goods required for those purposes are not, contrary to what Solon had said, without boundary: external things, sufficient for autarky and the good life, need not be excessive.[81] Stated more directly, the good life, for which the household provides the leisure and necessary external goods, sets the end of wealth acquiring and thereby its boundaries, the maximum as well as the minimum. Beyond those limits, surpluses of useful goods become in fact (and at best) useless. This connection between the purpose of household wealth and the good life emerges plainly in an exchange from the *Oeconomicus:* Socrates has suggested to Kritoboulos that, contrary to appearances, he, Socrates, is sufficiently rich and that Kritoboulos is poor. Kritoboulos finds the suggestion laughable, but Socrates explains it in this way: "My things are sufficient to provide enough for me . . . but with the pomp you have assumed and your reputation, even if you had three times what you possess now, it seems to me it wouldn't be sufficient for you."[82] The choice of a way of life sets the need for wealth, and Socrates' wealth, though modest in comparison to Kritoboulos, is adequate for the leisure he needs above all for the pursuit of philosophy. Kritoboulos' pomp, however, and presumably his concern for his reputation are not easily secured by any amount of wealth.

The idea of the sufficiency of a certain level of wealth for autarky—for leisure and *ta kala* that fill it—and, correspondingly, of the idea of the uselessness within the household economy of surpluses beyond a certain threshold, is a note struck repeatedly in the *Politics* and the *Oeconomicus.* And it is one closely related to the second theme referred to above, the art of using as the core of household management, and of acquiring within the limits required by those uses. The tasks of the mas-

---

[81] Aristotle, *Politics* 1253b24–25, 1256b29–30, 1256b33–34, 1265a33ff., 1323b7–10; Aristotle, *Nicomachean Ethics* 1179a1ff.

[82] Xenophon, *Oeconomicus* 2.2–4. For further commentary on the idea of sufficiency see Gauthier, *Un commentaire historique des Poroi,* pp. 123–24. Veyne, *Le pain et le cirque,* pp. 138–39, argues that both the preservation of the noble's patrimony and ongoing competition with the magnificence of other households prevented this threshold from being reached.

ter, (pseudo) Aristotle writes, are to acquire and to conserve, to order property and to make use of it.[83] To make use of it means, in its most straightforward sense, to know how to manage one's slaves, how to train trustworthy stewards to oversee them, and how to educate one's wife to be a skilled guardian of the household's indoor affairs. More broadly, knowing how to use suggests the art of acquiring and employing with a view to the right end, the greatest achievable autarky of the household's free members and beyond that leisure, the space for *ta kala*. Those who do not rule their households with the purpose in mind of securing the good life may have many possessions but it is as if they are themselves governed by Xenophon's "invisible masters"[84] in their quest after still more wealth. Socrates has wealth because he has sufficient resources to open the possibility of a good way of life and he knows their proper use; Kritoboulos would still be poor with three times his already substantial possessions. For that reason there is nothing very peculiar about Socrates' instructing the wealthy in the economic art, for the core of that art is to know the purpose to which acquisition is to be subordinated, to understand how one ought to live. The "invisible master" ruling Kritoboulos, himself the visible despot, and making a mockery of his authority within the *oikos* is, we might assume, the search for wealth beyond that needed for a good life, *pleonexia*.

With this idea of the centrality of the art of using the household's goods we are led to the crucial notion of acquisition, of the *oikos*' wealth-gathering function. For the household master must know not only how to use but how or (better) in what measure to acquire. The art of household management, Aristotle writes, is among other things the art of acquiring (*chrēmatistikē*).[85] More exactly, *chrēmatistikē* is one of the skills used by the household ruler, the skill of supplying the things needed by the *oikos*. One kind of acquisition belongs particularly to the autarkic household economy—that is, to an enclosed economy without exchange—and that is the gathering of things produced by nature. But household economies of this sort, roughly that described in Hesiod's *Works and Days*,[86] are barely sufficient for the purposes of life and not at all for the good life. Autarky, therefore, requires the growth of the community, first to an association of many households and, in the end, to a city community.

[83] (pseudo) Aristotle, *Economique* 1344b26–27.

[84] Xenophon, *Oeconomicus* 1.18ff.

[85] Aristotle, *Politics* 1258a33ff.

[86] See Edouard Will, "De l'aspect éthique des origines grecques de la monnaie," *Revue historique* 212 (1954): 224.

With this growth, the art of acquisition also changes and must involve exchange, in the first instance with one's neighbors, and then with other communities. This sort of exchange beyond the confines of the household or of the early associations of them came into being, Aristotle argues, to make up for the deficiency of the household, which indicates that its end was also self-sufficiency. Money, as a means for facilitating exchange at long distances and for providing a conventional and comparable marker of needs, did not alter the underlying purpose (the quest for autarky) of this extension of the household economy to a larger exchange economy.

We are here presented with a theory of the art of acquisition as having a necessary place in the household, but one subordinate to *oikonomikē,* to household management as the art of using the property thus provided. The core view of the place of the economy is extended, as I suggested above and develop in more detail further on, to the larger community of households. This idea, which plays on an unusual sense of *chrēmatistikē,* is meant to stand in contrast to the word's customary meaning, that is, skill in wealth getting as an end-in-itself.[87] In that latter sense, wealth is understood as money, and money in turn not as an instrument for achieving autarky through exchange but as itself the specific object of economic activity. In other words, the art of acquisition which is properly subordinated to the purposes of the household (or to the self-sufficiency of the association of households)—in which money, where it is used in exchange at all, has a strictly functional role as the denominator of need[88]—is now transformed into something radically different. Detached from the ends of the household and the conception of the good life which stands at their core, wealth loses its connection to needs (broadly conceived) and with that loss also disappear the limits on wealth-acquiring—that it provide sufficient things for life and the good life. The amassing of wealth beyond use sharply alters the place of the economy within the community, from a set of instruments subordinated to use into a master, the "invisible master" of *pleonexia.*

Aristotle's critique of the acquisitive life in its ordinary meaning is not directed at the possession of a certain magnitude of money; even less is it a commentary on the rich.[89] Rather, that critique is aimed at the shifting place of acquisition in the economy, from an activity directed towards

[87] See Finley, "Aristotle and Economic Analysis," p. 41.

[88] See Will, "Origines grecques de la monnaie," p. 221.

[89] For Greek attitudes toward wealth see Gauthier, *Un commentaire historique des Poroi,* p. 124; Otto Erb, *Wirtschaft und Gesellschaft im Denken der hellenischen Antike* (Berlin: Duncker and Humblot, 1939), p. 62; Finley, "Aristotle and Economic Analysis," p. 42.

self-sufficiency and leisure to an end in itself, to one transformed into an endless hunting after wealth. Aristotle's references to the limits of household needs and correspondingly to the need for only limited wealth, especially the two (contradictory) citations from Solon on this topic[90] are intended to direct our attention to the subordination of wealth making to the material requirements of the good life and not to some determinate quantity of goods, to the standard of measurement governing wealth rather than to any specific amount of it. With this as background, we are in a better position to understand precisely what the critique of the acquisitive life was, for it is the mirror image of the case for the extended household as a model displaying the proper position of the securing of human livelihood within the community. The household's property, animate and inanimate, is meant to provide not only for the needs of life but for the prerequisites of praxis, *ta kala*, and the leisure of the master. Those who engage in the acquisitive life are, Aristotle writes, serious about the former—life and its pleasures—but not about the good life. This sort of unlimited acquisition, whether for the sake of more wealth alone or more rarely for the satisfaction of insatiable pleasures, produces a slavish life.

This judgment appears to rest on two distinguishable foundations. One is a ranking of ways of life which holds that the good life is identical with a pleasurable existence, a view that does not allow us to say of humans that they have a good different from or superior to that of animals. To drive home this point, Aristotle uses variations on the common word ("human-footed animal") for slave when comparing the people's love of pleasure to cattle's. The more direct condemnation of the acquisitive way of life dedicated to wealth for its own sake (rather than to unlimited wealth in the service of unnatural and insatiable desires) proceeds as follows. The life of wealth chasing is a constrained or violent kind of existence. A constrained life, one lived under compulsion, is of course unfree and servile: the origins of its actions are external and compelling, and it is accordingly not voluntary. And like the servile life, the actions of which also originate outside of the agent, it cannot yield virtuous and noble deeds, which must be voluntary in the sense of originating with the agent. Finally, the life dedicated to the acquisition of wealth is an unleisured one precisely because its end is not limited; its practitioners are engaged in an occupation as endless as its object, one that must consume their every hour.[91]

---

[90] Aristotle, *Politics* 1256b34; Aristotle, *Nicomachean Ethics* 1179a9–12.

[91] Aristotle, *Nicomachean Ethics* 1096a6, 1109b30–35, 1110a1ff., 1110b16ff. See Welskopf, *Probleme der Musse*, p. 220; Erb, *Wirtschaft und Gesellschaft*, p. 52.

Wealth seekers lead unleisured lives under constraint. The sense in which they may justly be described as unleisured is plain and emerges clearly when their existence is compared to, for example, that of the friends engaged in hunting and philosophizing together or to the studied unhurriedness of the great-souled man of the *Nicomachean Ethics,* Book 4, who flaunts his lack of occupation.[92] The meaning of being under constraint is perhaps less clear. The reason is that constraint, in an unqualified sense, is defined as action having an origin external to the agent, and thus actions performed for the sake of pleasure or honor (or performed without pain to their doers) are not held, in the strict sense, to be done under constraint. The actions of a slave are manifestly constrained because their origin is to be found in the master. Similarly, the deeds of a wage laborer, a *thēs,* are constrained in the (somewhat extended) sense that poverty and the need to survive compel him to act as he does (the absence of poverty, it will be remembered, is what allowed humans in Hesiod's golden age to live freely). The money-making life is clearly not constrained in the way that the slave's is, nor is it under the same sort of necessity as the wage laborer's life, for it suggests a desire (*erōtikōs,* the term is Xenophon's)[93] for wealth and profit rather than the necessity that comes of penury.

The answer, we may speculate, is twofold. On the one side, the love of excess of any sort, for food, sex, or money, carries with it the stigma of slavishness, of a loss of self-possession in what might be called the *oikonomia* of the soul—a loss of the proper ruling element, the rational part, of the soul and with that a subordination to the object of desire. On the other side, the money-making life requires entry into the market, into the world of purchase and sale, with the dependency that, in the Greek view, accompanied a complete withdrawal from the autarkic economy (whether that of the household or of the autarkic city and its surrounding countryside).[94] There is in this critique a recognition that to leave the shelter of the closed and self-sufficient economy to enter into that of trade is to subject oneself, indirectly, to the wills of others and to the vagaries of the commercial life. When we remarked above, with Edouard Will, on the centrality of the ideal of autarky (however incompletely it may in fact have been achieved) in ancient Greek thought, we might have added the reverse side of the medal, that its loss entailed a subordination to constraint, whether that of the type binding the slave, of the poverty ruling the laborer, or of the desire and dependency governing the wealth chaser.

[92] Aristotle, *Nicomachean Ethics* 1124b25.
[93] Xenophon, *Oeconomicus* 12.15.
[94] See Humphreys, "Economy and Society in Classical Athens," pp. 143–44.

The sense of the idea that traders lead a violent or constrained sort of life may be more clearly seen in this splendid passage from Alexis de Tocqueville, whose "archaïsme" (as François Furet has aptly named it) makes him a superb guide to the whole of the premodern world: "He who possesses a small commercial fortune [*une petite fortune mobilière*] almost always depends, more or less, on the passions of another person. He must bend either to the rules of an association or to the desires of a man. He is prey to the smallest changes in the commercial and industrial fortunes of his country. His existence is perpetually upset by the alternatives of well-being and distress, and it is rare that the turmoil that rules his destiny does not also introduce confusion into his ideas and instability into his tastes. The small landed owner, on the other hand, takes his direction only from himself. His world is narrow, but he moves freely in it. His spirit is calm as is his destiny; his tastes regular and unhurried as his work. And having need of no one at all, he has the spirit of independence even in the midst of poverty."[95] The last sentence illuminates the freedom of even the poorest of autarkic ways of life and at the same time points to the tranquillity of its time in opposition to the feverish agitation of the trader's existence. The earlier sentences reveal the external constraints on the person fully engaged in the market.

A second part of the critique of the life dedicated to wealth acquisition is directed at its consequences for the community. The classical concept of community, as we noted earlier, is centered on the idea of persons bound together by a *philia* or mutuality understood as a mutuality in both need (life) and something higher, a certain shared perception of justice or the good life. The person engaged in acquisition for its own sake has a different *philia* or, we might better say, *erōs,* that is, his desire for wealth without limit. This desire takes him outside of the binding, closed horizon of the *philia* of his community, whether the household or the city, and gives him another fatherland, that of wealth. It dissolves affective bonds and replaces them with ephemeral self-interest.[96] The acquisitive life is, in short, without a polis because its purpose and specific object, wealth, knows no limits and therefore no community, and as such it is a threat to the community. The thrust of this critique emerges more clearly if we

[95] Alexis de Tocqueville, "Etat social et politique de la France avant et après 1789," in Tocqueville, *L'ancien régime et la révolution* (Paris: Flammarion, 1988), pp. 67–68; my translation. A rather more critical judgment of Tocqueville as an idealizer of the premodern elite can be found in Veyne's *Le pain et le cirque,* p. 128.

[96] Lysias, *Orations* 31.6,7. See Erb, *Wirtschaft und Gesellschaft,* pp. 51–52; Edouard Will, "Trois quarts de siècle de recherches sur l'économie grecque antique," *Annales: Economies, Sociétés, Civilisations* 9 (1954): 17–18; Humphreys, "Economy and Society in Classical Athens," p. 136; and see also Humphreys, *The Family, Women, and Death,* p. 10.

consider it against the background of exchange within the framework of the community. When Aristotle, in Book 5 of the *Nicomachean Ethics,* comes to consider exchange, he argues three points: (a) exchange is necessary for the community; (b) need and reciprocity are the principles governing exchange; and (c) money is a conventional marker for need. For, he writes, it is exchange that, among other things, binds persons together in a city.[97] This is another way of saying that the political association exists in part to provide (to the limited extent possible for humans) an autarkic life for its members and that where that autarky is more complete because of exchange than in the (exchangeless) household, exchanges of goods are an essential moment of the polity. These exchanges, Aristotle makes clear, are meant to satisfy the diverse needs of the community, and it is precisely this need that is the ultimate foundation of exchange and thus the cement of the community insofar as it is an association for the purpose of life and autarky.[98] But citizens vary in their needs and so they must be provided with a commonly recognized measure if exchange is to be possible. Money is such a measure, but the problem still remains as to the proportional relation between those needs represented by money. Aristotle's answer, set out in his discussion of a four-term relationship—that is, two exchangers and their goods—is difficult to fathom. In particular, we who are accustomed to thinking of agents in the market as ciphers and equals have considerable trouble grasping what it means to say that as builder is to shoemaker so houses are to shoes. What is clear is that Aristotle is offering a theory not of price-setting markets but rather of exchange based on need, represented by money, and within the framework of the community, under its principles of justice and adopting its proper (hierarchical) order. The relations among the persons of a good economy would thus resemble, in their ordered, hierarchical quality, those of the *oikos.*[99]

The passages from the *Nicomachean Ethics* which I have sketched above are not intended to provide an explanation of market price formation, a phenomenon of which Aristotle was aware (witness his discussion in the *Politics* of the effects of monopoly), but which is not the subject of these pages. Indeed, not only is the market absent from Aristotle's analy-

[97] Aristotle, *Nicomachean Ethics* 1133a1–2.
[98] Aristotle, *Nicomachean Ethics* 1133b7ff.
[99] Aristotle, *Nicomachean Ethics* 1133a23ff., and Finley, "Aristotle and Economic Analysis," pp. 34, 38–39; Will, "Origines grecques de la monnaie," pp. 218–20. I noted above (with Humphreys) that this contrast between hierarchical exchange, whether in the *oikos* or in the exchange system imagined in the *Nicomachean Ethics,* book 5, and the "unnatural" equality of the market also suggests an antidemocratic argument.

sis here, but so too are traders; the person to whom he refers is, as Finley has pointed out, the producer of goods and not the *kapēlos*. And last, the object of their exchanges is the satisfaction of need and not wealth acquisition for its own sake; money is not the purpose but the instrument of the community, of its needs and its conception of justice.[100] What Book 5 is most concerned with, however, is the proper place of the economy, of the production of human livelihood within the community. Accordingly those pages may be viewed as extending to the economy of the city the principles governing the household: the economy as a tool or instrument of material need satisfaction and of the pursuit of autarky subordinated to the purposes and the status lines of the community. Against that theoretical background, the location of the economy as set out in the wealth-acquiring perspective emerges as perverse. Its driving purpose knows no limits and is not directed by the needs of the city; it transforms wealth from an instrument of the community into an end-in-itself and in so doing dissolves that community (and its order), its proper *philia* and purposes, and substitutes for them the constrained, leisureless life of wealth chasing. The argument between the chrematistic and the household conceptions of the economy is, then, above all a dispute over the place of the economy within the community; contained by that association, subjected to its ruling purpose as an instrument or tool in the service of its users, or governing the community, breaking its bonds of *philia* and need, and substituting for them the pursuit of wealth.[101] The debate over the location of the economy is, in ancient economic thought, a central moment in the analysis of what a community is, of the place within it of the good life as well as of the idea of freedom.

2.4 The Polis Economy

In the preceding paragraphs, we saw the core of the analysis of the *oikos* extended to a broader set of exchange relations, of those that ought to be the sort carried out within the city. That claim has, however, been much debated: Hannah Arendt flatly denies that the ancient economy

[100] Finley, "Aristotle and Economic Analysis," pp. 38–40, and Will, "Origines grecques de la monnaie," p. 218.

[101] This language I have adapted from Karl Polanyi as in, for example, his "Aristotle Discovers the Economy," in Polanyi et al., eds., *Trade and Market in the Early Empires* (New York: Free Press, 1957), p. 66. As I noted in the Introduction, however, much of the analysis of this book is sharply in opposition to Polanyi's claims about ancient and modern economic thought.

was anything but a private affair; others have presented it and its theoretical reflections as virtually a planned economy and social welfare state on
the socialist model, and still others have claimed to see the entrepre-
neurial spirit flourishing in the fourth century before Christ. The passages
from the *Nicomachean Ethics* which we have just been considering do
not provide an adequate answer because their concern is with the ethics
of exchange and not with the direct involvement of the community in
economic life. We must, then, look elsewhere and, in so doing, my intention is not to rehearse the debates over the importance of trade in the
ancient economy, or indeed to touch (except briefly and by way of illustration) on its actual workings, such as we know them. Rather, my
purpose is to analyze what is, I think, a quite clear application of the
conception of the household economy to elements of the public realm and
its role in economic matters, foreign and domestic.

The word *oikonomikē* was used principally to refer to the art of household management. Yet, as we have observed, elements of the idea of the
household are frequently and unforcedly extended in ancient thought to
the public or political world, and that even by Aristotle, who took Plato
to task for one such elision of the *oikos* and the city. Only very rarely,
however, are *oikos*-derived terms to be found in accounts of the city and
its economic activities.[102] Here is one such instance: "There are four
types of administration (*oikonomiai*) . . . that of the king, of the satrap,
political and private."[103] Xenophon's *Ways and Means,* though it does
not refer to the city's revenue raising as *oikonomia,* makes it plain that the
city can exploit its resources for rentier purposes just as private persons
do in their households.[104] The abundance of parallels between the household and the city, with the implied conception of the city as a "vast
oikos," leads us to suspect that we may indeed find an idea of the city
economy in ancient thought: "Since the city is a large family, its economy
will sometimes resemble a domestic economy, an *oikos,*" as Paul Veyne
remarks.[105] At the same time, however, it would also be reasonable to
assume that the ideal of household autarky, of an exchangeless, enclosed

[102] See Finley, "Aristotle and Economic Analysis," pp. 40–41 and n.

[103] (pseudo) Aristotle, *Economique* 1345b11–14.

[104] Xenophon, *Ways and Means,* in *Scripta Minora,* trans. E. C. Marchant (London:
W. Heinemann, Loeb Classical Library, 1946), 4.13, 14, 17.

[105] Veyne, *Le pain et le cirque,* p. 192. On the city/*oikos* assimilation see Gernet, *L'approvisionnement d'Athènes en blé,* p. 348; Humphreys, "Economy and Society in Classical
Athens," pp. 143–44, 155; Karl Polanyi, *The Livelihood of Man* (New York: Academic
Press, 1977), p. 41. Ober, *Mass and Elite in Democratic Athens,* p. 212, also discusses the
family/kinship aspects of the polis.

economy, could hardly be extended *tout court* to an economy significantly dependent on imports of foodstuffs and strategic materials and with a flourishing export trade in pottery, olive oil, and wine. Nor would such a simple unqualified extension allow us to account for the theoretical case presented by Aristotle, that the city is an association that, in some large measure, stands opposed to, and grows out of the failure of, the household as a community seeking to secure autarky. And last, it would seem to collapse that central distinction between the pursuit of life and of the good life and thereby weaken the ancient understanding of the distinctiveness of the political sphere. What we will be looking for is an analysis of the city economy which shares core features with that of the *oikos* but which recognizes the importance of trade and markets in the city and which, in doing all of this, does not conflate the virtue of the city and its citizens with the pursuit of necessities so central to the household community.[106]

Let us again take our bearings in this discussion from the master theoretician of the ancient economy, Aristotle. Writing in the *Rhetoric* about what the speaker in the political assembly should know above all, Aristotle says that he must understand the subject of legislation and be familiar with the various constitutions as well as with the causes of their prosperity and destruction.[107] This comes as no surprise to us, for we would fully expect, in the light of the *Politics,* that the principal concerns of the public deliberative body would be the best laws and the regime form. What is rather more surprising is that Aristotle lists two other matters in which the person addressing the assembly must be thoroughly versed: the provision of food (sustenance/*trophē*) and revenue (*poroi*).[108] Deliberation about the provisioning of food, Aristotle continues, involves knowledge of the kinds of foods produced at home, of what may be exported and of what has to be imported. The art of ensuring the city's food supply, in a not fully autarkic city, requires restrictions on exports of foodstuffs (olive oil, wool, and wine were the only major agricultural products to be exported from Athens; the export of grain was prohibited) and the encouragement of food imports. The city, in these policies, plays very much the same role as the household master does: ensuring or encouraging the

---

[106] For parts of this agenda see Humphreys, "Economy and Society in Classical Athens," pp. 137, 139; Will, "Recherches sur l'économie grecque antique." Mossé, "La vie économique d'Athènes au IVᵉ siècle: Crise ou renouveau?" in Franco Sartori, ed., *Praelectiones Patavinae* (Rome: "L'Erma" di Bretschneider, 1972), provides a good summary of the centrality of commerce to the economic and political life of fourth-century B.C. Athens.

[107] Aristotle, *Rhetoric* 1360a18ff.

[108] Aristotle, *Rhetoric* 1360a12ff., 1359b23ff.

nourishment of communities. Thus, just as the city must be concerned with *trophē*, so too in the household: "this branch [of wealth getting] which has to do with food . . . is by nature a part of household management." Revenue is also a vital concern of the city: for its defense needs, its public works of various kinds, and, as we shall see, for the possibility of a democratic polity. The statesmen, again like the household master, must know the sources and proper uses of revenue "for cities need revenue . . . just as a household may, but in greater degree."[109]

The search for sustenance and revenue does not, however, exhaust the economic concerns of the city in Aristotle's account. Without the necessary offices, Aristotle writes, it is impossible for the city to exist, and among those necessary offices are ones concerned with what he revealingly terms *oikonomikai*.[110] As an illustration of this economic management, Aristotle cites the fact that the city sometimes gives corn to its citizens—another aspect of the provisioning of sustenance referred to above. While we might with good reason suspect that Aristotle chose sustenance in the form of a direct providing of food because it is there that the function of the household most clearly merges with that of the city (inasmuch as it is a nonmarket, nonexchange transaction not directed toward wealth creation), he does list other necessary offices then existing in Athens: offices, for example, to oversee the market.

Although the precise extent of Athens' control over its internal food markets, and especially of its price-fixing activities, is a matter of dispute, the last notion mentioned above, laws for the marketplace intended to assist the city in securing its most basic needs, suggests that the political community intervened in the economy, partly to assure sustenance for the population against the possible exploitation of scarcity by the grain traders. We see this objective most clearly in Lysias' oration "Against the Corn-dealers." In that speech, he accuses the corn dealers of taking grossly high profits when the city suffers misfortunes and of purchasing excessive amounts of corn and holding it in store. In short, they sought to profit from the reverses afflicting Athens, and this in the most grievous way by taking advantage of the need for sustenance.[111] Lysias' condemnation points to the powerful ethos against the exploitation of necessity

---

[109] Aristotle, *Politics* 1259a35–36, 1258a17ff.

[110] Aristotle, *Politics* 1299a23–24, and also 1321b7–8.

[111] Lysias, *Orations* 22.5, 6, 8, 9, 14, 15. See Mossé, *Fin de la démocratie athénienne,* pp. 59–61, and Peter Garnsey, *Famine and Food Supply in the Graeco-Roman World: Responses to Risk and Crisis* (Cambridge: Cambridge University Press, 1988), pp. 74–75, 139–42.

and of wealth acquiring that is contrary to the needs of the city. And it also tells us of some of the measures that Athens had taken against that type of economic activity: limits on the size of corn purchases and on the amount of profit to be made on a sale, for example—measures enforced, so Lysias tells us, to keep prices low for the consumers' sake.[112] If the provisioning of food for the city's population required some control over domestic grain markets, it also came increasingly to occupy a central position in Athenian trade policy. As Athens was not able to live entirely from the resources of her own agricultural lands, and increasingly unable to acquire foodstuffs through force, cereal legislation (domestic and foreign trade) became an ever more important focus of public attention. Trade legislation, exemplified in the extension of legal protection to merchants and in maritime loans based on written contracts (available only to ships bringing cargo to Athens), was essentially an import policy in which the city did not itself (except in fairly rare circumstances) directly undertake the provisioning of the populace but rather sought to facilitate merchant activity in its port while restricting its own exports of foodstuffs and discouraging commercial assistance (e.g., loans) to agents not engaged in importing into Athens.[113]

We recall from the discussion of Aristotle's *Rhetoric* that the second major element of public deliberation about matters economic was the city's means of acquiring revenues, for as he argued in the *Politics*, the city needs revenues even more than does the household. At the height of Athenian power, one principal source of revenue was tribute from her empire.[114] With the waning of that power, other more peaceful means had to be found, and this need helps to explain the protection and inducements provided to the merchants of the emporium, a not insignificant source of wealth for the city.[115] And indeed one of the most intriguing economic documents from this period, Xenophon's *Ways and Means*, deals precisely with that transition from war and empire as the instruments of revenue raising to pacific trade. Among the more conventional

[112] Lysias, *Orations* 22.8–9. See also Aristotle, *The Constitution of Athens* 51.1–4; Rhodes, *A Commentary*, p. 578; Austin and Vidal-Naquet, *Economic and Social History of Ancient Greece*, p. 293; Finley, *The Ancient Economy*, pp. 169–70.

[113] On these points see Gernet, *L'approvisionnement d'Athènes en blé*, pp. 365–66; Austin and Vidal-Naquet, *Economic and Social History of Ancient Greece*, pp. 115–18, 291–92; Claude Mossé, "The 'World of the Emporium' in the Private Speeches of Demosthenes," in Peter Garnsey et al., eds., *Trade in the Ancient Economy* (Berkeley: University of California Press, 1983), p. 62; Will, *Le monde grec*, vol. 1, pp. 633–64.

[114] Aristotle, *The Constitution of Athens* 24.1, 3.

[115] See Mossé, "The 'World of the Emporium,'" p. 62.

of Xenophon's recommendations is that Athens should study the interests of the metics, for they are one of the best sources of revenue. To that end, Xenophon proposes that they be relieved of certain duties—for example, military service—and allowed some privileges—for example, that of building a house within the city. Other, more radical, fiscal innovations include the suggestion that the polis become a "collective concessionary," leasing out a public fleet or slaves to private persons, or that it become a more efficient exploiter of the city's silver mines.[116] However plausible or implausible these proposals may be, they are noteworthy for the fact that the underlying source of public revenues is rent derived from the economic activity of others. In other words, the city itself, like the ideal household, seeks to live from the productivity of others; that is, it envisions itself as a rentier city, whether empire and tribute or taxes on metics are the means by which that income is derived. Nowhere among Xenophon's suggestions is the idea to be found that citizens might engage in trade or that the interests of local producers ought to be encouraged or, at the very least, sheltered from foreign competition.[117] This omission, as I argue below, was not an oversight on Xenophon's part but was rather a consequence of a view of the purpose of economic activity in the city's life which closely mirrors the analysis of its location within the household community.

Democratic Athens had yet a third and more indirect source of revenue in addition to the two types just mentioned (empire and emporium): its wealthy citizens. Finley argues that the practice of liturgies as a way of seeing to the city's various needs, but above all as a manner of transferring wealth from the well-off to the poor, had its origins in an "age when the community was still inchoate, when the aristocratic households performed essential public services . . . by expending labour and materials at their private disposal."[118] This aristocratic ethos of the duty of assistance to the city and its poor is evident in Isocrates' statement that in former times those who possessed wealth came to the aid of the poor and delivered them from want and, on a more abstract level, in Aristotle's discussion of honorable expenditures (gifts) on services to the gods and the city. Such private patronage, with its implied relationship of the dependency of the receiver on the wealthy donor, could not flourish in democratic

---

[116] Xenophon, *Ways and Means* 2.1–2, 3.14, 4.1, 17ff. The phrase "collective concessionary" is taken from Mossé, "Le IVᵉ siècle," p. 112.

[117] See Gauthier, *Un commentaire historique des Poroi,* p. 240, and Polanyi, *The Livelihood of Man,* p. 198.

[118] Finley, *The Ancient Economy,* p. 151.

Athens.   Liturgies   became   depersonalized,   half-honorific,   half-compulsory gifts to the city as a whole; from private redistribution via gifts they became a form of civic redistribution.[119] The honorific side of liturgies consisted in the gift-giving ethos and, as Aristotle suggests in the *Nicomachean Ethics,* in the display of magnificence and the winning of honor which were a part of such gifts. Of its compulsory and menacing dimension we learn from many sources. In one of Lysias' orations ("On a Charge of Taking Bribes"), the pleader, a wealthy man, beseeches the city not to impoverish him, for his wealth is at their disposal.[120] And we learn from Socrates that because Kritoboulos is wealthy he is "compelled to make frequent and great sacrifices . . . to accomplish great things— breeding of horses and training of choruses . . . to support a trireme and to contribute so much that you [Kritoboulos] will be hard put to sustain it. And should you seem to have performed some one of these things inadequately, I know the Athenians will punish you no less than they would if they caught you stealing something of theirs."[121] In sum, wealth was subject to the claims of the democratic city not in the form of a gift but as being, in a sense, the common property of all. The resulting instability of wealth and the complaints about the treatment of the well-to-do at the hands of the city are evidence both of the considerable demands made on the wealthy and of the transformation of honorific liturgies into an all-but-compulsory revenue source for the city.[122]

What is more distinctive in ancient economic thought, however, is the use to which it was argued these revenues ought to be dedicated. Let us begin our exploration of this use by returning to Xenophon's *Ways and Means.* This work, often hailed as the most modern of ancient economic texts because of its recognition of supply-demand-price interactions and its emphasis on ways of extracting surplus revenues, sets out the use of these revenues in the following words: "in order that every Athenian may

[119] On the old relations between the wealthy and the poor see Isocrates, *Areopagiticus,* in *Isocrates,* trans. G. Norlin (London: W. Heinemann, Loeb Classical Library, 1929), vol. 2, secs. 32, 35. See also Aristotle, *Nicomachean Ethics* 1122b19ff., 1123a5; S. C. Humphreys, "The Work of Karl Polanyi," in Humphreys, *Anthropology and the Greeks,* pp. 69–70; Rhodes, *A Commentary,* p. 339; Polanyi, *The Livelihood of Man,* pp. 171, 178; Ober, *Mass and Elite in Democratic Athens,* pp. 199–202, 226, 240.

[120] Lysias, *Orations* 21.13–14.

[121] Xenophon, *Oeconomicus* 2.5–6. Paul Veyne's "L'évergétisme grec," in his *Le pain et le cirque,* especially pp. 185–209, contains a superb commentary on these practices.

[122] See Aristotle, *Politics* 1304b19ff., 1320a18ff.; Isocrates, *Areopagiticus* secs. 24, 25; Isocrates, *Antidosis,* in *Isocrates,* vol. 2, sec. 160; Weber, *Economy and Society,* vol. 2, p. 1361; Mossé, *Fin de la démocratie athénienne,* p. 154; Austin and Vidal-Naquet, *Economic and Social History of Ancient Greece,* p. 321.

receive sufficient maintenance [*trophēn*] at the expense of the community."[123] And, at the end of the text, Xenophon again writes that his proposals, if implemented, would allow the people to be "maintained in comfort and the rich no more burdened with the expenses of war"; surpluses beyond the revenues required for meeting those objectives might be devoted to the splendour of festivals, the restoration of temples, and so forth. The purpose, then, of the economic activity of the city is precisely the maintenance of the people and the further adornment of the city itself. When we say, with Xenophon, the maintenance or sustenance of the people we mean that in a political sense. For as Philippe Gauthier has argued in his magisterial commentary on *Ways and Means,* Xenophon is not writing about an economic *trophē,* food to keep the bodies and souls of the poor together, but a political one—a civic salary (*misthos*) in return for the fulfillment of political responsibilities and intended to allow for a full-time citizenry. Merchants, slaves, the mines at Laurion—all the veins that may be tapped for revenue—must be useful to the city, which means, in turn, that they be useful for the good life understood as political activity. Through the city's acquisition of revenues, largely at the expense of noncitizens, Athenians will be provided with those goods (time above all) required for the political life.[124]

Now Xenophon's scheme for a leisured citizenry was just that, a plan, and most Athenians did not in fact live entirely at the expense of the city any more than they lived, like Ischomachos, from the revenues of their estates.[125] Yet the object of his proposals accurately reflected the practices and values of the democratic city. Formerly, Isocrates tells us, only men "who could afford the time [*scholēn,* leisure] and possessed sufficient means should devote themselves to the care of the community,"[126] or, what amounts to much the same thing, only the wealthy could govern because they alone had the leisure to do so. For a democratic regime to be possible, or better, for that sort of democracy to exist in which the multi-

[123] Xenophon, *Ways and Means* 4.33. See also Ober, *Mass and Elite in Democratic Athens,* p. 202, for a discussion of Demosthenes' proposal for a still more extensive welfare system.

[124] See Gauthier, *Un commentaire historique des Poroi,* pp. x, 20–21, 23, 85, 168, 240, 244. On *misthos* as civic salary see also Edouard Will, "Notes sur *Misthos,*" in Bingen, Cambier, and Nachtergael, eds., *Le monde grec: Hommages à Claire Préaux.*

[125] See Mossé, *Fin de la démocratie athénienne,* p. 158; Austin and Vidal-Naquet, *Economic and Social History of Ancient Greece,* p. 119; Gauthier, *Un commentaire historique des Poroi,* pp. 31–32, 240.

[126] Isocrates, *Areopagiticus* sec. 26.

tude participates directly in the holding of offices, some means had to be
found whereby those who could not live from the rents of their property
might nevertheless be able to find the time away from necessary toil
required to be fully a citizen. Thus Aristotle observes that in democracies
sufficiently endowed with revenues pay is usually provided for a citizen's
attending the assembly or sitting on juries. Pay for public service is a
characteristic democratic device because it remedies that former condition in which only the wealthy could attend to the affairs of the community by permitting even the poor to be at leisure. The growth of democracy in Athens could accordingly be measured by the increase in paid
offices: twenty thousand persons, Aristotle claims, earned their living
from the common fund created from tribute.[127]

It would be wrong to imagine that the growth in the number of people
living, wholly or in part, at the expense of the city and the increase in their
salaries are to be credited simply to public spiritedness. For the urban
poor of Athens, the civic salary, living from the public purse, may well
have been the only alternative to the despised condition of wage labor.[128]
Taking *misthos* or pay from the community made one a sort of poor
rentier, a person leading a somewhat leisured life. And the salary associated with political offices seems to have carried with it, at least for the
proponents of democracy, not the stigma of dependency associated with a
contractual sale of one's labor to an employer but the more archaic value
of *misthos* as an "honorable recompense" for a civic service. For others,
however, the expansion of paid political offices under the democratic
regime meant that public service had, in effect, become a job—a way of
earning a living and a source of income for the poor: "Father, if the
archon say that the court won't sit today. Tell me truly, father mine, have
we wherewithal to dine?"[129] Whatever their motivation may have been,
the important point for us in this is that the poor sought as much as
possible to become rentiers and that they shunned, as best they could, the
life of the laborer as one inconsistent with citizenship and unworthy of a

[127] Aristotle, *Politics* 1293a5–7; Aristotle, *The Constitution of Athens* 24.3, and see also
27.3, 41.3, 62.2.
[128] See Mossé, *Fin de la démocratie athénienne*, pp. 156–57; Humphreys, "Economy and
Society in Classical Athens," p. 147. Ober, *Mass and Elite in Democratic Athens*, pp. 79–
81, 132–37, discusses state pay and democracy.
[129] Aristophanes, *The Wasps* 303–6. And see Isocrates, *On the Peace*, in *Isocrates*, vol. 2,
secs. 13, 129–30; Aristotle, *Politics* 1320a30ff., 1267b1ff., 1309a5–8. On pay and the
possibility of direct democracy see Veyne, *Le pain et le cirque*, pp. 203–5. See also Will,
"Notes sur *Misthos*," pp. 428, 430–31, 437.

free person.[130] Having no or too little property themselves, the community and its revenues were used as the source of their income, and
indeed the democratic city, drawing its revenues from tribute, liturgies,
and confiscations, had as one of the purposes of its fiscal policy just such
a quasi-rentier existence for its citizens. Philippe Gauthier writes that
Pericles' task was "precisely to secure a sufficient leisure for the large
majority of citizens so that all would have a really equal chance to participate equally in the government of the city. . . . The problem was no
longer political but economic. . . . And that is why Pericles devoted such
efforts to consolidating the empire. . . . The empire made Athenian
democracy into a 'leisured democracy.'"[131]

Herodotus tells us that Solon once said that "it is impossible for one
who is human to have all the good things together, just as there is no one
country that is sufficient of itself to provide all good things for itself; but
it has one thing and not another."[132] Autarky is a great good, but it
cannot be fully realized either by the individual or by the household and
perhaps not even by the city. Exchange between households, in the case of
the polis, or between cities seems therefore to be necessary. The task for
the household as for the city is to subordinate exchange, as far as is
possible, to the purposes of the community: for a people to obtain all its
food from its own soil would be best, Xenophon writes, but where that
cannot be achieved, it is wise to consider how trade can be used to
accomplish the city's ends, or, in Aristotle's elliptical phrase, the "city
should be involved in trade for itself."[133] Now, the political community
exists for the sake of life and of the good life, and we would expect that its

---

[130] See Xenophon, *Memorabilia*, trans. E. C. Marchant (Cambridge: Harvard University
Press, 1923) 2.7.3–4, and compare to 3.7.5–6. See also Mossé, *Fin de la démocratie
athénienne*, pp. 69, 160. Pericles' funeral oration suggests a less hostile view of labor.
Thucydides, *The Peloponnesian War*, pp. 104–5. For balanced assessments of labor and its
valuation in Athens see Garlan, "Le travail libre en Grèce ancienne," p. 10; Welskopf, "Free
Labour in the City of Athens," in Peter Garnsey, ed., *Non-Slave Labour in the Greco-
Roman World*, p. 23; Nicole Loraux, *The Invention of Athens: The Funeral Oration in the
Classical City*, trans. Alan Sheridan (Cambridge: Harvard University Press, 1986), pp. 182–
84. Loraux notes throughout her book how common this mixture was of aristocratic and
democratic values.

[131] Philippe Gauthier, "La cité," in Gauthier, ed., *Athènes au temps de Périclès* (Paris:
Hachette, 1964), p. 47. I have translated "à l'aise" as "leisured" rather than affluent or
comfortable because that is the sense required by the context of Gauthier's argument. And
see Aristophanes, *The Wasps* 654ff. For commentary on the uses of public property in
Athens see Erb, *Wirtschaft und Gesellschaft*, pp. 20–21, 33, 43, and Gauthier, *Un commentaire historique des Poroi*, pp. 248–49.

[132] Herodotus, *The History*, trans. David Grene (Chicago: University of Chicago Press,
1987), 1.32.

[133] Xenophon, *Ways and Means* 1.1 and 2.1; Aristotle, *Politics* 1327a28ff.

economic policies would be dedicated to those ends. And that is just what we have seen. Sustenance or food acquisition is one of the two principal goals of the city as an economic agent. The other major objective is revenue gathering, and the use to which that revenue is put, apart from helping to provide for the city's defense and for the magnificence of its temples and other public places, is to allow people in the democratic polity that leisure, the freedom from toil, which is needed if they are to participate in the deliberative and other affairs of the city—that is, in the good life.

A number of points from the preceding analysis should be underscored here. First, within quite limited confines—preventing the exploitation of food scarcity in the domestic market, prohibiting the export and encouraging the import of foodstuffs, and securing revenues—Athens did have a public economic policy, and the need for that sort of intervention and concern on the part of the city community was recognized even by the most ardent philosophical critics of the wealth-seeking life. The qualifier "within quite limited confines" requires emphasis, for this was not a state planned economy in any sense of that phrase, and much economic activity took place outside the polis' purview. This noninterference was, as Finley has written, most certainly not the result of a doctrine of laissez-faire but rather flowed from the city's purposes: to provision itself in a way adequate for the conduct of its political life. The *oikos* master attended to the necessary economic matters of his household as far as he had to and then proceeded to those activities for the sake of which the household economy functioned, namely the praxis of his leisure. So too with the city: it occupied itself with those things necessary for its non-economic purposes insofar as the former were required for the realization of the latter and not beyond that threshold.[134]

A second and related point also commands our attention: that the city's engagement in economic activity does not seem to have been driven by a desire to protect the interests of its producers or merchants against foreign competition or even, more positively, to promote its own export "industries" (pottery, for example). The growth of its productive infrastructure appears not to have figured prominently in Athenian eco-

[134] See Austin and Vidal-Naquet, *Economic and Social History of Ancient Greece,* p. 118; Finley, *The Ancient Economy,* p. 155; Finley, "Aristotle and Economic Analysis," p. 43. Vidal-Naquet puts the relationship between the ancient city and its economy this way: "One could say that the city was at one and the same time profoundly engaged in the economic world and that it was profoundly foreign to that world, because its own values were elsewhere." Vidal-Naquet, "Economie et société dans la Grèce ancienne," p. 145 (my translation).

nomic policy. Rather, its objectives were to encourage security of the food (and strategic materials) supply by facilitating imports and to amass revenues; in sum, it aimed at the "satisfaction of material wants." This is not, of course, to say that there was no commerce in Athens or that its practitioners were not deeply preoccupied with amassing private wealth. It is, however, to suggest that such activities were marginal from the point of view of the city and of its economic theoreticians, whose concerns lay elsewhere, with the food supply and with revenues and their distribution.[135] And finally, those last-named objectives show once again the intimate bonds between the ancient conception of the household economy and of the city's economic functions. In both instances, economic activity is understood as providing the material prerequisites for the good life of the community's free members. The notion of the household master as rentier and of the city living from its revenues, collected through imperium or taxes on merchants, points to a single vision of the proper place of the economy in the community, whether that latter is the *oikos* or the city. And that proper place is one subordinate to the community's purposes, central among which is the desire to be free of further involvement in the economy.

Without the necessary things, Aristotle writes, it is impossible either to live or to live well. It is not possible to live without these necessary things in the straightforward sense that humans must nourish and shelter themselves and reproduce their own kind. If what is necessary is not provided, the good life—leisure, free time to be filled with noble and virtuous actions—will not be available. The *oikos* and the city, as we have observed, are associations whose purpose is, in part, to provide the necessary things, and central to both communities is the knowledge of the proper use of its wealth, meaning the end to be served by the economy, that sphere dedicated to the provisioning of what is required for life and the good life. That end I have broadly characterized as praxis or free activity within the context of the community. Wealth, we may then say, is a totality of instruments useful for securing the needs of life and those things required for the leading of a good life.[136]

[135] See Austin and Vidal-Naquet, *Economic and Social History of Ancient Greece,* p. 123; Mossé, *Fin de la démocratie athénienne,* p. 61; Hasebroek, *Trade and Politics,* pp. vii, 24, 102; Polanyi, *The Livelihood of Man,* p. 198; Finley, *The Ancient Economy,* p. 160; Mossé, "The 'World of the Emporium,'" p. 58; Mossé, "Le IVᵉ siècle," p. 117; Vidal-Naquet, "Economie et société dans la Grèce ancienne," p. 133.

[136] Nussbaum's *The Fragility of Goodness,* chap. 11, and her "Nature, Function, and Capability: Aristotle on Political Distribution," *Oxford Studies in Ancient Philosophy,* suppl. vol., ed. Julia Annas (Oxford: Clarendon Press, 1988), pp. 145–84, contain the

2.5   Servitude

Thus far we have considered the location of the economy in the household and the city largely from the perspective of the purpose it is meant to fulfill. Another way of stating this, and one that tells us something important about the ancient Greek conception of the economy, is to say that we have examined the place of the economy from the point of view of the *oikos* master or of the citizenry; for the management of the household or of the city is carried out with a view to the needs of the (dominant) free persons above all. Among the articles of property managed for the sake of the free are human beings themselves, and the slave is one such instrument, a part of the wealth of the household and city. The slave and other persons absorbed in the production of human livelihood constitute, together with inanimate property, the necessary equipment of life which is the economy. The location of the economy and its subordination to the purposes of the community can be unpacked as the position within that community of those persons engaged of necessity in labor and production: the hierarchy of the community, household, or city thus emerges as something intimately bound up with its pursuit of the good life.[137]

We saw in our discussion of the *Odyssey* the special position occupied by the slave Eumaios in Odysseus' household. He is a part of that community and indeed a necessary one, for it is slaves and other menial laborers who must break their "knees with heart-sore labor."[138] The dancing depicted on Achilles' shield, the feasting of the suitors in Odysseus' home, and in general the freedom from the compulsion of toil characteristic of the master family are made possible by the presence of Eumaios and his kind. Yet, as we also noted, he is a stranger there, not merely because of his origins and the role of force in bringing him into the household, but because his function, as the bearer of necessity, makes him foreign to the good life and the binding *philia* of the free community. In the pages that follow, I return to the question of the location of the economy in the *oikos*, now, however, with a view to its relationship to

---

authoritative analyses of the importance of external goods to the Aristotelian account of the good life.

[137] Aristotle, *Politics* 1259b18ff., 1260a34–35, 1278b32ff., and (pseudo) Aristotle, *Economique* 1344a23–24; S. C. Humphreys, "Homo politicus and homo economicus," in Humphreys, *Anthropology and the Greeks*, p. 162; Olaf Gignon, "Die Sklaverei bei Aristoteles," in *La politique d'Aristote: Entretiens sur l'antiquité classique*, vol. 11 (Geneva: Hardt, 1965), p. 272; Weber, *Economy and Society*, vol. 2, p. 1342.

[138] Homer, *Odyssey* 20.118–19; for commentary see Lencman, *Die Sklaverei*, p. 294.

hierarchy within the community. This discussion proceeds in the following fashion: (a) slaves, laborers, metics, and the idea of community; (b) leisure and the servile classes; (c) scarcity, servitude, and technology. It should be remarked that the issue of whether there are slaves by nature, so central to the *Politics,* Book 1, is (for the most part) glossed over here, for two reasons. First, I take these arguments to be strictly cultural artifacts with no residual philosophical value. And second, much of Aristotle's analysis (and for us the most potentially interesting) of the function of the servile population rests on a theory of the place of the economy in relation to the ends of the household and city and not on an examination of the slave's soul. This emphasis is evident in, for example, the fact that in the later books of the *Politics* Aristotle merges the various branches of the servile class on the basis of their essentially similar role in the community.

2.5.1   Servitude, Community, and the Economy

Recall (from Xenophon's *Oeconomicus*) Ischomachos' telling his wife that "this household is what is common to us." Ischomachos might well have said something similar to his slaves and other servants, for they are, in a sense, a part of his *oikos.* Now, as we observed earlier, a central moment of the ancient understanding of community is the idea of a binding *philia* or mutuality among its members, and *philia* expressed in living together is the foundation for the relations between man and woman in the household. But what of the slave? Does he share a *philia* with his master? Aristotle's answer is mixed. The best friendships, he suggests, are those between persons equal and united in virtue. *Philia* there is too between the unequal, husband and wife, or parents and their children. But if the distance between individuals is too great there can be nothing in common, and where that is the case there can be no friendship. In tyrannies, for example, there can be little or no friendship between ruler and ruled, for as the tyrant Hiero tells Simonides, "Now I am deprived of those who take pleasure in me, because I have slaves instead of friends for comrades." And so also with masters and slaves, as Aristotle says: "master and slave have nothing in common [*ouden gar koinon estin*]: a slave is a living tool, just as a tool is an inanimate slave."[139] What we are seeing

---

[139] Xenophon, *Hiero* 6.1, in *On Tyranny,* ed. Leo Strauss (Ithaca: Cornell University Press, 1963), and Aristotle, *Nicomachean Ethics* 1161b3–5. Aristotle here and at *Politics* 1255b13 modifies this assertion somewhat, maintaining that there is a possibility of friendship with a slave, not qua slave, but as a human being.

here is a theoretical expression of the same ambiguity we found in Eumaios' position in Odysseus' household, that is, a person at once part of the household and yet a stranger within it. The slave is a partner in the master's life in this sense: that the slave is a living tool, and tools are a necessary part of the craftsmen's equipment. They are necessary, that is, so that the latter can practice his excellence but they are not a part of that excellence; between a craftsman and his tools there is a bond of necessity, though clearly not of friendship or mutuality. The same is true, Aristotle states, of the possessions of the household and the city: "Hence although cities need property, property is no part of the city. And there are many living things that fall under the head of property. And the city is one form of community . . . and its object is the best life that is possible."[140]

The slave is a part of the community as are all the things necessary for its purposes. The necessity of his presence there, however, does not mean that he shares in the purpose of the household; quite the contrary, he is an instrument of that purpose, of the master's praxis and the leisure required for it. That is precisely what is meant when we say that the slave is a part of the community but not a member of it in the proper sense, that of one who shares in its purpose and *philia*. One avenue of approach to an examination of the question as to why the slave does not participate in that *philia* is through the psychology of servitude. All of the members of the household are human and have souls, but souls like other composites are characterized (and ranked) by their ruling elements. The female, according to Aristotle, possesses the same soul as the male but with her the deliberative element does not have the authority that it does with the free male. The natural slave, however, does not possess the deliberative element at all nor does he have the power of foresight. The slave, in short, lacks the reasoning part of the soul, though not that irrational part which is accessible to reason.[141] In his accessibility to reason, the slave is recognized as a person; by the absence of deliberation, foresight, and choice he is rendered radically imperfect. The natural slave lacks just those capacities (deliberation and purposive action) which are essential to participation in any community that has an end beyond the animal-like pleasures of the moment. Self-rule or autonomy being impossible for him because of the nature of his soul, he does not have that freedom needed for virtue and the good life, public or private, and he cannot therefore

---

[140] Aristotle, *Politics* 1328a34ff.

[141] Aristotle, *Politics* 1252a32ff., 1260a13, and Aristotle, *Nicomachean Ethics* 1098a3ff. See W. W. Fortenbaugh, "Aristotle on Slaves and Women," in J. Barnes et al., eds., *Articles on Aristotle* (London: Duckworth, 1977), p. 136.

take his place in a community centered on a perception of justice and of the good life.

Aristotle's analysis moves beyond the level of psychology, however, in setting out the position of the servile in the community. We can see this move intimated in his conflation of slave and nonslave labor. Consider this passage from the *Politics*: "we speak of several forms of slave; for the sorts of work are several. . . . One sort is that done by menials . . . the vulgar artisan [*ho banausos*] is among them."[142] Vulgar artisans and other menials are often citizens, and Aristotle nowhere extends the psychology of the slave to them or to resident foreigners. The slavishness of their pursuits must then have other foundations. One of those foundations is that they work for others and are therefore subject to the will of another person. To be free, on this account, means at a minimum not to live under the restraint of one's fellows, for that latter condition is a central part of what it means to be a slave.[143] The free wage laborers, the vulgar artisan, even the musician who performs for an audience have in common with the slave a condition of submitting to the wills of others. The fact that they must work for others and that therefore they are not autonomous results from another slavish trait of their condition, that is, that they are not autarkic, which is to say that they cannot provide for themselves. It would seem that the minimum material requirement for a life befitting a free person was self-employment, a concept suggesting both the absence of a commanding employer and economic self-sufficiency. And it is possible that something like that was the ethos of classical Athens. Aristotle's judgment is, in that respect, more severe than that of his society. This severity is evident in his assessment of farmers, a group that would for the most part meet the requirements of an autarkic and autonomous life and whose occupation, unlike those of urban laborers, was widely held in esteem in the Greek world. Aristotle includes farmers among the "multitude" and the "laboring element" of the community, above the *banausoi,* to be sure, but in a better regime their function would be carried out by slaves.[144]

---

[142] Aristotle, *Politics* 1277a36ff.

[143] See Aristotle, *Rhetoric* 1367a32; Aristotle, *Nicomachean Ethics* 1125a1; Aristotle, *Politics* 1337b20ff. For further commentary see Will, "Notes sur *Misthos*," p. 431; Humphreys, "Economy and Society in Classical Athens," p. 147; Welskopf, *Probleme der Musse,* p. 119.

[144] Aristotle, *Politics* 1291a10, 1319a31ff., 1321a5–6, 1329a36ff., 1330a26–27. See Humphreys, "Economy and Society in Classical Athens," p. 148. For evaluations of attitudes toward other forms of economic activity see Mossé, *Fin de la démocratie athénienne,* pp. 60, 160, 163, 166; Welskopf, "Free Labour in the City of Athens," p. 23. Xenophon, *Oeconomicus* 4.2, supports Aristotle's denunciation of the *banausoi.*

With Aristotle's comments on the agrarian population we are brought closer to an understanding of what he meant by servility and why, contrary to Athenian political practice and opinion, he extended that category to include the lives of *thētes*, farmers, and vulgar artisans. The key idea here is constraint or living under necessity. The slave lives under constraint in the most transparent sense, that is, under the will of his master, and the freedoms denied him are equally plain—of working as he pleases, of going where he wishes. Wage laborers and *banausoi* also live under constraint, but their master is the many masters of the community. We might add to this that their ultimate master does not have a human face at all: it is the penury and the resulting lack of self-sufficiency which compel them to sell themselves to their employers.[145] And finally, independent farmers, self-employed and largely autarkic, lead lives under compulsion in this most extended sense that, like the farmer of Hesiod's *Works and Days,* their time and activities are necessarily consumed in the production of their own livelihood, with little space left them for virtue and the good life. The idea of a slavish existence, of leading a life under constraint and hence being denied access to the possibility of a good life, is at its most fundamental level a conception indifferent to the source of that constraint, whether one or many masters or constraining toil resulting from poverty. What matters more than whether that necessity emerges from the will of another or from penury is the loss of freedom it entails, the loss of happiness and the good life and, in relation to the community, the exclusion from the *philia* and purposes that are the binding threads of any properly ordered *koinōnia*—which is to say, any community that aims at something more than mere survival.

"Slaves have no city,"[146] said Athenaeus, and in the best cities, Aristotle suggests, the servile, those engaged in necessary toil, would also be, properly speaking, cityless. Aristotle, and Athens, knew of other economic activities conducted by persons who were in the full sense without a city—that is, the metics. Here again Aristotle brings together (and abstracts from the political/legal distinctions between these various groups) under the single heading of slavish all those engaged directly in the production of the community's livelihood: "foreign and slave metics."[147] Both slaves and foreigners are, in a literal sense, metics, people living with or beside us (*met-oikoi*) but not as partners in the political life of the city.

[145] See Bernhard Laum, *Die Geschlossene Wirtschaft: Soziologische Grundlegung des Autarkieproblems* (Tübingen: J. C. B. Mohr, 1933), p. 371.

[146] Athenaeus, *The Deipnosophists,* 7 vols., trans. C. B. Gulick (Cambridge: Harvard University Press, 1967), 6.263c.

[147] Aristotle, *Politics* 1275b37–38, and see Rhodes, *A Commentary,* p. 254.

That latter assertion has a legal/historical meaning in that neither the slave nor the resident alien had citizenship or full legal personality. It also reflects the contempt and suspicion in which such outsiders and their occupations were held, not only the drudge labor of the slave or *banausos,* but also the commerce of the metic (or of the Athenian engaged in trade, domestic or foreign).[148] More abstractly, the metic resembles the slave in existing, literally and figuratively, at the margins of the city. That is, he is divorced from the political community and does not share in the citizen's activities or honors; he is under the laws of the city, but does not participate in the making of them or in the perception of justice which is their foundation.[149] The metic as an artisan or trader, then, belongs to that group of persons, engaged in the provisioning of the community, the household, or the city, who though a part of the city must nevertheless remain, like the slave, an *étranger absolu* in relation to that community. In Pierre Vidal-Naquet's words: "Athens had need of merchants and slaves. But neither merchants nor slaves were Athens; they were an *elsewhere* of democracy, an elsewhere which made it possible."[150]

2.5.2   Servitude and Time

We have seen some of the specific reasons given for the fact that the servile and others are outsiders—the psychology of the slave's soul, the lack of autonomy of the *banausoi* and *thētes,* the penury and subjection to constraining toil of the farmers, the unlimited pursuit of wealth by traders. The *Politics* offers a further aspect of their condition which once more unites them as persons who are, in the most profound sense, slavish, unfree, and without a community: "The slave has no leisure."[151] The slave's time is at the disposal of his master and it is employed to provide the master with the leisure required for *ta kala,* the noble and beautiful actions appropriate to a free person. Leisure is essential to the good life and it is also crucial to *philia,* to friendship expressed in living and acting

---

[148] See Gauthier, *Symbola,* pp. 111–13; Hasebroek, *Trade and Politics,* pp. 8, 22; Mossé, "The 'World of the Emporium,'" pp. 58, 61. And see Ober, *Mass and Elite in Democratic Athens,* pp. 272, 275, 277.

[149] See Aristotle, *Politics* 1278a38, 1324a16ff., and Lysias, *Orations* 22.5 on metics and the city's laws and 31.6–7 on the true *philia* of the commercial man. See also Gernet, *L'approvisionnement d'Athènes en blé,* p. 348, and Humphreys, "Economy and Society in Classical Athens," p. 144.

[150] Pierre Vidal-Naquet, *La démocratie grecque vue d'ailleurs* (Paris: Flammarion, 1990), p. 15 (my translation). See also Vidal-Naquet, *Le chasseur noir,* p. 214.

[151] Aristotle, *Politics* 1334a19.

together. The slave, and other menials whose time is devoted to the necessary things, have no leisure for *philia,* public or private: "Lack of leisure to join in the concerns of friends and of the city . . . is another condition of those that are called mechanical." The slave lacks the time to cultivate his own excellence through, for example, horsemanship, hunting, or philosophy or to share in the activity of the political community. He lacks the time, as we have said, because the production in which he is forced to engage by his masters consumes his hours so as to free time for his owner's praxis.[152]

Leisure is lacking also for those engaged in toil of other kinds, those not directly and permanently under the household master's supervision. The "vulgar artisan" is leisureless and so too are farmers and all those of moderate property, as well as the merchant, though in his case it is likely that the endless pursuit of wealth, *pleonexia,* is responsible for usurping his time.[153] The reason for their being without leisure is the necessity of constraining toil. The leisure denied them by that constraint is as essential to the virtue of a citizen as it is to the private excellence of the master or to friendship.[154] Those immersed in the life of provisioning, whether as producers or traders, are therefore outsiders for yet another reason: they do not have the leisure necessary both with a view to virtue or to the excellence of a citizen. That these occupations, legally free or not according to the form of the regime, are constrained and radically unfree, slavish, is revealed in precisely that absence of leisure, for, as Socrates said, leisure is the sister of freedom.

We have now seen the idea of a household economy from its underside, that is, from the perspective not of the masters but of those engaged in provisioning them. This latter group, including (for Aristotle) all those who produce or traffic in the things required by the *oikos* or the city, is an indispensable part of the community. The slave is needed to provide for the livelihood of the master family in the household and for the leisure of the master himself, and a city must be equipped with those whose lives are consumed in producing what the polis needs for securing the wants of its members. Without them, there would be no city, for the political association is one that aims at life and the good life. At the same time,

---

[152] Xenophon, *Oeconomicus* 4.3, and see Isocrates, *Areopagiticus* secs. 26 and 45, for these uses of leisure. See also Welskopf, "Loisir et esclavage," p. 163, and Welskopf, *Probleme der Musse,* p. 215.

[153] See Aristotle, *Politics* 1291b23, 1292b24ff.; Schlaifer, "Greek Theories of Slavery," pp. 174–75; Welskopf, *Probleme der Musse,* pp. 218, 220.

[154] Aristotle, *Politics* 1278a10–11, 1329a1–3, 1269a35.

however, they are, like Eumaios, a part of the community in a special sense. For leading constrained lives, lives under necessity (whether that of a master or of penury makes no difference), they can have no share in that higher common purpose which makes a community what it is. They are strangers or outsiders within their own households or cities. They are, we might say, rather like the instruments or tools to which Aristotle often compares them: things necessary and useful, but distinct from and subordinate to the intended purpose.

For the household master to be free from that necessity which threatens all persons, the necessity that arises from the human incapacity for complete and effortless self-sufficiency—from the grim poverty and scarcity that afflict all of humankind and that promises to bind him to toil for no end greater than that of sustaining life alone—it is necessary that the burden of provisioning the community be shifted to others. Similarly, for the citizen to be free from that toil which would necessarily keep him from the exercise of his political prerogatives, he must either live from his property as a rentier or from the city in the form of sustenance or salary. To the greatest extent possible, the free must guard their freedom by ensuring that they live from the constrained activities of others: of slaves, of the empire and its tribute, of metics, and so forth. Otto Erb's judgment "rentier or nothing, that is, a slave, unfree, without rights"[155] may be too sharp and certainly does not capture the actual condition of most Athenians, but it does express a cluster of ideas which stands at the very center of the ancient conception of the household economy: that to be a member of the community one must be free; that to be free includes not being subject to the will of another, master or employer, but extends beyond that to freedom from the constraint of necessity, especially the necessity to provide for one's own livelihood; lastly, that expanded sense of freedom in turns demands that one strive to be a rentier, to live from the toil of others, foreigners or slaves. Hierarchy within the household and city, imperium, or the effective peaceful exploitation of foreigners (as proposed by Xenophon) are essential to these communities and to the realization of one of their principal purposes, namely the greatest possible suppression of the economic sphere, the production of human livelihood, for the sake of their free members, indeed as a condition of their being free.[156]

[155] Erb, *Wirtschaft und Gesellschaft,* p. 21.

[156] Friedrich Oertel, commenting on Bücher, succinctly expresses the historical reality of this "preponderance of force" (to borrow John Dunn's phrase): "[Athens'] economy rested on force," in Oertel, "Anhang" to Robert von Pöhlmann's *Geschichte der Sozialen Frage und des Sozialismus in der Antiken Welt,* 3d ed., 2 vols. (Munich: C. H. Beck'sche Ver-

2.5.3   "If Thus Shuttles Wove": Scarcity and Domination

The *philia* of the community, its freedom, and its governing purpose, the life of *ta kala,* required a shifting of the economy and its characteristically constrained activities onto a segment of the population at once a part of the community, that is, as its necessary equipment, and foreign to its ends and the mutuality of its full members. In a word, hierarchy, domination, and exclusion were central and indispensable to this community. The importance of this thought for the ancient conception of community and economy is illuminated for us by the following sentences from the *Politics:* "if every tool could perform its own work when ordered . . . like the statues of Daedalus in the story or the tripods of Hephaestus which the poet says 'enter self-moved the company of the divine'—if thus shuttles wove and quills played harps of themselves, mastercraftsmen would have no need of assistants and masters no need of slaves."[157] Were there machines which could produce by themselves without need of humans, then the hierarchy of the *oikos* would no longer be necessary.

Hesiod's portrait of an age in which the earth's fruits were given to humans with little or no expenditure of effort on their part carries much the same meaning: slaves do not appear in the poem's story about that time but only in its account of the period in which the evils of Pandora's jar had spread grim poverty and toil among humankind. And we learn from Athenaeus of other representations of this now-disappeared life when "things needful came of their own accord." The earth provided humans with their livelihood, cakes sought out the mouths of the hungry, and fish baked themselves—sustenance was provided without toil. Under such conditions "what need had we of household servants?"[158] Athenaeus suggests that these visions of a golden age in which nature's generous provisioning made servitude unnecessary came increasingly to be the object of mockery, and it is likely that Aristotle's passage on Hephaistos' tripods is meant to convey just how fantastic that vision was thought to be.[159] The reality of the human condition, as the ancients saw it with

---

lagsbuchhandlung, 1925), vol. 2, p. 518 and also 544. For additional commentary see Hasebroek, *Trade and Politics,* and Gauthier, *Un commentaire historique des Poroi,* p. 240.

[157] Aristotle, *Politics* 1253b33–1254a1.

[158] Athenaeus, *The Deipnosophists* 6.268b, d, and see also 267e–f.

[159] Athenaeus, *The Deipnosophists* 6.269e. See Raymond Weil, "Deux notes sur Aristote et l'esclavage," *Revue philosophique de la France et de l'étranger* 172 (1982): 340; H. C. Baldry, "The Idler's Paradise in Attic Comedy," *Greece and Rome* 22 (1953): 59; Joseph

their unequaled clarity of vision, was that the struggle for livelihood
required sweat and toil and bound humans in a web of compulsion from
which the only escape for some was the servitude and wasted lives of
others. The earth not being spontaneously bountiful, it was best to have
slaves, and if one was too poor to own slaves, women and children could
fulfill their functions. It is tempting to speculate that Hope (as Hesiod
recounts, Zeus ordered Pandora to keep *Elpis* in her jar so that amidst all
the travails inflicted through her, Hope at least would not be denied
humankind) refers to the wish that a world without toil and slaves might
again be the human condition.[160] But whether Aristotle's comment on
the shuttles weaving and the quills playing of themselves is evidence that
Hope had not yet escaped Pandora's jar, and with this the promise of a
different future, or whether it is a plain rejection of that fantastic vision is
less important for us than what it reveals about the ancient conception of
the economy: the centrality of a certain type of scarcity to the human
estate; the necessity of toil and the exclusion, as far as possible, of that
necessity from the community and from the lives of its free members;
servitude as the means of effecting that exclusion, as long as the dream of
a bountiful nature and of a life without toil remains nothing more than
that, a sweet dream.

2.6   Pandora's Jar: The Idea of the Economy

In these pages, I have written as if it were plain that the Greeks did have
a concept of the economy, of scarcity, surpluses, and maximization (of a
sort). That assumption itself, seemingly unproblematic, is in fact much
challenged. This issue is more than a merely exegetical matter because on
its outcome depends, for students of political philosophy and normative
political economy, whether we, living in and thinking about such a profoundly altered social and economic landscape, can still hope to learn
from these authors who considered an economy now long dead. One
path, and by far the most radical, which this challenge follows is that

---

Vogt, *Ancient Slavery and the Ideal of Man,* trans. Thomas Wiedermann (Cambridge:
Harvard University Press, 1975), pp. 28–29; Garlan, "Le travail libre en Grèce ancienne,"
p. 17. An account of a less fanciful ancient Greek picture of an age without slaves can be
found in Beringer, "Freedom, Family, and Citizenship in Early Greece," p. 45.

160 Hesiod, *Works and Days* 96, and for commentary Seth Benardete, "Hesiod's *Works
and Days:* A First Reading," *Agon* 1 (1967): 154–55; West, *Prolegomena and Commentary
to Hesiod,* pp. 169–70; Baldry, "The Idler's Paradise in Attic Comedy," p. 51.

marked out by Karl Polanyi and his circle. Very schematically, it proceeds as follows. The noncapitalist, nonmarket economy, including (with some reservations) that of the ancient Greek world, was of a "substantive" type, which is to say that it was an "instituted process," that is, embedded and patterned through an array of noneconomic institutions, in which the interaction of humans and nature yielded the material means for the satisfaction of their wants.[161] This "sociologized" conception of the substantive economy, as one critic has called it, leads to the further idea that the economy as a distinct sphere of inquiry is dissolved into an analysis of the institutions in which it is embedded. There was then no ancient concept of the economy as a distinct and coherent sphere of activity, and so also was there no economic theory, for the possibility of the latter, it is maintained, depends on the recognition of an autonomous, law-governed cluster of phenomena called the economy—and such cannot be said to exist in societies with an embedded economy.[162] The additional claim is made that the substantive concept of the economy is entirely distinct from its modern (sometimes specified as post-eighteenth-century) counterpart, that is, the "formal" conception. That latter idea focuses not on the institutions in which the economy is embedded (for it originates in a world characterized by the disembedded economy) but on "means-ends" rationality, which is, in turn, often identified as the utilitarian calculus, with Jeremy Bentham as its greatest exponent. Its corollaries, according to Polanyi, are concepts of scarcity, surplus, and wealth maximization, and, in its operational analysis, the "formal" approach seeks to understand scarcity-induced choices among means for the realization of rank-ordered ends. The transhistorical claims of the "formal" conception are a crucial part of the reason for the Polanyi challenge, which asserts, in sum, that this conception may be valuable for unpacking the workings of a full-blown, autonomous market economy but not for the study of premarket societies, which is to say "all" earlier societies.

In its most stringent form this interpretation asserts the "invisibility" of the precapitalist economy. This supposed invisibility stems, as we have just observed, from (a) the nonexistence or marginality of markets, which

---

[161] See Karl Polanyi, "The Economy as Instituted Process," in Polanyi, Conrad M. Arensberg, and Harry W. Pearson, eds., *Trade and Market in the Early Empires* (New York: Free Press, 1957), pp. 248, 250; Terence K. Hopkins, "Sociology and the Substantive View of the Economy," in Polanyi et al., *Trade and Market in the Early Empires*, p. 299.

[162] The critic is Scott Cook, "The Obsolete 'Anti-Market' Mentality: A Critique of the Substantive Approach to Economic Anthropology," *American Anthropologist* 68 (1966): 328. See also Polanyi, "Aristotle Discovers the Economy," p. 71, and Finley, *The Ancient Economy*, p. 22.

are defined, in essence, as autonomous (of noneconomic institutions) price-making mechanisms; (b) the absence of a concept of scarcity, the latter notion being held to be a product of the conceptualization of a pervasive market economy; (c) the absence of an idea of surplus as the goal and consequence of economic activity; (d) finally, economizing, or rational action based on scarcity, and the choices induced by that condition are consequently historically finite concepts constructed for the post-eighteenth-century world.

These arguments are open to a range of challenges, but I restrict myself to a sketch of those criticisms that bear on the analysis presented here. Let us begin with a challenge to Polanyi's rejection of scarcity as a concept useful for understanding premarket economies and economic thought. If this rejection is taken to mean the denial of scarcity simply, then it is manifestly untenable, for while we know of some goods that are not scarce, we know of no postscarcity societies. The more modest version, that needs and therefore scarcity have a socially determined component, is a sensible proposition but one that cannot perform the service demanded of it by the substantivists, namely the denial of economizing behavior (the "formal" means-end theory of behavior) as a characteristic of precapitalist societies.[163] Once we acknowledge that the idea of scarcity may also be a useful way of describing conditions in which (non-market) goods are in short supply and can be secured only by the payment of a (monetary or a nonmonetary/shadow) price, it becomes clear that one important error of the Polanyi-type argument was to conflate scarcity as a pervasive feature of the human condition with its market variant and thereby to dismiss it as a category for analyzing premarket societies.[164]

[163] See Cook, "The Obsolete 'Anti-Market' Mentality," p. 333; George Dalton, "Economic Theory and Primitive Society," *American Anthropologist* 63 (1961): 4–5; Harry W. Pearson, "The Economy Has No Surplus: Critique of a Theory of Development," in Karl Polanyi et al., eds., *Trade and Market in the Early Empires,* pp. 322–23. See also George Dalton, "A Note of Clarification on Economic Surplus," *American Anthropologist* 62 (1960): 483–90. Amartya Sen, "Poor, Relatively Speaking," in Sen, *Resources, Values and Development* (Oxford: Basil Blackwell, 1984), and Sen, *Poverty and Famines: An Essay on Entitlement and Deprivation* (Oxford: Clarendon Press, 1981), pp. 9–23, contain fascinating conceptual examinations of the ideas of poverty and deprivation.

[164] Neil J. Smelser, "A Comparative View of Exchange Systems," *Economic Development and Cultural Change* 7 (1958–59): 176–77; Edward E. LeClair, "Economic Theory and Economic Anthropology," *American Anthropologist* 64 (1962): 1180–87; Robbins Burling, "Maximization Theory and the Study of Economic Anthropology," *American Anthropologist* 64 (1962): 804, 810–13. But see also Edouard Will's warning against conflating the modern and ancient senses of the word "economic" in Will, "Bulletin historique: Histoire grecque" *Revue Historique* 238 (1967): 439–42.

Scarcity and the economizing behavior it induces among agents are features of all known societies, though defined and institutionalized in different ways. It is just that latter addition that makes Polanyi's analysis valuable (though this is, as he recognizes, by no means his insight alone), for, as Maurice Godelier and Robert Bates have argued, without something like it the notion of economizing behavior remains a quite sterile theory of purposive action under one set of conditions, that is, economizing under scarcity.[165] A similar counter can be made to the rejection of surplus-creation as a characteristic of nonmarket-directed production. If the substantivist argument amounts to the claim that not all societies seek surpluses denominated in monetary terms and that not all societies produce for price-setting markets through which profits are realized, then it is not contentious. Surpluses can be embodied, for instance, in material subsistence insurance (food stocks), in leisure, or in conspicuous consumption. And those surpluses may be secured outside of the context of the market, for example, in the Homeric world, through war. This is only to repeat, in another form, the argument just made: surpluses may well be socially defined and secured through an array of institutions, of which the market is only one. Such a modest reformulation of the idea of surplus would not, however, likely satisfy the substantivist, for it again calls into question the notion of the radical exceptionalism of the ancient economies which underpins their analysis.[166]

As I have suggested, one background claim of Part One has been that the ancient Greeks did have a concept of the economy and that, in their analysis of the phenomena associated with it, ideas of scarcity, surplus,

---

[165] Maurice Godelier, *Rationality and Irrationality in Economics*, trans. Brian Pearce (New York: Monthly Review Press, 1972), pp. 9–15; Robert H. Bates, *Essays on the Political Economy of Rural Africa* (Cambridge: Cambridge University Press, 1983), pp. 138–40.

[166] See Douglass C. North, "Markets and Other Allocation Systems in History: The Challenge of Karl Polanyi," *Journal of European Economic History* 6 (1977): 703, and Burling, "Maximization Theory and the Study of Economic Anthropology," p. 817. Michael Hechter's "Karl Polanyi's Social Theory: A Critique," in Michael Hechter, ed., *The Microfoundations of Macrosociology* (Philadelphia: Temple University Press, 1983), criticizes Polanyi from a rational-choice perspective, though its substantive concern is with the theory of the state in modern market societies. A conceptually related critique, this time directed at Finley, can be found in Gerald A. Gunderson, "Economic Behavior in the Ancient World," in Roger L. Ransom, Richard Sutch, and Gary W. Walton, eds., *Explorations in the New Economic History: Essays in Honor of Douglass C. North* (New York: Academic Press, 1982), pp. 236–37, and M. W. Frederiksen, "Theory, Evidence, and the Ancient Economy," *Journal of Roman Studies* 65 (1975): 164–71. Paul Veyne's brief remarks ("Débat sur l'oeuvre de Karl Polanyi," *Annales: Economies, Sociétés, Civilisations* 29 [1974]: 1375–80) concerning Polanyi on the noneconomizing character of precapitalist economies remain one of the most trenchant critical pieces on this subject.

and maximization figured prominently. Polanyi-type claims of the kind expressed in (b), (c), and (d) above are consequently not useful for an understanding of ancient economic thought. A modified version of proposition (a) does, however, capture a crucial aspect of classical Greek economics and one that gives a distinctive cast to its notions of scarcity and surplus. In the pages that follow I begin with that first thesis, the nonautonomy of the economic sphere (and of ancient economic science) as a central moment of the household conception of the economy and proceed from there to its other related features including those of scarcity, maximization, and surplus.

The idea of the *oikos* economy (and its reflection at the level of the city) had at its center production for the satisfaction of need. Need in turn was conceived of, in the first instance, as the requirements of human existence but beyond that of the possibility of praxis, of unconstrained activity, for the household's free members. To those needs, we saw added a third: the achievement of the greatest possible autarky, or material independence, of the community, which meant, for the individual, freedom from constraining toil and from the necessity, out of penury, to come under the authority of another through the sale of labor. For the city, autarky meant a minimum of dependence on other communities and its intervention in trade in order to secure the needs of the citizen (free) community. In short, production and trade were understood as instruments in the service of sustenance, of independence, individual and political, and of the praxis of free persons. Put in another way, economic activity was subordinated to a set of purposes held by the *oikos* or the city.

We can, with this background, agree that the ancients had no (or only the thinnest) concept of an (autonomous) economic sphere, *if* by the latter is meant a group of phenomena—the interactions of individuals in pursuit of their livelihood—generating laws on their own and independent of the intentions of the dominant community.[167] They were, it should be added, most certainly familiar with the workings of economic laws of the sort commonly embraced under that heading. Aristotle, in his discussion of Thales and the olive presses, shows that he knew of the effects of monopoly on price and of the pursuit of riches through control of a market.[168] Lysias' orations provide abundant evidence of an aware-

---

[167] On the absence of an idea of the autonomous economy see Will, *Le monde grec,* vol. 1, p. 201; Austin and Vidal-Naquet, *Economic and Social History,* pp. 9, 13; Cartledge, "'Trade and Politics' Revisited: Archaic Greece," p. 5; Vidal-Naquet, "Economie et société dans la Grèce ancienne," p. 136.

[168] Cf. Polanyi, "Aristotle Discovers the Economy," pp. 66–67, 86–87.

ness of hoarding, famine, and the profits to be reaped from a cornered market in times of production shortfalls. And Xenophon, in both his *Oeconomicus* and *Ways and Means,* understood supply-demand-price relationships and the value of the good organization/discipline of production within the household.[169] But as has been argued earlier in this Part (and which I summarize below), these few and marginal insights into economic laws typically appear in a context that attempts to show how the city or household may exploit them too for its own noneconomic purposes. I have already observed that I do not wish to venture the anachronistic assertion that the Athenian economy was planned: the city intervened in matters crucial to it, ensuring food supply and revenue acquisition, but beyond that much economic activity was outside of its purview. What I do suggest is that at the levels of both the household and city, the economy was considered as a means to ends outside the economic sphere itself.

To claim that the ancients did not and could not have had a concept of the economy simply[170] is to commit the mistake of identifying the economic as such with those traits peculiar to its market form and then to deny the presence of both in the precapitalist world. Aristotle, Xenophon, and others did have a conception of the economic, one far more important than the list of prosaic insights sketched above. At its core it includes the two branches of wealth getting, the one devoted to providing for the needs of the household and the city and the other to the pursuit of unlimited wealth; the hierarchical categorization of persons engaged in the provisioning of the necessary things—slaves, *banausoi,* farmers, and traders—and finally the art of managing them, at its highest point, required the knowledge of the ends that such management ought to serve. The economy consisted of that bundle of activities, persons, and things (e.g., land) which provided the necessities required by the household and the polis in order that they might be free of the constraint that was attributed to the economic sphere. Indeed, that very distinction between things and activities necessary for human livelihood and the world of *ta kala,* of noble and free actions whether of a political or nonpublic kind, demanded of Aristotle a clear and distinct concept of the economy. This

---

[169] For parallel arguments see Maurice Godelier, "Politics as a Relation of Production: A Dialogue with Edouard Will," in Godelier, *The Mental and the Material,* pp. 197–98; Mossé, "Le IVᵉ siècle," pp. 117, 219; Mossé, "Xénophon économiste," p. 170.

[170] Cf. Finley, "Aristotle and Economic Analysis," p. 49, but compare to Finley, "Trade and Politics in the Ancient World: Classical Greece," in *Deuxième conférence internationale d'histoire économique, Aix-en-Provence, 1962,* vol. 1 (Paris: Mouton, 1965), p. 33.

recognition of the economy and this normative/theoretical rejection of
the autonomy of the economic sphere are combined in the ideal of the
rentier and rentier-city and in the ways in which that ideal was, however
partially, approached in practice. Xenophon's Ischomachos knows the
economy and what is needed for its proper management (i.e., for the
increase of his property), and he knows its value to him (i.e., that it
provides him with those things necessary so that he may participate in the
affairs of his city and of his friends). That latter principle, given a much
richer philosophical exposition by Aristotle, reveals the source of the laws
and the purposes to which the economy is subordinate; the former idea
displays the recognition of the economy. In the combination of the two,
we see the outlines of one of the centerpieces of the ancient Greek understanding of the household economy, namely, its distinct but subordinate
and nonindependent quality. In the following pages, I discuss the notions
of scarcity and surplus in ancient Greek economic thought with the end
before me of returning one final time to that core idea: the contained and
embedded economy.

The importance of the concept of scarcity for classical economics is
apparent above all in the fanciful images of life sustained without toil or
expenditures of any other sort. These images are to be found in the
Homeric poems, in Hesiod's dream of a golden race of men, as well as in
Aristotle's *Politics*, Book 1, and in the literary references of Athenaeus. All
of these texts point to a world in which the things necessary for life are
given through the abundant generosity of nature or through self-moving
instruments of production, a world in which there was no scarcity. And
where there are no scarce goods there is no economy:[171] Hesiod's golden
men do not toil, Aristotle's owners of self-moving shuttles do not have
slaves. We can easily imagine that there is no commerce between persons
under such conditions and that autarky, material self-sufficiency, is not a
problem or a task but a given. The central properties of the ancient
conception of the economy: constraining toil, hierarchy, trade, and the
struggle for autarky and the good life are not to be found in this imaginary world without scarcity. Unlike that fantastical world, the actual one,
as the ancients understood it, imposed grim poverty on persons, required
of them expenditures to provide for their daily and recurring needs, and
made the good life and autarky things to be struggled for in the face of the
poverty of the human condition. Scarcity and neediness were the human
lot. The genealogy of communities which Aristotle elaborates on in *Poli-*

---

[171] See Carl Menger, *Principles of Economics*, trans. James Dingwall and Bert F. Hoselitz
(New York: New York University Press, 1976), pp. 94–96, 98–99, 100–101, 289–90.

tics, Book 1, is an account among other things of the ways in which persons have sought to deal with that fundamental fact of scarcity or, in other words, to provide for their needs including the need for a life dedicated to activities beyond those that provide the essentials of human livelihood.

That latter thought should lead us to consider in some more detail just what was understood by scarcity. The portraits of a world without scarcity provide us again with a valuable starting point. They typically represent not a surfeit of wealth of any material sort but rather a world without toil in which the necessary equipment of life is given to humans without effort on their part. What the grim poverty of the human estate threatens is not so much subsistence or survival but the possibility of a life beyond toil, the pursuit of *ta kala* or of the life of the citizen: "For in an empty belly no love of the beautiful can reside."[172] To this question of the possibility of praxis must be added another crucial and related good threatened by human neediness: the freedom that is intimately bound up with material autarky. The lack of things necessary, that menace which looms over humankind, threatens to reduce them to drudgery without end, to put them under the authority of others, and to rob their city of its independence. Autarky and scarcity stand, therefore, in the "sharpest opposition."[173] The scarcity problem for ancient economic thought is generated not by the difficulties in securing an income floor, a minimum of those things essential for human livelihood. Rather, it arises from the consequences of neediness for the pursuit of other, noneconomic, ends. Scarcity, to repeat, threatens not just survival as such but the possibility of the good life. And it does that by compelling the expenditure of time on the production of necessities, by taking the farmer of the Homeric world away from the singing and dancing depicted on Achilles' shield, away from Zephyr's breezes and the enjoyment of one's choice wine, and away from the shared virtues and pastimes of friends and citizens. The insufficiency of means imposes costs of a specific sort, costs denominated in time expended under constraint (whether of necessary toil through penury or the constraint of a master) and drawn from that reservoir of hours available for the noble and free activities of leisure. Time as a precondition for the good life and for the community of friends or citizens engaged in forms of it; time as the fruit of freedom from constraint—it is that which was, perhaps, the most important of scarce goods.[174]

[172] Athenaeus, *The Deipnosophists* 6.270b.

[173] Laum, *Die Geschlossene Wirtschaft,* p. 371.

[174] See Ronald Frankenberg, "Economic Anthropology or Political Economy?" in John Clammer, ed., *The New Economic Anthropology* (New York: St. Martin's Press, 1978),

The theory of the household economy also saw a place for surplus. Here, as in the case of the ancient analysis of scarcity, there is both a tangible and a nontangible dimension to the idea of surplus. Human neediness imperils the possibility of a life beyond the daily struggle for physical preservation. A surplus of economic goods (property and persons) is therefore vital in order to allow for a surplus of that different and most precious cluster of (interrelated) goods: leisure, community, and noble praxis. The first part of that proposition defines surplus in relation to a threshold of economic goods sufficient to secure survival and the lowest level of autarky, that of the self-sufficient direct producer. At that level of possessions, physical needs and a minimal independence (that of freedom from a master, and hence above the level of the *thēs* and slave) have been secured, but freedom from the necessity to toil and consequently freedom for other goods have not. In a sentence, the surplus of time, for praxis and community, that is, those needs left after the requirements of life have been attended to, is made possible by surplus economic goods, the excess over what must be provided so as to meet the lowest acceptable levels of material well-being and independence.

Concepts of scarcity and surplus there certainly were in ancient economic thought, and so too the idea of economizing. These ideas and the behavior to which they refer are to be found in forms not much different from those attributed to actors in modern markets: exploitation of scarce supply, conventional economic motivations (material-wealth acquisition), and so forth. But in the theoretical literature with which we are concerned, and quite possibly for many citizens of Athens as well, they had a rather different cast. That is, scarcity, surplus, the husbanding of resources, and the choice of their best allocation were concepts defined with reference to a view of the good life and citizen activity. Scarcity was understood as a shortfall measured against the benchmark of a leisured and autarkic life. If wealth meant "not having to work,"[175] scarcity involved having insufficient equipment for that end. The size of one's property and the management of it were the instruments at hand which, when present in sufficient abundance, permitted a cessation of economic

---

p. 70, and for some of the peculiarities of time as an economic good, e.g., that it cannot be stored or saved but must be expended, see Tibor Scitovsky, *Human Desire and Economic Satisfaction: Essays on the Frontiers of Economics* (New York: New York University Press, 1986), pp. 74.

[175] Austin and Vidal-Naquet, *Economic and Social History,* p. 16, and G. E. M. de Ste. Croix, *The Class Struggle in the Ancient Greek World* (Ithaca: Cornell University Press, 1981), p. 122.

activity. Economizing in such a view would be centered on the economization of time as the room for the pursuit of political or other free and noble activities, which is simply another way of saying that economizing would amount to preventing, so far as was possible, the encroachment of the economy, with its necessary expenditures of time and effort, on the lives of citizens.

We can better understand this notion of scarcity and economizing by looking at a microlevel illustration: the management of the *oikos*. The despotic management of the household economy emerges from the purpose governing it, the confinement within the smallest possible circumference of the master's engagement in economic activity. Under conditions of scarcity and a seemingly nature-imposed necessity, the satisfaction of the master's wants for the things of the good life required the transfer of economic activity to others. In order for the *oikos*' dominant member to achieve that detachment from the realm of material provisioning, it was necessary that he escape so far as was possible from the activity of supervising his laborers. Hence the household head, if he could afford it, employed an overseer (*epitropos*) to rule his slaves and other servants. Xenophon's *Oeconomicus* provides us with a homely but telling glimpse into the use of such overseers. Ischomachos has the leisure to discuss economics with Socrates just because he has seen to the good management of his *oikos*. His excellence as an economist of the ancient type, that he is *oikonomikos,* is demonstrated precisely by his detachment from economic activity. In particular, this detachment is an effect of his having trained a steward, the person directly responsible for the expenditure of labor in the household's outdoor production. The overseer serves to free the master from the tasks of supervision by acting to prevent shirking, which is especially to be feared among those too much enamored with wine drinking, sleeping, and sex. Incentives, material and honorific, and direct discipline are his principal instruments in this effort. The objective of this discipline is, to repeat, not the production of more things or of things more cheaply made; it is rather the creation of the material foundations of the master's praxis.[176]

The discipline of the household economy has as well a second branch, that of its indoor affairs. Here it is the wife who assumes the role of the overseer, governing the indoor servants (themselves primarily female).[177]

---

[176] Xenophon *Oeconomicus* 12.9–14, 13.9, 14.6, 9, and Aristotle, *Politics* 1255b30ff., 1260b3ff.

[177] Xenophon, *Oeconomicus* 3.15, 7.3, 22, and (pseudo) Aristotle, *Economique* 1343b23–1344a7.

The wife has an important and directly economic function in the *oikos*—supervision of domestic labor—and accordingly she contributes to its noneconomic purposes as does the overseer in the fields. It is crucial also to observe that it is her gender and its place in the social cosmos of antiquity which assigns her this function. This division of labor rests on an underlying conception of what is "appropriate" for females and males to do. There are male and female functions, and such social/political appropriateness permeates the organization of the household and of the city. In sum, this is (in Godelier's phrase) a profoundly political economy, alike in the purpose and limits of economic activity and in the saturation of that sphere by the status norms of the *koinōnia.*[178]

If ideas of scarcity, surplus, and economizing behavior make ancient economic thought recognizable as a teaching on economics (undermining, thereby, claims of the radical exceptionalism of the Greek economy), the preceding paragraphs signal to us those of its features which gave that body of thought its distinctive form. Its defining horizon (the notion that economic activity and the material goods it requires and produces are instruments in the service of another and different purpose, a central characteristic of which is precisely the absence of further economic activity), means that the material economy has a limit, a threshold beyond which further expansion, new acquisitions, more commerce, advances in technology or production techniques, and so forth are not sought. Not only are they not sought but, and this is the core of Aristotle's and Xenophon's critique of the chrematistic life, the pursuit of them (the further investment of time in them) is judged perverse and, in a sense, irrational, for it draws down on just that good which the economy is to produce, the leisure and freedom its direct production of (material) goods is intended to yield. Such choices were not, as Godelier has argued in another context, "irrational" but rather represent an appropriate allocation of that most scarce of goods, time, within the horizon of a rank ordering of its various possible uses.[179] In that world, the squandering of time on additional economic activity was deemed perverse as, in a mirror image, would time away from production and wealth creating be judged slothful, or even sinful, in a later society. This is to say, in brief, that

[178] Xenophon, *Oeconomicus* 7.29, and Hesiod, *Works and Days,* 64ff. The Godelier reading can be found in Maurice Godelier, *The Mental and the Material,* trans. Martin Thom (London: New Left Books, 1986), p. 212.

[179] Godelier, "Politics as a Relation of Production," p. 212, and see Mossé, *Fin de la démocratie athénienne,* pp. 66–67, 102, 156–57; Mossé, "The 'World of the Emporium,'" p. 61; Keith Hopkins, Introduction to Garnsey et al., *Trade in the Ancient Economy,* p. xiii; Finley, "Land, Debt, and the Man of Property," p. 72.

concepts of need, surplus, and maximization in ancient economic thought contained within them a boundary or set of limits and that the idea of that boundary formed the basis of the denunciation of *pleonexia* and of market-oriented life generally.

Similar properties have been observed in noncapitalist peasant economies, for example, "target incomes," hostility to the market, and a generally conservative approach to innovation and economic expansion. Such societies, however (if we accept for the purpose of this analysis that these accounts of the workings of the precapitalist peasant village are accurate), have subsistence as their target, are hostile to markets because they fear that their precarious existence is threatened by the uncertainties of the market, and are noninnovating and risk-averse for that same reason, that is, the "safety-first" principle.[180] The economic thought we are considering here, and in some significant measure its corresponding practices as well, were not driven so much by these subsistence concerns as by a conception of the good life and the requirements of citizen activity. Its economic conservatism, the hostility to a life consumed in toil or in the markets, in general the idea of limits which enclosed economic activity, were not the reflections of a risk-averse society working at the margin of subsistence. Quite the contrary, they appear as a choice of how best to use a surplus created by a slave or servile population (in the household economy) or via empire, tribute, and taxes (in the city economy).

This idea of the economy we might designate an embedded and contained one. It is embedded not (or not only) in the general sense that its various functions are moments of the operations of overarching social institutions or, to borrow Finley's phrase, as a consequence of the heavy encroachment of political and status claims on the economic sphere.[181] Rather, the ideal of the embedded economy meant the subordination, insofar as this was possible, of all aspects of the securing of human livelihood to the purposes of the free community, whether those be praxis (private or political), the autarky of the household or of the city. What this ideal points to is a conception of wealth and its acquisition which like a thread runs through and unites the works we have been considering: that wealth is an instrument, a means, and not an end-in-itself and that like all instruments it is governed and limited by its proper end. To lose sight of the purpose for which wealth is nothing more than a servant is to bring down on oneself the fate of King Midas, who could not nourish

[180] See James C. Scott, *The Moral Economy of the Peasant* (New Haven: Yale University Press, 1976), especially pp. 13, 18, 24, 40.
[181] Finley, "Aristotle and Economic Analysis," p. 49.

himself because everything he touched turned to gold. That nourishment of human life, now more broadly construed than in the Midas fable, is the end in relation to which a measure of wealth is necessary.

The phrase "the contained economy" expresses that end: by "contained" is meant that the range of effects of the grim poverty of human existence and the resulting struggle for livelihood were to be kept within the smallest possible compass. Chief among those effects, the impact of which was to be minimized, were constraints on time (the necessity of toil) and the threat of a radical loss of independence in relation to others, to the *thēs'* employer, for example, or to foreign cities. The idea of the contained economy was bound up with a conception of the good life which, however much distance there may have been between its philosophical and popular expressions, had as its core the two related qualities of leisure and autarky. And it was precisely those two properties that the uncontained economy threatened by consigning persons to ceaseless toil or to the constrained life of commerce. Such a theory, it should be underscored, was concerned with a wide array of activities associated with the production of human livelihood and not, as some modern commentators intimate, with market activity alone. *Pleonexia,* we might say, is one, but only one, form in which the securing of human livelihood impinges on that space needed for other and higher human possibilities. The rejection of the chrematistic life rests on the same foundation as the fear of penury, for under both sets of conditions the good life is denied to humans.

We have already suggested that this conception of the economy contained in order to provide a type of life worthy of a free person, with its attendant idea of the fitting use of surplus, differs markedly from the "moral economy" of precapitalist peasant communities, the latter resting on an idea of scarcity and on the contained economy as a form of risk insurance. A second and different interpretation of nonmarket societies (and, incidentally, of nonmarket institutions within capitalist societies such as the firm and the family) is provided by the "new economic historians." On this reading, nonmarket mechanisms for the exchange of goods and services (including those of the ancient Greek world) are to be found where the transaction costs of the market, that is, the costs of "defining and enforcing property rights" (which may be defined expansively so as to embrace investments in the legitimacy of the prevailing order—in ideology, for example) exceed its expected benefits.[182] In short, this view

[182] Douglass C. North, *Structure and Change in Economic History* (New York: W. W. Norton, 1981), pp. 105–6, 181; Douglass C. North, "Markets and Other Allocation Sys-

suggests that forms of economic organizations are selected according to the "minimization of transaction costs" principle.

At least as applied to the world of classical Athens, this theory is misleading. For to the extent that Athenian citizens sought to avoid the market, to become rentiers whenever possible, and insofar as the city attempted to keep foreign commerce at the margins of its existence, necessary but something best done by outsiders and at a distance from the city and its political life, this choice does not seem to have been made on the basis of a calculation of the "costs" of an alternative exchange regime, for example, the transacting of exchanges in a market. Nor in the contemporary theoretical accounts of the ancient contained economy do we find such a selection criterion. We do read of opinions such as these: citizens do not work; citizens should be provided with a political *misthos* allowing them to carry out their citizen activities; the free are leisured; leisure is a prerequisite for the good life, public or private, and so on. These opinions reflect a choice as to a way of life; one that, in its many forms, required the containing of the person's involvement in the economic sphere. Aversion to the market (as well as to other productive functions, e.g., necessary physical labor and the sale of one's labor) had as its foundation not a theory of the costs of enforcement and measurement associated with the market mechanism but rather a view of the instrumentality of the economy for the sake of the good life, a view that, to repeat, required the greatest possible exclusion of it from the lives of free persons.

To make sense of the idea of an ancient comparative evaluation of and selection among different possible orders, one might recast the "costs" of these different economic mechanisms in terms of leisure and activity expended in the economic sphere rather than in the currency of property rights and their enforcement or of the tasks associated with the measurement of commodities. This idea can be put better in the following way: there are distinct, and hierarchically arranged, spheres of rationality. In one, let us call it the sphere of economic preferences, all goods have a price and are fully comparable: the loss of some good y can be compensated for by an increase in some other good z. These Jon Elster designates Archimedean preferences. Non-Archimedean preferences, on the other hand, are "non-comparable and do not lend themselves to the economic approach. . . . Where preferences have the Archimedean property, we can

tems in History," pp. 708–11; and Gunderson, "Economic Behavior in the Ancient World," p. 237n.

talk as if people maximize utility along a single dimension; otherwise the hierarchy of values must be explicitly recognized."[183] The heart of the Greek conception of the *oikos* economy, the choice to use surpluses to avoid (or contain) further economic activity, belongs in the sphere of rational but non-Archimedean and therefore noneconomic preferences. It is rational in the thin (instrumental) sense, that is, as a choice under scarcity as how best to achieve the desired end state. And it is non-economic because leisure, autarky (freedom), and the good life are goods that are not comparable with those of the economic sphere and that accordingly resist being traded off against them. In different ways both the "new economic historian" and the "moral economist" of peasant so-cieties fail to capture this dual aspect of the ancient conception of the economy.

The related concepts of the embedded and contained economy were plainly not able to serve as the basis of an independent economic science, that is, a science seeking to explain the autonomous lawlike properties of those phenomena called economic and without reference to a master science, that of the good to be served by the economy. Ideas of scarcity, surplus, and economization played a central role in ancient economic thought, and when these theorists turned their attention toward the mar-ket they had no difficulty discerning the causal relationship of, for exam-ple, supply, demand, and price. The economy was not theoretically "in-visible" or even "indistinct" to them. It was, however, conceptually subordinate to the study of the purposes it was to serve and to the order of the communities of which it was a part. Thus although Ischomachos will discuss with Socrates how he wins the loyalty of his stewards and other details of the running of his estate, and although Xenophon will analyze the movements in the price of silver, it is evident that what they are in fact examining is how to manage one's household in order to have the leisure to join in the affairs of city and friends and how to exploit the city's natural resources so as to be better able to support its citizens. Even in Hesiod's *Works and Days* we find a similar approach: how to be autarkic and lead a just life in the countryside. When Aristotle writes that it is base to consider what is useful and that a master's science is therefore a low one, what he means is that knowledge of that sort ranks with knowing how to use a hammer or work a loom—necessary, no doubt, but secondary to knowing what sort of house one should have or what

[183] Jon Elster, *Ulysses and the Sirens: Studies in Rationality and Irrationality* (Cambridge: Cambridge University Press, 1984), p. 127.

pattern of design in the fabric would be most beautiful—secondary, in other words, to the question of how one should live. Ancient economic thought was, after a fashion, "embedded," that is, visible as a discrete area of inquiry but subordinated to an overarching, and determining, analysis of the political and ethical ends (to politics as the "master science") that it was to serve and that provided the theory of the embedded economy with its governing laws.

Greek economic thought was also a theory of the contained economy. We have just sketched one facet of that idea: contained with a view to the possibility of the good life. The idea of the contained economy had another vital dimension, that of hierarchy within the community which made containment and hence the good life possible in the first place. Hence the centrality of ideas of order and rule, of the "domination moment," in ancient discussions of the household economy.[184] One road that this argument follows, and an anomalous one from the point of view of the analysis presented here (for reasons offered earlier), is that of natural slavery—the notion that the distinction between those who are free and those who are by nature slavish rests on the character of their souls. More intriguing is a second line of argument, one that grasps the freedom of the person in the light of his or her relation to the economic sphere. That sphere is understood as one in which compulsion reigns, whether induced by poverty and appearing in the forms of the unceasing necessity to labor or of submission to an employer or, in its most radical guise, caused by the subordination of slave to master. Being "inside" the contained economy entails, in varying degrees, a constrained and unfree life, one without leisure and so with limited possibilities for the cultivation of excellence and for sharing in the higher *philia* that binds the truly human communities.

The servile are, in that sense, "homeless," constrained, leisureless, and unable to participate in that chosen way of life which is the core of a community that is something more than an assembly of gregarious animals united in the search for livelihood. Yet they also are an indispensable moment of that community, the *oikos*, or the city, for without them, as Aristotle implies in his remarks on the shuttles moving themselves, the economy would not be contained. It would embrace everyone, and so, Aristotle writes, the poor (those without slaves) must treat their wives and children as attendants and presumably must themselves come to lead

---

[184] Otto Brunner, *Neue Wege der Sozialgeschichte* (Gottingen: Vandenhoeck and Ruprecht, 1956), pp. 43–44.

something very like a servile life. If nature were so abundant that there was no scarcity, or if *per impossibile,* machines were capable of producing on their own, the economy could be contained without hierarchy, without transferring its burdens onto the shoulders of the servile. That not being the case, however, a human solution must be found to the scarcity and containment problems: slaves and servants, one's wife and children, the domination of the seas, and tribute from the city's allies. It is thus that the ancient theory of the economy moved from general propositions about scarcity and the neediness of the human condition, from theories of the good life and its relation to the production of human livelihood, to the necessary hierarchy that stands at the very center of their idea of community.

It would be as false to deny the often repugnant character of the theory (and practice) of the ancient economy as it would be unprofitable to belabor any moral judgment of it. Its legacy for us is of two kinds. In the first place, it provides us with a conceptual language for thinking about the moral location of the economy: the place of the production of human livelihood in the cosmos of our goods, and the permeation of the social mesh of production by those values. Ancient economic thought did this by drawing us into a way of reflecting on the economy as an instrument not only of wealth-getting but also as a necessary part of the external equipment of freedom and of the possibility of the good life thereby made open to us. This idea of the instrumentality of the economy is nowhere more in evidence than in Xenophon's *Oeconomicus.* There the dialectical ascent of Socratic discourse drives us to consider the question of what the use is of the things, the wealth, that we produce and own. And from there we are led further, to inquire about the ranking of the ends it might serve. The seemingly so counterintuitive conclusion of the discussion between Socrates and Kritoboulos, that Socrates is wealthy, is intended to focus our attention on the moral architecture of the household and on the place of the economy within it. Against that background, the Socratic conclusion makes perfectly good sense: Socrates is truly *oikonomikos,* and so a fitting teacher of economics. The art of household management, economics, must, that is to say, be embedded in a higher-order theory of the good.

The second aspect of the legacy of this tradition is its understanding and indeed recommendation of a certain type of moral economy, one characterized by hierarchy and domination. And we must not be so naive as to believe that this part of ancient economic theory was an unfortunate overlay, the scarification of an otherwise beautiful and noble creation. The analysis and advocacy of servitude were not the result of ideological blinders or of theoretical error; rather they stemmed from a clear-eyed, and unapologetic, recognition of the conditions of freedom, community, and the good life in a world into which Pandora had let loose grim poverty. For freedom in this view meant not only not being subordinate to the will of another person, itself a circumstance thought to be often the result of penury, but also not being subject to the constraining necessity of toil or of the marketplace. It was also closely bound up with the "sister of freedom," leisure, since to be servile (or poor) was not to dispose of one's own time but to have it at the discretion of the seasons and endless labor or of the master. The poverty of the human estate threatened to rob persons of the leisure that was one of the hallmarks and treasures of freedom. And, in challenging the space needed for the pursuit of activities beyond those dedicated to the production of the necessities of physical existence, that scarcity was ultimately inimical to a life of praxis, of free and noble activities as well as to the sharing of them with the community. Properly ordered and contained through hierarchy, the economy might, however, be transformed into an instrument of the good, insofar as it was within the power of humans to limit the effects of the grim poverty that was their lot. It is both of these facets of Greek economic thought which capture our attention: the theoretical embedding of the production of human livelihood in an account of the good and a portrait of the beautiful economy, first set before us in the scenes of dancing and the grape clusters heavy with wine wrought by Hephaistos on Achilles' shield, together with its conceptual underpinnings, the subtly interwoven account of the relationship between the economy, time, the good life, and the hierarchical community devoted to it.

THE MORAL ECONOMY
OF THE
LIBERAL HOUSEHOLD

In *Democracy in America,* Alexis de Tocqueville writes that the household of the *ancien régime* was composed of two small nations, masters and servants, each placed permanently in its position, within one great nation. Those by nature inferior were ruled; those who were their superiors ruled, and thus the question hardly arose of the source of obligation on the one side or of dominion on the other. The authority of the household head was supreme not only over the servants but over the children and the wife as well. Tocqueville argues that the democratic revolution, with equality as its centerpiece, has dissolved the fixed hierarchy of the traditional household. Relations between master and servant, husband and wife and even between parents and children have been fundamentally modified. A temporary and freely made agreement between master and servant, an exchange of goods and/or services satisfying their respective preferences, replaces the former bonds of subjection and the pursuit of the lord's purposes alone. This contract is now the sole source of the master's legitimate power and the only reason for the servant's obedience. The vileness of the lackey's position is gone: "In a democracy there is nothing degrading about the status of a domestic servant, because it is freely adopted and temporary."[1] Similarly, in the relation between husband and

[1] Alexis de Tocqueville, *Democracy in America,* trans. George Lawrence and ed. J. P. Mayer (Garden City, N.Y.: Anchor Books, 1969), p. 579.

wife, the husband is no longer the *kurios,* the lord over his spouse, bringing her (as Odysseus does with Penelope) from her father's rule to the household under his own authority. The wife "freely accepts" the matrimonial bond. Conjugal society, that of a couple voluntarily joined together, replaces the lordship of the *pater familias:* "freely accepts" and "voluntarily" in a liberal sense, that is, where unmarked by status or hierarchy neither party is wholly the object of contract but each, bilaterally, consents (within parameters to be analyzed below) to the union.[2] The one surviving, and qualified, trace of domestic despotism is to be found in the relations of the parents to the infant child, and there time ultimately provides the liberal corrective, as the age of maturity brings the children to full equality.

In this part, I explore the classical liberal challenge to the *oikos* model of the household, its implications for a new understanding of the human community and for the location of economy within it. As we saw, the ancient concept of the household and of the place of the economy within it were, at their root, hierarchical. For the ancients could envisage the possibility of a community, or at least one befitting free human beings, only on the underlying foundation of servitude. That is, the material requirements of praxis, of participation in the affairs of the city or of friends, were such that under conditions of scarcity (with the resultant demand for time and activity to be expended in the production of livelihood) the binding *philia* essential to community and the good life were achievable only if this burden, inseparable from the human estate, was shifted to the servile population. The allocation of persons into these servile positions was, in turn, thought of in status terms—for instance, in terms of the "appropriateness" of certain forms of labor for females or of the inferiority of slaves. In that sense, one could say that relations of rule and subordination in the world of production were mediated through the community, its dominant moment and its ethos, and were accordingly established pre-economically. The theory of the household economy, with servitude at its center, was thus a response to the problem of providing the external goods necessary for freedom and the good life in a world afflicted by grim poverty.

This contractarian concept of the household and polity had as its principal antagonist precisely the *summum malum* of domination (hierarchy in the ancient despotic and early modern patriarchal ideas of the community), of rule private or public without the freely given consent of those

2 Tocqueville, *Democracy in America,* pp. 593, 600.

subject to it. It seeks to reconstruct the idea of community on egalitarian and voluntarist foundations; and that reconstruction, in turn, leads it to offer a new vision of the purposiveness of the community and so ultimately to a theory of the free and in a sense uncontained economy. Our task here, then, will be to map out these efforts to refound the idea of the community and from there to proceed to the place of the economy within it. In discussing the contractarian rejoinder to the *oikos,* I focus on John Locke, though with not infrequent references to Thomas Hobbes, Jean-Jacques Rousseau, and Immanuel Kant. The reason for this emphasis is that for an understanding of liberalism Locke is clearly more central than either Hobbes or Rousseau, in both of whose writings markedly illiberal arguments are to be found (for example, in Hobbes's absolutist conclusions and the insecurity of property under his best regime, and in Rousseau's partial adoption of the idiom of ancient political thought, especially in his remarks on citizenship and the importance of the public sphere). For my purposes Locke's considerable interest in normative issues surrounding the economy makes him more valuable than Kant.

3. Despotic and Conjugal Households

The contractarian tradition, for all of its internal variations, had in its founding works at least one common thread: the debate with the patriarchal view of the family and its extension to the political sphere.[3] It is possible to distinguish two broad and relatively distinct lines of reasoning in that patriarchal tradition: one, a naturalistic strand that argues that society is not an artifact and that seeks to ground that notion in the idea of the family as a natural association. Further unpacked, this naturalistic strand is bound up with ideas of hierarchy and rule as abiding characteristics of the political world, a thought again derived from a picture of the household community. Notions of equality and its corollary, the idea of the origin of obligation in consent, clearly have no place in such a theory nor do instituted limits (limits derived in one fashion or another

---

[3] Here I am interested only in that contractarianism which set the foundations for liberalism, and thus I ignore those variants employed for patriarchal purposes. For comments on the contractarian arguments pressed into the service of patriarchal theories see Mary Lydon Shanley, "Marriage Contract and Social Contract in Seventeenth-Century English Political Thought," in Jean Bethke Elshtain, ed., *The Family in Political Thought* (Amherst: University of Massachusetts Press, 1982), pp. 81–84.

from the wills of the subjects) on the ruler's household or political power. The naturalistic core of this view is what most plainly unites early modern patriarchal theorists with Aristotelian political philosophy.[4] A second strand focuses less on the natural character of the family and political associations than on the specific form of family rule and its importance for political life. The little monarchy of the household, combined with the idea of God's gift of the world to Adam and his successors, yields not merely a conclusion about the ontological status of political life but also the belief that only one sort of regime is proper to that life—the monarchical form. If the former line of reasoning draws the patriarchal argument toward Aristotle, the second leads it into disagreement with him, because it is evident that he did not seek to demonstrate the unique appropriateness of monarchy on the basis of patriarchal rule in the household.

Here I use Sir Robert Filmer's variant of the patriarchal argument as an exemplar of this sort of reasoning. Filmer builds from the claim that every person "is born subject to the power of a Father." No one is born free, for there is a "natural subjection" within the household, the absolute power that the lord of the family holds by nature (and divine ordination) over the members of the household. This picture is then extended from the authority of the father (understood to mean the panoply of powers including those belonging to the lord as husband and master) to the political realm: what the father is to his family and servants so the king is over many families. The powers of fathers and kings differ not at all in kind but only in latitude. In his "In Praise of the Vertuous Wife," Filmer expresses the heart of that point in these words: "In the fifthe commandement three duties are enjoyne[d] 1. Betweene Superiors and inferiors. 2. Towar[des] Æqualls. 3. Towardes Our selves. of the first kind some are Privat or Publique. Privat as [the] duty of the wife, of Parents and Children, or serv[ants] and Maisters . . . Publi[que] as the office of a Kinge."[5] The arguments deployed to arrive at these conclusions are not sophisticated, and surely Locke was right in his assessment that they are but a "Rope of

[4] See Peter Laslett, Introduction to Robert Filmer, *Patriarcha and Other Political Works*, ed. Laslett (Oxford: Basil Blackwell, 1949), p. 27, and Gordon J. Schochet, *Patriarchalism in Political Thought* (Oxford: Basil Blackwell, 1975), p. 23.

[5] Sir Robert Filmer, "In Praise of the Vertuous Wife," in Margaret J. M. Ezell, *The Patriarch's Wife: Literary Evidence and the History of the Family* (Chapel Hill: University of North Carolina Press, 1987), p. 169. See also Filmer, *Patriarcha*, pp. 57, 63, 72, 74, 76. Ezell argues, however, that in practice the power of English patriarchs was considerably less than the Filmerian claims might suggest. In particular, female migration, the deaths of fathers, and the assumption of their powers by their wives combined to reduce the dominion of the household lords.

Sand." Nevertheless, they do convey an image of political life as a natural hierarchy modeled on the family which Locke felt compelled to attack at length and which, in different guises, Hobbes and Rousseau also addressed. The patriarchal family/polity continuum, with its naturalistic and hierarchical conclusions, is not the only line of reasoning employed by Filmer. Central too is the Adamite argument. God, Filmer writes, had given Adam private dominion over the world; there was no natural community of property. Together with this private dominion, and the political power it conferred not only over household members but over all persons, God provided for that dominion to be passed on to Adam's successors. This gift of private dominion to Adam and his lineage is, Filmer asserts, the "fountain of all government and property."[6] It is because the Greeks were ignorant of Scripture that the true origins of government and property were concealed from them, and it is largely (though not exclusively) for that reason, he concludes, that Aristotle, the "grandmaster of politiques," failed to grasp that monarchy is the sole divinely appointed and natural regime. The Adamite argument for the origins of monarchical succession suggests yet another difference between Filmer's and Aristotle's use of the household as the beginning point for the study of the polity: for Filmer, monarchical authority and paternal power are identical and not merely (as they were for Aristotle) subspecies of the universal relation of ruler and ruled.[7]

If we seek to extract the central ideas from this tapestry of interwoven classical and scriptural notions, it will be evident that its core is that monarchs rule by right and according to nature, and that this right is not bestowed on them, conditionally or otherwise, by their subjects but belongs to them as the proprietors of their extended families, a proprietorship that is the result of God's initial gift to Adam. Dominion over the earth and its creatures is unlimited, and it is held over persons who are subjects of their king as children are the wards of their father, and wives the subjects of their husbands.[8] The natural inequality of power pervades the polity as its does the family: there are lords and subjects, their rela-

---

[6] Filmer, *Patriarcha*, p. 71; see also p. 64.

[7] Filmer, *Patriarcha*, pp. 76–85 passim, and Filmer, *Observations upon Aristotle's Politiques,* in Filmer, *Patriarcha and Other Political Works,* p. 187. See Schochet, *Patriarchalism in Political Thought,* p. 146, and for an accurate analysis of Filmer's misreading of Aristotle's account of monarchical rule see p. 21.

[8] For further analysis see John Dunn, *The Political Thought of John Locke* (Cambridge: Cambridge University Press, 1969), p. 61; James Tully, *A Discourse on Property: John Locke and His Adversaries* (Cambridge: Cambridge University Press, 1980), pp. 57, 143; Nathan Tarcov, *Locke's Education for Liberty* (Chicago: University of Chicago Press, 1984), p. 9.

tionship is fixed, and the obligation to obey on the one side and the entitlement to rule on the other flow directly from the general principle of natural social hierarchy (evidenced in the family) informed further by the scriptural specification of the original proprietor and the manner of his succession. Interleaved with this account of natural (political) subjugation is a theory of Adam's (and his successors') dominion over the world as the fountainhead of government and of property. There never was, according to Filmer, a commons; rather, there was Adam's ownership of the world. And the extension of property to others was by his permission or grant. Once more we see here important (Christianized) elements of ancient Greek, and particularly Aristotelian, economic thought: a version of the despotic model of the household economy, with power political and economic intimately bound together and residing in the master, by whose grace others may participate in it.

To overturn the Filmerian view that "we are all born slaves, and we must continue so; there is no remedy for it: Life and Thraldom we enter'd into together, and can never be quit of the one, till we part with the other," Locke thought it necessary to attack the foundations of that theory.[9] And so the contractarian reconstruction of the idea of the family proceeds from the claim that even in that seemingly most enduring of societies, the household, there is no natural authority, or at least none such as would dislodge the primacy of the juridical person in thinking about its legitimacy. For Locke, there were two ways (at times in obvious tension with each other) to force this breach in the patriarchal argument. One move was to expand on an intellectual embarrassment Filmer had himself observed in his efforts to draw on Aristotelian naturalism, namely, that Aristotle had insisted on the difference between the household and the polis. Parental power does differ from the political, Locke maintains, in its origins, limits, and duration, and it is distinguished from the latter in such a way that were a monarchy merely a large household its powers and duration would ill suit those who make the case for absolutism.[10] There was a second strategy, however. For as important as it was for Locke to construct an argument by means of which to distinguish household and political authority, it was still more crucial to dismantle the very groundwork sustaining the naturalism of the family (and thereby that of the political association), that is, the premises of natural subjection within

[9] John Locke, *First Treatise* (hereafter 1T followed by the section number), 1T.4, in Locke, *Two Treatises of Government*, ed. Peter Laslett (New York: New American Library, 1963).

[10] John Locke, *Second Treatise*, in *Two Treatises of Government* (hereafter 2T followed by the section number), 2T.2, 77, 86, 169.

the household community: that we are "born slaves" and because women are inferiors and under the rule of their fathers and husbands, daughters are therefore the objects of their lords' contracts and wives bound by their husbands' lawmaking. The reason for this is that underlying Lockean contractarianism is a set of related theological and philosophical anthropological principles which require that relations, public and private, be treated as relations between juridical persons. We are, Locke writes, "born Free," not slaves, nor are we born superiors or subordinates, contract makers over humans as objects of contracts. This foundation leads to a rethinking of all human communities, and the establishment of equality and voluntariness as key elements shaping relations of power within them. Thus, despite Locke's insistence on distinguishing authority in the household from its political counterpart, his analyses of the various types of associations do, in one of the branches of his argument, converge in an egalitarian/voluntarist reconstruction of the idea of human communities.[11] No doubt this reconstruction at the level of the family brought Locke himself into some considerable philosophical embarrassments, and the resulting tensions are apparent to the eye. What these tensions reveal, I think, is precisely the direction of this remaking of the household: they occur just where the contractarian drive of Locke's analysis encounters relations that appear to him as less amenable to egalitarian, voluntaristic redefinition. That is, these predicaments are to be found where the logic of his argument threatens to take him further than he is willing to go: relations between husband and wife are one such embarrassment, paternal/parental governance another. In the former, Locke does, with some missteps, draw many of the conclusions demanded by his argument; in the latter, he shifts his emphasis onto a more egalitarian, passive understanding of personhood. On these matters, Hobbes was (as we shall see further on) at once more radical and less red-cheeked.

The road to Locke's egalitarian and voluntarist conclusions proceeds from the argument for our shared status as persons: that because we are one and all the servants of our Creator, the property of Him who has made us, and because we are endowed equally with those faculties necessary to our callings, there cannot be any natural and permanent subordination among us. "And Reason, which is that Law [of nature], teaches all Mankind . . . that being all equal and independent, no one ought to harm another in his Life, Health, Liberty, or Possessions. For Men being

---

[11] See Tully, *A Discourse on Property,* pp. 133–34, and Geraint Parry, "Individuality, Politics, and the Critique of Paternalism in John Locke," *Political Studies* 12 (1964): 163–64, 166.

all the Workmanship of one Omnipotent, and infinitely wise Maker; all the Servants of one Sovereign Master, sent into the World by his order and about his business, they are his Property, whose Workmanship they are, made to last during his, not one anothers Pleasure." Humans, in short, "should also be equal one amongst another without Subordination or Subjection, unless the Lord and Master of them all, should by any manifest Declaration of his Will set one above another."[12] This enterprise then moves, haltingly but with a striking radicalism, to the contractualization of the family. And it is that project which we shall now examine in more detail.

3.1   Wives and Children

"[B]y the law of God, of nature, of reason and by the Common Law, the will of the wife is subject to the will of the husband."[13] Locke answers this core patriarchal thesis with the argument that God in no way set Adam over Eve but only "fortels" her subordinate position and that of wives thereafter in relation to their husbands. There was no gift of dominion over her; nor is there, as the patriarchal theorists assert, a relation of superior and inferior which would command obedience and make rejection of the husband's laws a sin "both against *god* and *man*."[14] The implication of the Lockean rejoinder is that consent must enter into the account of whatever legitimate relations of rule there may be between husband and wife. Nor is the magnitude of the domestic authority of the husband over his wife of a political sort, for it does not confer on the husband the power of life and death over her. Consequently, it provides but a poor foundation for the case on behalf of absolutism (or of any form of political power): when Locke calls it the "Father's Empire" (*Second Treatise* §65), he is no doubt speaking half in mockery of this paternal power. The half that is in earnest is the claim that the subordination of wife to husband has a "Foundation in Nature." The meaning of this latter notion is far from clear, but it might be ventured that the most plausible reading of it is that Locke saw that "Foundation" in female "weakness" coupled with God's "curse" on women, the "lunging forth [of] her Children in Sorrow and Pain." This particular dilemma is by no means

---

[12] Locke, 2T.4, 6.

[13] Lord Chief Baron Hale, quoted in Ezell, *The Patriarch's Wife*, p. 2.

[14] Filmer, "In Praise of the Vertuous Wife," p. 174, and Locke, 1T.47. See also the essay by the seventeenth-century patriarchal theorist Robert Whitehall, "The Womans Right Proved False," in Ezell, *The Patriarch's Wife*, especially p. 215.

Locke's alone, however. For example, Mary More, a seventeenth-century advocate of greater equality for women, was forced into similar contortions in her essay "The Womans Right," interpreting this biblical passage in the light of the Cain and Abel story as saying that a superiority and power of "Eldership" was thus conferred, but no considerable inequality between husbands and wives, or dominion.[15] In any case, this statement rests uneasily with the fundamental propositions of Lockean contractarian theory, and it is one of those embarrassments to which I referred above. What we can say on the basis of those underpinnings is that this "curse" scarcely provided Adam or husbands generally with the right to the scepter of rule over wives. Quite the contrary, the conjugal union in which this "curse" is realized is a voluntary one for the sake of procreation and the preservation of the species. It is a contractual union that can be nullified (within the limits set by positive law) by either party, which is to suggest that whatever Locke may have meant by the "weakness" of women or by the "Foundation in Nature," he must be understood as arguing that, at the primordial level, the parties to this conjugal union are persons equal and free and that accordingly their union must be by compact.[16]

Parental rule over children is also said by Locke to be given by nature. The relationship of parents to children is plainly not (as in the case of the relationship between the parents themselves) a voluntary association nor (as in the case of the rights of a conqueror over the vanquished in a just war) is it the consequence of a forfeiture of rights by the subordinate member. Being the result of neither contract nor conquest, parental authority would then seem to be by nature, meaning not the product of artifice (force or consent) but something given to humans as an enduring part of their earthly estate. And Locke suggests something like that when he states that parental power rests on "begetting." But just as was the case with his discussion of the conjugal relation, Locke's assertion of the naturalness of parental authority becomes, on closer inspection, rather more

---

[15] Mary More, "The Womans Right," in Ezell, *The Patriarch's Wife*, pp. 196–97.

[16] For accounts of the voluntariness of central household relations (husband/wife and master/servant) see Locke, 1T.43, 47, and 2T.78–81. For feminist critiques of Locke's analysis of women in the household, and for an argument that his theory remains patriarchal in that respect, see Teresa Brennan and Carole Pateman, "'Mere Auxiliaries to the Commonwealth': Women and the Origins of Liberalism," *Political Studies* 27 (1979): 183–200, especially pp. 191–92; Susan Moller Okin, *Women in Western Political Thought* (Princeton: Princeton University Press, 1979), p. 200, and Shanley, "Marriage Contract and Social Contract," especially p. 93. A general statement of this line of criticism may be found in Susan Moller Okin, "Justice and Gender," *Philosophy and Public Affairs* 16 (1987): 42–72, especially p. 43.

nuanced. Children are "begotten, not as their [i.e., the parents'] own Workmanship, but the Workmanship of their own Maker."[17] What kind of power, then, can rightly be had over those who are God's workmanship? Not arbitrary unlimited power, since the child is, like all persons, placed in the world at God's pleasure and for his purposes, not those of the infant's parents. Though the state of their reason does not yet permit them to be active contracting agents, they are nevertheless persons in a passive sense. That is, they are as equal as all persons with respect to dominion over one another; they are born to equality and freedom and not to thraldom. In its foundations, then, parental government properly understood shares in certain central qualities of all just human associations: the equality and freedom of persons (even if temporarily unequal in the degree to which these attributes have come fully into being) and the absence of enduring and natural relations of subordination among them. The authority of the parents, thus construed, does not derive from a right to rule based on an abiding superiority over their charges but rather from a duty to care for those who are born to freedom and who are not yet able to exercise it.[18]

The power of parents is that of the guardian over the person, protecting God's workmanship until such time as the child, having become capable of reason, achieves that autonomy and equality that she was born to but not in. Parental government is thus temporary (restricted to the time of the imperfection of the child's reason) and limited (by the rights— property, broadly understood—which inhere in the child even in his state of imperfection). It differs from political authority in its origins (begetting), its purpose (guardianship, preservation of the species), its magnitude (in power over life and death), and duration (temporary). Both the differences between parental and political power and the foundations underlying Locke's understanding of all proper human communities provide the demonstration as to why Filmer was wrong to deduce principles of political absolutism from the despotic and hierarchical household.

3.2   Masters and Servants

"Master and Servant," Locke wrote, "are Names as old as History, but given to those of very different conditions."[19] The condition of the ancient slave is that of an outsider forcibly drawn into the household com-

17 Locke, 2T.56 and 1T.98.
18 Locke, 2T.58, 65.
19 Locke, 2T.85.

munity, there to be used by the master, in the service of his purposes and in perpetuity. The servant of Filmer's patriarchal household is in a similar position: he is under the private dominion of his lord, an arrangement consistent with nature and Scripture. Now, in the liberal household too there are servants, persons who are "put into the Family" of the master, who come under his discipline and whose product ("the Turfs my Servant has cut . . . ") belongs to him. Yet the Lockean servant is not part of the "body economic"—or, rather, of that body economic found in the ancient or patriarchal household, the contained sphere essential to, but at the periphery of, the free community. His is not a fixed, subordinate status within the hierarchical household, subject to the will of the master, not a naturally subordinate existence whose servile activities are justified in terms of the goods provided to his betters, as the fruit of the original gift of private dominion, or in terms of a relation of inferior and superior. Rather, this servant enters the household as a free, equal, and independent person. He does indeed come under the discipline of the master, but in the only manner in which two persons, between whom there exists no relation of natural authority, can enter into a condition of ruling and being ruled, that, is by consent (a voluntary alienation of services on the one side and money or goods on the other) and for the satisfaction of their respective preferences as they understand them.

The importance of the concept of consent in Locke's account of master/servant relations will only be sketched here (I discuss it in greater detail further on). The idea is, first of all, an expression of the contractarian rejection of the naturalism (meaning what has not or could not possibly have been consented to) of the body economic, for it rests on the underlying notion that among equals, legitimate authority can be established only by a voluntary act of alienation. Second, the idea of consent or voluntary alienation carries with it limits on instituted authority. The prudential construction of those limits might, for example, ask what an individual seeks to gain from submitting to authority, and it suggests (in the Lockean version) the idea that unlimited rule over oneself is so bad a bargain as to be virtually irrational because, quite apart from any question of the relative value of the goods transferred in this sort of exchange, its unlimited quality means that the servant or subject has no way to enforce his side of the bargain in the future. Locke's natural-law construction of the limits of alienation through contract provides yet another way of drawing the boundaries of authority: that humans are God's workmanship and are put into the world to last at his pleasure, not their own. Accordingly, they are no more at liberty to dispose of their own lives (which is just what submission to unrestricted authority amounts to) than they are to take the lives of others, save where self-defense or the preservation of others requires it. The contract between master and servant must then be limited to an agreement about the services or goods to be rendered by the servant, and the power of the master presumably cannot extend beyond that needed to see to the "discipline" of his laborers in fulfilling their contractual obligations.

A second type of limitation is that on the time of service: "there is nothing degrading in the status of a domestic servant, because it is freely adopted *and temporary.*" The master/servant relation must be a temporary one; their relationship has to be limited not only in the manner (the scope) of its exercise but in its duration as well. Indeed, the temporary character of the servant's place in the household is one of the principal features (together with its origins in consent rather than in a forfeiture of rights through the prosecution of an unjust war) distinguishing the free servant from the slave. We may say that this limitation extends the understanding of what cannot be alienated from physical preservation of life to life conceived as the person's capacity freely to dispose over time. Some time may indeed be exchanged against wages, for instance, but to relinquish all of one's days is to make a slave's bargain: to bind the will of the future self as well as of the present one and so to preclude forever the possibility of an elective withdrawal from the master's authority.[20]

3.3   Hobbes and Rousseau on the Family

Because Locke was by no means the only classical contractarian philosopher concerned with the household and its proper order, I must make a brief historical excursus into the reflections of two of his fellow contractarian theorists on the family. Hobbes, whose political conclusions are decidedly absolutist and illiberal, developed a critique of the naturalist conception of the household and offered in its place a notion of a community by artifice as a counter to it, ideas that are in their way still more far-reaching than those of Locke. This radicalness can be seen in the following passage from Hobbes, which appears on its surface to belong to the naturalist school: "that a great family, if it be not part of some commonwealth, is of itself, *as to the rights of sovereignty,* a little monarchy."[21] There are two qualifications that render the analogy between

[20] For this intertemporal dimension see Serge-Christophe Kolm, *Le contrat social libéral* (Paris: Presses Universitaires de France, 1985), pp. 76, 194.

[21] Thomas Hobbes, *Leviathan,* ed. Michael Oakeshott (Oxford: Basil Blackwell, n.d.), p. 133 (emphasis added), but see p. 45 on the differences between family and civil govern-

the family and monarchy imperfect: first, the inability of the family to provide for the protection of its members, which is the purpose of the political association, and the other, suggested in the passage itself, that in a commonwealth the family is a private association and thus is subject to the sovereign—that is, the father has such powers "as the law permitteth, though not further."[22] Nevertheless, "as to the rights of sovereignty," the household taken by itself is a small monarchy, which means, in Hobbes's account, both in the magnitude of the family sovereign's power and, more crucially (for our purposes), in its origins.

Hobbes is arguing here that all associations among persons (save one) are voluntary, that is, that the powers of fathers and sovereigns by compact and by conquest are in an important sense of a piece and what they have in common is the voluntary (and thus obligation-creating) character of their associations. The sole exception is the society of master and slave, which, because it involves no act of consent and hence no relationship of obligation, is hardly of interest to Hobbes. His conflation of all types of obligation-generating authority, through the discovery of a voluntary foundation underlying them, leads him to the view that the family too is an artificial institution.[23] That families are ruled by fathers is not, according to Hobbes, the result of males' being the "more excellent sex," that is, is not justified by nature but is rather the consequence of civil law made in commonwealths that "have been erected by the fathers, not by the mothers of families."[24] Indeed, where there is no contract, dominion over the child belongs to the mother, the father being unknown (or identified only at the mother's will) and the female having the power to provide or withhold nourishment from the infant. Men and women, then, are not so distinguished by differences in strength or prudence that the dominion of the male over the female can be understood as being according to nature but must rather be conceived as coming into existence through covenant.[25]

If the radicalness of Hobbes's voluntarism is apparent in his commentary on male authority within the household, it is still more evident in his

---

ment. On the radicalism of Hobbes on the family see Brennan and Pateman, "'Mere Auxiliaries to the Commonwealth,'" p. 185, and Susan Moller Okin, "Women and the Making of the Sentimental Family," *Philosophy and Public Affairs* 11 (1981): 66.

[22] Hobbes, *Leviathan*, p. 153.

[23] See R. W. K. Hinton, "Husbands, Fathers, and Conquerors," *Political Studies* 16 (1968): 55, and Richard A. Chapman, "*Leviathan* Writ Small: Thomas Hobbes on the Family," *American Political Science Review* 69 (1975): 78.

[24] Hobbes, *Leviathan*, p. 131.

[25] Hobbes, *The Elements of Law Natural and Politic*, ed. Ferdinand Tönnies (Cambridge: Cambridge University Press, 1928), p. 104.

analysis of parental power. Dominion over children, Hobbes argues, is not acquired by the act of begetting but "from the child's consent, either expressed, or by other sufficient arguments declared."[26] The reasons Hobbes provides for the consensual origin of parental authority do not include an exploration of what such infant consent could mean but are rather directed to the argument that a right established by begetting would place power (impossibly, for Hobbes) in the hands of two masters and that the end of the child's submission to authority being self-preservation, this authority properly belongs to whomever will provide nourishment, whether or not they are the child's natural parents. The notion of children's consent to parental authority, besides being manifestly counterintuitive, also runs against Hobbes's own arguments about authorization and obligation, according to which children, fools, and madmen cannot be "authors" and thus cannot covenant, with the result that there is no law, justice or injustice, in relation to such persons. These problems notwithstanding (or, rather, precisely in their light), what is clear from the above is the fundamental Hobbesian drive to establish authority on a voluntary and not a naturalist foundation. The absolutism of Hobbes's concept of authority, including authority of the sort exercised by parents over children,[27] so foreign to Lockean political thought, should not conceal from us the extent to which he shared (and, in this instance, went beyond) Locke's rejection of the idea of natural subordination among persons.

"[A]s if master and servant were not introduced by consent of man, but by difference of wit"—so writes Hobbes, attacking Aristotle's distinction between masters and natural slaves. Nature has made humans equal, he continues, or if it has not, their equality must in any case be "admitted" because without that assumption there can be only that pride which hinders humans from establishing a condition of peace. The little "kingdom despotical" of the master over his servant differs not at all, in point of the magnitude of the master's power, from that exercised by parents over children, or by the sovereign over the commonwealth, though with the creation of the polity, the sovereign's power determines that of the rulers of private and subordinate associations.[28] Unlike Locke, Hobbes treats the servant not as a hired laborer but as one who is vanquished in

---

[26] Hobbes, *Leviathan*, p. 130; Hobbes, *De Cive*, trans. Thomas Hobbes, in Bernard Gert, ed., *Man and Citizen* (Garden City, N.Y.: Anchor Books, 1972), p. 212.

[27] See Hobbes, *Leviathan*, pp. 107, 133, 176; Hobbes, *The Elements of Law*, p. 105.

[28] Hobbes, *The Elements of Law*, p. 100; Hobbes, *De Cive*, p. 207; Hobbes, *Leviathan*, p. 133.

war and enters the master's household through submission to conquest. Yet in that act of submission the servant comes to be distinguished from a slave, for in exchange for a grant of life he voluntarily assumes an obligation to his master. It is that obligation, arising from his free will and based on a covenant, which binds him and not the chains that hold the slave.[29] The servant, then, differs on the one side from the slave in that he is a contractual member of the household, attached to it by bonds of obligation originating in his will and, on the other side, from the free persons of the home in that he is subject to a master as well as to a sovereign and insofar as he is denied "the honour of equality of favour with other [non-servile] subjects."[30] However, because all are by nature free and roughly equal, the servant is subject to that sort of authority which most concerns Hobbes, that which carries with it obligation and duty, namely, authority arising out of an act of the will.

Rousseau's writings, though anomalous in relation to the early liberal tradition because they seek to embrace at one and the same time the idiom of individualism and the critique of naturalism, and the cohesiveness of the ancient polity, are suffused with that passionate hatred of unauthorized, or personal, power which is characteristic of social contract theory. Rousseau's political writings also represent a departure from the English contractarian tradition (the Lockean in particular) we have been considering in that, as Judith Shklar has written, he maintained "that a deep damage is done to men by work, property and obligation under conditions of radical inequality. It is inequality that deforms all three and renders them occasions for vice and oppression."[31] These and other profound differences notwithstanding, Rousseau shared with the contractarian tradition a hostility to the idea of natural hierarchy and to conceptions of authority founded on and justified by that hierarchy: "Since no man has any natural authority over his fellow man, and since force produces no right, there remain only conventions as the basis of all legitimate authority among men."[32] Like Hobbes and Locke, Rousseau

[29] Hobbes, *Leviathan*, pp. 132, 141; Hobbes, *De Cive*, p. 207. For a valuable analysis of Hobbes's notion of contractual obligation see Jean Hampton, *Hobbes and the Social Contract Tradition* (Cambridge: Cambridge University Press, 1986), pp. 55–57.

[30] Hobbes, *The Elements of Law,* p. 105; and see Hobbes, *De Cive,* p. 217.

[31] Judith Shklar, *Men and Citizens: A Study of Rousseau's Social Theory* (Cambridge: Cambridge University Press, 1969), p. 50; see also Patrick Riley, *Will and Political Legitimacy* (Cambridge: Harvard University Press, 1982), pp. 99–100, 122.

[32] Jean-Jacques Rousseau, *On the Social Contract,* in Rousseau, *On the Social Contract with Geneva Manuscript and Political Economy,* trans. Judith R. Masters, ed. Roger D. Masters (New York: St. Martin's Press, 1978), p. 49.

was forced to address the competing naturalist and hierarchical conception of political authority, together with its central metaphor of the patriarchal household.

Rousseau's approach was two-sided: he sought both to distinguish between the household and the polity as sharply different forms of rule and to weaken as far as possible the ideas of natural authority and inequality within the set of family relationships. The first of these two lines of argument proceeds by listing the characteristics of paternal government and then contrasting them to those of the polity. In the household, the father is the sole commanding authority; he rules over the children by nature, and the duties of his gentle authority are dictated by natural feelings; the servants in his home owe him their labor in exchange for the livelihood he provides them.[33] None of these attributes applies to the political relation of ruler and ruled, or better, to legitimate relations of political authority. The distinction, then, between the family as it is and the polity as it ought to be is such that the metaphor of the family is ill-suited to convey any sense of what legitimate rule is in the broader, artificial political community.

Painted with somewhat wider strokes, we can say, with Rousseau, that the family is the *only* natural society. Yet Rousseau, no slavish adherent of rigorous argumentation, goes on to state, in his second line of attack, that the family is a prototype of political society in that its members alienate their freedom for the sake of self-preservation. The direction of his reasoning here, if not the details of its execution, is clear: the father has only temporary power over the children, which is necessary during the period of the latter's inability to be masters of themselves. Paternal authority (and for Rousseau, unlike Hobbes and Locke, it is more unambiguously paternal than parental) is transient and directed to the benefit of the weak. In other places, Rousseau seems to make a more radical argument, that the family is a free and voluntary association altogether, with its only bonds being "affection and freedom."[34] The tendency of these various

[33] Jean-Jacques Rousseau, *On the Social Contract* (Geneva Manuscript), in Rousseau, *On the Social Contract with Geneva Manuscript and Political Economy,* trans. Judith R. Masters, ed. Roger Masters (New York: St. Martin's Press, 1978), pp. 169–70; Rousseau, *Second Discourse,* in Rousseau, *The First and Second Discourses,* trans. Judith and Roger Masters, ed. Roger Masters (New York: St. Martin's Press, 1964), p. 165; Rousseau, *Political Economy,* in Rousseau, *On the Social Contract,* p. 209. For a discussion of Rousseau on the family see Judith Shklar, "Rousseau's Two Models: Sparta and the Age of Gold," *Political Science Quarterly* 81 (1966): 25–51, especially pp. 28, 40–47.

[34] See Rousseau, *Second Discourse,* p. 147; Rousseau, *Emile; or, On Education,* trans. Allan Bloom (New York: Basic Books, 1979), pp. 429, 459; Rousseau, *Social Contract,* p. 47.

pronouncements is to moderate or deny entirely the idea that essential to the concept of the family is the lordship central to the patriarchal household. The fear of domination of one person over another which is so central to Rousseau's political thought thus finds its way into his analysis of the family. The family, in its principal task, the rearing of children, must cultivate the independence of the child so that when he grows to maturity, he shall not be a servant, either of his desires or of other persons—a task made difficult by the weakness of the child, which simultaneously enchains him and makes him want dominion.[35] The core of Rousseau's thinking about the family is consistent with the analyses of his more systematic contractarian colleagues. That is, he seeks to reconstruct the family on grounds that do not claim for the household master a right by nature (or Scripture) to rule over the inferior members of the family but rather focus on the temporary, limited power of the father which is his as a trust: to see to the welfare of those in his household. Like them, Rousseau also (and not entirely consistently) distinguishes between the natural association of the family and the conventional community of the polity in order to differentiate among the different origins and limits of their powers.

The centrality of the restructured household in early contractarian theory is, as I suggested at the outset of this part, directly related to the importance of the family in traditional arguments for natural or divinely prescribed hierarchy in human associations. The variety of its formulations contain one central thread: the attempt to demonstrate the (limited) consensual origins and the limits of authority within the household and, where that is deemed impossible (particularly in the case of the parent/child relationship), to insist on the remaining core of personhood at work even there and to distinguish between the residue of natural (nonconsensual) authority and the public power to be found in the political community. The idea of the remade household, then, is a part of the contractarian solution to the problem of establishing authority on a legitimate foundation and of ending thereby the curse of servitude, political and private. Its contribution to that endeavor is largely negative, for its function is to undo one of the crucial underpinnings of the hierarchical, naturalist concept of the community: the natural order of the household as an exemplar of the human community as such.

[35] See Rousseau, *Emile*, pp. 66, 85, 88–89, 236; Guy Besse, "J.-J. Rousseau: Maître, laquais, esclave," in Jacques d'Hondt, ed., *Hegel et le siècle des lumières* (Paris: Presses Universitaires de France, 1974), p. 88.

4. Lions and Pole-Cats:
Domination as the *Summum Malum*

A second governing metaphor of contractarian theory, the state of nature, supplements the critique of the patriarchal household by reinforcing its rejection of an original, hierarchical community and by adding to that a more full-blooded theory of the person and of the contract by which they come to form a polity. It is to that topic that we now turn. State-of-nature arguments, it is now commonly accepted, were not intended to provide a historical account by which to refute those who held that humans are born to thralldom or that Adam was their first ruler. The philosophical purpose served by state-of-nature stories is rather the setting out of an anthropology, a concept of human being and of the conundrums inherent in their condition, upon which to build a theory of the just community and of the place of power within it. That the question "What is it to be a human being?" is answered in the first instance through the examination of a counterfactual preassociational world is merely the first indication of the break with the classical tradition: in Aristotle's *Politics,* the resolutive-compositive method finds its analytical basic unit in the family, in a structured, hierarchical community characterized from the outset by the presence in its midst of rulers and ruled. In classical contractarian writings it is the individual that functions as that basic analytical unit. But state-of-nature theories were intended to be more than useful vehicles for setting out a philosophical anthropology. They are also, as Robert Nozick has argued, constructions whereby the necessity of political community, as well as the nature of power exercised in that realm, could be analyzed.[36] These three issues, "What is the individual?" "Why politics?" (or "Why a community of the political sort?"), and "What are the limits and extent of political activity?" form a cluster of concerns centered on a single principal problem: fearing mastery or domination without right, in a phrase, the despotic *oikos* model of human communities, they ask how legitimate authority of one person over another can be conceived.

4.1   A Scepter to Rule

Locke writes that God gave Adam "a Spade into his hand, to subdue the Earth, [rather] than a Scepter to Rule over its Inhabitants." Neither

[36] See Robert Nozick, *Anarchy, State, and Utopia* (New York: Basic Books, 1974), pp. 3–9.

God nor nature established the dominion of one person over his fellows. Being each and all the servants of their Maker, whose workmanship they are, and being endowed with a common nature, faculties, and powers, there cannot be supposed any relations of natural subordination among them.[37] Locke's argument here is again more complex than the preceding propositions would suggest. It is, in the first instance, an account that postulates a roughly equal endowment of faculties, a theory of our common nature. Second, it is a theory of an economic task: that humans are put into this world to labor, to subdue nature and not to rule one another. And third, it intimates that all persons exist in a primary jural relationship, the duty and obedience they owe to their God. The identity of their status, as John Dunn has noted, flows from their shared relation as servants to their God.[38] The Lockean thesis of an egalitarian natural condition thus embodies a claim about a rough, substantive equality and a thesis about a common and undifferentiated set of duties toward God and one another. In such a condition, Locke concludes, all power and jurisdiction must be reciprocal: no one can rightfully hold dominion over another under circumstances in which nature has not distinguished between persons and in which duties and rights are held in common.[39]

A person who is under the determination of someone other than himself lacks liberty. No one is justly under such dominion in a state of nature characterized in the manner just outlined. Accordingly, the natural liberty of human beings is to be free of any superior power on this earth, not to be subject to the will or authority of any person. It is not, however, for Locke, to be free of law, for the state of nature is not licentious but is bound by natural law, and thus while persons in that state are free to dispose over their actions and possessions, that liberty is not unbridled. Being put into this world at their Maker's pleasure and about his business, they are not at liberty to waste their lives or those of others. Their bodies and the world that is given to them for their comfort and nourishment are, as it were, held by them in usufruct, the conditional gifts of their sole Master.[40] Locke's concept of the state of nature is, then, a construct that sets out a jural condition independent of political society and that yields a concept of the person as a (limited) self-proprietor,

[37] Locke, 1T.45, 67 and 2T.6.

[38] Dunn, *The Political Thought of John Locke*, pp. 121, 126, 157.

[39] Locke, 2T.4, 54, 172; see Raymond Polin, *La politique morale de John Locke* (Paris: Presses Universitaires de France, 1960), p. 182.

[40] Locke, 1T.42, 88; 2T.6, 22. See also Dunn, *The Political Thought of John Locke*, pp. 174–75; Polin, *La politique morale de John Locke*, pp. 131, 171–72, and Polin, "Justice in Locke's Philosophy," in Carl J. Friedrich and John W. Chapman, eds., *Nomos 6: Justice* (New York: Atherton Press, 1963), p. 270.

bound by obligations to God but in relation to his fellow human beings, equal, free, and without subjection. The weak hands of natural law in this world are, however, insufficient to secure and make operative that jural condition. For though humans are juridical persons, endowed with rights and obligations, they are also fallen creatures, and so are no fine observers of natural law or respecters of others' equal and free status. The "pravity of mankind" is such that "Robberies, murders, rapes, are the sports of men set at liberty from punishment and censure."[41] The desire to dominate others, to subject them to one's unrestricted will for the sake of gain, pleasure, or glory seems to be written in the human heart.

So much is this passion to rule a part of fallen humankind's condition, that children love it more than they do their own liberty: "I told you before that Children love *Liberty;* and therefore they should be brought to do the things are fit for them, without feeling any restraint laid upon them. I now tell you, they love something more; and that is *Dominion:* And this is the first Original of most vicious Habits, that are ordinary and natural. This Love of *Power* and Dominion shews it self very early."[42] The desires born of that love of dominion are, Locke adds, the "Roots of almost all the Injustice and Contention, that so disturb Humane Life." It is against this background that Locke's analysis of the state of war and the state of nature must be understood. The state of nature embodies the idea of a nonpolitical yet law-governed community. But in light of the depraved, dominion-seeking characteristics of fallen man and given the absence of an authority able effectively and consistently to enforce law and secure the rights and obligations of individuals, the state of war, the assertion of force without right over others, must constantly threaten.

The evil of this situation, of the actual or threatened violence of one person against another, can be construed in a variety of ways. On a theological reading of Locke, the drive for dominion violates God's law, which gave no such power to humans; and the condition it gives rise to, the state of war, obstructs them in the pursuit of their divinely given callings.[43] In order that all may take care of their "own eternal happiness" and of their "temporal lives here upon earth; the state whereof being frail and fleeting," they must be ensured against the violence of

---

[41] John Locke, *A Letter Concerning Toleration* (Indianapolis: Library of Liberal Arts, 1955), p. 47, and Locke, *An Essay Concerning Human Understanding,* ed. Alexander Fraser (New York: Dover, 1959), vol. 1, p. 72. For commentary, see Dunn, *The Political Thought of John Locke,* pp. 126–27, and Riley, *Will and Political Legitimacy,* p. 69.

[42] John Locke, *Some Thoughts concerning Education,* in *The Educational Writings of John Locke,* ed. James L. Axtell (Cambridge: Cambridge University Press, 1968), p. 207.

[43] See Dunn, *The Political Thought of John Locke,* especially p. 126.

their fellows. A second path is to take at its face value the self-ownership language of the Lockean theory of the person, to embed exclusionary rights in that definition and to read out of that the "hedges" against invasion by others. A third, almost Kantian, way of reading the objection to domination would take as its starting point a secular construction of the juridical concept of the person, in which primordial status is accorded to autonomy (rather than to exclusionary rights derived from property in one's self). To be a person means to be free in the sense of disposing over one's actions and goods within the context of natural law. A human coerced into obedience to another is treated as something to be used for the master's purposes alone. And because this freedom is the foundation of the argument for equality, to be a slave of another (that is to be subordinated through illegitimate force) is to have the second principal characteristic of the human jural condition violated, that is, equality with respect to subjection.[44] It is also, of course, possible to give the attack on domination a strategic or Hobbesian gloss. Here the emphasis is shifted from the fact of creation and the purpose of the Maker and from the secular juridical concept of the person to the notion that the person's first and strongest desire is for self-preservation, a desire whose fulfillment is constantly imperiled by the will to dominate and the lust for glory. What is more, felicity and the conveniences of our temporal existence remain insecure and subject to invasion in an environment where the pravity of humankind is restrained only by natural law.[45] The creation of an effective jural condition, the public sword, thus becomes the prerequisite of self-preservation and felicity.

It is the "corruption and vitiousness of degenerate men" especially evident in their desire for dominion over others that is the *summum malum*, the condition to be remedied. For domination, apparent even in the first cries of babies, strikes at the freedom and equality God has given humans, attacks the status of humans as persons, denies them the tranquillity needed to pursue their callings, and threatens their commodious life on earth. Domination, as Locke makes clear, is not necessarily a condition of violence; rather, its essence is the subjection of other humans

---

[44] For the most part in these pages, I adopt a reconstruction of Lockean self-ownership, one detached from its theological moorings. I also reconstruct it as a way of speaking about freedom rather than as a privileging of property rights over autonomy. The former approach is almost certainly contrary to the author's intentions though it does allow his arguments to speak to those living in a very different intellectual context, and that is its justification. The latter, a wedding of Locke and Kant, is historically more sustainable though far from being beyond challenge.

[45] Locke, 1T.88 and 2T.123.

to an arbitrary and absolute will, and it is therefore inherent in communities structured as natural hierarchies. Such a condition must always carry with it the threat of actual violence (hence the justice of killing a kidnapper), but its core is the idea that because no one is made by God or nature to rule over others the exercise of dominion without consent or for purposes other than those that the ruled could be expected rationally to accept constitutes itself a sort of violence against their persons.

If the violence of persons, understood as the acquiring of dominion over others against their will or of such a magnitude as to be threatening to their status as persons is, for Locke, the supreme evil, this is so (to reduce the preceding analysis to a single point) because humans are self-owners.[46] In this idea of self-ownership, of being the proprietor of one's own person, we find the basis of Lockean egalitarianism (no one is born with the scepter of rule) and of his concept of freedom (autonomy over one's actions and possessions, consistent with the law of nature). This self that is owned contains, in Locke's account, a core of two linked assets—control over actions and self-preservation—and an extended definition, that is, property in the more conventional sense. In contrast to Aristotle, for whom the question of justice in relations between master and slave or father and child can arise only by analogy (because they are the master's own property[47]), Lockean self-ownership, the heart of the juridical concept of the person, creates a jural space of rights against others and obligations both to oneself (and God, as in the prohibition on suicide) and to others as self-owners. The pragmatic insecurity of that jural space—given the pravity of humankind in its search for dominion, in its trespassing on the core or extended assets of other selves—is the one great reason that they seek the "sanctuary" of civil society. That is, the right and indeed the obligation to ensure self-ownership creates, when coupled with the threat of those who desire dominion, a condition in which humans, lords over their own persons and possessions and subject to no earthly power, yield a measure of their autonomy to the authority of civil government. This they do in order to "limit the Power and moderate the Dominion of every Part and Member of Society" or, in the words of the *Letter Concerning Toleration,* to provide against the "fraud and violence of others."[48]

[46] Locke, 2T.27.

[47] Aristotle, *Nicomachean Ethics* 1134b8ff.

[48] Locke, 2T.222; Locke, *Letter Concerning Toleration*, p. 30; and see Dunn, *The Political Thought of John Locke*, pp. 67, 126–27; John Dunn, "Consent in the Political Theory of John Locke," *Historical Journal* 10 (1967): 177.

Inasmuch as power is not given to some in virtue of their natural superiority over others, and because it is also not a gift from God to Adam and his royal descendants, authority over persons can be acquired, according to Locke's argument, only by force or by consent. In other words, Locke's attack on natural hierarchy and divine authorization reduces all noncontractual claims to power to veiled arguments for enslavement, for power unlimited and wielded without right. It is against that "preponderance of force," as Dunn calls it, whether of the regally attired absolute monarch or of the lowly highwayman, the "lion" and the "pole-cat," that a properly constituted government serves as a hedge, buttressed by the right of the citizens to cashier society's true rebels, those who would, through the unwarranted ingathering of political power, reintroduce the state of war, of force without right, into the polity.[49] The passion for dominion (no matter whether it is clothed in the eloquence of Filmer's Adamite argument or in the unvarnished demands of the rapist or thief), with all of its noxious consequences for the status of persons as autonomous beings, for their relationship to God and for the possibility of a commodious life on earth, is a central part of Locke's answer to the question, "Why political community?"[50] His analysis, as it proceeds from that point, is intended to show how and to what extent legitimate authority can be exercised over persons among whom there is no natural or God-given hierarchy, no tolerable unauthorized relations of domination and subjection.

In the Hobbesian theory of the state of nature, humans are by nature equal and free, though these terms carry a profoundly different sense than in the Lockean version just discussed. As we saw previously in our analysis of the Hobbesian household, his argument is directed against notions of natural hierarchy among persons and particularly against the Aristotelian version of that theory. But the ideas of equality and liberty which he uses to counter the naturalist argument draw on a psychological and materialist analysis of the individual rather than on the theological/juridical foundations set out by Locke. That is to say, equality is understood on the one side as a rough similarity of power and prudence: "They are equals, who can do equal things," and "Nature hath made men so equal, in the faculties of the body and mind." On the other side, there is the "similitude" of the passions—the desires, fears, and hopes

<hr />

49 Locke, 1T.1–3; 2T.93, 226; Dunn, *The Political Thought of John Locke,* p. 177.
50 Locke, *Essay Concerning Human Understanding,* vol. 2, pp. 208–9; and see Dunn, *The Political Thought of John Locke,* p. 67; Hampton, *Hobbes,* p. 271.

that are virtually the same in all persons.[51] Where such equality obtains, particularly that of power or strength, there is neither by right ("The right of nature . . . is the liberty each man hath, to use his own power, as he will himself") nor in fact (strength and prudence being roughly equal) effective subjugation.

The human condition is for Hobbes one in which there is no natural hierarchy, no entitlement (and indeed no power or ability) by which a supposed superior may govern his inferiors. There is rather an equality of weakness and a hope for felicity and self-preservation. Yet this condition is also one of unceasing strife: "For as amongst masterless men, there is perpetual war, of every man against his neighbour."[52] The reason for this strife among the equal and masterless is that humans seek dominion over one another, a tendency encouraged by their rough equality—that is, the equality of strength generates an equality of aspiration. Humans, then, have a general inclination, a "restless desire," to secure power upon power. The underpinnings of this argument for an unrelenting desire for power may be schematically described (with some overlap) thus: (1) the desire for felicity in conditions of scarcity; (2) the desire for self-preservation; (3) vainglory. Felicity is a continual progress of desire never reaching an endpoint or *summum bonum*, and of the power of persons in their ability to secure the goods they desire for themselves. But where, as is most frequently the case, their appetites are for the same objects, desire can be satisfied only at the expense of others. Competition with a view to imposing one's will on another by denying him the object of his appetite is, accordingly, one of the sources of the drive for dominion. A second source of this drive is that in the masterless condition the preservation of mere life, to say nothing of a "delightful life," coupled with the reasonable anticipation of the likelihood of threats to one's person or possessions, leads them to seek still greater power not because they savor power as such but because they are certain that the only way to protect themselves against their predators is to subdue any possible source of threat. And last, the passion for glory, the thirst for the pleasure some find in dominating their fellows, leads to conflict.[53]

The desire to dominate, whether hotly motivated (passionately, e.g., for glory) or coldly motivated (rationally, for self-protection through preemption), when combined with the premise of a rough equality of strength and prudence yields a set of perverse effects, consequences that

[51] Hobbes, *De Cive*, p. 114; Hobbes, *Leviathan*, pp. 6, 80–81.
[52] Hobbes, *Leviathan*, p. 140.
[53] Hobbes, *De Cive*, pp. 100, 115, 259; Hobbes, *Leviathan*, pp. 39, 56, 63–64, 81.

defeat the aspirations even of those who conquer others for the wholly rational reason of self-preservation. The liberty that masterless men have is "unfruitful," Hobbes writes, for it is shared by all who may act according to their wills and hence must seek to deprive one another of their liberty, each in order better to be able to pursue his felicity. Similarly, their equality of power renders that power itself useless because it cannot secure for them either the satisfaction of their desires or even, with any certainty, their self-preservation and a bare commodious life. These masterless men, free and equal, who by nature wish to rule themselves find that this requires ruling others, if only for security; yet they are unable to do so effectively. Each is therefore constantly exposed to domination or the threat of it and no one can count on remaining masterless for long.

The demand for liberty from the one effective power on earth, the combined power of the commonwealth, is self-defeating, for it produces not felicity or liberty but unceasing exposure to the violence of the domineering private sword. It is then, for Hobbes, the perverse consequences of one type of domination, that fought for by masterless men (and more practically, that which is advanced by those who seek to weaken the only power capable of banishing private violence and domination, namely the sovereign), that render that form an evil. This *summum malum*, the war of all against all, is not conceived by Hobbes in the juridical fashion of a Locke, or in the moral/juridical manner of a Kant. The perverseness of domination is measured not against the sanctity of a person's autonomy or self-ownership (arguments that Hobbes's minimalist concept of liberty and the will would hardly permit him to make) but rather against its consequences: unending threats to self-preservation and to the enjoyment of one's life in this world and the possessions that make it delicious.[54]

The foresight of these consequences causes humans, "who naturally love liberty, and dominion over others," to lay down their liberty and the private power through which they have sought dominion. Fear leads them to give up their lust for dominion and to seek the sanctuary of society. And because there can be no peace without subjection—that is, where

[54] See Hobbes, *De Cive*, p. 216; Hobbes, *Of Liberty and Necessity*, in *The English Works of Thomas Hobbes*, ed. William Molesworth (London: John Bohn, 1840), vol. 4, pp. 244–45, 260–61, 273; Hobbes, *Leviathan*, pp. 38, 136–37, 139; Riley, *Will and Political Legitimacy*, pp. 40ff. Jean Hampton's "Two Faces of Contractarian Thought," in Peter Vallentyne, ed., *Contractarianism and Rational Choice: Essays on David Gauthier's Morals by Agreement* (Cambridge: Cambridge University Press, 1991), makes the argument that Hobbes's rational choice approach needs a Kantian corrective, respect for persons as ends-in-themselves, in order even to get off the ground as a theory of society. See pp. 46–55.

individuals have been stripped of the power (liberty) to do as they will—
the human condition is one exhaustively described in two types of domination: that of the master, of the private sword, and that of the protection
provided by the sovereign.[55] The absolutism of the Hobbesian sovereign,
and the analysis of the defects of constrained government, flows directly
from the evil against which the commonwealth is the remedy. The obvious, and powerful, rejoinder is that it is unreasonable to imagine that for
fear of "pole-cats" rational humans (those pursuing the ends that Hobbes
himself attributes to rational agents) would give themselves over to a
"lion." Their security is preserved less well by an unfettered sovereign,
armed with state power and rendered immune from any sanction, than it
would be in a condition of anarchy, of the violence of equals. It is worth
observing that on either the juridical or prudential accounts of the *reasons* for government, the Lockean form of limited government, a "hired"
or agency authority, is more consistent with fundamental contractarian
premises than is the Hobbesian absolutist regime, which is the recipient
of completely alienated powers (save, of course, for the nugatory power of
self-defense, which in Hobbes's account is inalienable).[56]

The choice between the private power and violence of masters and the
public authority of government stands also at the heart of Rousseau's
political theory. Invoking the words of Pliny the Younger, Rousseau
writes: "If we have a prince, . . . it is so that he may preserve us from
having a master."[57] The problem of domination and servitude clearly
occupies a central place in Rousseau's thought, and indeed much of his
reasoning, his republicanism, the critique of the private sphere (including
his attitude toward women) and of inauthenticity, and his theory of the
general will have their origins in the fear of domination. Rousseau argues
that the malaise of servitude flourishes with society, and grows together
with, and as a result of, property and the division of labor. Domination,
then, is not an ingredient in the construction of a prepolitical condition to
which government (either absolute or limited) is the answer as an authorized or hired authority but is rather rooted in the social condition itself, a
situation for which even the best government is only an imperfect remedy.

The child's cries at birth are for Rousseau, as for Locke, an expression
of the will to dominate; but unlike Locke's account, this drive to domi-
neer is said to emerge from the child's weakness, the source of all wicked-

---

[55] Hobbes, *Leviathan*, p. 110; and see Hampton, *Hobbes*, p. 278.

[56] For a brilliant game-theoretic analysis of the contractarian method and its implications
for regime forms see Hampton, *Hobbes*, pp. 256–84.

[57] Rousseau, *Second Discourse*, p. 164.

ness. Weakness creates dependency, and dependency in turn the desire to control others as best one can. Social (or, more precisely, bourgeois) man resembles the child in that the abundance of his needs, artificial and cultivated by luxury, and the passions tied to them make him dependent and weak.[58] The multiplicity of these needs in a society dedicated to the private, competitive world of *amour propre* extends the lateral bonds of dependence among its citizens, the subjection of one person to another, and the gross inequality that is a consequence of the social magnification of the (in themselves inconsequential) natural inequalities of intellectual and physical endowments. By contrast, the natural condition of humankind is one of independence (isolation) and of an extreme modesty of needs; in short, a condition in which domination and servitude can hardly exist.

Man, being a free agent and not by nature subordinated to others, there is, Rousseau writes, no worse evil than for one person to be at the discretion of another. The task, then, is to devise a regime in which dependence will be minimized.[59] Because dependence arises not only from the violence of the powerful against the weak but internally, as it were, from the passions and multiplication of needs, one crucial part of that strategy must go beyond the purely political in order to reach into the souls of socialized persons. This task forms a central part in the education of Emile, and its underlying idea is that if one is to be truly free one must become the master of the passions rather than their servant. For it is in the moderation of the passions, the control over them, that the person becomes free and independent. This notion carries two meanings, two senses of freedom: that of freedom within, threatened by the passions and secured by moderation, and that of external freedom. Because needs engender dependence the person in control of his needs or passions approaches the greatest possible self-sufficiency. In both cases, the core of the idea of freedom is the absence of a constraining master.[60] On the political level, this taming of the passions finds expression in the general will and, more broadly, in Rousseau's admiration for the asceticism and public-spiritedness of the ancient (especially the Spartan) polity. If the bourgeois is the person who judges all in light of his own passions and

[58] Rousseau, *Emile*, p. 48, 66–67, 88; Rousseau, *Second Discourse*, pp. 140, 156; Rousseau, *Letter to M. d'Alembert*, trans. Allan Bloom, in Rousseau, *Politics and the Arts* (Ithaca: Cornell University Press, 1960), p. 119; Rousseau, *Social Contract* (Geneva manuscript), p. 158.

[59] See Rousseau, *Second Discourse*, p. 163; Rousseau, *Social Contract*, p. 49; Shklar, *Men and Citizens*, p. 57.

[60] See Besse, "Maître, laquais, esclave," p. 96, and Shklar, *Men and Citizens*, p. 162.

needs—if, that is, his will is inclined toward private preferences and hence towards inequality—the general will subordinates the private and reasons in the "silence of the passions."[61] The bourgeois made into a citizen is, then, a person who has acquired a new will, one which tends toward the common, and therefore equality, rather than toward the inequality of the passions and private preference.

The general will is, of course, more than the soulcraft of Emile's tutor writ large. It is also a vision of a public institution meant to show how freedom can be consistent with authority and, what is more, how the public realm can suppress the inequality and domination inherent in the private sphere. Recall that for Rousseau there are two types of dependence: one of humans on nature or things, the other between persons. The former is beyond our power to alter and is not a moral relation, not a relation between two wills. Personal servitude is, however, alterable and it is also the form of dependence which most degrades humans, master and valet alike.[62] The idea of the general will is framed as an answer to domination among persons. Rousseau's argument for the general will is notoriously obscure, and as its more recondite features are of little importance to the theme of Part Two, I shall only briefly mention some of the principal ways in which it is a counter to relations of servitude and mastery.

The first, and most conventional, line of argument presented by Rousseau is that political authority, properly constituted (i.e., not simply a ruse of the wealthy and strong over the poor and weak as set out in the *Second Discourse*), is public power protecting against private domination. And because that public force is the execution of the (general) will of the legislative citizens it is a sanctioned power applying equally to all citizen/subjects. As the bonds between citizens as legislators and subjects are strengthened, those lateral, private ties of dominion are slackened. Second, and related to the preceding, because citizens obey only those laws whose making they have participated in, they obey no one but themselves. They thus exchange the self-determination of the isolated human for the self-determination of the common self, the public person of the general will. They obey but are not servants; command, yet are not masters. And last, in submitting themselves to the general will, they obey

---

[61] For a detailed analysis of the Spartan image in Rousseau's thought see Shklar, "Rousseau's Two Models: Sparta and the Age of Gold." On the bourgeois see also Rousseau, *Social Contract* (Geneva manuscript), p. 161; Rousseau, *Social Contract*, pp. 59, 67; Rousseau, *Emile*, p. 292.

[62] Rousseau, *Emile*, pp. 38, 85.

no one, no person but only laws. Because they have given themselves to no one in forming their political community, and because their laws are general and therefore blind to individuals, they have no master except their own wise laws. The indignity of the lackey, the submission to the will of another person, is here removed; personal authority is replaced by impersonal laws, applying equally to all and blind to distinctions among humans.[63] In sum, the legislative general will is the corrective to private dominion and the violence of some persons over others because it takes the private sword away from individuals and confers power only upon the results of their common deliberation and because it is the embodiment of their collective autonomy, of subjects who are submitted to no other authority than that in which they, as active citizens, are members. And finally, it is the appropriate remedy because, when citizens bow only before the law (general and blind) and not before other persons, the morally repugnant character of personal subordination is eliminated from their acts of obedience.

The state of nature theories we have been considering are, first of all, vehicles for attacking a view of the human community as a set of status relations, natural or by divine ordination. The literary form of this attack is the move "back" past the family, the basic association of the classical hierarchal argument, to a nonassociational situation. Before humans are members of communities they are individuals or, to speak outside of the historical metaphor of contractarianism, the question of what it means to be a person has an answer independent of what it means to occupy a position in relation to others. Indeed, it is the basic claim of state-of-nature theories that, contrary to the patriarchal-household model of the community, the properties of a rightful relation between persons can be fully grasped only against the background of a nonassociational theory of the person. Stripped of the illusory garb of status, power, and differentiation, the individual is shown to be equal and independent. As we have seen, the notions of equality and independence are given markedly different glosses—jural in Locke, psychological and materialistic in Hobbes and (in a different manner) in Rousseau. Nevertheless, beneath the variety of ways of unfolding the idea of equality lies a single, common thread: that no person rules by nature over another, whether that is understood

[63] See Rousseau, *Emile,* p. 473; Rousseau, *Second Discourse,* p. 163; Rousseau, *Social Contract,* pp. 75, 77, 108; Rousseau, *Political Economy,* p. 214; Riley, *Will and Political Legitimacy,* p. 120; Besse, "Maître, laquais, esclave," pp. 83–84; Alexandre Matheron, "Maîtres et serviteurs dans la philosophie politique classique," *La pensée* 200 (1978): 3–20, especially pp. 19–20.

as a statement about their juridical condition, their relationship to God, or their physical prowess. Similarly, we may say of the idea of freedom as a property of persons within a community that underpinning the diversity of views to be found in the contractarian tradition is one core argument, that only by an act of the will, a voluntary act, can one person rightfully be subordinated to another.

It is against this background that the problem of domination, of power in human relations, becomes so central—whether the power in question is that of governors over the governed, of husbands over wives, or of masters over servants. The claims of natural or divine entitlement to rule having been dissolved by the corrosive egalitarianism and individualism of the state-of-nature theory, the exercise of power must appear as an affront to human dignity, as a violation of the autonomy and equality that are key to the moral anthropology of the contractarians. And yet it is also apparent that the pravity of humankind, reflected above all in the will to dominate, makes the substitution of the public sword for the private a necessity if humans are to find a commodious life on earth and one consistent with their autonomy. How, then, can this necessary power of the political community be distinguished from mere private coercion, the "lion" from the "pole-cat"? Both involve submission and the loss of the means of self-rule; are they not, therefore, of the same species, the political differing from the private only in its strength and impunity? Or, in different words, what distinguishes the legitimate from the illegitimate exercise of authority? The *summum malum* (jural and practical) for beings with the characteristics of humans is domination or the threat of it. The central question of justice then becomes not who should rule and in virtue of what particular superiority but rather how can the power required to protect us from the dominating violence of others be rendered legitimate and not be itself yet another form of the violation of what it means to be a person?

4.2   Contracts and Contracting Agents

The liberal answer (of which we have seen intimations above) to this question of the legitimacy of the community is contained in the pervasive metaphor of contract. Embraced within the language of contract is a theory of the person, of liberty and consent to authority, and of the sort of obligation consistent with being a person. In the pages that follow, I am concerned principally with the concepts of person, will, and obligation which undergird contract theory and with how together they constitute one response to the problem of domination.

The person of contractarian theory is a particularly bloodless, colorless creature, and designedly so. The manifold distinctions that mark out human beings one from the other make no appearance here. The person is rather conceived as a bundle of jural characteristics which have a primacy over other qualities, whether natural or the accretions of history, which may distinguish actual subjects one from the other. The primacy accorded to this jural conception of the person plays a strategic role in the contractarian argument similar to that of its other governing metaphor, the state of nature. That is, it seeks to remove the consideration of what it means to be a person from its traditional locus embedded in the analysis of hierarchical associations with their rich descriptions of differential endowments and the power entitlements said to flow from them. The negative, leveling (resolutive) operation of the state-of-nature theory is the beginning point for the construction of the notion of the juridical person. The state-of-nature device, apart from its egalitarian drive, also provides the contractarian argument with a context to which all agents are equally subject (force or domination) and a reason, or desire, to escape their predicament (felicity, self-preservation, the establishment of a secure juridical condition). The latter features we have explored in the preceding pages; here we shall examine the attributes of the contracting agents.

To be a contracting agent, one must have something to alienate, that is, be a proprietor of an alienable asset and have the liberty to dispose of this good (and a reason for so doing), and there must be an institutional context that permits and secures voluntary bilateral exchanges by these agents. The minimal condition of proprietorship for a contracting agent is self-ownership: the words or deeds by which the contract is effected must be one's own if the binding agreement that is the object of the contracting process may have not only assets to be exchanged but persons to be obliged. That is the sense of Hobbes's observation that "a *person*, is he, whose words or actions are considered . . . as his own" and again "he that is called the *author* with regard to actions is called the *owner* with regard to possessions."[64] It is, in part, because of this minimal require-ment of self-ownership that madmen and children cannot be understood to be contracting agents: lacking the deliberative faculty, the power of reasoned choice, their words while undoubtedly those of the physical

[64] Hobbes, *Leviathan*, p. 105; Hobbes, *On Man*, trans. Bernard Gert et al., in *Man and Citizen*, ed. Bernard Gert (New York: Doubleday, 1972), p. 84; and see Tully, *A Discourse on Property*, p. 121.

subject are not owned by them in the somewhat richer sense of ownership—that they know the meaning of their utterances, that their (contracting) words designate obligations of which they are one of the parties. In sum, a person who does not know the meaning of his words (however laxly understood "know" may be) cannot be the subject of an obligation.

The contractarian idea of self-ownership extends beyond those elements required by contracting speech itself. Particularly in the robust Lockean account, self-ownership comes to mean proprietorship over one's physical person and actions: "Master of himself and *Proprietor of his own Person* and the actions or *Labour* of it."[65] And from this ownership of actions and labor emerges (with restrictions to be discussed below) a proprietorship over things with which labor has been mixed. Self-ownership here merges with the concept of the autonomy of the person, and indeed autonomy becomes the "*Liberty* to dispose, and order, as he lists, his Person, Actions, Possessions and his whole Property."[66] The contracting agent must, in short, be his own master, for he who does not dispose over his own person is incapable of creating an engagement or obligation, and thus there can be no contract with a slave because not being his own ruler he can neither undertake an obligation nor alienate anything.[67]

If we press the contractarian argument and ask it to give more substance to the idea of autonomy as self-ownership, it becomes apparent that choice is its central component. Choice (in the Lockean version) is an uncoerced act of the will in the alienating of one's assets, whether those be tangible, external assets (property) or a measure of one's self-government (natural liberty). Relatedly, choice is crucial because to covenant is to undertake an obligation to deliver now or in the future the promised good, and there is no obligation that does not arise from the exercise of the will.[68] Assets may be transferred in many ways, including by theft or other forms of violence, and obedience may be secured by force, but these situations are not contractual and coercion can leave no residue of duty or obligation—the transfer or promises may be annulled as soon as the aggrieved party finds the strength to subdue his conqueror (Hobbes alone among the major social-contract theorists denies this principle).

[65] Locke, 2T.44.
[66] Locke, 2T.57; and see Polin, "Justice in Locke's Philosophy," p. 269; Polin, *La politique morale de John Locke*, pp. 131–32.
[67] Locke, 2T.172; Hobbes, *De Cive*, p. 207.
[68] Hobbes, *Leviathan*, pp. 86, 90, 141.

Such a reading of the intertwined ideas of self-ownership, autonomy, and choice captures one key feature of the contractarian concept of the person as one who disposes over his property, broadly construed, and who therefore is the possessor of exclusionary rights against others—his property cannot be alienated without an uncoerced act of his will, which is to say, without his consent. One exegetical difficulty with this construction is that in the political sphere consent, or the free exercise of the will, has little direct behavioral/institutional specification, at least in the Lockean version that forms the reference point of these pages.[69] Although the contracting agent is to be understood as one who, having exclusive property in his person and possessions, cannot (save through an act of consent or will) have that property detached from him, the practice of political obedience, which involves a partial alienation of liberty, is not held by Locke to be just if and only if there is such an express act of consent. It is of course possible to read back into Locke's language of contracting agents and consent a full-blooded, democratic participatory politics, but the author's own words direct us to a more modest standard: that of uncoerced acceptance as sufficient manifestation of consent to be governed. Recast somewhat, this latter reading suggests that the ideas of self-ownership and autonomy are meant to establish a barrier to coercion rather than to set out a theory of institutionalized agency. Thus, in place of the proposition that only the power to which one has consented, that is, erected by an act of the will, can be called just and generate obligation we might substitute the claim that what has been extracted through coercion is an invasion of his property and cannot bear the title of a rightful transfer and hence can generate no obligation. This shift in emphasis seeks to create a barrier to coercion, to limit the scope of obligation, and, as Dunn has argued, that is precisely the role played by the notion of consent in Locke's broader theory of obligation.[70] These two interpretations of self-ownership and will are plainly not inconsistent, and indeed the richer account of agency seems to require the more limited theory of agency (as an exclusionary right against the coercive invasion of one's property) as its pragmatic precondition. Both constructions are part of a contractarian argument addressing a central predicament, domination and the free political community as its corrective. Historical fidelity demands the recognition of the special (and limited) function that agency

---

[69] This point has been made in Dunn, *The Political Thought of John Locke*, pp. 136–37, 142; Dunn, "Consent in the Political Theory of John Locke," p. 176; Hannah Pitkin, "Obligation and Consent," *American Political Science Review* 59 (1965): 996–99.

[70] Dunn, "Consent in the Political Theory of John Locke," p. 156.

and consent have in Locke's political thought, but the foundations of his argument permit (or more, invite) the extended reading outlined above.

4.2.1   Choice

A second key issue in this way of setting out the concept of the person as someone who is a self-owner, capable of alienating assets, undertaking obligations, and protected against coercion by an exclusive right of property in herself, is what ought to count as choice or consent.[71] That is, when is the person in such a condition that no choice, hence no agency or consent, can be attributed to her with the attendant consequences for the moral standing of the transaction in question? The most obvious case of a denial of choice which violates the liberal concept of the person at its root is slavery through force: here the victim is physically bound or otherwise restrained by violence and compelled to yield to a master's wishes. There is no choice, no possibility of an act of election, and hence no obligation between the two parties, and for that reason the master/slave relationship is of no use to the contractarian theory of the political community, even to the Hobbesian version of that theory with its markedly expansive idea of what can be counted as voluntary.[72] Beyond the slavery case, and other equally extreme situations in which the context excludes choice altogether, the question remains of what magnitude (or type) of restraint renders a seeming choice the mere appearance of one.

Now one of the basic currents of the Lockean argument is an attack on the notion that property can include dominion over persons, an attack that moves against the Filmerian position that Adam and his royal successors were given private dominion over the earth and its creatures. The issue becomes, by extension, whether the power acquired by those with superior economic assets, land, tools, or whatever, makes a sham out of the apparent free agency of the contracts entered into with them by those lacking such endowments but needing food and shelter in order to live. The consequences of this question for the relationship between liberal political philosophy and markets is discussed at the end of Part Two; for now, I wish to explore it briefly from within the confines of contract theory simply.

[71] This exclusive right ceases when a person forfeits her jural status by employing illegitimate force against others.

[72] See Hobbes, *De Cive*, pp. 207, 216; Hobbes, *Leviathan*, pp. 132–33; Locke, 2T.172; Rousseau, *Social Contract*, pp. 49–50; Chapman, "*Leviathan* Writ Small," p. 81; Hinton, "Husbands, Fathers, and Conquerors," p. 57.

One controversial reading of Locke's idea of consent (suggested by James Tully) holds that if, for instance, economic necessity causes a decision to be made it is thereby rendered involuntary. Indeed it can be treated, under a certain construction of necessity, as a coerced outcome. This analysis relies heavily on two passages from Locke's *Two Treatises* (1T.42 and 2T.85) in which the contractual nature of the master/servant relation is established and in which Locke maintains that "a Man can no more make use of another's necessity, to force him to become his Vassal, by with-holding that Relief . . . than he that has more strength can seize upon a weaker, master him to his Obedience, and with a Dagger at his throat offer him Death or Slavery."[73] This is read as saying that for a person to meet the requirements of a free, contractual move into servitude there must be the possibility of choice, an option for preserving his life in some other manner. What this line of interpretation offers then is an understanding of Locke which takes him to be attacking, virtually as a piece, the Adamite argument for royal proprietorship over the body politic and the power of despotical lords over the propertyless.[74] The critique here attributed to Locke is centered on the idea that the state power of the monarch and the economic power of the lord, if absolute, are coercive in the sense that they leave their subjects, private and public, with no scope for choice and hence render them not contractual citizens or servants but slaves. The radicalness of this reading consists above all in the fact that it directs our attention away from the more restricted and conventional picture of coercion as the violence of unrestrained public power to the possibility of another source of coercion, less visible but no less effective—private economic power.

My principal interest in this issue is with a query of the following kind. Consider from a different angle the relationship between the lord, his economic assets, and the free individual driven by necessity into servitude (*not* vassalage or slavery): that of choosing under constraint. Let us imagine the following situation, adapted from Nozick's *Anarchy, State, and Utopia:* twenty-six single men and twenty-six women wishing to be married and sharing a common preference ranking for the twenty-six candidates of the opposite sex. If A marries A^1, then B whose first preference (ex hypothesis) was for A^1 will not have his/her first choice realized and thus can achieve only a less desired result by marrying B^1. At the end of the list, Z has no option (save celibacy) other than to marry Z^1. However

---

[73] Locke, 1T.43; Tully, *A Discourse on Property,* pp. 136–37.
[74] Tully, *A Discourse on Property,* p. 146.

undesirable that may be in Z's view, if he does marry her it is by choice and is voluntary.[75] Not only does such a choice intuitively seem voluntary, constrained though the option environment is, but a correction of that environment designed to yield a different outcome might well infringe on A's right to make his/her (legitimate) choice freely. The reason it appears voluntary is the absence of coercion of the conventional type, that is, the direct subordination of one person to another achieved through the application of force. Now imagine again our lords and servants. Let us assume that the lords have acquired their property not by theft or other forms of violence but legitimately through inheritance or (more implausibly) through the sweat of their faces. All available land has been brought into individual hands (assisted by the existence of money), but some persons find themselves without land and therefore without the means to sustain themselves from their own properties. These latter have the choice of starvation or (contractual) servitude. It is, to say the least, not at all clear that on Locke's argument this is not a choice, that the highly restricted option set renders the situation illegitimately coercive. Second, it is even less evident what coercive measures could be justly used against the lord who has legitimately acquired his estate and whose power over the servant derives from the confluence of his and others' exercise of their industry, that is, from the scarcity of land.

It will be objected to the above analysis that Locke, in his well-known proviso that there be "enough, and as good left in common for others"[76] and in his insistence on the duty of charity, sets limits on property acquisition or, more precisely, sets the theoretical groundwork for the commonwealth to redistribute property so as to meet the requirements mandated by that proviso. There are several possible rejoinders to this objection. First, Locke's claim is that unequal industriousness (and hence unequal acquired economic assets) in fact produces such wealth that all are better off, even those who are mere "day Labourer(s)," that is, nonowners of land. In this way, the greater industriousness of some, and their greater wealth, serve the same function as the commons had previously, that of providing the means whereby the lives of God's creatures may be preserved on earth. Second, and independent of the preceding proposition, the "enough, and as good" limitation is not addressed to the problem of choice. Locke is not arguing that in order for the free person to submit herself contractually to servitude she must have the option of taking

[75] Nozick, Anarchy, State, and Utopia, pp. 263–64.
[76] Locke, 2T.27.

advantage of free land. Rather, Locke derives this limitation from the purpose for which God has given humans the things of nature: to provide for the "Support and Comfort of their being." Thus, even on a stringent reading of the "enough, and as good" proviso (one holding that Locke meant for the commons to remain open), the existence of the commons is a remedy not to the problem of constrained option sets and their effect on choice (though that might be one of its consequences) but is aimed rather at ensuring the preservation of all humankind.

Third, Locke distinguishes between justice and charity in relation to property. Both give "every Man a Title," the former to the product of his honest industry and to his rightful inheritance and the latter to "so much of another's Plenty, as will keep him from extream want."[77] Is this the same sort of title, though? That is to say, is the duty of charity one that generates a publicly enforceable claim on the property of persons? Locke's *Venditio* manuscript makes the case that a seller acts justly as long as he makes no distinction among his buyers; whatever price he exacts, and however dire the distress of his customers which allows him to charge a high price for his goods, as long as he treats them equally "he transgresses not against Justice" though "what he may doe against Charity *is an other case.*"[78] Charity (like love) is a Christian duty, and to violate it is, in Locke's moral universe, a sin; the grain merchant who allows humans to starve by refusing to lower his prices is culpable before God for their deaths. But Locke does not suggest that he is culpable before the civil power, which cannot concern itself with the salvation of souls or the fulfillment of Christian duties. Raymond Polin makes a similar point, arguing that "the love of neighbours which is present in us as creatures and the reason which is present in us as men recommend the duty of charity. It cannot oblige us, because charity is in the realm of faith."[79] Though Locke does recommend in his (often draconian) letter on the treatment of the poor that they be cared for "out of the stock of the kingdom," and while in his educational writings he insists on the importance of instilling a spirit of generosity and liberality (charity) in matters concerning property as a counterweight to the child's will to

[77] Locke, 1T.42.
[78] Locke, *Venditio,* in Patrick Kelly, ed., *Locke on Money,* 2 vols., in *The Clarendon Edition of the Works of John Locke* (Oxford: Clarendon, 1991), vol. 2, p. 498, emphasis added. Kelly, on the contrary, stresses the traditional, scholastic theory of price which (he argues) Locke develops here. See Patrick Kelly, *Locke on Money,* vol. 1, p. 98.
[79] Polin, "Justice in Locke's Philosophy," p. 276; and see Locke, *Letter Concerning Toleration,* p. 17, and Locke, *Pacific Christians,* in Lord King, *The Life of John Locke* (London: Colburn and Bentley, 1830), vol. 2, p. 64.

dominate, expressed in acquisitiveness, he does not (and could not) make this case on the basis of the poor's (supposed) publicly enforceable claim-right to the surplus of their more industrious fellows.[80] In sum, the story of the *Venditio* manuscript deals with two manifest evils: famine and property violation, and, proceeding from the point of view of political justice, it treats the second of these as the greater ill, thereby confirming the primacy accorded to the conception of the *summum malum* as the direct invasion of self-ownership by others. We may also surmise from the *Venditio* story that Locke does not consider the merchant's taking advantage of the extreme distress of the food buyers to be an invasion of their self-ownership, which is to say that, liberally speaking, he does not consider the monopoly owner of grain to have coerced the buyer.[81] Had Locke thought that there was coercion involved, his theory would have allowed, even required, a political corrective; and of that remedy there is no trace.

We might say then that Locke's account of justice is composed of a core, the "stock" of the person articulated in the notion of proprietorship as the right to self-ownership and its corollary, the right of alienation, and a set of moral duties which stands outside of that core and which includes charity. The broad construction of the Lockean proviso, one in which the right to the property of others (derived from the "enough, and as good" proviso) dominates exclusionary rights, threatens to reduce all of an individual's endowments, including their person, to something (coercively) alienable. And it is for that reason that some contemporary theorists have favored a rather more restrictive reading of the proviso.[82] The legitimate

[80] Locke, "Poor Law Reform," in H. R. Fox Bourne, *The Life of John Locke* (London: Henry S. King, 1876), vol. 2, p. 382; Locke, *Some Thoughts Concerning Education,* pp. 213–14. Though the arguments I have sketched in these paragraphs represent the burden of Locke's account of property (here, property in food), justice, and the power of the magistrate, the textual evidence is not wholly consistent. Consider the rather different approach suggested by this passage from Locke's *Letter Concerning Toleration,* p. 40: "But if peradventure such were the state of things that the interest of the commonwealth required all slaughter of beasts should be foreborne for some while . . . who sees not that the magistrate, in such a case, may forbid all his subjects to kill any calves for any use whatsoever?" I am grateful to James Tully for insisting on the importance of this passage, though it does not bear the theoretical weight that he attempts to place on it.

[81] I share David Zimmerman's thought that the owners of *natural* monopolies do not act coercively, though they may well exploit others. The conclusion is different, as Zimmerman argues, if the owner has set out to corner the market. See David Zimmerman, "Coercive Wage Offers," *Philosophy and Public Affairs* 10 (1981): 121–45, especially p. 137. The underlying principle of this argument, that scarcity, in and of itself, does not create a coercive relationship between those who must bargain within its confines is also applicable to the sale-of-labor problem discussed in the preceding pages.

[82] See David Gauthier, *Morals by Agreement* (Oxford: Clarendon Press, 1986), pp. 202–4, and Nozick, *Anarchy, State, and Utopia,* pp. 178–82.

exercise of core rights in economic exchanges may produce the terrible consequences described in the *Venditio* piece, may, that is—in the modern jargon—produce negative externalities without anyone's (including the victim's) core liberal rights having been violated. This does not mean that the community should remain indifferent to such a plight. On the contrary, Locke writes in the *Letter Concerning Toleration* (p. 24) that "we must not content ourselves with the narrow measures of bare justice; charity, bounty, and liberality must be added to it. This the Gospel enjoins, this reason directs, and this that natural fellowship we are born into requires of us." However, two things in this passage merit observation: first, a distinction is made between justice on the one side and charity and liberality on the other, and second we are enjoined to go beyond the requirements of "bare justice" not by the magistrate and his laws but rather by the Gospel, reason, and natural fellowship.

What the preceding argument suggests is that the foundation for a corrective redistribution is not to be found in the core and that the principles contained in that core will have to govern such redistributive measures as may be thought desirable on other grounds. That ground might be Christian charity or a secular moral conviction of obligation toward those who are suffering. The state can become the executor of these noncore values in a liberal, contractarian manner if individuals agree to allow the body politic to attach their property for the purpose of assisting those who become destitute as the result of such externalities, in other words by means of a public social insurance scheme. Indeed, if certain elementary propositions concerning public goods and collective action are adopted, state-enforced welfare measures would be the only effective way of securing the common goal of relief for the destitute.[83] The idea of a right of the poor to the property of others would, on the other hand, be illiberal because it would attack the heart of liberal self-ownership, and in practice it would lead to a coercive redistribution of property.

This analysis leads to two related conclusions about consent and coercion. The first is that the idea of choice as a condition of voluntariness is given an expansive definition by Locke and even more so by Hobbes. It is expansive in the sense that it recognizes choice and hence voluntary alienation as being possible in a highly constrained environment of options, so long as those constraints are not the result of injustice—of violence or theft, for example. Here is an illustration: consider the threat to inflict death (outside of the context of a just war or self-defense generally) in

---

[83] See Kolm, *Le contrat social libéral*, pp. 242–43, 256–57. But cf. Nozick, *Anarchy, State, and Utopia*, pp. 265–68.

order to secure some good or service. The transfer that emerges thereby is not binding because no one legitimately has the right to the life of another (apart from those circumstances just mentioned). A rough economic analogy would be a situation in which the lord's property had been acquired by theft and then used to employ laborers made landless by that theft. This too would be illegitimate in Locke's view because of the juridical flaw in one of the party's endowments: the lord no more freely disposes over his stolen property than the unjust conqueror does over the lives of the vanquished. In neither case is it the limits of the range of options, or their unpleasantness, which undermine the transaction but rather the morally flawed claims/actions at the core of each: to the persons or property of others. To say then that the contractarian person is a self-owner whose (alienable) assets can be transferred only by a free act of his will and that such a free act necessarily implies choice and therefore options is to grasp at its heart the sense and import of the Lockean concept of the person. But as we have just seen, this fundamental point of contract theory does not commit its proponents to the view that limited or unpleasant options render choice coerced and unfree. This is so both because the theory contains an idea of choice in which the presence of options, without further specification as to the range or desirability of those options, is considered sufficient to allow the choice to be counted as voluntary and because (for Locke) a patterning of the option environment threatens to infringe on the rightly held endowments of some persons. It should be observed that at that level of generality much of the above could just as well be said about Hobbes, but at the risk of some considerable conflation. For Locke, as generous as he was in the end in admitting constrained choices as voluntary, was more philosophically attentive than Hobbes to the conundrums posed by these issues of voluntariness and of choices under constraint.

The second point to be drawn from the analysis of the preceding pages, and to which I briefly alluded before, concerns the contractarian idea of coercion. Illegitimate coercion is understood here exclusively as the actual or threatened use of violence of persons against persons. Conceived in this fashion, unjust coercion becomes on the one side the direct violence of the robber or conqueror and, more broadly, dominion arbitrary and absolute, that is, unlimited private unauthorized dominion. Other determinants of behavior, including some that could plausibly be represented as coercive, are considered and put aside or do not appear at all in contract theory, though they do in Rousseau's writings (e.g., private power flowing from economic inequalities) and in this way serve (as we noted above) to distinguish his arguments from those of his British counterparts.

To be dominated or coerced, then, is to be subordinated directly to the will of another person, a point that can be illustrated by drawing again on Nozick's twenty-six men and twenty-six women wishing to marry and with a single ordering of preferences: if A directly subjugates Z to his will, threatens his life let us say, and compels him to marry Z^1 (rather than Z's first preference, A^1) this act is recognized as coercive. If, on the other hand, A exercises his liberty to marry A^1, being indifferent to or even unaware of Z and his wishes, and so on through the remaining twenty-five couples, the fact that Z is left with his least-desired choice (Z^1), the resulting determination of Z's behavior is not seen as coercive—in part because Z *has* a choice (i.e., not to marry) but also in part because his will has not been directly subordinated by the wills of the preceding, independent decision makers. The restriction on Z's will, that he cannot have the partner he most desires, is a consequence of two factors: a scarcity situation and the presence of other humans who justly and noncoercively exercise their wills by "appropriating" some of those scarce "goods." The poverty of the human estate (together with the thwarted desires and constrained wills it produces) is not a part of the liberal idea of the *summum malum,* for it is not seen as an important element of that form of unfreedom which is its central concern, that which arises from the unauthorized hierarchy of the ancient and later patriarchal conceptions of the community.

In light of the above discussion of the expansiveness of what may be counted as freely chosen, it might seem at first blush paradoxical that in a theory of the person the centerpiece of which is the idea of self-ownership (widely construed) there should be limits placed on the voluntary alienation of oneself. Yet the idea of limited self-alienation plays a crucial (if varied in the extent of the limits prescribed) role in contract theory, and this for two broad sorts of reasons: (1) the contractarian idea of the person and (2) the purposive nature of the contracting act. One set of reasons consists of those related to the contractarian concept of the person. In Locke's account, this strand of argument has a markedly religious cast: the person does not have the rightful power to alienate his existence to another for the same reason that he lacks the power to dispose arbitrarily over the lives of others. God has placed us in the world at his pleasure; he has made us and we are his, so that in relation to God we are usufruct possessors of ourselves, though in relation to other persons we acquire the status of self-owners simply. Our persons not being (in relation to God) wholly our own, we are under an obligation not to employ them in ways contrary to his laws—for instance, by disposing of them through suicide or alienation to an arbitrary, absolute power.

It is possible to construct a case with an outcome similar to the one we have been considering here but which does not employ the theologically grounded idea of usufruct possession or the secular language of rights/property in oneself as the foundation of the argument for limited alienation. Rather, what is foundational in this Kantian version is the concept of self-ownership understood as autonomy. The core idea is that to be a person means to be autonomous, and they who give up that autonomy thereby reduce themselves beneath the level of humanity. A person who sells herself into slavery has destroyed the humanity within herself. Man, considered as an end-in-himself, cannot alienate that in him which distinguishes him from the rest of nature, that is, the freedom or autonomy that is higher than any price: "But man regarded as a *person*— that is, as the subject of morally practical reason—is exalted above any price; for as such (*homo noumenon*) he is not to be valued as a mere means to the ends of others or even to his own ends, but as an end-in-himself." Or again with Rousseau: "To renounce one's freedom is to renounce one's status as a man, the rights of humanity and even its duties."[84]

A second way of approaching the question of the limits of alienation is through the notion of the contracting act itself. The idea of a contracting act as the foundation of a legitimate political community is understood, as we observed above, against a background of personal domination and violence or the threat of it. That context provides the contracting parties with purposes: self-preservation, felicity and a commodious life, the opportunity to pursue their callings in peace and tranquillity. These purposes determine in their different manners both the degree of what each must alienate and what each expects to gain from the bargain. Because the transfer is essentially one of privately held powers (in virtue of the principle of self-ownership) to a public authority for the purpose of securing the good of each, the transferred powers must be sufficient to allow for the attaining of those goals, yet the transfer or alienation must not be

[84] Immanuel Kant, *The Doctrine of Virtue* (Part Two of *The Metaphysics of Morals*), trans. Mary J. Gregor (New York: Harper and Row, 1964), p. 99; Kant, *The Metaphysical Elements of Justice*, trans. John Ladd (Indianapolis: Bobbs-Merrill, 1965), pp. 97–98; Rousseau, *Social Contract*, p. 50.

of such a magnitude that the governing purposes of the parties to the contract process are defeated in the very attempt to realize them.[85]

In Hobbes's argument, self-preservation is the overriding end for which humans submit to the authority of the commonwealth. And the powers needed to ensure the peace being great, the sole power that a rational agent would reserve to himself (more precisely: which could no more be alienated than, for example, the desire to breathe) is that of doing what he may to save himself. To yield that power would be to surrender just what is to be preserved, and such a bargain is therefore contrary to the purpose of the contracting act and cannot therefore be admitted.[86] For Locke, on the other hand, the purpose is best expressed as the securing of self-ownership (life, liberty, and property) consistent with similar protection for others. To create that protection, the public authority must have the power of life and death, of making and enforcing binding laws. But a call for more power, or for those same powers wielded by an arbitrary (unrestrained) will, would make the bargain absurd, for it would suggest that to avoid the threats of roughly equal persons ("pole-cats") humans give themselves over to the mercy of a much more irresistible force, government ("lions"). And "a Rational Creature cannot be supposed when free, to put himself into Subjection to another, for his own harm."[87] In addition to her obligations to God which require her to preserve herself and all humankind as far as possible, and hence not to give herself over to an authority whose power is so unrestricted as to pose a constant threat to life and property, the rationality of the contract procedure leads Locke to the same conclusion, namely, the retention (inalienability) of certain rights, including the right of judging whether government has met its fundamental duties and, in extremis, cashiering it. We might therefore better describe the Lockean contract process as one establishing government in a fiduciary manner, a "hired" authority, rather than in the language of the full-blooded alienation or surrender model of the transfer of powers.[88]

[85] For examples of this kind of reasoning across the contractarian tradition, see Rousseau, Social Contract, pp. 49–50, 64; Hobbes, Leviathan, pp. 64, 84, 109; Locke, 2T.124, 129–30.

[86] Hobbes, Leviathan, p. 86; Hobbes, De Cive, pp. 181–82, 216.

[87] Locke, 2T.164.

[88] As with much else in Locke's political thought, it is possible to derive the right to rebellion from theological premises. See Dunn, "Consent in the Political Theory of John Locke," p. 158. For an extended analysis of hired versus surrender models see Hampton, Hobbes, pp. 116, 119, 123, 258, 263.

4.2.2   Persons and Contracts

The contractarian concept of the person turns, then, on the idea of self-ownership. Unpacked, the notion of self-ownership displays all persons as equal just because the self is construed (primarily) in a jural sense; that is, the self is an expression of rights and obligations indiscriminately held by humans, either by nature simply or through their common submission to their Maker. The essence of the contractarian concept of equality is that—however the set of rights and duties is specified—there is no differential endowment of such attributes in advance of a voluntary act of alienation. Only by forfeiture, by reducing oneself through violence to the level of a beast, can a person quit this condition of jural equality. A secondary strand of the argument for equality is that which sees persons as being similar or identical in their substance, whether physical or psychological, and in their circumstances. This argument may mean, as in Hobbes's account, that humans are all equally without the power to ensure themselves over the long term against the violence of their fellow predators and that their hopes, fears, and the prudence they use in pursuit of their desires are roughly the same. In the Lockean version, the argument is that all are equally compelled by their fallen nature to earn their sustenance in the sweat of their faces and in an environment in which others cannot be counted on to be strict observers of justice or abstainers from the fruits of their labor.

The notion of the contracting person drives, as we have seen, to the conclusion that among humans conceived of as indiscriminately endowed with identical clusters of rights and duties there can be no just nonconsensual relation of dependence or subordination. There may of course be de facto subjugation as in the case of the relations between parents and children in which subordination is justified till such time as the child quits the age of minority and enters that condition of freedom to which it is born. The idea of independence suggests that in light of their juridical equality no person has a rightful claim to exercise dominion or authority over another in virtue of a supposed superiority. The primacy of the definition of the person as an equal jural being in contractarian theory precludes or renders inconsequential references to real or supposed superiority; even if such superiorities of strength, wisdom, or virtue are acknowledged, they cannot constitute the ground of a claim to rule. The third characteristic of the contracting person, autonomy, can be seen as embracing the two preceding qualities, equality and independence. Not being subject by nature to the dominion of others, a person is by right her own master in relation to them even if (or, for Locke, precisely because) as a creature of God she is also bound by obligations to her Master. She is free, that is, within the limits of reason (prudential reason, i.e., the search for self-preservation and felicity) and of divine obligation, to rule over herself, to do as she has a will to do.

"Sir R. F.'s great Position is, that *men are not naturally free.* . . . But if this Foundation fails, all his Fabric falls with it, and Governments must be left again to the old way of being made by contrivance, and the consent of Men."[89] So Locke argued. What the contractarian concept of the person offered was just such a challenge to the foundation of the naturalistic, hierarchical justification of rule over persons. The activity of these persons (equal, independent, and autonomous) in relation to one another and particularly in those interactions that give rise to direct power (husband over wife, master over servant, ruler over subject) can no longer be held to rest on some prior claim to authority. Will, in the shape of the "consent of Men," therefore becomes the *force créatrice* in the establishment of relations of power between persons.[90] Now, as has been suggested earlier in these pages, the ideas of will and consent can be read out of the contractarian argument in two principal ways: as a quasi-metaphorical way of expressing the limits of legitimate obligation (political or in the household) and as a robust theory of autonomy with several consequences, such as, universal franchise or, in the more ambitious Rousseauian form, direct (not represented) participation in the making of laws. The first reading is most explicitly set out in Kant's writings on contract theory, and its thrust is to use (hypothetical) consent as a benchmark against which to judge the legitimacy of laws or other social arrangements, leaving entirely to one side the actual manner in which those laws or arrangements are made. It asks, in effect, the question, "Would law x be one to which a rational person would give her consent?" where the latter part of the question is understood to mean consistent with her status as a juridical person. Laws that violate that status fail the test; those that meet its standards are said to be consistent with the dignity of the person, independent of whether or not her agreement has actually been sought. In this fashion, the ideas of will and consent become an expression of the limits of what may be done in relations between persons— boundary markers, as it were, distinguishing law from mere force. The robust version, beginning from the same concept of the person, would

[89] Locke, 1T.6; emphasis in the original.
[90] See Karl Olivecrona, "Appropriation in the State of Nature: Locke on the Origin of Property," *Journal of the History of Ideas* 35 (1974): 213.

accept these limits but go on to give the will a behavioral role in forming (or, more minimally, consenting to) the laws to which it must submit.

I wish to underscore not so much the differences between these two accounts but rather their fundamental similarity. Each seeks to attack a view according to which individuals are assigned their places (by nature or God) and in which rightful power flows from the ranking of those assigned situations. On either construction, authority that rests on that sort of ground is illegitimate, the violence actual or menacing of a social order that denies the status and protection of equal personhood to its members. Both, in short, see the principal evil as the subordination of one will to the arbitrary (i.e., private, not authorized) will of another (an evil that would include all naturalistic, hierarchal *oikos*-model societies), and they equally seek the remedy to that ill in the notion of the person as the bearer of certain inviolable attributes, assembled under the rubric of self-ownership. Autonomy in this conception, insofar as it is an attribute of persons in their relation to one another (and putting aside autonomy as a psychological or moral possibility *in foro interno*), is thus directed against a specific alternative and is in turn shaped by the direction of its attack. That specific object of the contractarian critique is the violence of persons broadly conceived as the illegitimate exercise of the power of a will over other wills, and its remedy consists in the notion of the autonomous person as a being whose self-ownership sets limits on his treatment (subordination) to the exercise of those powers which are consistent with his status as a person (autonomy as exclusionary right) and in the extended account to the exercise of that power in which he has directly participated.

4.3   The New Body Politic

The contractarian concept of the person as an equal, independent, and autonomous being yields an understanding of community and membership in it radically at odds with the organic notion of the body politic. That latter metaphor, together with its corollaries of the hierarchal family by nature, political fatherhood, and the great chain, had to be supplanted by a new image of community, one consonant with the equality and the primacy of its members' (equal) juridical status as persons.[91] Similarly, membership in that community had to be reconstructed in the light of the

[91] See Michael Walzer, *The Revolution of the Saints* (Cambridge: Harvard University Press, 1970), pp. 149, 174, 180.

contractarian theory of voluntary alienation as the sole rightful vehicle for the transfer of a person's assets or powers. We have already seen intimations of this transformation in the concept of the community in the contractarian analysis of the household and its relationships. I shall now briefly sketch its application to the idea of the new body politic.

First, a tentative and thin definition of the body politic: the core of the body politic is power of life and death and of "all less Penalties" for the purpose of securing and preserving the *bona civilia*. What distinguishes this power from that of, say, the slave master over his slaves or of the galley captain is, among other things, that it is held by right: "*Political Power* then I take to be *a Right* of making Laws."[92] The juridical endowments of the contractarian person do not include an unequal distribution of power—no one is born with a right to rule, no one is born to thralldom, or indeed to any form of subjugation whatsoever, save to that temporary and limited power of parents over children in the period of their minority. The rightful power of the body politic, not inhering in any one person or one group of its members, must therefore be composed out of the powers of them all, transferred in a measure equal for all to the body politic. The mode of this transfer is already implied by the quality of self-ownership: it has to be voluntary.

The formation of the body politic must be viewed (metaphorically) as being by artifice, an act of the will expressed in consent (at least in a privative sense in that no one can rightfully be forced to submit to the community except in those circumstances in which, by his enjoyment of the benefits of the community, he has tacitly consented to its authority). The new body politic is also to be understood as a community of equals. Equality here means not an economic equality, or one of virtue, wisdom, or honor but rather is tied to the jural concept of the person as a being endowed (each and all) with certain rights and obligations. Central to the jural idea of equality is the notion of equality with respect to jurisdiction or dominion, that is, that no person possesses a right to rule others. The coercive authority of the body politic is, accordingly, one of the universal or equally applied force of law: the standing rule must be "common to every one of that Society." Thus just as the contracting act itself is one in which all are on an equal juridical footing, unmarked by humility or deference derived from unequal status, so in the body politic all are equal in their subjection to the law.[93] Here again, it is possible to give the idea of civic equality an expansive reading such that all who are subject to law

[92] Locke, 2T.3; emphasis in the original.
[93] Locke, 2T.22; see also Immanuel Kant, *On the Common Saying: 'This May be True in Theory, but it does not Apply in Practice'* in *Kant's Political Writings*, trans. H. B. Nisbet,

must be coequal participants in the making of it. But on both the minimalist and expansive constructions, the bedrock condition derived from the idea of the contract person and the equal endowment of rights and duties is that no one is by nature (i.e., in his primordial, juridical status) subject to a coercive power that is not, at the same time, equally binding on all other members of the community.

The contract agent is a purposive being, and the contracting act is an exchange or alienation intended to achieve some end held by each agent individually. Applied to the foundations of political authority, that end is specified in contract theory as preservation of the person (physically and/or as a juridical being) and, more widely, as the securing of property and a felicitous life against the threat of predation, whether from one's fellows or at the hands of an arbitrary and absolute government. The dominant purpose of the contractors is thus composed out of a notion of the person and a context in which he is active. As we have seen, this purpose is one of the criteria by which the magnitude of the alienation (or "loan") of individual powers to the community is established. That same purposiveness also serves to set limits on the powers of the body politic by directing it to the proper end, the protection and preservation of persons, their lives, (residual) liberties, and estates. It is the unity of this end which gives the new body politic its cohesiveness. And the contract community has as its end nothing more than the aggregated composite of the purposes of individual rational agents understood as (abstract) jural persons: their preservation as autonomous, self-determining individuals insofar as the exercise of this self-determination is consistent with the exercise of the same right by others.

The body politic comes to be the "umpire" for "a peaceable decision of all their Controversies, and a bar to the state of War amongst them."[94] It may indeed be the case that the use to which individuals put their publicly ensured capacity for self-direction matters enormously: that, for Locke, fulfilling the duties of one's calling is the end that freedom serves or that, for Kant, the negative liberty of the political sphere may encourage a greater degree of moral self-legislation. But both are, in their different ways, equally clear in pronouncing that the body politic, at its core, has this function above all: that of securing self-direction understood as the

---

ed. Hans Reiss (Cambridge: Cambridge University Press, 1971), p. 75. Similar arguments are to be found in Rousseau, *Social Contract*, pp. 62–63. Hobbes is clearly the exception here: Hobbes, *Leviathan*, p. 56, and Hobbes, *De Cive*, pp. 168, 170; and see Walzer, *Revolution of the Saints*, p. 214.

[94] Locke, 2T.227, 87.

freedom from arbitrary external direction by other wills. The contractarian concept of the person (as an autonomous self-owner), the idea of the contracting act (as a voluntary alienation for individually held purposes), and the context that shapes the parties in determining the degree and purpose of their alienation (as the threat of domination that renders their persons insecure outside of the sanctuary of legitimate government) all drive the theory toward the idea of the body politic as umpire, as an instituted set of "hedges"[95] meant to free humans from the threat of force (violence or domination, i.e., the arbitrary exercise of the will of one person over another). Not only are the self-chosen activities conducted within (and consistent with) the protective sphere of the body politic's hedges not a matter over which the public authority can properly wield its power, but the artificial community, the new body politic, must be understood as existing in order to allow, to the extent possible, such self-direction.[96] The night-watchman conception of the minimalist state may be too emaciated a view of the liberal regime, but what it as a metaphor successfully captures in the contractarian tradition (Hobbes excluded) is a basic drive that requires the justification (as a prima facie evil) of extensions of public power, measured against the benchmarks of the jural nature of the person and of the body politic as a purposeful extension of that nature. Phrased differently, as long as the web of human relations retains its voluntary, bilateral character calls for the force of the public world to interfere in that web are inherently suspect. The primacy of the nonpublic or private spheres, the extent to which it is they that trace out the normative boundaries of the public—these rest on a claim about the priority of the autonomous, jural person and of the justice inherent in the voluntary arrangements between them.

4.3.1   The Impersonality of the Contractarian Community

If the scope and purpose of the body politic's power flow from underlying conceptions of the person and of alienation of individual autonomy as an end-directed (contracting) act, it is also the case that this power assumes a special character, magistery, or impersonal authority in place of the intensely personal notion of power embodied in the *pater familias* of the patriarchal family-based accounts of politics.[97] The heart of this conception of public authority is nicely set out in the following statement of

[95] Locke, 2T.57.
[96] See Parry, "The Critique of Paternalism in John Locke," pp. 164, 166, 174, and Polin, *La politique morale de John Locke*, p. 146.
[97] See Walzer, *Revolution of the Saints*, p. 159.

Kant's: "This [republican] constitution is the only enduring political constitution in which the *law is autonomous and is not annexed to any particular person*. It is the ultimate end of all public Law . . . for, as long as . . . the other forms of the state represent so many distinct moral persons as invested with supreme authority, it must be recognized that only a provisional internal justice and no absolutely juridical state of civil society can exist."[98] A similar understanding is to be found in Locke's political thought, where the body politic is said to consist of those under a "common establish'd Law," who have "a standing Rule to live by, common to every one of that Society." Political power as the rightful exercise of authority over life and death thus takes on yet another attribute, the impersonality of rule-governed and legitimate authority. What power is not impersonal and rule-bound can only be "arbitrary," by which is meant power exercised according to the will of its possessor and not by a standing, common rule independent of his will. Political power that is not rule-bound is, in short, private—the force of a master over his slave (but not that of master over servant, which is a contracted, that is, rule-determined, relationship) and cannot therefore be a part of a body politic.[99]

The impersonality of power within the new body politic (and the contractarian household) flows from several sources. (1) The abstract quality of the person, considered as a bundle of jural endowments, and the contract process by which these uniform endowments are alienated or lent to the public sphere suggest that the composed or artificial community thereby achieved will share in the impersonality of its makers and of their exchanges. (2) The idea of the contract process itself as a partial alienation of powers for the sake of the preservation of the person undermines the legitimacy of an arrangement in which power is transferred to an unrestricted will because the latter is antithetical to the notion of the person as a rational end-seeker, that is, because it is exceedingly difficult to reconcile with those purposes said to be inherent in the person as either a jural being or a self-interested actor.[100] (3) Because the body politic is meant to be a partial remedy to the pravity of humankind, to the willful and often coercive self-preference of humans, and because providing those in such a depraved condition with unrestricted force seems an unlikely solution, it is necessary to constrain not only the wills of private

[98] Kant, *Metaphysical Elements of Justice*, pp. 112–13; and see Rousseau, *Social Contract*, p. 67; emphasis added.

[99] Locke, 2T.22, 87, 163, 200, and 214. See also Dunn, *The Political Thought of John Locke*, p. 128; Polin, *La politique morale de John Locke*, p. 149; Rousseau, *Social Contract*, p. 52.

[100] Thus the oddity of the Hobbesian argument when set against its contractarian foundations. See Hampton, *Hobbes*, pp. 121–22, 264.

persons but also, and all the more so, those who hold state power. This is to say that the private wills of governors must be made into civic wills, if not through a political/moral denaturing of their souls then through institutional arrangements that will direct their ambitions to the *bona civilia,* respectively through the Rousseauian and the *Federalist* solutions.

The fourth foundation for the impersonality of the contractarian conception of political power is perhaps the most important one, though also the least explicitly articulated. Its principal idea is that there is something particularly degrading in submitting to the will of another person, though not in submitting to the equal or greater power of impersonal political authority. Personal power, the violence of human beings, and not power itself is the *summum malum* here, an idea whose provenance is again the rejection of the paternalistic and naturalistic conception of the private dominion of some over others. Obedience to law removes the poison, as it were, from the act of submission by making that act not a genuflection before another person but rather obedience to objective authority. This idea can also be read simply as asserting elements already contained in the three preceding points—that the equality and freedom of the person generate a vision of the body politic which in its lawmaking activity must be indifferent to distinctions among those persons, an indifference more reliably secured under a rule-governed arrangement than under the free-ranging power of a sovereign's will. It is of course true that these considerations figure prominently in the contractarian argument, but there are traces of another line of reasoning, one eloquently set out by Rousseau: "Whoever has other masters than the laws is worthless [*est un méchant*]" and again "One is free though subordinated to laws, but not when one obeys a man."[101] Rousseau unfolds these propositions, in the language of the *Social Contract,* as being derived from the ideas of freedom (in obeying the laws, one is only obeying oneself and is therefore autonomous) and of equality (the laws are blind and so are indifferent to distinction). Yet there is something more to Rousseau's argument, and it is apparent in that passage from his *Emile,* cited earlier, where he distinguishes between the morally neutral condition of dependence on things and the deplorable state of dependence on others, concluding that "if there is any means of remedying this ill in society, it is to substitute law for man"—which is to say, to substitute the greatest possible dependence of individuals in relation to their city (laws) for direct dependence among persons.[102] The subjection of one will to another, personal domination, is the main evil.

---

[101] Quoted in Besse, "Maître, laquais, esclave," pp. 84–85; my translation. See also Matheron, "Maîtres et serviteurs," pp. 19–20.

[102] Rousseau, *Emile,* p. 85; Rousseau, *Social Contract,* p. 77.

The remedy for that predicament consists in limited power exercised for the good of the individuals (understood as jural persons) who compose the community and in the "autonomy" of the law, that is, its detachment from the wills of persons or, what amounts to much the same thing, the objectivity (impersonality) of the law.

The contractarian community can, in summary, best be understood as a special sort of protective association, a public juridical space whose members are considered as identically endowed jural agents and as voluntary, purposeful members of the community. This public or juridical space consists, on the one side, of the residual rights and liberties of the person and, on the other side, of the submission to the artificial (i.e., self-forged and fastened) chains of civil society. The first-mentioned element of the contractarian community may be viewed as shaping or restricting the public domain in two ways: (1) by a theory of inalienable rights, ones that no rational person could be assumed to have transferred voluntarily, and (2) through a notion of the rational purpose of individuals, namely, the preservation of those liberties and of a felicitous life. The second of the two elements contains within it the idea that membership in the body politic, and submission to its authority, is neither coercive nor inegalitarian; that is to say, the notion of the self-forged chains of civil society precludes arguments that there are such things as natural bonds of subjection between persons. It also brings to the fore the idea that legitimate public coercion must bind all equally, because from the definition of the contract (jural) person, his rights and his purposes, there can be deduced no inequality of subjugation to the public authority. And last, in the notion of artificial chains, is contained the abstractness not only of the juridical persons who form the community but of the power exercised over them, that it is not attached to individuals but is rather the objective and autonomous core of the new body politic.

5. The New Body Economic: The Contract Community and Its Economy

5.1   The Economies of Despotic and Liberal Households

The economy of the despotic household, analyzed in the *oikos* literature and discussed in the preceding section, could be understood as one in which, to use Amartya Sen's words, "family behaviour would . . . be just a reflection of the head's choice function, and family welfare—in terms of revealed welfare—would then have to be seen as the maximand implicit in the head's choice function."[103] Recast in the language of ancient political economy, we might say that the *oikos* economy was governed by the household's free members and above all by the master, and that it was aimed particularly at his welfare. With that proposition, we have located the seat of economic purposiveness in the despotic household. Now, the welfare that was the specific object of this purposiveness consisted of the provisioning of the household in the necessities of its existence but also something more: the liberation of the master from the constraints inherent in that provisioning. Together, these two propositions yielded a theory of what we termed the embedded and contained economy: embedded, that is, in the "choice function" of the household's free persons and contained in the sense that its operations were to be kept at a distance from the master in order that, being free from the demands imposed by the production of the household's livelihood, he might devote his leisure to other more valuable activities. The preferences of the other persons within that household would hardly matter at all except in an instrumental way. Xenophon's recounting (in the *Oeconomicus*) of the discussion between Ischomachos and Socrates makes plain that this economy is not "invisible" or "indistinct" but it *is* subordinated, and the science that seeks to unpack its laws will look to the end determining them and so to the master and his purposes. Ancient political economy is, as Godelier has suggested, a pervasively political economy—here in the sense that it is concerned with hierarchy, the place of the economy within that hierarchy, and relatedly in the search for the good life.

This Aristotelian manner of conceptualizing the economy as a moment in the structure and activity of the despotic household pervaded economic thought into the early modern period. Blending readily with patriarchal accounts of the body politic, it provided a means of thinking about the economy as part of the royal household, the nation as one household with the sovereign as its just master. The richness and variety of this tradition of economic thought are beyond the scope and purpose of the argument here, and so I shall do no more than to outline, in the broadest strokes, its underlying continuity with the classical political economy of Aristotle.[104]

---

[103] Amartya Sen, "Economics and the Family," in Amartya Sen, ed., *Resources, Values, and Development* (Oxford: Basil Blackwell, 1984), p. 373.

[104] Keith Tribe, *Land, Labour, and Economic Discourse* (London: Routledge and Kegan Paul, 1978), and Tribe, "The 'Histories' of Economic Discourse," *Economy and Society* 6 (1977): 314–43; Otto Brunner, "Das ganze Haus," in *Neue Wege der Sozialgeschichte*

What characterizes this continuity of the ancient and modern preliberal economic thought is above all the primacy of the idea of the body politic, with its distinctions between persons, over the economic world—or, in other words, the inability to conceive of economic activity without prior reference to the hierarchy and purposes of the nation as household. Thus, economic categories came to have, as Keith Tribe has shown, "a determination which escapes the realm of the economy" and which is rooted rather in the form of the body politic itself.[105] The status or position of persons within that hierarchical community is, accordingly, decisive in determining their economic activity: the relation of the subject to his lord is prior to, and shapes, the relation of both to the land. So too with rent, distribution, trade, and other features of economic life—all are conceived as the outcome of a prior order in which persons occupy differently ranked positions and in which the task of household management is to preserve that proper order for the benefit of the nation/household.[106] And last, as in the Aristotelian account according to which the household can be properly grasped only through an understanding of its dominant moment, the master or the free family, so here the sovereign and his administration constitute the unity that binds the subordinate persons and activities into a coherent whole. Political economy, as the study of the royal household, is thus built around the idea of the just and wise regulation of that national household, with, as Tribe has argued, "the monarch's guiding presence" being an indispensable ingredient.[107]

We saw at the beginning of Part Two that liberal contractarian theorists attacked the patriarchal household model in two ways: (1) by reconstructing the family as a quasi-contractarian conjugal union in place of the hierarchical household of superiors and inferiors and as the temporary and limited jurisdiction of parents over children and of master over

---

(Gottingen: Vandenhoeck and Ruprecht, 1956); Mark Blaug, *Economic Theory in Retrospect*, 4th ed. (Cambridge: Cambridge University Press, 1985); W. Stark, "The Contained Economy: An Interpretation of Medieval Economic Thought," in *Pre-Capitalist Economic Thought: Three Modern Interpretations* (New York: Arno Press, 1972); Joyce O. Appleby, *Economic Thought and Ideology in Seventeenth-Century England* (Princeton: Princeton University Press, 1978).

[105] Tribe, *Land, Labour, and Economic Discourse*, pp. 33, 35–36.

[106] See Tribe, "The 'Histories' of Economic Discourse," p. 328; Tribe, *Land, Labour, and Economic Discourse*, pp. 28–33, 36, 82; Brunner, *Neue Wege der Sozialgeschichte*, p. 36.

[107] Tribe, *Land, Labour, and Economic Discourse*, pp. 81–82; and see Tribe, "The 'Histories' of Economic Discourse," p. 328.

servants and (2) by challenging altogether the appropriateness of the household metaphor for the understanding of the political association. In its Lockean version, the rejection of a theory of political community which drew its fundamental tenets from the notion of an organic, natural, and hierarchical household had, among its many consequences, the dismissal of the notion of the king as *pater familias* presiding over his private dominion. It also signaled the rejection of the idea of a right to power grounded in virtue or on a putative superiority over others. In the most general terms, we may say that the contractarian tradition sought to undermine the idea of the natural hierarchical community, whether that of the household or of the polity. Thus in place of the private dominion of the household master or king, we find (in Locke's writings) the individual as proprietor of his person and goods with exclusionary rights against others. In place of the right of the *pater familias* or sovereign to exercise his power, we see contractual and/or limited power over (potential) equals in the home and the rightful power of the body politic as composed from the transferred powers of individuals. Last, in place of the master as the purposive/legislative center of the community, we find the new political community whose purpose, like its powers, is composed out of those attributable to all rational individuals.

In brief, the contractarian argument sought to refashion the moral architecture of the community: to level the hierarchical household, private and public, to draw the analysis of the political community back to a starting position of equally endowed juridical agents and to reconstitute the body politic from that foundation as a free association of equal persons transferring their natural powers for the sake of the preservation of these persons. In this section, our attention has been concentrated on the contractarian polity as an answer to the *summum malum* of the exercise of arbitrary power over others. Contract theory provides a remedy for the violence of arbitrary power by putting forward an idea of legitimate rule, constrained (in the Lockean variant) in its exercise and voluntary (on either the thin or rich understandings of consent) in its origins. But it is reasonable to postulate that although the critique of the household conception of politics has as its central concern the nature, use, and extent of public coercive authority it will in addition fundamentally alter the way of thinking about the relationship between economy and community. That is, if contract theory decisively rejected the model of the hierarchical household, it would also have to rethink the location of the economy in that moral architecture, which previously had been conceived as an embedded moment of the *oikos* hierarchy. It is that reconceptualization to which I shall now turn.

5.2   Spades and Scepters

Earlier we saw Locke writing that man was given "a Spade into his hand, to subdue the Earth, [rather] than a Scepter to Rule over its Inhabitants." The "penury of his Condition" requires that he secure his livelihood in the sweat of his face.[108] Just as Pandora's gift made humankind into the *zōion oikonomikon,* so here too the nature we are given, to be economic creatures, occupies a central place. The juxtaposition of the spade and scepter suggests, however, that the evil to be righted is less the grim, freedom-constraining poverty of this estate than it is the use of force (rule without right) to "command [persons] to work."[109] The scepter of rule, the heart of the despotic household, is not a legitimate remedy for that condition. The central problem then becomes one of arranging the economy so that its operations do not violate the autonomy of the person, understood as his or her freedom from unauthorized coercion. In sum, the issue of the consequences of the neediness of the human condition for a life free and without constraint, and for the possibility of the good life, so crucial to the ancient *oikos* theory of the economy, is here replaced by the search for an answer to the "preponderance of force" in human affairs.

On the microlevel, some of the normative economic consequences of the leveling of the hierarchical household are evident in the encounter between master and servant set out in Locke's *Second Treatise* §85. These two persons, one ready to perform a service for money and the other willing to pay for it, exchange their different wares, each having in mind a preference, for money or for the value of the service rendered, to be realized thereby. Furthermore, their exchange act is not marked or influenced by their (extraeconomic) status; they meet not as master and servant, superior and inferior, but rather on that liberally level plane of juridically equal persons exercising their right to alienate goods. In short, the hierarchical status community vanishes here as the necessary background to human interactions of virtually every type, and in its place we find the conception of contracting agents equally endowed with rights—a

108 Locke, 1T.45, 2T.32.
109 Locke, 1T.45.

conception deeply indifferent to distinctions between persons. Locke's sketch of the exchange between master and servant illuminates several important characteristics of the new economy: that the purposes of economic actors can no longer rightfully be determined from above, over-determined, by the master's utility, but must rather reside with the individual; that exchanges are the result of freely made (liberally speaking, noncoerced) choices in pursuit of these goals; that the exchange is unmarked by distinctions between persons of an illegitimate sort. The body economic thus loses its despotic quality by which the maximand of the master and the free family members determine the activities of the household's subordinates. It now becomes a composite of juridically identical persons voluntarily interacting in ways selected to advance their various ends. Insofar as the community, in the form of the public authority, is something more than the aggregate of these choices and the interchanges flowing from them its activities ought to be directed principally (though not necessarily exclusively, for reasons set out above) to umpirage, to ensuring that coercion does not mar their dealings.[110]

5.3   The Autonomy of the Economic Sphere

This cluster of characteristics of the liberal body economic is embraced in the idea of the autonomy of the economic sphere, an idea that at once defines the economy in opposition to the despotic household conception and sets it in a new location in the community. In the moral-economy literature associated with Karl Polanyi and his circle, the autonomy of the modern economic realm is taken to mean, on the one hand, roughly its "disembedded" quality, that is, its status as an independent and distinct institution and, on the other hand, its naturelike workings independent of the community, operations that come to subordinate that community in all its aspects to laws not of its own making.[111] This picture of the autonomous economy, characterized as the "juggernaut" market, captures (albeit more than somewhat perversely) a part of the shifting conception of the economy and its location. A more complete account of the meaning of this reconceptualization, which I shall now venture, would have to contain the following ideas: (a) the shifting locus of the pur-

[110] See Kolm, *Le contrat social libéral,* pp. 27–30.
[111] Karl Polanyi, *The Great Transformation* (Boston: Beacon Press, 1957), pp. 55, 57, 68–76.

posiveness of the economy from the household master to all agents; (b) the moral self-sufficiency of the market, as well as (c) the Polanyi-type depiction of the nondesigned, yet lawlike character of the economy.

(a) The idea of the disembedding of economic activity from the context of the despotic household entails, among other things, the transfer of purposiveness (preferences) and choice from the master to all agents equally. Disembedding in this part of its meaning amounts to another way of expressing the move from a hierarchical community dedicated to the master's want satisfaction to an association of persons self-legislative within a set of constraints, such as protection of the fundamental rights of others and limits on what can be alienated. That exchanges of goods generally and in particular of key goods—that is, those bound up with the "stock" of the person (labor for example)—would have to occur as the efflux of the preferences and uncoerced choices of individuals and not as the consequence of a process of overdetermination is a fairly plain deduction from the liberal contractarian (Lockean) theory of the person and of the proper mode of intercourse among them. The economic/institutional outcome of that theory is not, of course, uniquely determined; it need not, for example, necessarily terminate in a market or in a capitalist market. We could imagine independent and self-sufficient households that do not exchange with one another but merely allocate goods and services within their own confines. The fundamental principles of liberal exchange would apply to those transfers, but they would not constitute an explicit market with a price mechanism. The market (again, not necessarily of a capitalist type) does nevertheless represent the dominant liberal institutional solution (in the sense of according with the principles of individual preference and choices) to large-scale exchange activity in an environment characterized by an extensive division of labor.[112]

We might designate as "autonomous" or "disembedded" the economy that emerges from the application of such a theory of the person in the following sense: that the control over economic activities is taken from the household despot or his royal analogue, and that ends and choices become the rightful property of autonomous individual agents. This shift

---

[112] See Serge-Christophe Kolm, *Le libéralisme moderne: Analyse d'une raison économique* (Paris: Presses Universitaires de France, 1984), p. 37. For recent efforts to read a stronger connection into the relation between markets and a free society see John Gray, "Contractarian Method, Private Property, and the Market Economy," in John W. Chapman and J. Roland Pennock, eds., *Nomos 31: Markets and Justice* (New York: New York University Press, 1989), p. 27, and Narveson, "The Justice of the Market," in that same volume, p. 266.

can better be represented, from the perspective of the liberal reading of it, as the disembedding of the economy from its location in one specific sort of community (the hierarchical, despotic household) and its re-embedding in another, different type—which is to say, the radical subordination of economic life to the preferences and choices of individuals. In Serge-Christophe Kolm's words: "Liberalism is the total subordination of the economy and politics to culture [i.e., to the desires, needs, and tastes of individuals]."[113] This property is sometimes (and usually critically) represented as the impersonality of market society. That critique, we might observe, has its origins in the Aristotelian theory of money and the market rendering all that they touch homogeneous, equalizing things unequal and thereby upsetting the proper order of things—a critique that, in its ancient form, paralleled certain objections to democracy.[114] And so it is impersonal, this economy: just as authority at the political level acquires this abstract quality, detached from the characteristics of individuals, so the market is impersonal in that there we are free from the bonds, affective or coercive (or both), of the more intimate world of the *oikos* and thus at liberty to establish voluntarily these ties elsewhere. Adam Smith's butcher, brewer, and baker do not know one another, and still less their customers. Yet all have meat, ale, and bread on their tables each evening; and their providers receive a fair income. There is to be sure an anonymity, a distance, in their relations but also a recognizable freedom at least in comparison to the community of the *oikos*. In the market, as in the political realm, this impersonality was taken as emancipatory.[115]

(b) The idea of the autonomy of the economic sphere also suggests that, being wrested from its embedded position within the despotic household and subordinate to the master's legislation, the economy does not thereby collapse into anarchy, but generates laws of its own. The consequentialist

---

[113] Kolm, *Le contrat social libéral*, p. 46.

[114] M. I. Finley, "Aristotle and Economic Analysis," in M. I. Finley, ed., *Studies in Ancient Society* (London: Routledge and Kegan Paul, 1974), contains a good discussion of the difference between the market conception of persons and those found in ancient economic thought.

[115] Adam Smith, *An Inquiry into the Nature and Causes of the Wealth of Nations*, ed. R. H. Campbell and A. S. Skinner (Indianapolis: Liberty Classics; reprint of vol. 2 of the Glasgow edition, 1981), vol. 1, pp. 26–27. See also Gauthier, *Morals by Agreement*, p. 102. Sen, drawing on Smith's *The Theory of Moral Sentiments*, correctly observes that this passage from *The Wealth of Nations* should not be read as arguing that self-love is the only or best human motivation; see Sen, *On Ethics and Economics*, pp. 22–28. A further corrective along similar lines can be found in Stephen Holmes, "The Secret History of Self-Interest," in Jane J. Mansbridge, ed., *Beyond Self-Interest* (Chicago: University of Chicago Press, 1990), pp. 267–86.

side of this argument—namely, the case that these laws produce economic optimality without design or at least without an overdetermining
plan—I do not address here; rather, I focus strictly on theorizing about
the law-governed character of these free exchanges.[116] Once the possibility of a distinctive realm of lawlike phenomena is acknowledged, economic science as opposed to the study of the *oikos* master's purposes and
management of his household can come into being as an independent
mode of inquiry.[117] Locke's essay *Some Considerations of the Consequences of the Lowering of Interest and Raising the Value of Money*
provides a foundation for the conception of the economy as an autonomous (independently law-governed) sphere and thus also for a
self-standing science of economics. The issue Locke addresses in *Some
Considerations* is whether the price of money can be regulated, that is,
whether the government can set a rate of interest without consideration of
the prevailing market rate. Locke answers that it cannot be so regulated
and that even were such controls possible the consequences would be
negative. The heart of Locke's argument is that money is a commodity
like any other and that it is the want of money which regulates its price or,
as Locke calls it, the "natural interest of money." Thus just as a lack of
land brings tenants, the shortage of money brings borrowers, and in the
balance between the number of buyers and sellers present in the market,
the natural price will emerge.[118] This basic law governing the price of
money is not the consequence of supervening conscious human agency
(which can only ineffectively and unprofitably try to impede its operations) but is rather conceived on the model of a natural law, albeit one
composed out of the many free decisions of persons seeking to maximize
their self-interest (to buy cheap or sell dear) within constraints (lack of
land or shortage of money). The irresistible character of this controlling
law of the economy, its independence from the body politic, and its
quality of being rooted in the free decisions of (maximizing) individuals

---

[116] The limitations of the "invisible hand," particularly in regard to externalities and
public goods, are discussed in Kolm, *Le contrat social libéral*, pp. 201–7. Amartya Sen,
Poverty and Famines: An Essay on Entitlement and Deprivation (Oxford: Clarendon Press,
1981), deals with different aspects of the "invisible hand's" failures. I touch on some of these
issues in the context of a discussion of Marx.

[117] See William Letwin, *The Origins of Scientific Economics* (London: Methuen, 1963),
p. 178, and Tribe, "The 'Histories' of Economic Discourse," p. 340.

[118] John Locke, *Some Considerations of the Consequences of the Lowering of Interest and
Raising the Value of Money*, in Patrick Kelly, *Locke on Money*, 2 vols., in *The Clarendon
Edition of the Works of John Locke* (Oxford: Clarendon, 1991), vol. 1, pp. 211–14, 219–
24, 249–50.

set the stage for the rethinking of the economy as an autonomous, self-legislating sphere—a rethinking that, William Letwin maintains, in its specification of a body of fundamental laws of the economy contributes mightily to the development of modern economic science much as Newton's laws of motion did for physics.[119]

What is particularly important in this aspect of the autonomous economy is the liberal quality of the laws that govern it. By that I mean the following. Statements about the "naturelike" character of the laws of this sphere point to the fact that they are not the product of human design.[120] If we recall the critique of the hierarchical community and its offshoot, the despotic household economy (with the locus of economic regulation in the master's hands), we can better grasp the moral (and not merely instrumental) value attached to the undesigned regulation of the economy. Another way of putting this is to say that the laws of the "invisible hand" are invisible precisely because they are not the emanations of someone's will, so that in turn, the power they have over agents in the economy is not coercive in the liberal understanding of that term. They are the (unintended) efflux of the exercise of individual choices; no supra-individual agency intervenes here to guide (illiberally) the conduct of human affairs. And they operate in a manner that is indifferent to background, noneconomic distinctions between persons.

(c) The autonomy of the economic sphere has a third, and perhaps even more striking, expression in Locke's notion of the justice of the market. The sense of this autonomy discussed in the preceding paragraphs throws

[119] Letwin, *Origins of Scientific Economics*, pp. 177–78. This estimation of Locke's importance to economic theory is of still greater antiquity; see for example the opinion of the Florentine Physiocrat Gianfrancesco Pagnini, cited in Kelly's introductory essay to *Locke on Money*, vol. 1, p. 1. For a reading of the watershed importance of Lockean political economic thought see Louis Dumont, *From Mandeville to Marx: The Genesis and Triumph of Economic Ideology* (Chicago: University of Chicago Press, 1977), pp. 47–59. A quite different interpretation of Locke as a premodern economic thinker in whose works the economy is still indistinct can be found in Tully, *Discourse on Property*, pp. 158, 161, and Tribe, *Land, Labour, and Economic Discourse*, pp. 36, 46. Kelly, in the essay cited above (pp. 68, 95–96), gives a more balanced assessment, placing him in part among the Mercantilists, in part among the heralds of classical economic theory. For convenience' sake, I write here as if these laws were, or are, fully and well understood. For a valuable cautionary note see Frank Hahn, "Reflections on the Invisible Hand," *Lloyds Bank Review* 144 (1982): 1–21.

[120] See F. A. Hayek, "The Results of Human Action but Not of Human Design," in Hayek, *Studies in Philosophy, Politics, and Economics* (Chicago: University of Chicago Press, 1967), pp. 97–98. For an important qualification of the idea of the absence of design see Amartya Sen, "The Profit Motive," in Sen, *Resources, Values, and Development*, pp. 91–93.

light on the independent, law-governed (on the model of the laws of nature) character of the economy. This third meaning of autonomy goes beyond the attempt to formulate a causal account of economic activity in that it attributes justice to those discovered laws. Locke, in his *Venditio* manuscript, asks: "what is the measure that ought to regulate the price for which any one sells so as to keep it within the bounds of equity and justice?" And his answer is, in brief: "The market price at the place where he sells." The "measure" is not the commodity's "natural value," for example, the use of wheat in nourishing humans, but its "merchant value," or the ratio of money to the commodity in question, that is, the measure that not only does in fact regulate price but that also *ought* to regulate it so that it stays "within the bounds of equity and justice." There is then no other "measure set to a merchants gain but the market price."[121] The distinction between natural and merchant value and the establishing of the latter as the measure of the justice of exchange requires that all persons be treated equally—that the same price be charged to all buyers in the market ("for justice has but one measure for all men")— and that coercion not be the instrument for setting the value of the goods to be exchanged. We might (following David Gauthier) recast this so as to say that a (perfectly competitive) market constitutes a "morally neutral zone" in the sense that it needs no moral/political constraints. More exactly, the introduction of such external constraints on the voluntary bilateral transactions of the market would be to reinstate the partiality and compulsion for which the market was meant to be a corrective. It thus further separates itself from a theory of justice in economic matters in which an overdetermining community and its distinctions between persons were crucial.[122]

The above analysis is not meant to suggest that Locke could have fully understood or set out the laws of a capitalist economy. Yet if it is the case that one of the signal moments of the transition to classical political economy is the belief in the "efficacy of individual freedom in economic affairs," then Locke's argument for the efficiency of the market in which buyers and sellers come "to a pretty equal and fair account" suggests that he rightfully belongs to that tradition. So also do the naturelike (in the sense of self-regulating) qualities of the economic processes he describes tend to place him in that tradition. There are to be sure elements of

[121] Locke, *Venditio*, pp. 496, 498. For a discussion of natural and merchant value see *Venditio*, p. 497, and Locke, 2T.37.

[122] Gauthier, *Morals by Agreement*, pp. 84–85, 96. Compare to Aristotle, *Politics* 1257a25ff. and Aristotle, *Nicomachean Ethics* 1131a15ff., 1133a20ff.

Locke's economic thought which indicate the gap between his views and those of a full-blooded liberal conception of the economy, for example, the highly coercive treatment of the poor which he advocates in his document on the poor-law reform and the elaborate scheme he devised to stem the export of manufactured woollen goods from Ireland.[123] Nevertheless, what clearly emerges from Locke's economic writings is, as Louis Dumont writes, a vision of the autonomous economy in *statu nascendi*—an economy populated by contracting agents, governed by its own rules, and containing within itself principles of justice.[124] However inchoate Locke's economic thought may have been, judged from the standpoint of classical political economy, the essential features of a disembedded, contract-based, self-regulating economy are there, and they are present, as I have suggested, not by happenstance but rather because they flow from key propositions in his political philosophy: the dissolution of the despotic or patriarchal household model, the idea of the juridical, contractarian person as proprietor, and the purpose of the body politic as being the preservation of that person in her juridical status.

Taken together, the preceding arguments can be amplified into a theory calling for the virtual detachment of the economy from the political sphere. Or better: one in which government stands ready to enforce contracts, preserve the peace, and so forth and otherwise is called upon only in cases of market failures. This final argument for the autonomy of the economic sphere, and so correspondingly for as minimal a state as is consistent with a solution to the conundrums that make it necessary in the first instance, is thus the sum of the particular lines of reasoning set out above. If markets are efficient in producing wealth, government intervention is likely to thwart the creation of wealth, and with that the well-

[123] Locke, "Poor Law Reform" and "Encouragement of Irish Linen Manufacture," in Bourne, *The Life of John Locke*, vol. 2. See also Karen I. Vaughn, *John Locke: Economist and Social Scientist* (Chicago: University of Chicago Press, 1980), pp. 120–21. Kelly's introductory essay to *Locke on Money*, vol. 1, gives an excellent overview of the modern and premodern elements of Locke's economic thought. In particular, Kelly points to limits on Locke's confidence in "untrammelled individualism" and accordingly to his emphasis on the need for statesmen to guide the economy (pp. 95–96). He also argues for the importance for Locke of the public over the individual good: "I think every one . . . is bound to labour for the publick good, as far as he is able, or else he has no right to eat" (p. 16, and see also p. 70).

[124] See Dumont, *From Mandeville to Marx*, p. 47. Dumont also emphasizes the importance of Locke's critique of Filmer to the development of this conception of the economic sphere. It is also evident that, for Locke, there is a market both for labor and land. See Locke, *Some Considerations of the Consequences of the Lowering of Interest and Raising the Value of Money*, pp. 236–37, 249–50, and Polanyi, *The Great Transformation*, pp. 68–69, 71, 112.

being not only of the industrious improvers but also of those who, in the face of the scarcity of the means of production (here, land), must depend on the owners of that wealth for their livelihood. So too, if the market is nothing other than an ensemble of voluntary (within the horizon of the contractarian definition) exchanges it must have a prima facie case to be allowed to proceed unimpeded, at least for those who subscribe to a theory the central good of which is freedom, liberally understood. And last, if the distributive consequences of these transactions have a certain justice, derived from the quality of the actions which bring them about—and that is just what Locke suggests in the *Venditio* essay—they rarely require or permit external correction. The state, which is what the public realm is reduced to, compensates for the "weak hands" of natural justice in the world. Where some would not be able to see their agreements made binding, nor others their injuries compensated, the state provides for the rectification of their condition. Beyond that, claims such as that made in the Lockean proviso are in effect claims about responses to market failures. Precisely where one sets the boundary markers for the "enough, and as good" qualifier, whether, for example, at the point at which survival is threatened, at which the quality of life or self-realization is imperiled, is uncertain. Also unstated is the rank ordering of the remedies: coercive redistribution, charity, and so forth. What is clear, however, is that both in the specification of the ills to be relieved and in the instruments of that remedy the burden of apology is shifted onto those seeking to disrupt voluntary transactions. This shift reflects a view according to which such disruptions, savoring of paternalism, must be justified against the moral force sheltering the free arena of the market.

This sketch of the liberalism of Locke's economic thought can be made to stand in still sharper relief by contrasting it to Rousseau's (considerably less developed and not always consistent) observations on political economy. Again, Rousseau's argument stands uneasily between two worlds, the ancient and the liberal. Moving within the horizon of that latter discourse, Rousseau insists on the importance of personal property, of its proximity to the foundation of the social compact and on its inviolability. And part of that insistence is the (almost Lockean) rejection of Filmer's attempt to break down the distinction between the public or royal economies and private ones.[125] The ancient refrain in Rousseau's

---

[125] On property rights see Rousseau, *Political Economy*, pp. 214, 224–25, 229–30, 235, and on Filmer see pp. 209, 211–12. Judith Shklar correctly emphasizes the importance of property rights even in the midst of this his "most rigorously Spartan picture" as she describes the *Political Economy*. See Shklar, "Rousseau's Two Models: Sparta and the Age of Gold," p. 36.

Political Economy is apparent in its organic imagery with the body politic being the embracing form and relatedly in its emphasis on citizenship ("where I ought to have started," Rousseau writes) and the subordination of the economy to the end of making good citizens. Central to the body politic's well-being is precisely the regulation of economic activity in order to ensure the minimum possible distance between the rich and poor so that no one shall be forced to sell himself and no one able to buy another. For the reciprocal need that drives market exchanges is, for Rousseau, one of the principal sources of servitude, and nowhere are its effects more damaging than in the traffic of persons which constitutes the core of a market in labor. Accordingly, the governing premise of his economic thought is that the political must be made to serve as a counterweight to the unfreedom of the private world.

Rousseauian political economy lacks any notion that the economy is morally self-sufficient and it wants an analysis of the independent laws of the economy. It is almost as if we can hear the voice of the embedded, classical Greek conception of the economy in this passage from Rousseau's *Political Economy:* "I believe it was this great maxim ["to work much more carefully to prevent needs than to increase revenues"] that gave rise to the marvels of the governments of antiquity. . . . And it is from this, perhaps, that the common meaning of the word *economy* is derived, referring more to the wise handling of what one has than to the means of acquiring what one does not have."[126] Such words could as well have been written by Xenophon or Aristotle.

The sources of this difference between Locke and Rousseau are many and profound, and an examination of them in detail is not required by the argument presented in these pages. We can, however, say that they are grounded in two related Rousseauian theses: the superiority of the public over the private in a well-ordered regime (the republican or classical side of Rousseau's thought) and the degradation of the private dependence of persons on one another. The former leads Rousseau to condemn the commercial spirit insofar as it draws the attention of citizens away from public affairs and transforms them into bourgeois, that is, persons who gladly alienate their civic freedom, their participation in public affairs, for the sake of the pursuit of their private interests.[127] The second thesis flows directly from the above: to the extent that the community is weak-

---

[126] Rousseau, *Political Economy*, p. 227. For the organic imagery see Rousseau, *Political Economy*, pp. 211–13, and on labor and commerce see for example Rousseau, *Political Economy*, pp. 221–22, 234; *Social Contract*, p. 75; *Second Discourse*, p. 140; *Emile*, pp. 184–85.

[127] Rousseau, *Social Contract*, pp. 101–4, 54n.

ened in relation to the private, the equality and freedom of all persons as citizens are diminished, to be replaced by the inequality and domination inherent in the commercial world. When Rousseau wrote that we give ourselves princes in order that we shall not have masters, he meant that the public or political must function as a potent antidote to the private, the realm of property and personal dominion. Judged from that standpoint, the Lockean notions that government is the umpire among self-chosen and private activities, the "Guarantee for the performance of all legal Contracts,"[128] and that the market has itself a certain moral rectitude are plainly at odds with the true purpose of public authority. This and his extended and explicit critique of the world of commerce distinguish his analysis from Locke's, and that fact directs our attention once again to Locke's sharp break with the traditional mode of analysis of economy and society.

5.4   Labor

I now turn to two other themes, important for an understanding of Locke's normative political economy and for the contrast between that theory and its ancient predecessor—namely, labor and leisure. It will be recalled from the analysis of the Aristotelian household economy that the labor of slaves, wage workers, and other subordinate members of the household (and the political) community was said to be purposive within the context of that community, that is, it served to allow the free members the time or leisure necessary to pursue the good and noble activities of citizenship—philosophy and so forth. Work done under compulsion, whether by the economic compulsion of need or by the drive of avarice or by the authority of the master over the slave, was considered a degraded condition and a form of unfree activity suitable only for those of an inferior station. In large measure, this view rested on the idea that the goods of human life could be developed only in leisure, in free and unconstrained time. Those whose functions within the community denied them that time were incapable of achieving excellence; and their lack of leisure was the precondition for permitting the community—household or polis—to fulfill the purpose for which they exist, the cultivation of the excellence of man and citizen. We might reasonably anticipate, then, that the attack on the organic, hierarchical household and its economy which

---

[128] Locke, *Further Considerations Concerning Raising the Value of Money,* in Patrick Kelly, *Locke on Money,* 2 vols., in *The Clarendon Edition of the Works of John Locke* (Oxford: Clarendon, 1991), vol. 2, p. 415.

forms a central motif of the contractarian project would also have consequences for the way in which labor and leisure are understood. And indeed that is just the case. Let us begin by examining briefly the Lockean concept of labor, a concept that can be divided into these elements: labor as part of the juridical person and as a moment of the human condition generally. The juridical person, we recall, is first of all a self-owner, a creature with property in his own being, and this primordial sort of proprietorship is the great and original foundation of all property. But (for reasons to be set out below) our bodies are something more than mere natural possessions; they are meant to be put to use and that use is human action, as Locke says: "The *Labour* of his Body and the *Work* of his Hands, we may say, are properly his."[129] Labor belongs to the individual, it is her property, an essential extension of her fundamental stock, and a part of what it means to be a juridical person. Just as ownership of one's physical self is part of the jural idea of the person, so too is proprietorship over that self-in-motion, that is, over labor: all persons are, juridically speaking, laborers and that condition is unmarked by status or other forms of differentiation.

Labor is, for Locke, something more than an element of the concept of the juridical person; it is also a duty and a fundamental part of that person's earthly condition. God put a spade, a tool, into Adam's hand—a spade "to subdue the Earth." The father of humankind was made a "day labourer for his Life"; the supposed original and absolute monarch of the world, on examination, appears no different from the lowliest English worker. The lesson of Adam is twofold: on the one side, it reinforces the juridical equality of the person as self-owner and laborer by reducing the father of all humankind to a laborer himself and thereby inviting the question as to who can claim to be above labor if the Creator made the first human with a tool in his hands? On the other side, it points to the dignity of labor—that by their actions humans are to subdue nature, to exercise their industriousness and rationality in making use of the things of nature which God provided them for their preservation and comfort.[130]

Put in a negative light, labor is something commanded of human beings by their Maker and required of them by the "penury of [their] Condition"; in short, it is humankind's curse as well as the expression of their rationality and the fulfillment of one of their obligations to God.[131] Yet even here the equality of labor is manifest: Locke typically refers to the

[129] Locke, 2T.27; emphasis in the original.
[130] See Locke, "Labor," in Kelly, *Locke on Money,* vol. 2, pp. 493–95.
[131] Locke, 2T.32, 35. In his "Labor" manuscript (Kelly, *Locke on Money,* vol. 2, p. 494), Locke refers to "that horid ignorance and brutality" in which most workers are kept.

genus labor and does not distinguish among its types. This equality can be construed, as Dunn has shown, as part of the Puritan rejection of the hierarchical cosmos of callings and its replacement by an egalitarian notion of the calling in which distinctions are made only according to the effort expended in the pursuit of one's allotted task.[132] With some violence to historical accuracy, this view of labor can be recast in secular terms so as to say that it is by labor of all sorts that humans subdue nature and produce wealth—in brief, that the external goods of human society are the work of the industrious and not the slothful. The contempt for indolence ("It is degrading to have no work"[133]) and its corollary, the striking reversal of the ancient aversion to labor, rests in large measure on a critique of the unproductive consumption-oriented aristocracy. There may well be a related basis for it, however—in the association of the leisure of some with the despotic economy in which that free time is purchased by the unfreedom of others. Whatever reading is given to this conception of labor, as rooted in the Puritan idea of the calling or as founded on something more secular, the essential point for our purposes is that labor activity has been detached from the background of the hierarchical community, individualized in the idea of the juridical person as a self-owner, provided with a type of dignity, and made a central and equal part of the human condition.

5.4.1 The Alienation of Labor

According to Locke, labor can be sold and indeed, under conditions in which private appropriation has rendered land an exceedingly scarce commodity, many or most will be driven, for want of another feasible alternative, to sell their labor to others. On the one hand, labor emerges as something dignified, as the exertion of rationality and industriousness in the mastering of nature and, on the other hand, as an alienable good and one that appears to subordinate the propertyless laborer to the owners of property. This distinction between labor as an activity and as a commodity has been said to give Locke's theory of labor a problematic character; that is, the move from the first understanding (labor as an essential and dignified activity) to the second (labor as a alienable good,

---

[132] See Dunn, *The Political Thought of John Locke*, pp. 219–20, and Walzer, *Revolution of the Saints*, pp. 169, 209–10. Cf. Tarcov, *Locke's Education for Liberty*, p. 127.

[133] Quoted in Samuel Brittan, *A Restatement of Economic Liberalism* (Atlantic Highlands, N.J.: Humanities Press, 1988), p. 195. See also Locke's comments on the evils of idleness in "Labor," in Kelly, *Locke on Money*, vol. 2.

generating new relations of power between persons) involves a "morally suspect" change, as E. J. Hundert calls it, in the nature of labor and of the person who must alienate it.[134] The underlying issue here is whether Locke viewed wage labor as consistent with the autonomy of the person (if we assume that he had a theory of wage labor at all).

Locke did have a theory (or the rudiments of one) of wage labor, and this theory is entirely consistent with the fundamental principles of his contractarianism and with those of liberal contractarianism generally. Again, this is not to make the plainly anachronistic case that Locke saw and sought to justify a pervasive free labor market where one did not in fact yet exist, nor is it to make the equally implausible case that the servants discussed in the seminal "Turfs" passage of the *Second Treatise* are fully identical to the industrial wage laborers of nineteenth-century England.[135] The argument presented here is rather that the principles of a free labor market are inherent in Locke's analysis and that the common features of later wage-labor relations can be justified on Lockean grounds, even if Locke himself, in the historical circumstances in which he wrote, hardly could have foreseen a generalized system of wage labor. My purpose in making this case is to add another dimension to the preceding argument: that the disembedding of the economy from the hierarchical community had as one of its principal features the transformation of labor from an occupation tied to subordinate status into a moment of the human estate and into a commodity or, less jarringly, into a good freely alienable by its rightful owner.

Let us begin by returning to a reading of Locke according to which he did not have a theory of wage labor and, more important for our purposes, according to which his concepts of freedom and the person would have led him to condemn capitalist wage labor. This analysis has two branches. (1) A free person can be held to submit herself voluntarily to the condition of being a servant of another person only if there is an alternative of a specific sort available. Where no such alternate means of providing for herself exists, the individual is bound by necessity and hence cannot be said to have contracted freely. (2) Labor is defined as the

---

[134] E. J. Hundert, "Market Society and Meaning in Locke's Political Philosophy," *Journal of the History of Philosophy* 15 (1977): 37, and Hundert, "The Making of *Homo Faber:* John Locke between Ideology and History," *Journal of the History of Ideas* 15 (1972): 8, 10.

[135] For critiques of this sort of historical conflation see Peter Laslett, "Market Society and Political Theory," *Historical Journal* 7 (1964): 152, and Hundert, "Market Society and Meaning in Locke's Political Philosophy," p. 41. The "Turfs" passage is in Locke, 2T.28.

actions of a person determined by his will, and so it is (liberally) impossible for a person voluntarily to alienate his labor in the sense of giving his actions over to the direction of another. To sell one's labor, which involves the superintendence of the employer over its use, would be to reduce the seller to the level of a slave or vassal, for the person who is directed in his activity has lost all autonomy. What Locke is describing in the "Turfs" passage is therefore not a sale of labor power, but of a service, the crucial distinction being that in the former the employer directs him *in* his work, in the latter merely *to* his work. The Lockean concept of a legitimate alienation of labor would, on this reading, constitute an objection to and not a justification of capitalist wage labor.[136]

The first branch of that argument I have addressed in the preceding discussion of contract and choice, and I shall add to it here only two passages from Locke which suggest that even the most severe constraints on available options do not render the labor contract unfree: "The Authority of the rich Proprieter, and the subjection of the Needy Beggar began not from the Possession of the Lord, but the Consent of the poor Man, who preferr'd being his Subject to starving" and again "as for the Workmen, who are employed in our Manufactures . . . these the Clothier, not having ready Money to pay, furnishes with the necessaries of Life, and so trucks Commodities for Work, which such as they are, good or bad, the Workman must take at his Master's Rate, or sit still and starve."[137] In both passages, the option allowed the needy beggar or the workman is not access to the commons, another job, or charity, but work or starvation. The second of the two passages, a descriptive account forming a part of a larger discussion of the market, offers no normative gloss whatsoever on the fact that these workers must take the master's rate or perish. The first passage explains why there is no need for a critical normative comment: there is an uncoerced choice, however unpalatable and constrained, and therefore a voluntary contract.

The second branch of this argument builds on the historical circumstances of labor in Locke's time, on Locke's statement that the servant provides his master with "the Service he undertakes to do"—that is, with the self-directed completion of a task set by the lord—and, more broadly,

---

[136] See Tully, *Discourse on Property,* pp. 136–42, and Tully, "A Reply to Waldron and Baldwin," *Locke Newsletter* 13 (1982): 43–44. For a parallel analysis, see Tribe, *Land, Labour, and Economic Discourse,* pp. 49–50, and Laslett, "Market Society and Political Theory," pp. 152–53.

[137] Locke, 1T.42; Locke, *Some Considerations of the Consequences of the Lowering of Interest and Raising the Value of Money,* p. 237.

on a reading of Locke's theory of autonomy and its consequences for the individual's control over his actions. Although the historical background that may have shaped Locke's views on the nature of the servant's labor is not of direct interest here, it is worth observing that Locke does not restrict his observations on wage labor to the servant resident in the master's home but also discusses the "day labourer" and the workmen in "our manufactures." It is by no means certain from Locke's references to these categories of hired labor that he assumed them to be self-directed task executors rather than mere hired hands. And we also know that seventeenth-century farm servants were (as E. P. Thompson notes) "subject to an intense labour discipline" that often required the farmer-employer to work exceptional hours himself to ensure that the servants did not evade work because of an absence of supervision.[138] In short, there is reason to question the claim that Locke's laborers, whether servants or workmen, were conceived by him as self-directing task performers.

What is more important in this second branch is the idea that Lockean self-proprietorship is to be understood as the quality of being the master of one's actions, where mastery means control over what cannot be alienated and in which self-ownership is retained. This idea seems to follow from Locke's principle that freedom is the liberty to dispose over one's whole property and "therein not to be subject to the arbitrary Will of another, but freely to follow his own."[139] But if we look closely at this last definition, its issue becomes less clear: for "not to be subject to the arbitrary Will of another" means not to be bound by constraints that one has not voluntarily accepted, that is, contracted for, which in turn is just the sense of the conclusion of the definition "but freely to follow his own." What is contracted for is not, in Locke's view, submission to an arbitrary will, and if we add other features of his contract theory, that power established by contract is restricted in magnitude, in purpose, and in time, we may conclude that though contractual slavery is impermissible for Locke the contractual sale of a finite amount of labor time under supervision is not. This reading is confirmed in Locke's statement that the Jews sold themselves into drudgery, not slavery: "it is evident, the Person sold was not under an absolute, arbitrary, Despotical Power. For the Master could not have power to kill him, at any time, whom, at a certain

---

[138] See E. P. Thompson, "Time, Work-Discipline, and Industrial Capitalism," *Past & Present* 38 (1967): 77–78.
[139] Locke, 2T.57.

time, he was obliged to let go free out of his Service: and the Master of such a Servant was so far from having an Arbitrary Power over his Life."[140] What distinguishes drudgery from slavery is contract, the limited power and the duration of that power over the servant. There is no condemnation of drudgery, as there clearly is of slavery, and the moral dividing line between the two estates does not have to do with whether the Jews sold themselves to self- or other-directed labor but rather with whether they contracted and under what conditions (specifically, the extent and duration of the supervising power) they consented to work.

It is surely quite possible, then, that Locke did not theorize about capitalist wage labor but that the legitimate relations between master and servant, whose principles he did set out, are readily extendable to such transformed conditions, and that there is nothing in those principles to indicate that Locke would have judged the sale of labor power to be a form of slavery. The reasoning that allows this extended application of the justification of master/servant relations is that neither the constraints limiting the worker's options on entering into the contract with his employer nor the subsequent supervision of labor activity are crucial benchmarks for Locke by which to discriminate between a condition of slavery and one of free service to another.[141] Rather, what is a central concern of Locke's is that the submission be by consent, that restraints on choice be themselves just, and that the act of submission not yield a permanent and unlimited subjection to the master. Indeed, the employer's supervision of his labor might well be considered an integral part of any contract (e.g., that which creates civil society) in which goods are delivered over time; that is, the element of enforcement vital to the performance of contracts that are not frictionless.

The preceding analysis brings to light the centrality of contract in the alienation of labor. The importance of this fairly straightforward observation for the study of the place of labor in Locke's political economy is that the idea of labor contracts, sometimes decried as the "commodification" of persons or as the creation of a "fictitious" commodity, was intended to reinforce the dissolution of the hierarchical-household conception of the economy. It does this by detaching labor from the position of persons

---

[140] Locke, 2T.24; for further analysis see Jeremy Waldron, "'The Turfs My Servant Has Cut,'" *Locke Newsletter* 13 (1982): 14–15.

[141] I have argued that Tully's distinction between selling one's labor and selling the product of that labor, the former counting as servile and the latter as free, is not to be found in Locke, although something quite like it is employed by Kant. See Kant, *On the Common Saying*, p. 78 and note, and Kant, *Metaphysical Elements of Justice*, p. 71.

within the community and by freeing it from the community's (for example, from the *oikos* master's) purposes. In other words, it extends the metaphor of the juridical person to the economic sphere such that each of the contracting parties confronts the other not in a relationship of superior and inferior but as commodity owners freely exchanging their wares. The contract neither rests on nor produces a liberally meaningful, juridical, distinction between persons. Second, it involves no overdetermining theory of the community good to be served by labor; some such good may be the result of economic activity, but contract theory does not deploy it in order to explain why the contracting agents do (or should do) what is contained in their agreement. It is sufficient to assume that each seeks the satisfaction of his own preferences and chooses the actions he deems appropriate to those ends. Polanyi has described this change in the condition of labor in these words: "To separate labor from the other activities of life and to subject it to the laws of the market was to annihilate all organic forms of existence and to replace them by a different type of organization, an atomistic and individualistic one. Such a scheme of destruction was best served by the application of the principle of freedom of contract."[142] That same phenomenon might also be (liberally) described as the freeing of labor from the hierarchical household model in which it was subject to the master's welfare function and the passing of control over labor to its owner to be used by him at his discretion and for his purposes.

5.5   Time, Leisure, and the Liberal Economy

In the Aristotelian account of the household economy we saw that the labor of the slaves and servants was grasped as the precondition of the freeing of time, or the creation of leisure, within which citizens could cultivate excellence. Providing time as leisure was understood as one of the central purposes of the community and of its economic activity. Once more we would expect that the critique of the organic household as a metaphor for analyzing economic and political life should yield a substantial revision in the way of thinking about time, labor, and community.

At its core, the contractarian community has no dominant purpose apart from the preservation of individuals' self-chosen activities, and, in particular, it could not allow of a (publicly sanctioned) purpose that

[142] Polanyi, *The Great Transformation*, p. 163.

required the subordination of some for the sake of the excellence of others.[143] In other words, it can neither prescribe an excellence that leisure is to permit nor can it tolerate the idea of a (publicly sanctioned) hierarchy of tasks oriented to the providing of the possibility of virtuous activity for one group. The rejection of a hierarchy of tasks, established supraindividually—that is, independently of the preference rankings of individuals in the choice of their own life plans—is an unproblematic deduction from the idea of equal juridical persons as autonomous, purposive agents; the dismissal of the idea of a certain type of *summum bonum* is rooted in the translation of the good into individual preferences.[144] To be more faithful to Locke's argument, and to the liberal case for neutrality, we might recast this to say that the good, to the extent that it can legitimately be identified by the body politic, is indistinguishable from the publicly secured ability of each to adopt and pursue his preferences insofar as that pursuit is consistent with the opportunity of others to do likewise without unreasonable (coercive) restraint. What this reformulation does is to permit the notion of, for example, a religiously grounded equivalent to the *summum bonum*—that is, a set prescription for the good life, as a matter of private duty before God—while at the same time acknowledging that from the point of view of the community or body politic only the sum of individual freely chosen activities, protected by the authority of the community are to be recognized as public or community goods. Liberal neutrality, in other words, is not necessarily an agnostic stance on the question of the good life, but it is a rejection of the idea that in a free society the public sphere, that locus of force, can in any way pronounce on the matter.[145]

If two of the principal background elements in the transformation of the idea of time or leisure are the attack on the hierarchy of activities (and persons) and the critique of the notion of the good to which those activities, and the persons who perform them, are purely instrumental ("living tools"), so too is the new, egalitarian theory of labor a key component of that revision. Labor of whatever sort is a part of the human condition, its curse as well as the ennobling application of our reason in subduing

---

[143] This thought invites comparison with Michael Oakeshott's account of *universitas*, an association of agents united "in . . . their joint purpose." See Michael Oakeshott, *On Human Conduct* (Oxford: Clarendon Press, 1975), pp. 204–5. I am indebted to an anonymous reviewer for Cornell University Press for suggesting this idea.

[144] See Locke, *Essay on Human Understanding*, vol. 1, p. 351; Hobbes, *Leviathan*, p. 63.

[145] One of the best contemporary statements of liberal neutrality can be found in Ronald Dworkin, "Liberalism," in Stuart Hampshire, ed., *Public and Private Morality* (Cambridge: Cambridge University Press, 1978), pp. 113–43.

nature. Free time, then, comes to be viewed (nonpolitically and from the perspective of our callings) as repugnant idleness and sloth or as (literally) re-creation, moments in which the person is restored so as to be able to begin his labors anew. More politically, it may be seen as having been intimately associated with a community in which the power of the scepter enabled some to compel others to take up the spade in their service. Stripped of the connection with a governing conception of excellence and of the domination over human beings which was a part of it, and made a subordinate moment of a universal human activity (labor), leisure comes to be suspect insofar as it is not derivative from and preparative for still more labor.[146]

The final and more characteristically contractarian facet of the new position of time is as a central element of the legitimate contract itself. A significant part of what distinguishes slavery from the condition of servants or day laborers is that the latter belong only temporarily under the discipline of the master.[147] What they dispose of in contracting away their labor is time as well as energy or exertion. They cannot, on this view, alienate their whole time because in so doing they would be attaching themselves in perpetuity to their master's household (or manufactory) and to his rule, to a condition in which termination would be impossible. As a self-proprietor, the contract agent is the owner of his time; his subordination to a master can be only a voluntary act, the creation of an artificial community of the household through the contracting act, and that community of master and servants must, according to this theory, be limited both in time and in the magnitude of power thereby given to the master. Time, in short, becomes one of the objects of contract, a good or property to be alienated by its owner, within limits and for his own purposes. The freedom of time is thus conceived, as is the contractarian notion of freedom generally, not as the absence of constraint or necessity imping on its use, but rather as an expression of a legitimate, voluntary use, or transfer of it. He who has freely consented to give some measure of his time over to another for the latter's use can be said to have exercised that self-mastery or autonomy which stands at the center of what it means to be a (contractarian) person. Control over time, in which control is taken to mean disposition over time and the voluntary alienation of it as a part of one's property, places the idea of time within the broader

---

[146] See Locke, "An Essay Concerning Recreation," in King, *The Life of John Locke*, vol. 2, pp. 165, 167, and Hobbes, *Leviathan*, p. 224; Hobbes, *De Cive*, pp. 266–67; Rousseau, *Emile*, p. 195.

[147] Locke, 2T.24, 85.

argument for individual self-ownership and thereby further separates it from its ancient moorings in the structure and purpose of the organic community.

6. Public Homes, Private Homes: Society and Economy in Classical Liberalism

The core of the liberal contractarian project is the preservation of autonomy, which raises the question of legitimate power, of what sort of authority and under which conditions dominion or rule can be exercised by some humans over others. The *summum malum,* the perennial evil of human affairs, is in this view the state of war, conceived not as a condition necessarily involving actual violence but as a situation in which power is wielded without right. The identification of this state as the evil to be transcended followed, as we have seen, from a critique of the patriarchal-household justification of the natural or divinely prescribed hierarchy of the premodern community. That critique resolved the community into a level plane, populated by autonomous individuals, each the bearer of certain rights embraced, in the Lockean account, under the overarching concept of self-ownership. The quality and liberty of these self-owners destroy the foundation of the hierarchical account of community, an account rooted in inequality, but when this liberty and equality are combined with the pervasive will to dominate others, they lead to a new need for political authority, princes to protect individuals from masters. This refashioned body politic could not, given its theoretical origins in the notion of persons freely disposing over themselves within the limits of natural law, be conceived of save as the result of consent to the use of public coercive authority for the composed purposes of individuals.

What I particularly stress here is the importance of the community of the ancient and patriarchal household model as the background shaping the early liberal conception of autonomy and equality. The idea that the community, whether of the household or of the polis, is characterized in the first instance by its dominant moment, the just rule of some over others independent of consent, the subordination of the wills of the latter to the best or ruling elements is precisely what the liberals had to undermine, and virtually every major strand of the contractarian argument forms a part of that critique. Thus the state-of-nature image undermines the ancient conception of the community and creates a context in which the attributes of the person can be analyzed without reference to a log-ically prior community and therefore also without reference to hierarchy and domination. The notion of the jural person is similarly intended to answer not only the inequality of the *oikos* model (by setting out a concept of the person from which position and differentiation are absent and in which all agents are considered the bearers of identical initial juridical endowments) but also its domination moment (by defining the jural person as the carrier of exclusionary rights against others, a self-owner or master with the liberty to dispose, within limits, over herself).

Running through and uniting these various contractarian arguments is a theory of the autonomous agent and, by extension, a notion of just relations between such agents. There are, to be sure, profound differences among the contractarian philosophers as to the nature of autonomy and over what can count as a free act of the will. But as important as those distinctions are, there is a common thread binding their arguments to-gether, one best grasped in the distinction between autonomy and hetero-nomy. To have a free will is to be self-legislative, to give the law to oneself; to be subject to the will of another is to exist heteronomously, to be governed from the outside and hence to lose that central property, that proper function, of the will, self-determination. This idea can be re-phrased in Lockean terms, with a shift in foundations (from the legisla-tive capacity of reason to a property right in oneself) but with no loss to its concluding point: persons as self-owners have a right to that power by which they may dispose of their alienable assets (their property, broadly construed). Any other mode of attaching their assets—that is, any man-ner of securing their obedience or of taking their tangible property which does not acknowledge their rightful power over these assets in virtue of self-ownership—is a violation of just what it is to be a person.

Both the Kantian and Lockean constructions of will as autonomy have a moral resonance in the idea of self-legislation over the passions, but our concern is more with their public dimension, with the manner in which this concept of the will shapes the understanding of relations between agents. Here, as we saw, the early liberal argument expresses itself in the idiom of consent and contract: self-legislation does not preclude rule by others, but it does specify the manner in which one autonomous will can rightly become subordinate to another (or, more generally, the way in which powers or property can be transferred between persons) and that is by an act of consent, a free, purposive giving or lending. I said that the contours of what can count as a free transfer vary sharply across the contractarian tradition, and so do the limits on what can be transferred.

Held in common among them, however, is the minimum or privative condition that what is extracted by force alone, which seeks no sign of voluntary submission or alienation, cannot be said to be voluntary or contracted for. However lacking in actual or behavioral political content the idea of consent may be in contractarian thought, its role as a hedge, marking out the boundaries protecting the person from illegitimate coercion, is unmistakable. And this idea of protective boundaries brings into focus again the centrality of domination as the evil to be addressed: power exercised without the actual consent of the governed or, on the minimalist account, such an exercise of power inconsistent with what could have been rationally consented to, is nothing other than violence. But when that power is acquired by, or consistent with, consent, no matter how constrained the option set may be within which the choice is made, violence is transformed into legislative authority, robbery into a rightful transfer of property, and the relations between persons which thus emerge are consistent with the fundamental right of autonomy.

Will as expressed in choice and the creation of a public space that ensures the possibility of choice (not necessarily of a wide range of choices, but rather the mere absence of coercion, of that which excludes the possibility of an individual's veto over the exchange) is the essence of the contractarian concept of autonomy and of the body politic as its guarantor. This vision of autonomy stands at the center both of the concept of the jural person and of one of their free associations, the political community. It also, as we have shown, pervades the understanding of other associations, particularly those of the family and of economic interchange between persons. The structure of the family is recast so that its relations of authority are characterized by a mix of consent and equality as the defining properties of the person and by the limited power and duration of these relations. The fundamental independence of the adult members of the household is particularly evident in the assertion that the wife can leave the marriage at will: she can dissolve the community and absent herself from her husband's jurisdiction and that without having to return to the jurisdiction of another *kurios*.[148] Similarly, the servant occupies his position in the household not as a bound, inferior member of a community producing for the sake of the well-being of his superiors but rather as a commodity owner, alienating his labor under the temporary

---

[148] On divorce in the ancient world, see S. C. Humphreys, "Women in Antiquity," in Humphreys, *The Family, Women, and Death* (London: Routledge and Kegan Paul, 1983), p. 46, and Raphael Sealey, *Women and Law in Classical Greece* (Chapel Hill: University of North Carolina Press, 1990), pp. 36, 65, 76–78.

discipline of the master for his own purposes—an authority relation perhaps, but one created by and dissolvable at his discretion.

In the contractarian world, populated by independent, autonomous jural persons, the relationship between these individuals and their community is radically transformed. The community is no longer a dominant structure determining the lives of persons embedded in the varied ranks of its hierarchy and subordinating them to its purposes. Rather, it is reconstructed as the efflux of the will of each, alienating certain rights for the sake of individually held purposes, the better to secure their liberty and property. The public community, one might say, becomes nothing but the compounded power assembled from the alienation of individual powers and forming an agency whose end or purpose is the sum of purposes attributable to rational persons. And in proportion as the despotic household model of the community is dissolved, as the community's ruling moment loses its dominating presence to be replaced by the body politic as a free, voluntary protective association, so the distinctness, the visibility, and independence of the private interchange of individuals, of the now autonomous economy, increases. The location of the economy within the community thus shifts as relations between persons are rethought and set on a new foundation: it is no longer embedded in the overdetermining preferences of the household despot, nor therefore is it saturated by the political, by status, by conceptions of appropriateness and (preeconomic) hierarchy or indeed by any of the other manifold ways in which the *oikos* created a profoundly political economy.

The movement from the *oikos* conception of community and economy to the contractarian understanding of self-ownership, consent, and voluntary alienation as the cement binding together legitimate relations among persons marks a watershed.[149] The liberal reconstruction of the household and bodies politic and economic does not claim to have dissolved relations of power and authority in the economy or elsewhere. Aristotle's shuttle had not become self-moving, scarcity had not been conquered, and masters and servants had not disappeared from the face of the world. Nor were individuals thought to have achieved that self-sufficiency, that freedom from constraining necessity which Aristotle attributes to the gods and certain creatures. But that this ideal situation was perhaps not even necessary is suggested by the silence of classical liberal thought on those dimensions of the ancient analysis of freedom, economy, and com-

---

[149] This movement, described as one from status to contract, receives its classical formulation in Sir Henry Maine, *Ancient Law* (New York: Henry Holt, 1864), especially pp. xl and 163.

munity. The threat to freedom lay rather in the preponderance of force in human affairs, private and public, centered on illegitimate hierarchy; the classical Greek solution to the burden of constraining toil had contributed mightily to that threat. Against this *summum malum* of the violence of persons, force or power without right, the contractarian argument offered the corrective: a theory of justice in which individuals are equal in their initial independence from the power of others, free as proprietors over their persons. And their relations, whether economic or those of the new body politic, are constructed on the foundation of a voluntary alienation. There may indeed (as Locke suggests) always have been masters and servants and those names may never disappear from the human community (as he intimates by his silence on the future in the *Second Treatise* §85). But contract gives the relation of power among masters and servants a "far different condition," one in which the essential (i.e., juridical) equality and autonomy of each is preserved and in which accordingly no violence or domination exists between them. Freedom as the right (within limits) to self-determination in relations with others is thus restored and made the centerpiece of the contractarian community, economic and political.

Let us pause to reflect one last time on the economic variant of that ill which classical liberalism sought to remedy and on the nature of the remedy for it. As we remarked, the ancient political economy of Aristotle and Xenophon saw economic activity as an embedded moment of the community it sustained. This quality of being embedded means specifically that the economy was subordinated to the purposes of the free community, which included not only the provisioning of its material sustenance but also the providing of unbound time, leisure, so that some might pursue higher activities, citizen duties or philosophy. It also means that the economy was embedded in the hierarchical structure of the household and polis, that it was contained as much as possible through being made the burden of the community's inferior members. The liberal critique of that understanding of community—the attack on a dominant, overdetermining purpose governing the economy and its agents as well as on its corollary, the hierarchy of persons and activities—was bound to alter radically the manner in which virtually all aspects of economic life were conceived. This critique replaced the purpose of the dominant segment of the community with the composed purpose of the new body economic, composed, that is, out of the individual preferences of its members. In place of the hierarchy of the household metaphor, liberal theory offered the concept of the juridical person, detached from a context of ruler and ruled, and equally endowed with the basic rights inherent in self-ownership or autonomy. And last, instead of determining forms of association and activity by a person's prior standing in the community, it postulated contract and self-chosen activity as the only legitimate means of establishing relations between persons and assigning them their functions within the community. The relationship between the general critique of the community understood as a hierarchical household and the idea of a private economy, one detached from control by the despotic lord or a body politic distinct from and standing above individuals, goes beyond a mere pleasing analogy between political contractarianism and economic contract. Rather, the autonomy of the economic sphere flows directly from the concept of the juridical person as a self-owner freely alienating his goods without any prior background distinctions between him and his fellow bargainers and from the notion of the legitimacy of the pursuit of individually set ends. Similarly, the inclusion of labor within the circumference of the autonomous economy is also a direct consequence of self-proprietorship and the right to alienate what is one's own (under certain restrictions, discussed above).

One result of this disembedding of the economy, then, is that it gives birth to an autonomous economic domain, where autonomy carries not only a privative signification (i.e., detachment from the control of the master or of the overdetermining body politic), but a positive one as well. That is, the economy generates its own laws and indeed has a self-sufficient justice within its operations; self-sufficient in that within its domain (once secured against coercion and with enforceable contracts) transactions and their outcomes have an equity and justice that requires no external intervention to bring them about. This autonomy makes a truly independent economic science possible, a science devoted to the study of economic phenomena and of their laws considered as a discrete sphere, one no longer overdetermined by the purposes and laws of the *oikos* despot. For all of their decidedly illiberal features, Locke's economic essays venture such an attempt to comprehend the laws of the disembedded economy, and that attempt distinguishes these writings sharply from those of the classical Greek tradition in which the idea of a purely economic science, detached from a consideration of the good life or of the good of the city, is hardly thinkable or is considered a perversion of the true understanding of the economy.

This vision of the free economy, of the moral and law-generating autonomy of economic phenomena, emerges from a critique of the idea of the hierarchical household as a model for the analysis of the larger community of the body politic and is a central moment of the contractarian reconstruction of the relationship between persons and community. And it is in this manner that the long-enduring problem of domination, most vividly expressed in reflection on the condition of the slave, a condition which has in Sir Henry Maine's phrase "at all times either shocked or perplexed mankind," is at last laid to rest.[150]

[150] Maine, *Ancient Law*, p. 157.

PART THREE

MARX AND THE NEW HOUSEHOLD ECONOMY

7. The Dissolution of the Old World

Frederick Engels, writing about the family, observed that the idea of expressing the passage from the premodern to the modern world as a move from status to contract had been developed by Marx in the *Communist Manifesto,* years before it was given its classical formulation by Sir Henry Maine.[1] Marx thought that this moment of the transformation wrought by the mighty solvent of the "bourgeois revolution" was apparent even in the microcosm of the household. There capitalism destroys the traditional patriarchal order, sets the family on a contractual foundation, makes wives less dependent on husbands and children on their parents by drawing them one and all into the larger economy. This destruction of the traditional family, which might on its face seem a brutal development severing the noneconomic and affective ties of the household, is to be welcomed, Marx argues, for it is, in miniature, the end of the direct domination and exploitation of the female and child members of that

[1] Frederick Engels, *The Origin of the Family, Private Property, and the State,* in *Karl Marx and Frederick Engels: Collected Works* (New York: International Publishers, 1975–), vol. 26, p. 186. This edition of the collected works is cited hereafter as *MECW.*

community on the basis of their inferior status.[2] The ending of the patriarchal household economy, and of the relations of hierarchy and domination which were crucial parts of it, occurs through the changes to the family's internal structure and through the increasing absorption of the household into a social economy in which individuals are stripped of status positions and in which power is not constitutive, *ex ante*, of their relations with others.[3] Yet also central to Marx's analysis of the liberal household is the view that it brings about the destruction of the patriarchal order, the wrenching of individuals out of the hierarchical nexus of the premodern household, in a manner that simultaneously transforms them into commodities, inputs into the production process, whether by absorbing them into the surrounding social economy or by remaking the family itself into a small enterprise. We see here Marx's fundamental ambivalence toward the liberal family (and toward liberalism as such): a recognition of its accomplishments vis-à-vis the old order in creating a microcommunity of free and equal persons—each disposing over him- or herself in an association untainted by status—and an argument that these persons become self-owners only then to find that the voluntariness of their contracting acts is severely cramped and that they are once more subordinated, now via the market. A good household would retain core liberal norms of freedom and equality, or, better, it would redeem liberalism's promise by abolishing one of those very institutions (the market) which it had developed as the vehicle of emancipation.[4]

This suggests that Marx accepted core elements of the liberal way of characterizing the shift from the ancient *oikos* conception of the economy to its modern successor. And that acceptance is one of the contentions I argue for in these pages. In particular, he adopted as his own the view that this transition could be described, in part, as one from status to contract, with the concomitant idea of the dissolution of the antique (despotic *oikos*-model) economy and its social relations and their replace-

[2] Marx, *Capital*, vol. 1, trans. Ben Fowkes (New York: Vintage Books, 1977), pp. 620–21; Marx, *Zur Kritik der politischen Ökonomie (Manuskript 1861–1863)*, vol. II.3.6 of *Karl Marx. Friedrich Engels Gesamtausgabe (MEGA)* (Berlin: Dietz Verlag, 1975–), p. 2052 (this edition of the collected works is cited hereafter as *MEGA*); Marx and Engels, *The German Ideology*, in *MECW*, vol. 5, pp. 180–81; Marx, *Results of the Immediate Process of Production*, trans. Ben Fowkes, App. to *Capital*, vol. 1, p. 1083; Marx, *Capital*, vol. 1, pp. 620–21. And see Marx, "The British Rule in India," in *MECW*, vol. 12, and Engels, *The Origin of the Family*, pp. 186–87.

[3] On this last point see Jon Elster, *Making Sense of Marx* (Cambridge: Cambridge University Press, 1985), p. 327.

[4] Marx, *Manifesto of the Communist Party* (hereafter *Communist Manifesto*), in *MECW*, vol. 6, p. 502.

ment by an economy and society grounded in a far different set of rela-tions. This acceptance of the liberal theory of the new moral economy is to be found in the two currents, analytical and normative, that coexist, often uneasily, in his writings. On the one side, he granted that a basic change had occurred in the organization of the economy, that the laws of the precapitalist and capitalist economies were fundamentally different and that something like the concepts of modern economic science were needed to comprehend the latter's laws.[5] At the same time, he acknowl-edged much of the normative force of the liberal critique of the precapital-ist world and made elements of it his. Yet standing behind this picture of the acceptance of the analytical and normative value of liberal political economy is a theory also of its limits. To understand the watershed in human history represented by capitalism, Marx turned to his teacher in so many things, Aristotle, and above all to the *Politics,* Book 1. There Marx found a way of classifying economic formations which was pro-foundly to influence his account of capitalism. And there too he discov-ered elements of a theory which would give him a critical purchase on capitalism, a way to think about the limits of liberalism. Marx was not able, however, to accept the essentially despotic character of the ancient vision of the good economy, and this rejection, in the name of something very like the liberal ethic of autonomy, led him to attempt an outline of what we might call a new household economy, combining (or attempting to combine) central elements of the *oikos* model with the achievements of liberalism.

In the pages that follow, I want to reconstruct this, Marx's analysis and critical embedding of liberalism. Here is the framework for that recon-struction: (1) I examine Marx's arguments concerning the liberal (and above all, Lockean) rejoinder to the premodern world. I begin by focusing on those claims of liberalism which Marx accepted and in substantial measure made his own. I then proceed to the more characteristically marxist analysis, which I read out as a move beyond the discourse of liberalism, one that locates the watershed represented by capitalism in a different language, drawn from Aristotle and expressed by Marx in his "general formula" of capital. That crucial element of his thought I seek to unfold at increasing levels of specificity: ends, communities, classes, etc. (2) I then turn to the locus of Marx's critical discussion of capitalism and especially of markets. The guiding thread of that critique, I suggest, is something quite like the liberal idea of freedom. And that thread I follow

[5] Marx, *MEGA,* II.3.6, p. 2268; Marx, *Capital,* vol. 1, p. 258.

through Marx's account of the origins of the capitalist market, the meaning of choice within it, classes and markets, the perverse effects of the market, and the relationship of the market to the command-governed microeconomies of the firm. (3) In the last pages, I explore further Marx's overarching Aristotelian theory of economic formations, now with a view to his concept of communism as the new *oikos*. Here I am concerned with the way in which Marx conceived of communism as an embedded and contained, use-value driven economy reproducing at the social level the world of the *oikos*, though wedded to core liberal desiderata. I conclude with a critical analysis of what I take to be the failure (and the remaining value) of this venture.

7.1   From Status to Contract

For Marx, the historical rupture represented by the emergence of an economy of the capitalist type could be portrayed, in part,by employing the conceptual language of classical liberalism. That is, this shift might be described as the dissolution of the despotic economy (and state) and its replacement by an economy and other social institutions at the center of which stood a new sort of agent, the person: juridically free, equal, and independent and legitimately bound to other persons only through a voluntary agreement, a contract. Accordingly, the collapse of the old society and the emergence of the new might be expressed, as we noted at the outset of Part Three, as the move from status to contract.

The newness of this world, which systematically undermines the premodern household—as it dissolves all other antique institutions—is nowhere more apparent than in the place of labor within it. We have already seen this watershed in Locke's *Second Treatise* §85, where he writes of a new master/servant relation, one founded on contract, temporary and limited in its character, and reflecting their free choice as to the best way in which to realize their preferences. That Lockean contrast between the patriarchal household and its political analogue, with their hierarchical and unfree character, and the contractual household (including its laboring population) based on the idea of the person is also to be found in Marx. The ancient economy, Marx argues, rested on "direct domination" and servitude, where by "direct" is meant a relationship in which contract between the principals plays no important role. Where labor has some access to its own land, as in the case of serfs, the relation between lord and peasant will take one form of extraeconomic coercion; in the case of slavery, the laborer is a thing, a commodity pure and simple. Relations of personal dependence among household members and in the larger society are also, for Marx, permeated by the centrality of the community or, in less ambiguous terms, by the presence of the political dimension: here political relations are, to use Godelier's phrase, at the same time relations of production.[6] The preservation of that community in its social/political order was among the central determinants of the economy. The relative insignificance of exchange and the pervasive presence of the political community and with it of inequality and unfreedom were defining characteristics of the premodern world, according to Marx. To this sketch we might add one further and related property: that the dominating influence of the community, the dependence of persons on that community, and the restrictions on its inferior members combine to limit individuality in these societies.[7]

In this (designedly) selective portrait of precapitalist society, Marx comes close to Locke's summary of the patriarchal world, domestic and political. And in his account of the classical liberal remaking of that economy and society, Marx once more is in some considerable accord with the tradition. At the heart of this transformation is the change from relations of direct domination to relations between individuals mediated through the market (noncoercive exchanges) and resting on the idea of the juridical person. The creation of a virtually all-absorbing market sphere, one that came to embrace both labor power and land as commodities and that determines the worth of activities and things according to their exchange value presupposes the dissolution of all "fixed" relations of dependence. It also entails, Marx maintains, the dissolution of all noneconomic distinctions among individuals, for in the market they meet as bearers of their commodities in the straightforward sense of being mutually indifferent and "equally worthy."

The commodity is a "born leveller." If relations of dependence and a priori inequality disappear, in their stead emerge new relations, founded

[6] Marx also uses "natural economy" to convey this idea of the absence of market mediation. See Marx, *Capital*, vol. 1, pp. 173, 452; Marx, *Capital*, vol. 3, trans. David Fernbach (New York: Vintage Books, 1981), pp. 731, 930; Marx, *MEGA*, II.3.1, p. 229. And see Marx, *Capital*, vol. 3, p. 926; Marx, *Grundrisse*, trans. Martin Nicolaus (New York: Vintage Books, 1973), p. 498; Frederick Engels, *Draft of a Communist Confession of Faith*, in *MECW*, vol. 6, p. 100. On political relations as relations of production: Marx, *Grundrisse*, pp. 492–93, 503; Marx, *Capital*, vol. 3, p. 1021; Maurice Godelier, *The Mental and the Material*, trans. Martin Thom (London: New Left Books, 1986), pp. 220–24.

[7] Marx, *Grundrisse*, pp. 84, 226, 541. See also David Miller, "Marx, Communism, and Markets," *Political Theory* 15 (1987): 182–204.

on commodity exchange and presupposing nothing but the property right of each to her self and to her goods. The self is here dominant and equal; and because the will of the individual is said to be embodied as well in each person's objects, the transfer of goods and services (activities) can legitimately take place only with the consent of the parties. In short, there can be no appropriation by force. The decomposition of the precapitalist world, of its many-tiered structure permeated in advance by political and status position, and of individuals embedded in that structure of hierarchy and rule, produces a society the foundation of which is the *person*. The community of such persons, of juridically equal and free agents, is one bound together by mutual need: money, the cash "nexus" (in a word, the economy), is their true community, and money (capital) is as impersonal, in the sense of being untainted by status, as are the "abstract" persons (the "bearers" or "functionaries") who are its owners.[8]

Central among the goods absorbed into the market is labor power: previously much labor was held as a good owned outright, as a chattel belonging to the slave owner, or as dependent and bound to the land. The free laborer is not a chattel, and her labor power, sold only for a temporary period, is a commodity over which she is proprietor, which is invested with her will and which can only be alienated via an act of consent. The laborer, in other words, is a person, and without her (in this dual aspect of laborer/person) capitalism would not be the social and economic system that it is. When Marx writes that labor power is a commodity belonging to its owner, a core part of what he intends by this is that the commodification of labor, the drawing of labor power out of its non-market ties to the master or lord and land, and its newly acquired position as a good to be exchanged in the market, give the laborer a field of choice that was not previously hers. The market in this sense among others is an institution that serves an emancipatory end, and its extension (spatially, as the world market, and internally, as the process of commodification) is one of the characteristics separating the bourgeois world from its antecedent formations.[9]

[8] Marx, *Grundrisse*, pp. 223, 241–43, 246; Marx, *Capital*, vol. 1, pp. 178–79, 247; Marx, *MEGA*, II.3.6, p. 2267. Marx, "Reflections," in *MECW*, vol. 10, pp. 590–92. For a different reading of Marx on freedom and money see Shlomo Avineri, *The Social and Political Thought of Karl Marx* (Cambridge: Cambridge University Press, 1968), p. 164.

[9] Marx, *Grundrisse*, pp. 289, 293, 463–64; Marx, *Capital*, vol. 1, pp. 271, 452; Marx, *Theories of Surplus Value*, trans. Emile Burns, Jack Cohen, and S. W. Ryazanskaya, ed. S. Ryazanskaya and Richard Dixon (Moscow: Progress, 1963–71), vol. 3, p. 431; Marx, *Capital*, vol. 3, p. 1019; John E. Roemer, *Free to Lose* (Cambridge: Harvard University Press, 1988), pp. 80–81.

This introduction of choice into relations between persons, the idea of contract and consent as barriers against coercion, does not express, for Marx, the whole of the emancipation wrought by the market. For it leaves out this consequence of self-ownership: that the producer, being now a free agent, is responsible for herself and accordingly learns to govern herself—in a word, to become autonomous in a way not previously possible.[10] Not only is the market, then, a means of enlarging the sphere in which choice is exercised but it is in addition an education in self-government because, in renouncing the master, it thereby throws the person back upon herself and her own decisions. That the master or lord does not appear in the market is yet another of its core properties for Marx. As we observed above, there is no politically or socially fixed relation of subordination in the market: the web of relations among persons here is not one penetrated by any extraeconomic ordering of them. Market society reduces actors, as it reduces all other things, to a purely economic standing, and it rejects as illegitimate all noneconomic gradations among persons as it also banishes coercion (liberally understood).[11]

This picture of the bourgeois world—with its emphasis on the idea of the person as embracing juridical freedom, equality, and independence— is strikingly close to Locke's, as was Marx's sketch of the precapitalist world. And Marx considered Locke's formulation to be liberalism's "classic expression" and the basis of all subsequent English political economy. In this normative sense, as well as in key explanatory aspects of his work, Marx's analysis is embedded in the liberal tradition of which he was in other respects so critical. The world of the (more or less) pervasive market was in certain important ways sharply different from and superior to precapitalist societies. The position of the producers in the modern economy, and that of the capitalists as well, are determined in no small part by the market institutions through which their relationships must be mediated in a capitalist economy.[12] This fact alone radically distinguishes capitalism, and calls into being the need for a new political economy.

That basic economic institutional change produces a society normatively superior—in its way, freer, less coercive, and more egalitarian

---

[10] Marx, *Results of the Immediate Process of Production*, p. 1033; Marx, *MEGA*, II.3.6, p. 2135.

[11] Marx, *MEGA*, II.3.6, p. 2130, and II.3.1, pp. 116–17; Marx, *Capital*, vol. 1, pp. 270–71; Marx, *Results of the Immediate Process of Production*, pp. 1025–27.

[12] Marx, *Capital*, vol. 3, p. 1021; Marx, *Theories of Surplus Value*, vol. 3, p. 431.

than earlier economic formations.[13] I repeat this point here for emphasis, because Marx's language is on occasion swept away by his savage indignation at what he took to be the fundamental flaws of this society. In those moments, he wrote as if there were in fact virtually no difference between, for example, the slave economy of antiquity and the modern, market-based economy; as if contract, the absence of coercion, and the juridical status of persons were but so many illusions (together with the "legal fiction" of contract), which, intentionally or not, concealed the existence of slavery in capitalism. Such a claim, conflating as it does all economic formations into one type, is too coarse a theoretical premise for an author who maintained that identifying the *differentia specifica* was key to explaining the varied ways in which human beings had historically organized the production of their livelihood.[14] To assert that one of the principal and defining institutions of a capitalist economy, the market, did not distinguish that formation from economies in which the market was absent altogether or was, at most, marginal would be to commit an error of numbing grossness. And that mistake Marx did not make. Nor did he advance the almost equally implausible case that there is no significant normative difference between an economy in which part of the population belongs, *tout court,* among the conditions of production without so much as a trace of consent or of a recognition of their status as persons, and one in which they (in part) dispose over themselves, share in the general wealth they produce, and are not marked out in advance or because of their function as inferiors.[15]

Whatever Marx's motivations may have been in adopting that sort of language (perhaps a desire to remove, rhetorically, the bloom from the rose of the theory and society he was seeking to criticize), his analysis aims to confront a much more subtle, nuanced task: on the one hand, to explain the main distinguishing features of capitalism, properties in which its moments of freedom and equality are located. And, on the other hand, to show how the freedom of the bourgeois world recoils upon persons in such a way as to restrict, significantly and perversely, that very freedom. Indeed, this claim can be further sharpened: that elements of the capitalist economy reproduce some of the characteristics of the despotic

[13] Suggested at Marx, *Grundrisse,* pp. 158, 161, and Marx, *Results of the Immediate Process of Production,* p. 1025. David Miller, *Market, State, and Community* (Oxford: Clarendon Press, 1989), pp. 210–14, provides a valuable summary of this aspect of Marx's argument.

[14] Marx, *Critique of Hegel's Philosophy of Right,* in MECW, vol. 3, p. 12. On the "legal fiction" claim see Marx, *Capital,* vol. 1, p. 719.

[15] Marx, *Grundrisse,* pp. 245, 283, 420–21.

economy in opposition to which classical liberalism defined itself. That this re-creation takes place in the presence of—more, as a consequence of—some of those very freedoms that were to correct premodern servitude and that the remedy for it is a reinstitution of the centerpiece of the ancient theory of the *oikos* is the paradox that stands at the heart of Marx's life project: at the center both of what is most fertile in his work and of the logic that led his doctrine to its end.

Marx maintains that, as central as the characteristics of the market mentioned above are to the capitalist economy, it would nevertheless be misleading to analyze them apart from their context. As we proceed, we shall explore elements of that context as Marx saw them in bourgeois society: the historical antecedents that create the immediate preconditions of markets, nonmarket sectors in capitalism, and so forth. For the present, what I am looking for is a theory of a grander sort, the one that Marx employs in order to set out the bourgeois world in its historical specificity and that forms the basis for his criticism of it, the theory Marx draws on in order to understand the revolution he thought had transformed the entire structure of society and, in so doing, had created a civilization that towered above that of all earlier epochs.[16] One candidate for such a dividing line between epochs is the magnitude of the market itself. This might be measured, crudely, by the proportion of transactions which occur in the market as opposed to whatever other institution may exist for the provisioning of human beings. With this as a criterion, we might say that capitalism is distinguished from earlier economic formations by the fact that in the latter only a small portion of goods are exchanged in the market. A way of refining further this magnitude-of-markets approach would be to look, with Polanyi, for the commodification of goods previously withheld (in greater or lesser degree) from the market, specifically labor and land.[17]

Both of these understandings of the explosive expansion of the market under capitalism figure in Marx's account of the system's distinctiveness. Neither, however, could provide the clear and distinct line of demarcation for which he was searching. The reason is this: for Marx, markets external or, more rarely, domestic have existed throughout much of history, but while premodern and capitalist markets are distinguished by their size, they are different in another respect, which in turn has explanatory pri-

[16] Marx, *Capital*, vol. 2, trans. David Fernbach (New York: Vintage Books, 1981), p. 120.

[17] Polanyi, *The Livelihood of Man*, p. 43. See Marx, *Capital*, vol. 1, pp. 172–73, 183; Marx, *Grundrisse*, pp. 419, 673–74; Marx, *Capital*, vol. 3, p. 1019.

macy over their magnitude. This essential difference (which we shall further examine below) lies in the fact that the process of "social metabolism," as Marx sometimes calls the production and exchange of goods, can be subordinated to the needs of the traders or their communities or it can be an instrument in the search after ever greater surpluses. This manner of differentiating markets and economic formations according to the final purpose being served closely parallels (and is taken from) the approach to be found in ancient Greek reflection on the economy, above all in Aristotle's *Politics*, Book 1, and *Nicomachean Ethics*, Book 5, but also in Xenophon's *Oeconomicus*. That is, it is adapted from a theory in which exchange within the framework of the community and for the satisfaction of its needs is opposed to trade for unlimited gain. When Marx writes that the tendency to create the world market and to subjugate every moment of production is contained in the concept of capital, he means that markets themselves adopt different forms and that these forms require explanation in the light of a theory of the order in which they are embedded.[18]

A second possible dividing line between epochs (and one more visibly marxist) is the way in which "surplus labor" is extracted from the direct producer.[19] This approach would hold that the distinguishing fissure line between socioeconomic formations is the type of exploitation, the sort of compulsion by which a surplus, however denominated, is transferred from its producers to the dominant class. Here exploitation is the overarching idea, the basis of a general theory of economic formations, while the manner of extraction provides the conceptual dividing line between them. This too forms a part of Marx's account: economic relations between producers and employers in a capitalist economy are mediated through the market, and it must also be there that at least a part of the story of exploitation is to be found. A slave economy, on the other hand, extracts surpluses through direct domination and coercion. This way of classifying grand economic types is deficient, for reasons similar to those urged above against the market-magnitude approach. In the first instance, it is too coarse-grained a criterion: all economies (or at least those above the most rudimentary technological level, including socialism) involve a surplus transfer and in that technical sense exploitation is a feature of all of them. What we require is rather a theory that explains the

---

[18] On aspects of this see Marx, *Capital*, vol. 1, pp. 172–73, 182–83, 198, 207; Marx, *Grundrisse*, pp. 408, 419; Marx, *A Contribution to the Critique of Political Economy* (Moscow: Progress, 1970), p. 50.

[19] Marx, *Capital*, vol. 1, p. 325.

changing reasons for exploitation: to what ends are surpluses created and transferred? To distinguish forms of exploitation according to the manner in which they are extracted is not adequate: the techniques and institutions that effect this transfer, the degree of pressure on the direct producers, are phenomena themselves in need of explanation.[20] And it is the end or purpose of the economy which provides the key to that explanation.

If the size of the market and the mechanisms of surplus extraction do not permit us to account adequately for the specificity of capitalism, there is a theory that does, according to Marx, and it is first picked up in his remarks on the "cell form" of bourgeois society, the commodity. Commodities are material things, products of the human interchange with nature and, across all economic formations, things to satisfy human needs. Insofar as these goods are exchanged, the end in view is the same: meeting needs. Commodities in a capitalist economy also have that property of being things useful, and if that were their principal defining trait, this economy would hardly be distinguishable from its antecedents. They have, however, this second property: they are things that have "exchange value" and the quality of containing more value than was used to create them. This latter property is the peculiar form given to goods in a capitalist economy, and it constitutes the pervasive form of wealth in this society. It was, for Marx, the key to be used to unlock the core of that system.[21]

Commodities, then, bear that double set of attributes (use and exchange/growth) which Aristotle first analyzed in the *Politics*, Book 1. Only in the capitalist economy it is the commodity's exchange value in the sense of being a vessel of expanded value, and not of whatever usefulness it may possess, which governs production by giving it its guiding purpose; "as the president of General Motors once said, his job wasn't to make cars, but to make money."[22] What Marx is venturing in this analysis of the commodity into its constituent elements, and the defining of the dominant component, is the starting point—the "cell form"—in the light of which the peculiar properties of the bourgeois world will emerge in sharply defined relief. And what Marx reads off of the commodity is the

---

[20] See Marx, *Capital*, vol. 1, pp. 344–45.

[21] See Marx, *MEGA*, II.3.1, p. 247; Marx, *Capital*, vol. 1, pp. 125–26, and Marx, *Results of the Immediate Process of Production*, p. 974. And see Aristotle, *Politics* 1256b30ff.

[22] Quoted in Will Kymlicka, *Liberalism, Culture, and Community* (Oxford: Clarendon Press, 1989), p. 107. See also Marx, *Capital*, vol. 1, p. 273, and vol. 3, p. 132; Marx, *Grundrisse*, p. 708.

idea of capital—in other words, of all the phases of the "social metabolism" of the economy, including its production and circulation components, as being directed toward the creation and realization of surplus value or, in its phenomenal form, profit. Phrased in more conventional terms, it is the expansion of wealth, not bound by need because not aimed at use or consumption, that is the goal of capitalist production.[23] In all forms of society, Marx writes, one form of production predominates over all others and "bathes" them in its "general illumination." Such in bourgeois society is the production of goods for the sake of profit. It is just that characteristic which captures the *differentia specifica,* the "general illumination" of the epoch, which gives all aspects of the capitalist economy, including its form of exploitation and the extent of its commodification of persons and things, their distinctive hue.[24]

We have already seen traces of Aristotelian political economy finding their way into Marx's analysis of capitalism: in the distinction between things made with their use as the goal and those in which exchange value is the determining purpose, as well as in the distinction between exchange for (and limited by) need and exchange for the sake of accumulation. Now, it will be remembered that in the *Politics* these ideas are elements of a more basic portrait of two types of economy, characterized by their end or purpose and, correspondingly, by the sort of stewardship exercised over them—*oikonomikē* and *chrēmatistikē.* The former was the art of ruling a household with a view to the proper, and finite, ends to be served by the economy; the latter was, in one of its branches, the mad Midaslike pursuit of wealth for its own sake and destructive of the possibility of the good life. Marx's phrase a "general illumination" suggests that the components of his argument we have been considering are themselves parts of a grander characterization of capitalist and noncapitalist economic formations. That is indeed the case, and once more we find here Marx's profound debt to Aristotle's economic analysis.

[23] Marx, *Capital,* vol. 3, pp. 324, 352, 354, 358, and vol. 1, pp. 769, 918; Marx, *Grundrisse,* pp. 270, 590; Marx, *MEGA,* II.3.1, pp. 75, 84. I use "profit" and "surplus value" almost interchangeably in Part Three of this book, though of course they are different, but related, entities for Marx. This theory is a discredited one, and, in any event, it does not bear directly on the arguments presented here. For critiques see Ian Steedman, *Marx after Sraffa* (London: New Left Books, 1977); John Roemer, *A General Theory of Exploitation and Class* (Cambridge: Harvard University Press, 1982); Elster, *Making Sense of Marx,* pp. 127–41. Amartya Sen, "On the Labour Theory of Value: Some Methodological Issues," *Cambridge Journal of Economics* 2 (1978): 175–90, looks at the labor theory of value from another perspective than that of value accountancy, that is, as a perspective designed to bring the centrality of human labor into clear focus.

[24] Marx, *Capital,* vol. 1, p. 769; Marx, *Grundrisse,* pp. 106–7.

Marx maintained that the core defining properties of a capitalist-type economy could be expressed in its "general formula," M-C-ΔM, in which M stands for money, C for commodity, and ΔM for valorized money or profit. Broken down into its elements, this formula consists of nothing more than two exchange moments, purchase (M-C) and sale (C-ΔM). And from Marx's point of view it is, as stated, deficient because it does not explicitly identify production as one of the crucial elements in the creation of surplus value.[25] However, if the M-C segment is understood to include the purchase of the factors of production and their employment (for Marx, especially labor power), this shortcoming is overcome. This "general formula" is clearly meant to capture more than the analysis of exchange into purchase and sale elements. Its central claim is rather to be found in the terminus ΔM. Understood in the light of that goal (surplus value), every one of capital's individual components—money, commodities (including labor), and activities (purchase, sale, production)— becomes a different mode of value, "value-in-process" as Marx sometimes writes.[26] The economy in all its aspects is absorbed into the valorization process of capital. Here is a second and related feature of this characterization: the terminus ΔM is not merely the endpoint of the process, but its purpose, its driving force and soul.[27] Indeed, Marx goes so far as to sketch a history of (bourgeois) economic thought, the guiding thread of which is the recognition of expansion-oriented accumulation as the "spur" and "highest law" of capitalism. A third notion contained in the schema of M-C-ΔM is that its terminus has no limit precisely because it is not tied to need or consumption but to the expansion of wealth. For that reason also, the process is self-renewing: every achieved stage of ΔM is the starting point of another iteration of the cycle, dedicated to securing yet a further growth of capital.[28]

Marx contrasts this idea of the core of capitalism to the concept of the (generic) precapitalist economy: C-M-C or its variants C-C (barter) or C (where C no longer stands for commodity but for the consumption and other goods of an autarkic household). Once more we have the possibility of exchange, of purchase and sale, mediated by money or through direct barter. What distinguishes this form of economic metabolism from that

[25] Marx, *Capital*, vol. 1, p. 257; Marx, *A Contribution to the Critique of Political Economy*, p. 123. For limitations see Marx, *Capital*, vol. 1, p. 266, and vol. 2, pp. 109–43.
[26] Marx, *Capital*, vol. 1, pp. 255–56.
[27] Marx, *Capital*, vol. 1, p. 250; Marx, *MEGA*, II.3.1, p. 13.
[28] Marx, *Grundrisse*, p. 516; Marx, *MEGA*, II.3.1, p. 15. Marx's sketch of this history of economic thought can be found in Marx, *Ökonomische Manuskripte, 1863–1867*, in *MEGA*, II.4.1, pp. 374–78.

described in M-C-ΔM is that its terminus, C, is solely a use-value, some-thing to satisfy a need, to be consumed. All precapitalist societies are characterized by Marx as having economic systems dedicated to the fulfilling of needs, typically the opulent requirements of the dominant group and the more minimal needs allowed to the direct producer. This determining end of production lies outside the production/exchange cir-cuit itself: it is, therefore, in Marx's scheme, a noneconomic goal.[29] The property of being a noneconomic goal gives rise, according to Marx, to a number of important consequences. First, because it is consumption it is finite and limited. Marx does not make this connection directly, but it is clearly the thought linking use-value on the one side and the limits of production on the other. This in turn means that the explosive, expan-sionary quality of capitalism, the pressure to grow beyond every achieved state, is absent in these economies. Second (and relatedly), it involves the idea that the economy is embedded in the community or, better, that it is a profoundly political economy in the sense that its relations of produc-tion are permeated by the (noneconomic) positions of persons and that its (exploitation's) purposes, lying outside the sphere of the economy, ema-nate from the status and other needs of the dominant group.[30]

Earlier we saw that Marx's account of the double nature of the com-modity as use and exchange value could be traced back to Aristotle's discussion of goods in the *Politics,* Book 1. Now we are able to state more exactly just how deep Marx's debt is to the Aristotelian idea of the household economy. For his grand distinction between the capitalist economy, M-C-ΔM, and the generic precapitalist one, C-M-C, is in both its substance and method taken directly and explicitly from Aristotle and the ancient Greek tradition.[31] This method of conceptualizing the econ-omy is Aristotelian (I use this term here and in much of the following as a shorthand that embraces more than Aristotle's writings, and includes also Xenophon's) in that it directs our attention to the end or purpose, the *telos,* as the informing principle of economic activity, and also because it seeks, as we shall see, to discriminate among these possible ends and to

[29] See Marx, *Capital,* vol. 3, p. 449. On Marx's tendency to collapse precapitalist econo-mies into a single form see Elster, *Making Sense of Marx,* p. 273. On the goal of the precapitalist economy see Marx, *MEGA,* II.3.6, p. 2132, and II.3.1, p. 12; Marx, *Capital,* vol. 3, p. 443, and vol. 1, pp. 250, 253.

[30] See Marx, *MEGA,* II.3.6, pp. 2132–33; Marx, *Capital,* vol. 3, p. 970; Marx, *Grundrisse,* pp. 487–88; Marx, *Theories of Surplus Value,* vol. 2, p. 528.

[31] Marx, *MEGA,* II.3.1, pp. 15–16; Marx, *A Contribution to the Critique of Political Economy,* p. 137n; Marx, *Capital,* vol. 1, p. 253n; Marx, *Results of the Immediate Process of Production,* p. 1041n.

judge the corresponding economic formations in the light of a valuation of the ends being served.

Marx, with Aristotle and Xenophon, distinguishes, on the substantive level, between two broad types of purpose in the economy: that of the household, of things useful and necessary for life and the good life, and that of unlimited acquisition—*oikonomikē* (C) and *chrēmatistikē* (ΔM). When Marx writes that all precapitalist economies are oriented to the satisfaction of need, he means that in their varied ways they can be described as household-type economies: "*The art of household management* . . . the science whereby humans are capable of increasing the things of the house . . . the things of the house [are] its totality of goods . . . a good is what is useful to each and all . . . useful [is] everything which one knows how to use."[32] Observe that in this excerpt of Marx's from Xenophon's *Oeconomicus* VI.4, Xenophon and Marx focus on the idea of the household economy as one defined above all by the centrality of usefulness within it. And so too, on the larger scale of historical/economic formations, the notion of the *oikos,* with the economy subordinated to the needs of its dominant members, captures the crucial distinguishing trait of the premodern order of things, that is, of C-M-C or its variants.

The portrait of capitalism, on the other hand, is that of the chrematistic life magnified and transformed from a personal corruption into the "driving force" of the economic system as a whole, *pleonexia* writ large and depersonalized. Here wealth is the end, not in the form of consumption goods for the community's dominant group (a goal that would impose limits on growth of the economy) but as value, profit without limit— "abstract" wealth, as Marx occasionally terms it. The notions of the limitlessness of wealth not tied to need, of the pursuit of gain as destructive of a community built around need and the judgment as to its perverse consequences when compared to an economy ordered by need all figure prominently in Marx's account of M-C-ΔM/capitalism, and they are steeped in the ancient texts (foremost among them the *Politics*) which are the original source of this, the foundation of Marx's political economy. When one considers the many theoretical tributaries that flow from this picture of capitalism and of its antecedent forms—for example, the theory of the technological dynamism of capitalism (and of the economic conservatism of all earlier epochs), the theory of crises of overproduction,

---

[32] Marx, *Xenophon: Von der Haushaltungskunst,* in Marx, *Exzerpte und Notizen. 1843 bis Januar 1845, MEGA,* IV.2, p. 391.

and the theory of capitalism's emancipatory material results systematically turned into their opposites—the depth of Marx's debt to Aristotle is evident, and some of its detail is brought out in the sections that follow.

The idea of the watershed transformation involved in the move from C-M-C to M-C-ΔM economies gave Marx a neo-Aristotelian theoretical language different from that of classical liberalism with which to analyze the dissolution of the despotic *oikos*-model economy and the emergence of one characterized in large measure by contract, freedom, independence, and equality. Now, the Lockean language of self-ownership and of the rights that emerge from the dissolving of the relations of dependence typical of the old world yields to a more recognizably marxist portrait of the foundations of this change: the emergence of a capitalist market economy. At the core of this dissolution is the ending of a use-value-driven economy, of a consumption economy governed by the needs of the dominant group. With the ending of use-value/need as the direct and determining object of the economy (together with the reproduction of the community as a certain sort of ordered whole), all of the artificial (in the sense of exogenous) constraints on the economy also dissolve: gender, race, nationality no longer act as barriers to the expansion of the economy.[33] To be more precise, all aspects of the premodern world, from its status distinctions to its divisions between communities, are leveled by the bourgeois revolution, and their elements are transformed and absorbed into the new economic process, M-C-ΔM or the valorization of capital. Where the production of ever greater wealth, abstract and impersonal—that is, not bound by consumption and not individualized in the person of its owner as was the case with landed property—is the governing purpose and where, accordingly, there can be no little or no barrier to the commodification of things or persons, everything takes on an economic hue and becomes one of the moments in the creation of wealth.[34] What we see here, then, is a recasting of the language of dissolution: the end of relations of direct domination and of a noneconomic or

[33] Marx, *Grundrisse*, pp. 410, 502, 541; Marx, *Capital*, vol. 1, pp. 197, 209, 345; Marx, *MEGA*, II.3.6, pp. 2133, 2288; Marx and Engels, *German Ideology*, p. 73; Marx, *Theories of Surplus Value*, vol. 3, p. 448; Marx, *Communist Manifesto*, p. 509.

[34] See Marx, *Economic and Philosophical Manuscripts*, in *MECW*, vol. 3, p. 266; Marx, *Grundrisse*, pp. 156, 222, 408, 410, 530; Marx and Engels, *German Ideology*, pp. 73, 86; Marx, *Draft of an Article on Friedrich List's Book "Das nationale System der politischen Oekonomie,"* in *MECW*, vol. 4, p. 266; Marx, *Poverty of Philosophy*, in *MECW*, vol. 6, p. 113; Marx, *Theories of Surplus Value*, vol. 3, p. 448.

status hierarchy is understood in the light of the death of use-value-driven economies of the precapitalist type. The equality of persons and independence from relations of subordination which were central elements of one way of portraying capitalism are now understood as a function of the emergence of an economy whose god is wealth, not that of individuals, but wealth abstract, mobile and expanding, in a condition of "absolute becoming"; we see a discourse the very vocabulary of which savors of a standpoint grounded, at least in part, in the world before capitalism.

The impersonal nature of capital and its powerful expansionary drive—two related properties, as we have suggested—create a society in which all relations assume a purely economic form. The antique and profoundly political economy, one permeated by extraeconomic factors and seeking above all the satisfaction of the noneconomic needs of its dominant members, is replaced by an economy the binding cement of which is the cash "nexus" and which aims at the expansion of capital. Or, as Marx sometimes puts the point, the *seigneur* or lord departs the stage to be replaced by money (capital) as the economy's controlling force.[35] In less metaphorical terms, we might say that the overdetermining master of the *oikos*-model economy (with the resultant subjection of the economy to his needs) disappears. The economy and its workings are thereby emancipated and are subject to no law save that of the increase of capital. The economy, in short, is disembedded and becomes itself the all-absorbing structure and determining force over society. In such a world, the definition of humans as political animals, the assertion of the primacy of the political, makes little sense. And so too is a type of political economic analysis which takes its bearings from a conception of the good life, of how to make the best citizen, and so forth, singularly inappropriate. A form of analysis embedded in an overarching theory of politics or the good life is suitable for an epoch of the C-M-C type, with its subordinated economy; but in a system in which the autonomous economic process, impersonal and automatic, rules, in which the guiding hand is invisible precisely because it no longer resides in the dominant community, another sort of analysis is required.

For a new world, a new mode of explanation was needed: one which, in Raymond Boudon's words, "distinguishes classes of economic agents according to their function, which sees the foundation of value in labor and

---

[35] See Marx, *MEGA*, II.3.1, pp. 116–17; Marx, *Capital*, vol. 1, p. 179, and Marx and Engels, *German Ideology*, p. 397; Marx, *Economic and Philosophical Manuscripts*, p. 267.

which sets for itself the essential objective of analyzing the phenomena of growth."[36] Economics for the first time becomes a science independent of politics, the study of autonomous laws of production and exchange. And because those are just the laws now permeating all aspects of society as they are absorbed into the valorization process of capital, so economics becomes the master science of modernity.[37] It is for that reason that Marx's own political economy draws its principal concepts from modern economic analysis; and it is for that reason also that the analysis of purely economic forces occupies such a central place in his account of capitalism. The commodity, or embodied value, is the natural starting point for the study of bourgeois society, just as a conversation between Socrates and two *oikos* despots, Kritoboulos and Ischomachos, about the proper use of things was the fitting point to begin an examination of the household economy. It is not unreasonable to speculate that this idea of a watershed transformation, distinguishing the new society from all of its predecessors, penetrated even into the language of Marx's political economy. The ghostly literary world of *Capital:* of forces, collective workers, of capital endowed with will and capable of acting, with hardly so much as a trace of human actors in their individual guise, is not an inexplicable artifact of Marx's prose. Early in his life he had written that objects have become our language and that we could hardly understand a human language. By these remarks I think Marx meant that the language to express the properties of an economy indifferent to the intercourse of individuals and to their needs must take on the vocabulary of objects and impersonal forces, unlike the language of an earlier economy, one in which the human being (more accurately, one group among them) was the purpose of production.[38]

Marx's political economy, then, is firmly anchored in that modern theoretical discourse, the categories of which, insofar as they depict "value-in-motion," are, he writes, "valid . . . for the relations of production belonging to this historically determined [capitalist] mode of produc-

---

[36] Raymond Boudon, *La place du désordre: Critique des théories du changement social* (Paris: Presses Universitaires de France, 1984), p. 18; my translation. See Marx, *Capital*, vol. 1, p. 444n; Marx and Engels, *The Holy Family*, in MECW, vol. 4, p. 122; Marx, *MEGA*, II.3.6, p. 2268.

[37] Marx and Engels, *German Ideology*, pp. 409, 412, 414; Marx, *Grundrisse*, p. 104. See Georg Lukács, "The Changing Function of Historical Materialism," in *History and Class Consciousness*, trans. Rodney Livingstone (Cambridge: MIT Press, 1971), p. 92.

[38] Marx, *Comments on James Mill*, in MECW, vol. 3, p. 227; Marx, *Grundrisse*, pp. 487–88; Marx and Engels, *German Ideology*, p. 86.

tion."[39] That latter thought, together with the rather more elliptical reference just cited, suggests that Marx brackets this new idiom with critical qualifiers, with the language of a nonbourgeois, Aristotelian view of the place of the economy. That higher-order theory of the economy provided Marx the background with which to account for the historical novelty of the capitalist economy. This same theory suggested to him ways of understanding the unique defining characteristics of capitalism. And last, it provided him some critical purchase on the society he was observing, and a way of thinking about the one that would succeed it. Virtually all that is important in Marx's enveloping account and criticism of capitalism is fully intelligible only against the background of his reflection upon the *oikos*-model economy. Indeed, it is just that background that led Marx to stress the guiding thread he took up in his efforts to explain the bourgeois world: valorization, or the creation of ΔM.[40] In the discussions that follow, I trace out the main components of that effort—community, time, and freedom—keeping in mind always that, according to Marx, it is the shifting place of the economy in the architecture of the human community, from the *oikos* to the chrematistic pattern, that explains the world he saw before him.

7.2   Communities

7.2.1   The "Real Community" of Use-Value

One of the keys to understanding the premodern world, Marx thought, is the idea that there the community was the "presupposition," the foundation of production and exchange. What it means to say that the community is the foundation, and why that would be a distinctive attribute of prebourgeois economies, has to be explained, as also does the notion of community itself, a word that on its face has a rather too woolly, romantic, and undifferentiated character to appeal to an author who described the history of all hitherto existing societies as that of conflict between oppressor and oppressed.[41] That last proposition we can, in turn, use to

---

[39] Marx, *Capital*, vol. 1, p. 169. And see Marx, *Grundrisse*, p. 106; Marx and Engels, *German Ideology*, pp. 409–11.

[40] Marx, *Results of the Immediate Process of Production*, p. 977.

[41] Marx, *Grundrisse*, pp. 492–93, 509; Marx, *Capital*, vol. 3, p. 970, and Marx, *The Poverty of Philosophy*, p. 194. Kymlicka, in *Liberalism, Community, and Culture*, correctly captures the distance between Marx and contemporary communitarians along a number of

grasp Marx's understanding of the noncapitalist community and of the place of the economy within it. Every society capable of producing a surplus, some increment above the subsistence requirements of the direct producers themselves, has also witnessed the transfer of all or a portion of that surplus from the producers to those who, in one fashion or another, control the economy. In a word, exploitation is a property of all suprasubsistence economies.

Now, the transfer of the surplus product takes place between (let us say, for the purpose of simplification) two groups, which Marx occasionally (and popular marxism frequently) designates as classes. In that sense, any community can be disaggregated into (at least) two classes, those who directly create the surplus and those who "pump" it out of them. But this application of the idea of class to precapitalist societies is too theoretically blunt to capture Marx's meaning, and, taken literally, it collapses into one form the fundamentally different character of C-M-C and M-C-ΔM economies. Marx, to be sure, does employ the term "class" when speaking about ancient and feudal societies, but it is a loose and generic use, serviceable perhaps for making the point that the world before capitalism was founded on exploitation and accordingly that it was not an idyllic, organic community, but not valuable for any application beyond that.[42] The reason for this is that neither in its foundation, instruments, nor purposes was this exploitation or the group conducting it strictly eco-

---

conceptual lines. The attachment of some of the latter to a romanticized view of the family and/or the premodern community, and Marx's fairly clear-eyed grasp of their nature, is surely one of these lines of differentiation.

[42] See Godelier, *The Mental and the Material*, pp. 231–33, and for different interpretations see G. E. M. de Ste. Croix, "Class in Marx's Conception of History, Ancient and Modern," *New Left Review* 146 (1984): 94–111; Ste. Croix, "Karl Marx and the History of Classical Antiquity," *Arethusa* 8 (1975): 7–41; Ste. Croix, "Karl Marx and the Interpretation of Ancient and Modern History," in Bernard Chavance, ed., *Marx en perspective* (Paris: Editions de l'Ecole des Hautes Etudes en Sciences Sociales, 1985); Ste. Croix, *The Class Struggle in the Ancient Greek World* (Ithaca: Cornell University Press, 1981), pp. 31–111. Vidal-Naquet, "Les esclaves grecs étaient-ils une classe?" in his *Le chasseur noir* (Paris: Maspero, 1983), pp. 212–21. Finley, *The Ancient Economy* (Berkeley: University of California Press, 1973), pp. 45–61, 183. See also Max Weber, *Economy and Society*, ed. Guenther Roth and Claus Wittich, trans. Ephraim Fischoff et al. (Berkeley: University of California Press, 1978), vol. 1, pp. 302–7. Kostas Papaioannou, usually such a profound guide to and critic of Marx, is incorrect to attribute to Marx a single, purely economic theory of the foundations of class; see Papaioannou, *De Marx et du marxisme* (Paris: Gallimard, 1983), pp. 190–235. Ober, *Mass and Elite in Democratic Athens* (Princeton: Princeton University Press, 1989), pp. 192–247, is rather more sympathetic to the use of the idea of class in explanations of the politics of the ancient world.

nomic and that, as we shall see, distinguishes these phenomena from their capitalist analogues.

At the most basic level, what Marx intends when he writes that the community was the presupposition of production is that membership and status in that community were important prerequisites of access to major economic goods, for example, land. Status, expressed juridically and in other more amorphous social conventions, was prior to and permeated the economic domain: political relations were relations of production. In such a world, the purely economic idea of class has little applicability—power here precedes rather than emerges from the economy, and individuals coalesce into groups according to their various status positions in the community: master/slave, leisured/mechanical laborer, male/female. It is precisely this embeddedness in the noneconomic institutions and values of society which gives the exploitation relation of the precapitalist world its peculiar political cast.[43] The community with its status-based distinctions as the foundation of the economy and so of relations of exploitation is also, Marx argues, the "final purpose" of the economy: the reproduction of that community with its various and ordered strata, the making of better citizens, a "life appropriate to a certain status or condition" (*Standesmässige Existenz*), the "full human development" of the masters are some of the (noneconomic) governing purposes of the premodern economy which Marx identifies.[44]

And finally, the instruments by which these ends are achieved—the techniques of exploitation—are according to Marx themselves extra-economic. By "extraeconomic" is meant the use of coercion (broadly conceived) between persons, sometimes outright ownership of the laboring person, and in general the transfer of goods between their producers and the master group which takes place in a context marked by hierarchy and direct (nonmarket) domination. It is to be observed here that "extra-economic" instruments for the extraction of surpluses are typical, according to Marx, of "natural" economies, that is, of those economies in which markets and their voluntary, bilateral exchanges are not the principal modes of transaction, and especially not of those transactions associated with the employment and exploitation of labor.

[43] Marx, *Economic and Philosophical Manuscripts*, p. 266; Marx, *Capital*, vol. 3, pp. 754–55, 731, 1021. See also Elster, *Making Sense of Marx*, p. 327.

[44] Marx, *Results of the Immediate Process of Production*, p. 1030; Marx, *Capital*, vol. 1, p. 533. See also Marx, *Capital*, vol. 3, p. 970; Marx, *Grundrisse*, pp. 487–88; Marx, *MEGA*, II.3.6, p. 2133.

If we now descend from this rather general level to the characteristics of the microorganization of precapitalist production, we find (to the very limited extent that Marx addresses this matter at all) many of the properties of the former reiterated, *mutatis mutandis*. The cooperation of persons in production here rests on domination and servitude; it is not mediated by exchange.[45] This is to say, among other things, that relations of authority at the level of the production unit in these noncapitalist economies, the power of the *despotēs* or of the *pater familias* is, at its foundation, bound up with status, gender, or political authority rather than grounded directly in the economy or ownership of economic goods.[46] If the foundations of authority at the microlevel of the economy are political/status in nature, the purpose governing the organization of production (the division of labor, technical innovation, and pressure on the producers) is itself distinctive: use-value. "Its [the ancient economy's] way of looking [at production and the division of labor] was what was *better:* quality [only rarely is *pleiōn*, or "more," mentioned]; otherwise always *kallion* ["more beautifully"]."[47] This same use-value orientation also accounts for the conservative pace of technological innovation before capitalism. Saturable needs, a preference for consumption (broadly construed as leisure, citizenship duties, and so forth) over productive reinvestment, and the absence of a mechanism compelling the more efficient production of *pleiōn*, of ever more things, are among the reasons for this conservatism.[48] This same consumption/use-value-driven economic formation also rebounds on the consumption of labor and land, in short, on exploitation. Once more the finitude of the needs to be satisfied, the fact that there is an upper threshold beyond which further production and pressure on labor make no sense, shapes the microeconomy by limiting the exploitation of labor (and land). Overwork is an exception in antiquity and so too is the overuse of land.[49] This is not to say, it should be

[45] Marx, *Capital,* vol. 3, pp. 926, 930, and vol. 1, pp. 173, 452; Marx, *Grundrisse,* pp. 245, 498; Marx, *Theories of Surplus Value,* vol. 3, p. 400; Marx, *MEGA,* II.3.1, pp. 229–30.

[46] Marx, *Capital,* vol. 3, p. 1021, and vol. 1, p. 172; Marx, *Results of the Immediate Process of Production,* p. 1083.

[47] Marx, *MEGA,* II.3.1, p. 257 (my translation), and see also pp. 173, 246–47, 255, and Marx, *Capital,* vol. 1, pp. 487–88n.

[48] See Marx, *Capital,* vol. 1, p. 617; Marx, *Theories of Surplus Value,* vol. 2, p. 528; Marx, *MEGA,* II.3.6, p. 2133; Elster, *Making Sense of Marx,* p. 276; Robert Brenner, "The Social Basis of Economic Development," in John E. Roemer, ed., *Analytical Marxism* (Cambridge: Cambridge University Press, 1986), pp. 24, 28–29.

[49] Marx, *Capital,* vol. 1, p. 345; Marx, *Economic and Philosophical Manuscripts,* p. 266; Marx, *MEGA,* II.3.1, p. 173.

added, that for Marx the limited exploitation of labor was a consequence of a more humane society or of more nobly minded masters; rather, it was a function of the restricted need for surpluses inherent in a use-value-governed economy.

The story Marx offers us about the community before the bourgeois one, that of the "real community [*realen Gemeinwesens*]" as he once named it,[50] is an account of the *oikos*-model community and economy writ large, of the C-M-C type or one of its variants. In this community the economy is subordinated or embedded in noneconomic political and social institutions and subject to noneconomic purposes. Production, its techniques, discipline, and other relational aspects are here permeated by the political, religious, and social characteristics of the community. It is also, as we have observed, a contained economy. And that idea of containment is simply one way of highlighting the fact that, for Marx, the binding cement of this community is not purely economic. There may well be exchange of goods within and between these communities, and the interdependency associated with a growing division of labor does certainly create a bond of need, as Aristotle had recognized in Book 5 of the *Nicomachean Ethics;* but Marx saw (as also had Aristotle) that these exchanges could occur within the framework of the community and subordinated to its purposes.[51] In sum, the purposiveness of this community was displayed in, among other ways, the use-value orientation of the economy and, phrased negatively, in its stagnant quality—stagnant because of the absence of those institutions by which actors in these societies might be compelled, pressured, to generate economic growth.

If, as Marx writes, humans (or some class of them) are here the "end" of production, and if that end gives the economy its particular embedded nature, subject to the will of persons, it is also the case that this purposiveness which provides the community its coherence resides in the masters, in, for example, the ancient despot whose slaves make possible his "full human development" or with the head of the medieval patriarchal family who exploits his wife and children.[52] The precapitalist community, at its core, was exploitative, hierarchical and, for most of its members, unfree, and that lack of freedon was part of the price paid for the contained, human-controlled character of the economy. Marx's point,

[50] Marx, *Grundrisse*, p. 509.

[51] See Marx, *Capital*, vol. 3, p. 443, and Marx, *A Contribution to the Critique of Political Economy*, p. 50.

[52] Marx, *Capital*, vol. 1, pp. 171, 533; Marx, *Results of the Immediate Process of Production*, p. 1083.

however, is not to bring this type of society before the bar of historical-moral judgment but to seek to explain the way in which these phenomena were distinctive, and that explanation, as we have seen, focuses on the noneconomic properties of the foundations, instruments, and purposes of surplus extraction which are, in turn, but so many ways of expressing aspects of C-M-C and its variants.

7.2.2   The Bourgeois Community

Here, as with the prebourgeois community analyzed in the preceding pages, I intend only to lay out the boundary lines of Marx's idea of the community under capitalism, such as they flow conceptually from its "general formula," M-C-ΔM. A more detailed discussion of Marx's theory of market and nonmarket institutions in bourgeois society is offered in the following sections. Let us begin by reversing the order of our examination of Marx on C-M-C–type economies and start with what Marx took to be the characteristic microeconomy of capitalist production, the factory. The reader should be forewarned that the use I am about to make of Marx's reflections on the factory intentionally (though not, I think, unfaithfully) selects certain of its features, leaving to one side for the present certain other (and arguably the more important) of its properties.

"The power of activity which creates value by value existing for itself . . . is posited," Marx writes, "in production resting on machinery, as the character of the production process itself, including its material movements." The production process of capital is, in short, a visible exemplar of a broader social process, M-C-ΔM, the "automatic [i.e., not controlled by humans] subject" of which is value.[53] What Marx is arguing, in the most general terms, is that if we strip the production process (for the time being) of the commanding presence of the capitalist within it and therefore also of the element of prior planning and consider it as an assemblage of interconnected machines served by persons, we get a picture in miniature of the modern community embraced within the M-C-ΔM process. One notices immediately in Marx's metaphor the inhuman quality of capitalism, a language that, as we remarked above, pervades his writings: inhuman not primarily in the sense of cruelty or evil of any sort, but as not being subject to human control, as the opposite, in short, of C-M-C economies.

To exploit this analogy, we might begin by observing that under the

---

[53] Marx, *Grundrisse*, p. 693; Marx, *Capital*, vol. 1, p. 255.

roof of the factory there is indeed a community, an association of producers engaged in interlocking activity. This is a world not of isolated
individuals but of persons bound to one another through their functional
interdependence.[54] Within this nexus of (almost physical) interdependence, individuals occupy different positions with one major hierarchical
gradation, that between those holding supervisory positions and the primary producers themselves. The interlocking functions of the machines
require different types of operators, and they also call forth a coordinating supervisory role. The allocation of persons among the various tasks
and along the principal hierarchical divide is not (in this very adumbrated
account of the factory) the consequence of an a priori, extraeconomic
inequality among them. Rather, it is the result of "objective"—that is,
impersonal—forces, here the technological composition of the production unit and the resulting technical division of activities and power.
Distinctions of function and rank emerge in this microeconomy, but
strictly as a consequence of the objective laws of its operations and not
because of pre-existing rank or privilege. In contrast to our earlier characterization of the political economy of the ancient world, we could say of
capitalism that, according to Marx, relations of production are here not
internal to political relations. This description is one way of expanding on
the claim that the factory represents the "technological truth"[55] of
capitalism: the more general "truth" being that classes in the bourgeois
world are largely artifacts of the economic system, untainted by status.

A second component of Marx's use of the factory as a mirror held up
before the surrounding society is the origin and purposiveness of the
factory community. The association of workers in a factory is posited,
Marx writes, not by the workers but by capital, and so too are the towns
that concentrate producers geographically so that the needs of the new
spatiotemporally compressed production process and technology may be
met.[56] What Marx means by this (the details will be discussed further on)
is essentially that their community has its origins in something unfree,
coercive, a type of compulsion, and, more generally, that the community
is the creature of a process rather than of their wills, of the revolution in
the scale of production characteristic of capitalism. Inside the mechanized
atelier, the purposive quality of human action—the capacity of persons to
determine their behavior according to a concept of an end and to act in

---

[54] Marx, *Capital*, vol. 3, p. 731, and vol. 1, pp. 547–48; Marx, *Grundrisse*, p. 702;
Marx, *MEGA*, II.3.6, p. 2024.

[55] Marx, *MEGA*, II.3.6, p. 2059.

[56] Marx, *MEGA*, II.3.6, p. 2013; Marx, *Capital*, vol. 2, p. 221, and vol. 3, p. 172.

unison in pursuit of that end—is replaced by the subordination of these persons to the valorization process made visible here in actions and relations imposed by the needs of the system of machines.[57]

This community is an unfree one, in its origins and in its actual workings. To its members, being there out of necessity and being united in a purpose not of their own but, in a sense, selected for them, their community must seem to them an "alien bond."[58] It is alien not in the quasi-psychological sense that this term has acquired in some studies of Marx but in something like the way in which Eumaios, for example, was a member of Odysseus's *oikos,* though still and unalterably a stranger in it. There out of necessity and never fully participating in the purpose and hence *philia* of that household, Eumaios was in a recognizable sense homeless, without a hearth. His entry into the *oikos* was the result of an act of direct force, and the power ruling over him was intensely personal and violent, that of a king and a master. The homelessness of the factory community (and, by extension, of the bourgeois world) is less the consequence of such force than of the "violence of things," of constraint generated by an uncontrolled economy. The factory, in its technological aspect, serves as a useful metaphor for Marx by displaying the "objective" (again meaning: impersonal, not resting on direct domination) foundation of the alienness of the modern community.

If we now step back from the detail of Marx's image of the factory as a mirror, we will be in a better position to summarize his understanding of the community under capital. We might begin here by calling once more on Marx's "general formula" for capital. The universalism of the system described by that schema we have already observed: knowing no bounds, neither of religion, gender, or nationality, it is cosmopolitan on the world stage and all-absorbing domestically. What is left after this solventlike action is a community the "social bond" of which is purely economic, defined in terms of exchange value and money, in short, of the various moments and interconnections of the valorization process of capital: "an association founded on competition." Groups of individuals, distinguished functionally and vertically according to their roles in the valorization circuit of capital, do emerge, and these are classes in the strict, or capitalist, sense. This type of social gradation means, for Marx, that relations between persons and between groups are not masked by patriarchal, blood lineage or by any other kind of noneconomic position:

[57] Marx, *Capital,* vol. 1, pp. 284, 287, 290; Marx, *MEGA,* II.3.1, pp. 83, 86, and II.3.6, pp. 2014, 2020, 2022; Marx, *Theories of Surplus Value,* vol. 2, p. 548.
[58] Marx and Engels, *German Ideology,* p. 80.

rather, all are "personifications" or "bearers" of various aspects of economic relations. (This idea is explored in more detail below.) Marx's florid language should not conceal from us what is in fact a fairly straightforward claim about classes in bourgeois society (in contradistinction to superficially identical groups in the antique world): that they are the untainted artifacts, the efflux of the workings of an economic process indifferent to everything save surplus value (profit).[59] The capitalist, on this view, is the "conscious subject" of the M-C-ΔM process; the worker, "personified labor." Such power as the capitalist has over the worker is fundamentally different (both in its origins and, as we shall see, its purpose) from that of the precapitalist master. For it is only by virtue of the possession of money (capital), which is in its nature indifferent to its individual owner, that the capitalist has authority.[60] Conversely, it is the absence of capital, and not any extraeconomically established position of inferiority, that makes the worker a worker. It is just this indifference, the impersonality of the valorization process—in contrast to the intensely personal character of the hierarchical world before capitalism—that constitutes, according to Marx, the material and nonjuridical foundation of equality under capitalism.[61]

We might differently express this equality by saying that all are subject to the requirements of the capital circuit. And this idea leads to a second extension of Marx's factory metaphor: that of the purposiveness and freedom of this community's members. Recall that in the microcosm of the mechanized atelier (in the short account of it presented above), it is the movements and interconnections of the machines which cause the arrangements and actions of the persons who serve them and, in that sense, one could say, again allegorically, that purposiveness resides in things and thus restricts the agency of the individuals under their control. If we move from this rather *Modern Times* retelling of Marx to a more substantial (though still too general) level his argument can be stated as follows. The

[59] Marx, *Capital*, vol. 1, p. 179; Marx, *The Poverty of Philosophy*, p. 194.

[60] Marx, *MEGA*, II.3.1, p. 16; Marx, *Theories of Surplus Value*, vol. 2, p. 548; Marx, *Results of the Immediate Process of Production*, p. 989; Marx, *MEGA*, II.3.6, p. 2161; Marx, *Capital*, vol. 3, pp. 731, 1021, and vol. 1, p. 247; Elster, *Making Sense of Marx*, p. 327.

[61] Marx, *Grundrisse*, p. 246; Marx, *Capital*, vol. 1, pp. 151–52. François Furet is wrong to take Marx to task for not grasping the egalitarian currents at work in modernity, at both political and social economic levels; see Furet, "Le système conceptuel de la *Démocratie en Amerique*," in Alexis de Tocqueville, *De la démocratie en Amerique*, vol. 1 (Paris: Garnier-Flammarion, 1981), p. 40, and Furet, *Marx and the French Revolution*, trans. Deborah Kan Furet (Chicago: University of Chicago Press, 1988), p. 27.

governing purpose of the community under capital, a purpose common to all of its main moments, is that of the "valorization of value," the creation of surplus value, or, in its realized, money form, ΔM.[62] Individual agents in this economy are bound to one another as a function of the relationships between the various and connected movements of capital through its circuit. And it is those bonds, expressed in their end-directed form as ΔM, which are instantiated in individuals as their "subjective" wills. The mechanism by which the purposiveness of the system is translated into the intentions of its actors is what Marx calls the "silent compulsion" of economic laws—meaning, as I discuss below, an array of constraints which has the effect of requiring agents to adopt the process's ends as their own.[63] The agency of both the community and of individuals, agency here understood as the capacity for self-determination (as the setting of one's own ends), is diminished under capitalism, Marx argues. One additional and revealing consequence of this shift of the locus of purposiveness from the community (or its dominant group) to an all-embracing economic cycle is the breathtaking capacity for economic growth, intensive and extensive, of capitalism. That is, in place of the reproduction of the community and its vertical social order as the end governing the economy, we find a purpose, ΔM, which knows no limit because it is not bound by need of any sort. It was, paradoxically, only the detachment of the economy from the direct governance by the community which made possible the emergence of a material foundation that would, so Marx believed, allow the re-creation of a society governed by its own purposes and without servitude, ancient or modern.[64]

We have now unfolded the distinction between C-M-C and M-C-ΔM economies at two descending orders of generality: at the first level, an identification of the different ends being pursued, and on the second, a drawing out of that distinction into a somewhat more finely detailed portrait of the communities associated with each economy. That second level of analysis drew our attention to the consequences of the absorption of the formerly noneconomic spheres into the valorization circuit of capital, to the meaning of the shift of the location of the economy from one permeated by the political and social spheres to a process grown independent and determining of these spheres. I have traced this transformation

---

[62] Marx, *Capital*, vol. 2, p. 180.

[63] See Marx, *Capital*, vol. 1, pp. 254, 289; Marx, *Results of the Immediate Process of Production*, pp. 989, 1051.

[64] Marx, *MEGA*, II.3.1, p. 327; Marx, *Capital*, vol. 3, pp. 182, 957–59. Marx, *Economic and Philosophical Manuscripts*, p. 243.

and its impact on the community principally through a sketch of Marx's concepts of class and power, of interdependence and independence, and of purposiveness and freedom in the bourgeois world. The binding thread uniting these disparate elements was the end, C or ΔM, which informed and shaped in different ways each of the moments arrived at through an analysis of the two processes.

What I introduce now is another level of detail for the deployment of Marx's arguments. Here again the overarching structure of the account M-C-ΔM (and the contrast to use-value economies), is repeated as the specific object of our investigation: the shifting location of the economy. Now, however, we will, with Marx, expand on the M-C-ΔM formula and its thus-far unstated components. Those components are the market and the production process itself, that is, the social relations of production within the workplace and the idea of classes. These two spheres, so different in their organizing principles, mutually condition one another, Marx argued, and together they constitute the principal forms of the social economy of capitalism. In this third ply of Marx's analysis of capitalism, we will be particularly concerned with the normative/critical elements. The sections that follow will thus explore (1) the antecedent conditions of the capitalist market and the emergence of classes from market exchanges; (2) the idea of unfreedom in the market; (3) an array of its perverse effects.

8. Markets

We saw in the preceding pages a sketch of Marx's acceptance of core elements of the classical liberal portrait of the dissolution of the old world and its replacement by something radically new, a process that could be described as the shift from status to contract or, in other words, from relations of direct domination to market relations between juridical self-owners. We also observed that he sought to place this liberal idiom within another language: the move from a use- to a surplus-value economy. And insofar as this transformation also involved the destruction of the family as the center of production and its replacement by a social economy, this shift might be described as the emergence of a fully interdependent economy.[65] In somewhat different words, the proclaimed independence of

[65] See Marx and Engels, *German Ideology,* p. 76, and Marx, *Capital,* vol. 3, p. 943.

persons in liberal economic/political philosophy is an attribute of their relations as contrasted to the direct domination of an earlier epoch. They are independent of a priori relations of subordination, but when their circumstances are compared to those of the yeoman's household, for example, the magnitude and nature of their dependency, now of a different sort, becomes clear. It is an "objective" dependency, one arising from an extensive division of labor on a social scale and the resulting need for exchange and the market.[66] Cast on that level—that is, of the transition from an individual to a social economy—this dependency is not (yet) a part of Marx's critique of capitalism but only one element of his account of the emergence of interdependency. I cite this illustration here to provide an example of Marx's embedding of the liberal idiom (in this case, of the independence of the agent) in his own theoretical language (personal/juridical independence in the context of an interdependent—that is, social—economy). Now, two other central attributes of the market person were, as we noted, her equality as a juridical person and self-owner and her freedom, meaning her self-disposition in relations with others. These characteristics are likewise embedded in another story, that of the antecedent conditions of the market; and the study of those conditions and their reproduction forms an important component of Marx's explanation and critique of capitalism, and it is to them that I now turn. Once we have displayed these conditions, we shall also be able to see more clearly the specific color, the capitalist character, according to Marx, of this interdependent, social economy.

8.1   Coercive Transfers: The Origins of the Market

One way of framing Marx's story about the antecedent conditions of the market is to treat it as historical/moral in purpose. That is, we might consider this account of capital's "original sin" to consist of a set of propositions about the actual origins of capitalist markets, set out with the intention of demonstrating their illegitimacy and, employing Robert Nozick's idea of justice-preserving exchanges, the illegitimacy of the transactions shaped by them. The normative dimension of this point I discuss only briefly here, the reason for my brevity being that while arguments of this type certainly figure in Marx's writings, their underpinnings are not among his more original contributions. This is so because Marx seems almost to want to effect an ironic reversal of the fundamental

[66] Marx, *Grundrisse*, pp. 161, 163; Marx, *Capital*, vol. 1, pp. 202–3.

tenets of liberalism itself. And to do that, he introduces no new normative considerations, but only the well-known ones shown in their inverted form. We might therefore designate this inversion as a part of Marx's immanent critique of capitalism.[67] Here, in compact expression, is how Marx presents elements of the argument: (a) Capitalism, far from needing independent persons, requires a servile population of individuals in the sense of persons who have little choice but to sell their labor. (b) For this servility to be assured, capitalism requires not the expansion of property ownership but its contraction, that is, that a sizable portion of the population be free of all property ownership, except ownership of themselves (as Marx writes, *vogelfrei*—free as little birds), hence self-owners in the most narrow sense and with a highly constricted option set. Capitalism thus depends on a thorough expropriation of the population, on their detachment from the means of providing for their own livelihood. (c) This transformation was wrought neither by an idyllic, contractual transfer of property nor indeed by voluntary, bilateral exchanges of any sort. Nor was market pressure, under conditions of the independent ownership of the land, sufficient to bring about this change. Rather, the creation of the modern working class was, Marx writes, an event inaugurated by acts of violence, of an often state-led set of coercive measures.[68]

Marx, I think, savored the juxtaposition of norms and facts contained in these observations on the origins of the capitalist market. To the normative centrality of property, self-ownership (including crucially owner-

---

[67] For further discussion of this immanent critique see Steven Lukes, *Marxism and Morality* (Oxford: Clarendon Press, 1985), pp. 52, 58. David Gauthier, *Morals by Agreement* (Oxford: Clarendon Press, 1986), p. 95, captures the liberal rejection of initial allocations of this type by insisting on the fairness of initial conditions and on liberalism as the justice of inputs.

[68] For (a) see Marx, *Capital*, vol. 1, pp. 880–81; for (b), Marx, *Grundrisse*, pp. 463, 507; Marx, *Capital*, vol. 1, p. 507; and for (c) Marx, *Capital*, vol. 1, pp. 809, 915–16, 926, 938; Marx, *Results of the Immediate Process of Production*, p. 1083. I do not consider here a possibility that for Marx would most certainly have been a counterfactual: that the transfers that resulted in the core pattern of holdings creating and constituting a capitalist labor market had been nonexpropriative and pacific. It does seem to me though that if markets can be shown, independently of whatever "original sin" may have brought about their birth, to restrict freedom in comparison to some feasible alternative, then the justice of those origins (let us say, on some entitlement theory of holdings and transfers) is not theoretically central for an argument that focuses on autonomy. In the pages that follow, I pursue a line of Marx's analysis and criticism of markets that does not invoke the story of their origins. G. A. Cohen develops a parallel argument showing the limits of Nozick's historical entitlement claims and maintaining that if the securing of liberty is really the dominant desideratum, then the end result of even innocent (on Nozickean grounds) exchanges may be deleterious. See Cohen, "Robert Nozick and Wilt Chamberlain: How Patterns Preserve Liberty," in John Arthur and William H. Shaw, eds., *Justice and Economic Distribution* (Englewood Cliffs, N.J.: Prentice-Hall, 1978), pp. 246–62.

ship of one's own labor), and independence and reliance on the market rather than on coercive, state action, he contrasted what he took to be capital's "original sin": large-scale expropriation, the appropriation of unpaid labor, and servility as a consequence of expropriation and of the violent circumstances that created that servility. No doubt, he especially relished this contrast because, as he wrote in Section Two of the *Communist Manifesto,* the intent to expropriate was among the things of which the communists were accused. The double-edged irony of these observations aside, they provide one way of situating analytically and evaluating the properties of agents and the market institutions in which they interact, and of describing the dissolution of the premodern world. They do this by setting out the historical backdrop to the market—the reason that agents appear there at all and that many appear selling their labor power. It is this meaning of the dissolution of the old world that (among other things) is not adequately captured in the idiom of the move from "status to contract." On the level of evaluation, this background analysis suggests that the freedom and independence of market agents—while real enough when compared to the situation of persons in a society composed of relations of direct domination—are tainted and made questionable by their coercive origins. Cast back against the classical liberal argument (the Lockean one, in Marx's account), such a history, if true, would call into question (on liberal grounds) the justice of the market-creating transfer and so, by extension, of principal features of the modern market insofar as they flow from that original transfer.

8.2   Choice and Constraints

I do not intend to engage in an extended examination of the immanent critical aspects of this history of capitalism's origins for, as I said above, its principles are sufficiently familiar, and sufficiently nonmarxist, that further attention to them would not be profitable. What I wish rather to do is to look at these observations, but at a higher level of abstraction and as a background element in Marx's theory of classes, markets, and freedom. Here I take my bearings from Marx's argument that the relation between buyer and seller in the labor market is shaped by their respective class positions.[69] Before they even meet in the market they are proletarian

[69] Marx, *Capital,* vol. 2, p. 115; Marx, *Results of the Immediate Process of Production,* p. 1015; Marx, *Capital,* vol. 1, pp. 723–24.

and capitalist; market behavior is determined, not in its detail but in its broad and defining structure, by class. The market is thus embedded in—shaped by—class and, as we shall see, it reproduces those classes. One might read this as an analogue, at the level of social analysis, to Marx's distinction between value and price, deep structure and epiphenomenon. On this view, classes are not composed out of individuals, their behavior (preferences) and constraints, but, like a marxist equivalent of the Platonic forms, they seem to stand above these persons, mold them, and be analyzable independently of them. And Marx's language often supports just such a construction: class membership is like a fate, something that descends on one. It is a "situation of being assigned [*Angewiesensein*]."[70] Marx's manner of writing is here meant to convey a point, and I return to that point presently. Taken too literally, however, it can give a fundamentally inaccurate (and analytically inferior) picture of what Marx understood by class.

Consider once more Marx's story concerning capital's "original sin." If we put to one side the issue of violence and the presence of the state, what this story tells of is a fundamental shift in the pattern of basic economic endowments, a different distribution of the "social elements" of production or, in plainer words, of labor and the other core means of production.[71] Labor power becomes fully the property of its natural owner, who is under no juridical obligation to alienate (sell) it to an employer; it also, Marx maintains, becomes virtually their sole endowment. The means of (social) production—for example, factories—likewise come under private ownership, and laborers must be hired to run these various moments of the production process. This is, needless to say, a highly stylized and simplified picture, and I use it only to capture a part of what Marx means when he writes that class precedes and structures the market. There is nothing supramundane about this claim: it amounts to the assertion that market agents in a capitalist economy have various endowments. These endowment patterns may be traced out along a number of lines, but a fundamental one, for Marx, is those who possess labor power alone, and those who, having effective control over the instruments of production, but no direct control over labor, must now engage it in a market, for a price and from its proper owner.

This pattern of endowments constitutes one aspect of what Marx in-

---

[70] Marx, *Grundrisse*, p. 96; Marx and Engels, *German Ideology*, p. 77. Something like this is suggested in Louis Althusser and Etienne Balibar, *Reading Capital*, trans. Ben Brewster (London: New Left Books, 1972), p. 267.

[71] Marx, *Capital*, vol. 2, p. 462.

tends by class. And it explains in part why buyers and sellers appear in the labor market: given this pattern of endowments, individuals of both classes need each other—the one to secure income (wages) which are now the only recognized entitlement to commodities in the market, including sustenance, the other to create and maximize surpluses. The appearance of each in the market, the fact that only there can they arrange both to create and to share in social wealth—in short, their need for each other— sets up the vital relational dimension of the marxist definition of class. But notice how this relational aspect emerges: it is not the result of force, of an overdetermining master, nor does it emerge from unequal juridical status or political power.[72] Rather, it is a consequence of a pattern of initial endowments (how that pattern itself is arrived at makes no difference for its impact on class formation, though it certainly is of great normative importance) coupled with the optimizing behavior of the agents involved. The first element of this argument, the ownership or effective control over the means of production, is, from the marxist standpoint, a noncontroversial element of the definition of class. The second component, that individuals become capitalists or proletarians as they seek to optimize under a wealth constraint, that classes are formed in the market—this position, set out in magisterial fashion by John Roemer, is less obviously a part of the marxist tradition. Indeed, that it is able to reproduce something very much like the classical marxist typology of classes on microfoundations by generating class position out of a standard model of markets, endowments, and preferences, rather than by postulating it in advance, is, among other things, what gives it its novelty and its brilliance.[73]

The value of the Roemer construction of class for the reading presented in this book lies in its unpacking of the mechanism by which classes of a purely economic sort are generated by markets under certain assumptions about the initial endowments of agents. And though I am not interested here in defending Roemer against the received orthodoxy (much less

[72] Marx, *Grundrisse*, pp. 245, 283, 420–21, and Marx, *MEGA*, II.3.1, p. 183; also Erik O. Wright, "Varieties of Marxist Conceptions of Class Structure," *Politics and Society* 9 (1980): 323–70, especially pp. 324–25.

[73] See Roemer, *Analytical Foundations of Marxian Economic Theory* (Cambridge: Cambridge University Press, 1981), p. 202; Roemer, *A General Theory of Exploitation and Class*, pp. 14, 77; Roemer, "Why Labor Classes?" Working Paper no. 195 from the Department of Economics, University of California at Davis (December 1982), p. 1. See also Elster, *Making Sense of Marx*, pp. 326–27. For some representative attacks on rational choice marxism see Scott Meikle, "Making Nonsense of Marx," and Cliff Slaughter, "Making Sense of Elster," both in *Inquiry* 29 (1986): 29–43, 45–56.

in defending that orthodoxy), it is important that Marx's analysis can in fact be reconstructed in a way that takes us close, unexpectedly perhaps, to Roemer-type classes. We have seen Marx claiming that class is anterior to market behavior, and that assertion would appear, on its face, to rule out the Roemer approach. But we also saw that when fully deployed Marx's claim amounted to the proposition that the endowments (labor power and capital) of market agents were set before they appeared there and that they constitute one of the factors necessitating and shaping market exchanges. Marx also provides the material for the second element of the market-behavior theory of class: optimizing under constraints. This element might seem at first to be fundamentally at odds with the canonical marxist story according to which "compulsion" drives both capitalist and worker. Here again, a close examination of the substance of Marx's argument yields a more finely inflected picture than does his often florid choice of words. The worker, Marx writes, is forced through his own interest to sell his labor power: he is compelled by his needs. For the capitalist, on the other hand, it is the creation of surplus value in the context of a competitive market which acts as a force compelling certain behaviors from him.[74]

In a sense, then, persons in a capitalist market economy could be said to choose their class position, and that claim is, I imagine, among the most counterintuitive from a marxist perspective,[75] because it might be taken to echo the thought that occupation and income differences— loosely speaking, class position—are reflections of preferences, for instance, for security over risk-taking, for leisure over monetary income. The element of constraint, so important to marxism for both explanatory and critical reasons, would seem to be reduced here to the exercise of preferences. And it would therefore become exceedingly difficult to make sense of Marx's repeated references to the "illusion" of freedom in the market and to the "veiled slavery" underlying it. In fact, however, the idea of choice under constraint captures handsomely Marx's argument and its shadings. Recall that according to that argument, external compulsion is absent from capitalist relations, meaning that power emerges from market transactions but has no (theoretically interesting) *ex ante* existence.

[74] On these points see Marx, *Grundrisse*, pp. 245, 413; Marx, *MEGA*, II.3.1, pp. 174, 183; Marx, *The Poverty of Philosophy*, p. 118; Marx, *Capital*, vol. 1, pp. 381–82, 932; Marx, *Results of the Immediate Process of Production*, p. 1051.

[75] See John E. Roemer, "New Directions in the Study of Class," in Roemer, ed., *Analytical Marxism*, p. 90; Roemer, *General Theory*, p. 81; Adam Przeworski, *Capitalism and Social Democracy* (Cambridge: Cambridge University Press, 1985), p. 95.

The presence of persons selling (in the present) their labor power and of others buying it cannot be explained by coercion or status position. The worker, Marx writes, has a "wide field of choice," governs and is the proprietor of herself; she is not commanded or forced by some other person to sell her labor power. Yet it is essential to the marxist definition of class that she be constrained to sell her time and activity, for otherwise class position would in fact be strictly a function of preferences.[76]

This is one of the central paradoxes of capitalism for Marx: that "external" or direct compulsion is absent but not compulsion altogether.[77] Agents in a capitalist economy choose to engage in their various economic activities, but they do so in a context of constraints, for example, survival of the enterprise in a competitive market, the need for money-based entitlements to food and other consumption goods, and initial endowments. Those constraints are sufficiently powerful that workers require no "external compulsion" to deliver their services: the market, its constraints and the endowments of individuals active in it, replace the more direct and personal forms of coercion characteristic of the pre-modern world. Not only does it replace them, but it is more effective than they were in generating wealth-creating activity. The compulsion at work here is, Marx says, "silent," meaning not emanating from a person, the *oikos* despot for example. He also describes it as "material" or objective and therefore difficult to recognize, theoretically, for a (liberal) way of looking at the world accustomed to thinking of coercion in its premodern and personal forms.[78] It thus appears freer than economic behavior in the premodern world for two reasons: because of the absence of a visible master commanding it and because, relatedly, it must be free-willed, the object of choice. It is, however, as constrained a way of life with this important difference: that the constraints are no longer the master's whip but a highly restricted and unacceptable choice set. To repeat the central points: (a) the presence of that choice set is in fact one of the marks distinguishing the bourgeois from the premodern world; (b) the presence of that choice set gives the (misleading) appearance of a society without unfreedom, or none at least of a morally relevant sort.

Let us consider one of Marx's illustrations of these points, in Chapter

[76] See G. A. Cohen, *Karl Marx's Theory of History: A Defense* (Princeton: Princeton University Press, 1978), p. 72; Elster, *Making Sense of Marx*, p. 324.

[77] Marx, *MEGA*, II.3.1, pp. 174, 183.

[78] Marx, *Results of the Immediate Process of Production*, pp. 1027–28n, 1031; Marx, *Capital*, vol. 1, p. 899; Marx, *MEGA*, II.3.6, p. 2131; Marx and Engels, *German Ideology*, pp. 78–79.

33 of *Capital,* Volume 1, entitled "The Modern Theory of Colonization." Those pages, despite their title, have little to do with colonization, being rather an attempt to illuminate the nature of compulsion in capitalist society. The argument is presented in this manner. In the developed bourgeois world, the compulsion underlying the (labor) market is hidden: voluntary contracts are the means by which labor is bought and sold, and whatever element of restraint may be visible in it appears as something "natural" in the sense of not emanating from any particular will. But in the colonies, where land is cheaply or freely available, migrants decline to participate as laborers in the industries being founded there. They prefer instead—and the feasible choice set enables them—to return to the condition of independent producers. In the end, Marx concludes, those circumstances that in the European world "naturally"—that is, without the assistance of the state or of any authority whatsoever—populate the labor market with applicants must, in the new world, be artificially instituted through legislation, for instance, by a mandated increase in land prices. The core of Marx's argument here is the notion that only as a result of a highly constrained choice set, "the labor market . . . or the workhouse," does the labor contract, so essential to capitalism, occur at all. Alter the boundaries of that set, and people exit the labor market.[79]

We can express Marx's normative point in this chapter of *Capital,* Volume 1, by drawing on some analysis provided by David Zimmerman.[80] Zimmerman makes the case that we can count someone (Q) as coerced if agent P changes the range of options open to Q such that this change makes Q worse off than in some preproposal baseline situation. To avoid counterintuitive results such as saying that a slave is uncoerced who agrees to work still harder to avoid the (actual preproposal baseline) condition of being constantly beaten, Zimmerman suggests that we refine the idea of the relevant baseline to include alternative, feasible baselines, here nonslavery. Under this revised definition, P coerces Q if P prevents Q from having (or removes Q from) her highly preferred alternative baseline situation. Under this definition of coercion, the raising of land prices in order to deny the poor any option other than factory labor would unquestionably count as coercive. By extension, we can say that systemic constraints on alternative, feasible, and highly desired situations must also be reckoned coercive in an objective sense; that is, they are not the

---

[79] Marx, *Capital,* vol. 1, p. 936.
[80] David Zimmerman, "Coercive Wage Offers," *Philosophy and Public Affairs* 10 (1981): 121–45, especially pp. 124, 132–36.

direct result of human purposiveness but nevertheless a normatively interesting form of unfreedom.[81]

The market is an institutional shelter for bilaterally voluntary exchanges in comparison to the ways of appropriating labor typical of slave or serf societies. But Marx maintains that if we add two further assumptions to this depiction—that entitlements to all goods in a capitalist market depend both on effective demand and on a certain pattern of initial endowments—the end result is a severe set of constraints on choice. There is a third assumption at work here which, though not stated so boldly in Marx's writings, is a theme underlying his philosophy of history as the growth of human productive powers. The additional claim is that in order for this argument concerning constraint to function as a critique, the parameters of the choice set have to be malleable under some feasible alternative arrangement. Members of the earliest human economies who lived at the lower threshold of calorie consumption required for the sustaining of life may also have faced severely restricted options, but if those restrictions were incorrigible they would not constitute the groundwork for a critique, even under the wide parameters of critique allowed by Marx, for example, where the constraints need not emanate from a will or an unjust act in order to be counted as wrongs.

Here are two further and related points about this Chapter 33 of *Capital,* Volume 1. The first is that it underscores a key argument of Marx's, that capitalism and capitalist markets not only produce surplus value but, when they are functioning properly, they reproduce the relations necessary to capitalism, essentially those of capital on the one side and the sellers of labor power on the other. This is to say that on the assumptions sketched above—the existence of a pattern of initial endowments and of one dominant form of entitlement to goods—the market will attract both workers and employers. Or, to rephrase this, the constraints will be such that the exit option, while individually accessible, will not be so collectively. And that pattern is reproduced not through any artificially (nonmarket) induced restrictions but by the behavior of the agents themselves under the prevailing constraints.[82] This is the reverse

---

[81] This extension is suggested by David Zimmerman himself in "More on Coercive Wage Offers: A Reply to Alexander," *Philosophy and Public Affairs* 12 (1983): 165–71, especially p. 171.

[82] See Gerald A. Cohen, "The Structure of Proletarian Unfreedom," *Philosophy and Public Affairs* 12 (1983): 3–33; Jeffrey Reiman, "The Fallacy of Libertarian Capitalism," *Ethics* 92 (1981): 85–95, and Reiman, "Exploitation, Force, and the Moral Assessment of Capitalism: Thoughts on Roemer and Cohen," *Philosophy and Public Affairs* 16 (1987): 3–41.

side of the argument in "The Modern Theory of Colonization," which attempts to demonstrate the effect of relaxing one of the constraints (i.e., initial endowments, by the re-creation of something quite like the commons). This effect is that the market fails to deliver the goods necessary for the reproduction of capitalism. What we see traces of in this last line of analysis is one of Marx's variants of market-failure theory, according to which the high costs of some types of transactions, negative externalities, and free-rider problems may, under certain circumstances, make non-market institutions more efficient as ways of organizing production and distributing goods. The variant Marx presents here considers one class of failures, those in which the market is unable to generate pressures sufficient to permit the production and reproduction of capital as an ensemble of class relations: for example, at the origins of capitalism (when the necessary pattern of endowments is not in place) or where, as in the colonies, the choice set is opened beyond that of the labor market or the workhouse. In such circumstances, the state is called into action to correct market weaknesses, though in the normal course of things the market (together with the other premises noted above) ought to be able to reproduce the relations of capitalism without external assistance.

Here we have, then, the first stage of Marx's analytical and critical embedding of the liberal account of the capitalist market. Its governing theme is class as the backdrop to and product of the market, and that theme can be further decomposed into the following elements: endowments, entitlement, and choice. Together, the arguments embraced under this heading help shape Marx's theory of the community under capital and its freedom. The starting point (if we put aside Marx's historical claims) is that class constitutes the necessary background condition to the labor market because that latter institution rests upon a pattern of endowments: in Roemer's words, the endowments of those who in order to optimize must sell their labor power and of those who, conversely, must hire it—in short, those whose only alienable good is their labor power and those who own capital. In a system in which entitlements to the things necessary for life involve money or credit, and in which disposal over alienable assets is key to securing those means, the pattern of endowments will yield a constrained set of choices. All participants act in pursuit of their own interests and not from direct external compulsion, and in that sense they choose their class position. But the indirect type of compulsion, objective in form and mediated through a noncoercive market, Marx thought, acts as a significant constraint on freedom. The exercise of choice is thus not an adequate index of freedom under circumstances in which the choice set is highly (and corrigibly) restricted.[83] Conversely, the presence of classes, of groups of persons who in a plausible sense must do what they do in the market, is a potent indicator of the limits of freedom, even in the presence of choice.

8.2.1   Remarks on Classes and the State

Before proceeding to Marx's analysis of the consequences of markets for freedom, I want to make a few remarks on his idea of class and its relation to the political sphere. My concern in these observations, and hence my reason for clustering them in this section, is Marx's argument for the newness of classes of the capitalist sort, an argument that includes location vis-à-vis politics. It is, as I said earlier, the failure to recognize this aspect of Marx's thought which leads to the (inaccurate) charge that he was a theoretical "modernizer," seeing all societies in the light of the one before him.[84] Accordingly, let me begin with this theme, already mentioned in passing, the novelty of classes of the capitalist type. The absence of external compulsion—of something like the despotic power of Locke's *Two Treatises* (a human coercive agency)—means that the powerful forces at work in a capitalist market economy, fulfilling functions analogous to the sovereign's sword or master's whip (reproducing basic social relations and seeing to the transfer of surpluses from their direct producers to the dominant class), must here be "objective," "material"— in a phrase, "purely economic."[85] That classes, or their premodern ancestors, have always had an element of constraint in them and that, in Marx's story, they have always involved some type of exploitation is what allows us to unite classes in capitalist society and estates/status groups in earlier societies under a single theoretical heading, that of class in the loose, or generic, sense. What distinguishes the classes of the bourgeois

[83] This thought lies behind the extremely counterintuitive appearance of Hobbes's theory of obligation-producing, voluntary contracts under extreme constraint. See *Leviathan*, pp. 130, 132–33.

[84] A striking example of this sort of critique is Cornelius Castoriadis, "From Marx to Aristotle, from Aristotle to Us," *Social Research* 45 (1978): 667–738, the weakness of which is its reliance on a single passage and theme from *Capital*, vol. 1, concerning the comparability of goods in exchange. A second illustration is Dumont's *From Mandeville to Marx*, pp. 181–82, 184. A good counter to this view is Georg Lukács, "The Changing Function of Historical Materialism," in Lukács, *History and Class Consciousness*, which maintains that Marx's historical materialism was intended to be the "self-knowledge" of capitalist society.

[85] Marx, *Results of the Immediate Process of Production*, p. 1028; Marx, *Capital*, vol. 1, p. 899.

world, and brings them under a stricter construction of the concept of class, is that they are formed entirely by impersonal forces ("objective," "material," "purely economic": these terms are all, at their root, ways of describing the impersonality and status neutrality of capitalism) and reproduced by the operation of those same conditions: the choices of optimizing agents under a wealth constraint and in the context of a type of entitlement to goods. Not only in the process of their formation, but (as we shall see) in their consequences—that is, in the type of relations between persons which they produce—are they classes of a distinctive sort. That type can be described as "impersonal" or "purely economic," meaning that its principal attributes and causal factors are contained within the reproductive process of capital, a process that is literally indiscriminate (neutral) as between individuals. Phrased negatively, status, political tinctures of any sort—*ex ante* power, the overbearing presence of the community, and its dominant moment—are all absent from capitalist classes, their formation and reproduction. The shifting location of the economy, its depoliticization one might (loosely) say, can be expressed in the liberal idiom as the emancipation of individuals from the varied types of despotic economies. Marx would add this further context: that classes, in the sense of a group of persons compelled to carry out certain functions, re-emerge in a market economy of the capitalist type.

I hope that the reader will allow me a brief excursus here, to explain why I do not bring up two sets of issues that are standard topics in discussions of Marx: exploitation and class struggle. It is apparent from the preceding remarks that I have not made exploitation the centerpiece of this reconstruction of Marx's theory of class. That approach, perhaps best represented in the contemporary literature by Erik O. Wright and G. E. M. de Ste. Croix, captures a core claim of Marx's, that exploitation stands at the center of relations between classes in all epochs.[86] I have touched on it only lightly because (as I remarked earlier) it does not provide a key to the *differentia specifica* of classes, precapitalist and capitalist, that was such an important part of Marx's project. Of course, forms of exploitation can be distinguished, for example via a typology of the means for extracting surpluses from the direct producers, means such as direct coercion in contrast to indirect market pressures. But for my purpose in this section, that is, to grasp the meaning of Marx's distinction

---

[86] See Erik O. Wright, "Class and Occupation," *Theory and Society* 9 (1980): 177–214, especially pp. 179–80; Ste. Croix, *The Class Struggle in the Ancient Greek World*, p. 43, and Ste. Croix, "Karl Marx and the History of Classical Antiquity," pp. 15, 18, 20, 26.

between C-M-C and M-C-ΔM types of economies as it bears on the concept of class, the techniques of exploitation are only a part of the story and not the crucial one at that, though they can be easily incorporated into the argument set out here.

Second, I do not take up the much-belabored question of the place of politics in the idea of class, understood as the distinction between a class "in itself" and one "for itself." Much of the debate over this issue is of such a doctrinal character, and therefore so theological-political, as to be of little interest outside texts recounting the history of socialist thought. There is, however, an important problem underlying it, namely, that if the explanandum is social conflict (class struggle) as one of the prime "motor forces" of history, then it becomes vital to produce a concept of class which permits us to build from its objective, structural features (shared position in the economy) to an analysis of why those features would produce collective action by members of one class and why those actions would generate conflict with members of other classes. Clearly, to meet the full range of requirements, including the explanation of conflict, imposed on the idea of class by Marx's theoretical agenda would require more than a sketch of the differences between premodern and modern classes. I do not explore it here, not because it is of no significance nor (even less) because Marx provided a systematic and satisfactory account of it, but again because the full range of explanatory tasks demanded of the idea of class does not form a part of the issue occupying center stage in these pages: Marx's understanding of the shifting place of the economy.

Another challenge to Marx's idea of class, and one I do want to consider, has been put forward by Adam Przeworski. This argument, like the preceding one, raises the question of the political sphere and the relationship of class to it. Only now the assertion is not simply that any concept of class which can be deployed to meet the various explanatory demands made of it by Marx must account for collective action and conflict but that classes are constituted, formed, at least in part, in the political realm.[87] Przeworski's counter to Marx can be expressed in this fashion: classes are not "prior to" politics but are organized and defined within the political sphere. Marx was wrong, Przeworski concludes, to conceive of capitalism as a system of "isolated cycles of production," that is, as iterations of the M-C-ΔM circuit bounded by a historical (political) act of transfer, the expropriation of the direct producers, but self-operating (and in that sense nonpolitical) thereafter.

[87] Przeworski, *Capitalism and Social Democracy,* pp. 67, 70, 96, 234.

I want to use the Przeworski critique to place in bolder relief one of the arguments of the preceding pages, Marx's claim that characteristic of capitalism (in contradistinction to earlier social/economic formations) is the dominance of the economy over politics. The following argument may well, in a backhanded way, confirm Przeworski's criticism, though that is not my main purpose. Rather, I wish to show in another form how much of the liberal story Marx accepted, even while turning it back upon itself. Now, in the classical liberal account of the origin of the economy, it is a political act that settles property, money, and so forth.[88] That (thought-construct) political "act" is contract or consent, which ends the commons and establishes the legitimacy of unequal ownership and unlimited accumulation and so, by extension, grounds the new master/servant relation. Marx, too, sees the origin of the labor market in a political act, though hardly a consensual one. This political act is rather the directly coercive, often state-led expropriation of the independent peasantry. The market, in Marx's version of this tale, was at that stage still too marginal to produce and reproduce capitalist-type labor relations. What was needed before its operations could proceed without further state intervention was a redistribution of economic endowments. And it was as a result of that redistribution (expropriation), political in nature, that the working class was born—the working class understood as those who must sell their labor power in the market. Playing on Locke's paragraph from the *Second Treatise* on the master/servant relation, we might say that the first servant arrived at his master's door because of an act of expropriation, and that was capital's "original sin." Subsequent appearances at the employer's door will not, however, be the consequence of political force but of a pattern of initial endowments and of the market through which they are exchanged. Given that pattern of endowments, the market is a robust institution, capable of producing and reproducing relations of the capitalist form without (direct) state intervention. Force (politics) is the market's midwife, and it must tend over the market's first emergence. After that, no midwife is needed. Freely adapting Montesquieu: at first humans make institutions, and thereafter it is the institutions that make them.[89]

---

[88] John Locke, *Second Treatise* 2T.45, 50, in Locke, *Two Treatises of Government*, ed. Peter Laslett (New York: New American Library, 1963).

[89] This analysis contains something like Marx's answer to Robert Brenner's question (in "The Social Basis of Economic Development") as to what would have induced agents (lords or serfs) in a feudal society to quit their existing mode of production inasmuch as, in their different ways, both groups stood to lose from the shift to pervasive markets. Brenner criticizes both the canonical marxist account (growth of the productive forces) and a Smithian explanation focusing on trade and suggests in their place a structure of explana-

This claim leads to a second core element of the liberal story that Marx accepts—market neutrality, a thesis also brought to the fore by Przeworski's critique. Once the market becomes the pervasive mechanism for allocating goods and persons (labor) across society, its operations are neutral with respect to the political sphere: it makes no noneconomic distinctions between persons. Marx's often repugnant language in *The Jewish Question* is meant to express just that thought: Jews, who suffer under civil disabilities in the political sphere, are the equals of their political oppressors in civil or economic society. This is so because capital, unlike political institutions, is neutral in relation to its holders: the only passion it knows is the drive for more of itself. In its world, discrimination along religious, social, or gender lines has no place. Again, as we have observed above, neutrality may be formulated, in the canonical language of liberalism, as a consequence of the juridical equality of persons as self-owners. Marx accepts the neutrality description but recasts it as the indifference of capital toward all (noneconomic) distinctions. For Marx to agree that classes are formed within a political process would be to dilute a central element of his (and liberalism's) claim, that the market is blind to (extraeconomic) differences among its actors and that the market is the pervasive institution through which individuals in a capitalist society interact.[90]

By way of that last point, we are brought to a third reason for Marx's silence on the political sphere, generally and in his discussion of class formation, that is, the dominance of civil society over politics. When Marx describes Locke as the great ideologist of bourgeois society, he intends among other things that Locke had envisioned the shrinking of the political and the corresponding growth of civil, or private society: the dominance, in short, of the market over all other realms. Conversely, the modern reincarnation of the republican tradition, in imagining that a

---

tion centered on the emergence of markets as an unintended consequence of other actions. Marx's argument (in mocking the social-contract story of the origins of capitalism) suggests that no agent would (rationally) have opted for markets, and it also intimates that certain essential features of capitalism such as a supply of free labor were created as a byproduct of other events, e.g., royal attacks on feudal retainer bands and the Reformation breakup of church lands (see *Capital*, vol. 1, pp. 873–74, 878, 881–82). Marx's writings do not permit us to go beyond these intimations, but nevertheless the rudiments are in place for a response to Brenner's challenge.

[90] Recent literature on women's place in the economy shows just how ill founded was the optimism of Marx (and the liberals) on the neutrality of the market. For some contemporary observations on the continued ascriptive structuring of the labor market see Claus Offe, *Disorganized Capitalism* (Cambridge: MIT Press, 1985), pp. 13, 36.

restoration of something like the ancient primacy of politics and citizenship is possible, commits a basic error. Bourgeois society is simply not
compatible with the intensely political world of antiquity.[91] Here once
more *The Jewish Question* provides a key to Marx's thinking: not only
does the political sphere not penetrate civil society, but it is in fact civil
society that dominates, a point Marx makes (perversely) by stating that
the Jewish community, denied the political rights of the most ordinary
Gentile citizen, nevertheless rules through its economic power. Notice
that Marx is yet again developing a mirror image of the familiar liberal
account: the state is indeed minimal because it has been, as it were,
expelled from civil society, a possibility in turn opened up by the effective-
ness of the market mechanism (after the initial distribution is set) in
enforcing the behaviors required for the reproduction of capital.[92] Observe further that the market also appears as a sort of forum for freedom,
standing in normative contradistinction to unfreedom in the state: Jews,
Marx argues, were freer in the economic sphere, which is neutral and
therefore blind also to religion. The standard marxian reversal of this part
of the liberal story is that the depoliticization of the economy sets in
motion not autonomous agents but persons who, having lost their varied,
ranked status positions, now come under the impersonal forces of the
market and acquire, in that process, a new hierarchical ordering, new in
that it is the consequence of the different functional roles they occupy in
the reproduction of capital.[93] (Further on, I discuss the normative aspect
of Marx's theory of the minimal state.)

The core of the preceding argument is Marx's acceptance of the broad-
brush assertion that capitalism, in its most developed form, takes politics
out of civil society and emancipates its agents, at least in relation to the
world before capitalism. The state is a minimal one because its operations
are no longer necessary to the functioning of surplus creation and extraction. Politics or, more generally, nonmarket organizations reappear in a
variety of guises when the market fails. What is important to remark is
that Marx clings to a view of the capitalist economy largely free from
political institutions and that, accordingly, one of the defining properties
of classes is that they must emerge (in all but the first instance) from the

[91] Marx and Engels, *German Ideology,* p. 409; Marx and Engels, *The Holy Family,*
p. 122; Marx, *Capital,* vol. 1, p. 444n. See also Lukács, *History and Class Consciousness,*
p. 92.

[92] Marx, *The Jewish Question,* in MECW, vol. 3, pp. 166–67, 170–72.

[93] Marx, *The Poverty of Philosophy,* p. 118; Marx and Engels, *German Ideology,* p. 77;
Marx, *Capital,* vol. 1, p. 719; Marx, *Grundrisse,* p. 96.

workings of the economy and not, as with status groups, as a function of the political realm. In sum, they must be classes of the Roemer type. To assert that classes are constituted in the political sphere would be, for Marx, to reintroduce the political into civil society, to weaken the fundamental explanatory and normative propositions of the autonomy of the economy under capitalism, and to upset the ironic reversals that Marx was venturing against liberalism.

That these classes, formed and reproduced within the market/production sphere, move outside of that world and seek to draw the state back in to support them against the (different) types of market failure they endure and that in so doing they must organize themselves politically are claims readily assimilable to Marx's theory of the minimal liberal state and of its evolution into something rather more interventionist. What Marx needs, however, and what the Przeworski counter would deny him, is his vital starting point: of civil society not structured by politics, neutral, and without coercion of the traditional sort. In grasping that, we come to understand that the virtual absence of the state and politics from *Capital,* and indeed from much of Marx's mature writing, reflects a deep commitment to this (almost liberal) view of the bourgeois world.

8.3   Perverse Consequences

We have seen above one facet of Marx's explanation/critique of market society: the need for a specific initial redistribution of basic productive assets in order that the two principal classes of bourgeois society may (better: have to) meet in the marketplace. That initial distribution, on Marx's account, takes place in the absence of the market and therefore through the agency of the state, usually in some coercive form or other. The critique that stands at the heart of this contention we designated an immanent one, inasmuch as it rests on a prohibition against coercion and on a claim that subsequent transactions, structured by an initial unjust act, preserve that injustice and so are themselves called into question. To this immanent critique, we added a second line of analysis, that is, that class in a market society is a grouping of persons who, in an important sense, *must* act as they do given their endowments and the array of entitlements to goods open to them in a market economy. The element of constraint here is a consequence, according to Marx, of a pinched option set—labor or the poorhouse. The fact that it is the option set that constrains rather than direct coercion gives the functioning of a capitalist economy an element of voluntariness (choice) which obscures the (corrigible) limits of that choice and so the indirect compulsion at work there. That specification of unfreedom I took to be typically marxian, for although classical liberal authors recognized its factual base, they deemed the residue of contract in relations between the persons facing this constrained option set to be sufficient to render these persons free in the liberal sense, that is, uncoerced, choosing agents. In short, Marx's rejoinder is of this order: the liberal achievement of self-ownership, broadened into a claim of ownership over external things, rebounds upon the heart of self-ownership, autonomy, in ways that constrain the scope of its exercise. Let me suggest, provisionally, that a central element of marxism's dilemma is visible here. For while the above analysis of the impact of ownership of the world on ownership of oneself (autonomy) may well be accurate, the same logic can be played back against those who would deny property in the world: inasmuch as property is what we do things with, eliminating my control over property must, in some measure, also limit what I can do and so restrict my self-ownership.[94]

I now turn to a second way of thinking about markets and freedom. This we might call the perverse-consequences approach. By perverse I mean a twofold idea: in the sense of unintended and in its substantive signification as well—that is, contrary to the human good, including freedom.[95] These two facets are, however, only analytically distinguishable, for it is precisely perversity in the second sense which serves Marx as an index for the unintended and autonomy-denying consequences of the market, that is, perversity of the first sort. Before we begin with the first of these two strands of analysis, the unplanned yet lawlike character of the market, I address an important difficulty in understanding Marx's reflections on freedom and markets. This difficulty arises from his unfortunate tendency to write about the market as the "surface," the "phenomenal form"—in a word, the "exoteric" persona of capitalism. Behind that character mask there is another sphere, something called the "laws of capital" of which the market is merely the "executor."[96] The task of political-economic explanation on this reading is to penetrate beneath the

---

[94] I take this phrasing from Jan Narveson, "The Justice of the Market," in Chapman and Pennock, eds., *Nomos 31:Markets and Justice* (New York: New York University Press, 1989), p. 266.

[95] See Raymond Boudon, *Effets pervers et ordre social* (Paris: Presses Universitaires de France, 1979), pp. 5, 7, 10. Boudon also analyzes (pp. 202–5) some instances of perverse-effects arguments in Marx, for example the falling-rate-of-profit discussion from *Capital*, vol. 3.

[96] See Marx, *Grundrisse*, p. 552; Marx, *MEGA*, II.3.5, pp. 1630–31; Marx, *Capital*, vol. 3, p. 338; Marx, *Theories of Surplus Value*, vol. 2, pp. 218–19.

surface, to go deeper than the market, in order to discover the wellspring of the laws it enforces. This argument structure mirrors that of the value/price distinction, and like the latter it too gives birth to a version of the transformation problem: how to understand the causal relation between these two spheres and, just as important, how to make sense of the one (the "esoteric") level of this explanation, which has no behavioral or intentional content. Elsewhere, I ventured an analysis of this argument which made Marx into a functionalist of a sophisticated sort, one who sought to unpack the black-box causal mechanisms uniting the ends and the behaviors producing them.[97] Here I want to withdraw that reading and to offer in its place another and, I believe, more cogent one.

Rather than a two-tier causal account of capitalism, the "laws of capital" on the one hand and their executive branch on the other, we might attribute to Marx a single-layered story in which it is the (capitalist) market as an institution (a set of constraints), its agents, and the consequences of their interactions under constraint that together warrant a lawlike picture of the phenomena. The principal advantage of this move is that it enables us to recover from Marx a mode of explanation which does not force us to reject or adopt his metaphysics of appearance and essence. I might add that it also has a secure textual mooring, or such at least as one can hope to find in Marx's writings. Here the language of surface and inner phenomena, of the exoteric and esoteric aspects of the economy, is replaced by the idea that the laws of capitalism are not located in some hidden domain but rather are the efflux of (*ex ante*) uncoordinated decisions in a context of interdependency. "The laws of capital are in fact nothing other than the general relations of this movement [of competition among capitalists], its result on the one side, its direction on the other."[98] These general relations are amenable to an analysis of a lawlike kind because they are describable in a patterned (rule-governed) causal way, a causality Marx expresses as the compulsion that those interconnections (in the form of competition) exert on individual agents. Stated in plainer language, competition among capitalists functions as a coercive force, compelling them to pursue those ends (and the means appropriate to them) which are at the heart of capitalism and weeding out maladapted strategies. Similarly, Marx maintains that competition among workers in the labor market acts as a lawlike determinant of their behavior until the development of capitalism on the one side and the growth of trade unions

---

[97] See my "Explaining Capitalism: The Method of Marx's Political Economy," *Political Studies* 37 (1989): 612–25.

[98] Marx, *MEGA*, II.3.5, p. 1603, my translation; Marx, *Capital*, vol. 3, p. 365; Marx, *Grundrisse*, pp. 157, 197.

on the other reduce the salience of the material bases of that competition.[99]

What Marx wants to illuminate in speaking of the "laws of capital" is the notion that the processes of the capitalist market, while they are composed out of the consciously regulated acts of the wills of market agents, nevertheless appear to display in their totality an independence from these same persons, compelling them to act in certain ways. That property of unregulated but interdependent activity is, in one sense, truly independent of individuals, because it constrains them and generates unintended consequences. It would, however, be wrong to imagine these laws as independent of humans in the same way as, for example, the laws of nature are said to be. For the "laws of capital" are the product of human hands, the results of an uncoordinated social economy. We might speculate that Marx's use of the strong language of underlying causal forces determining the surface phenomena of the market was meant to convey the importance of constraints to the functioning of markets and thereby to undermine the idea that the market is a sphere of freedom because its particular moments are the decisions of individuals. If that speculation is accurate, Marx achieved his goal at the cost of some loss of precision in his statement of the second aspect, namely that the language of laws should not conceal from us the fact that these laws are the historically specific and humanly created artifacts of one particular organization of the economy. A careful laying out of the elements of Marx's analysis demonstrates that he did not need to leave the market sphere in order to make the arguments he did.

What the preceding observations bring to light is Marx's account of the generation of (independent) laws out of interdependent but unregulated economic activity. That captures a part of what Marx understands by the emergence of lawlike forces from an anarchical (in the *ex ante* sense, i.e., not planned) market. Another part, indeed a crucial one, of his theory of the law-governed character of the capitalist market is the purposiveness of its processes. It is not simply that market competition constrains persons to act in certain ways or that the actions of those individuals produce unforeseen consequences. Rather, these constraints and consequences are, in their varied ways, bound up with the overarching purpose of a capitalist economy: the creation of ΔM.[100] Once more, we find Marx

[99] Marx, *Capital*, vol. 1, pp. 254, 381, 433; Marx, *Grundrisse*, pp. 413, 651, 657; Marx, *Communist Manifesto*, pp. 492–93, and Marx, *Wage Labour and Capital*, in *MECW*, vol. 9, p. 225.

[100] Marx, *Results of the Immediate Process of Production*, p. 1051; Marx, *Capital*, vol. 1, p. 254.

writing as if this purpose resided somewhere else than in the persons who act within the constraints of the market, and that this end-state was, by a process unspecified (and perhaps unspecifiable) instantiated in the consciousness of capitalists, whereupon it becomes their "subjective purpose."[101] What Marx is seeking to draw out here is a thought much more credible than the idea that there is an "objective" purposiveness that is translated into a subjective one. And this thought is that competition in the market requires individuals to choose strategies—e.g., cost cutting, introduction of labor-saving technology, and so forth—which are best adapted to economic survival and expansion, that is, to the creation of ΔM. Competition does this by imposing penalties on counteradaptive decisions and rewarding the appropriate ones, leaving the decision between them to rationally motivated actors.

Contemporary nonmarxist work on the theory of the firm offers a second type of analysis which in certain respects dovetails handsomely with Marx's emphasis on the systemic purposiveness of capitalism. In the preceding account, we saw an argument according to which a competition-imposed survival criterion is transmitted to individual actors in the economy and becomes their purpose as they adapt to the constraints of the market (the "deliberate" model). Now, in this second version, provision is made for "blind" evolution: the actors may well aim at some satisficing solution and employ precedent and rule-of-thumb procedures, yet overall it will be the most profitable firms that survive.[102] The reason that the actual outcome imitates a world in which firms were conscious profit-maximizing units is that the market (competition) functions in the manner of a natural-selection mechanism, preserving the "right" procedures (quite apart from the actors' intentions) and eliminating the nonadaptive ones, yielding in the end a population of the most profitable firms. What interests me in the context of the present analysis is not directly whether economic behavior is intentional adaptation to the market with its constraints, punishments, and rewards, or whether the market selects out the appropriate behaviors—in which case there is no need to invoke an intentional explanation at all. Rather, it is the notion that the capitalist market is end-directed and that either (on model one above) its operatives respond rationally and match their behavior to that end or (on model two) the market weeds out some behaviors and rewards others. The reason for emphasizing this purposiveness of the market is

[101] See Marx, *Capital*, vol. 1, pp. 254, 433.
[102] See Richard R. Nelson and Sidney G. Winter, *An Evolutionary Theory of Economic Change* (Cambridge: Belknap Press, 1982), pp. 4, 9–11.

that, for Marx, capitalist markets are structured not simply by a set of (unequal) endowments, an extensive division of labor, and the constraints on economic behavior which flow from these attributes, but also by their governing end, ΔM. Marx knew (and his C-M-C formula states) that markets predate capitalism and that what distinguishes early markets from capitalist ones is more than the latter's pervasiveness: it is also the systemically induced purpose that drives exchange, consumption, or, in Marx's phrase, the growth of value, that is, of profit.

In sum, when Marx set out to analyze markets of the capitalist type, the portrait he finally drew had the following central features: (a) markets are structured by the class position of their members, where by class position is understood their (unequal) endowments. (b) These markets are also structured by a pattern of entitlements, which in a pervasive capitalist market economy can be expressed as a money entitlement, that is, the power to purchase and sell. (c) Beyond these two initial premises, the market is structured in the sense that its operations consist of individual choices with no *ex ante* coordination at the level of the economy as a whole. (d) Those individual choices in an interdependent (or social, as Marx sometimes calls it) economy interact with one another and set in motion lawlike processes. (e) These processes are lawlike in three senses: (1) they can be described in regular, causal-pattern language. (2) They are like natural laws in that they bind or act as a force of compulsion upon persons and appear to have an existence independent of them. In reality that independence of the laws of capital is partly fact, partly illusion—the former because those laws are not the product of human design, the latter because they are of human making. (3) They are end-directed in the sense that the various operations of the market compel its leading agents to pursue profit and in the sense that it adjudicates between those who are successful in this and those who fail. The first species is preserved, the second perishes. (f) And last, the capitalist market is, because of the nature of its determining end, ΔM, explosively expansionary, transforming virtually all goods into commodities and all labor into wage labor, thereby making the market the main institution for transactions. It is this combination of traits that Marx thought defined the particularity of the capitalist market and that set the foundation for the second strand of his perverse-effects analysis, designed to show the coexistence of individual choice and unfreedom in the market.

Below, I consider this second branch of Marx's perverse-effects account of the market under two headings: "Overproduction and Undersatisfaction" focuses on a specific (and, according to Marx, unique) form of

capitalist economic crisis, that of overproduction, as revealing the consequences of its entitlement structure and its final purpose. The second
discussion, "Economies of Time," brings into view more clearly the
centrality of the determining goal of the capitalist market by showing
both the source of the drive to introduce labor-saving technology and the
way in which that same source dictates a certain, according to Marx
suboptimal, employment of that technology. As will become clear in the
paragraphs that follow, Marx gave considerably more weight to the second of these arguments, thinking, I suspect, that it captured the core
perversity of capitalism: a disembedded economy, ruled by the laws of the
valorization of capital and not by those of human need, and producing as
a result unnecessary deprivations of freedom and other goods. The first
argument, on the other hand, because it gives a certain priority to the
consequences of a pattern of entitlements over the aspects of anarchy and
the ΔM purpose, may well have struck Marx as an excessively legalistic
approach insofar as it concentrated on the results of exclusionary rights in
property. There is, however, another and still deeper reason for Marx's
interest in capitalism's drive toward labor-saving improvements in production and its particular employment of those improvements, and that is
his interest in time spent in noneconomic activity as a forum for human
freedom and development. That concern, which Marx shared with the
ancients, makes his analysis of the economy of time under capitalism
something more than a surrogate way of speaking about the issue of
perverse effects. In what follows I thus devote greater attention to it.

8.3.1   Overproduction and Undersatisfaction

The first sort of perverse effect of the market that I consider is that
revealed in crises of overproduction. That type of crisis, Marx thought,
was peculiar to capitalism: previously there had been, to be sure, overcon-
sumption but not overproduction, and there had been crises of under-
production due, for example, to the calamities of war or nature. One
important factor accounting for the absence of overproduction and its
attendant crises in the precapitalist world was, according to Marx, the
fact that the purpose governing production was need and not expanded
value.[103] Capitalism, however, being directed to the creation of profit, is
capable of overproduction, not in relation to the satisfaction of "absolute

---

[103] Marx, *Communist Manifesto*, p. 490; Marx, *Theories of Surplus Value*, vol. 2,
pp. 501–3, 528.

needs" but rather in relation to effective, money- or credit-backed demand. Capitalism, Marx writes, can overproduce commodities (i.e., as vessels for expanded value) while simultaneously underproducing in relation to the satisfaction of needs.[104] In short, crises of overproduction can take place in the midst of underconsumption, the latter sometimes occurring even among the makers of the surplus commodity itself. The possibility of this form of crisis is written in the nature of the commodity, that is, something made in order to achieve additional value in its sale. If we use the language of Marx's description of the complete production/circulation cycle, we could say that M-C-ΔM opens up the possibility of just this sort of crisis: a surfeit of things in the midst of undersatisfied need for just those things.

Marx maintained that the perversity revealed in this type of crisis is threefold. The first and most obvious sense is that the crisis itself is neither intended by its agents nor is it in their interests (as capitalists or workers). A second meaning of the idea of perversity in this context carries with it a normative valuation of economic institutions which permit the undersatisfaction of material needs in the presence of abundance. Here again, I think, Marx meant to intimate the unintended nature of the process that produces such results. No capitalist may wish for that outcome, yet it will nevertheless emerge from the decisions they make in the course of optimizing under competitive pressures and from the underlying entitlement structure of the market. The third aspect of this form of crisis, simply a further unfolding of its unintentional quality, is that it is the consequence of the convergence of the following properties of capitalism: (a) the market-enforced pursuit of profit (ΔM), (b) a system of entitlements (effective demand), and (c) an unregulated economy that causes the consequences of (a) and (b) to emerge unhindered, generating a crisis of one sort for the capitalist, often in the presence of a very different type of dilemma for other persons in the economy.

The core of this form of crisis, the overproduction of commodities and undersatisfaction of material needs, is to be found in the idea of effective demand, which can be approached by the employment of either the language of the purpose of capitalist production (ΔM) or that of property relations and the power over commodities which flows from one type of entitlement. The first idiom directs us to the thought that commodities are produced in order to function as the bearers of enhanced value (and not directly for the satisfaction of need); the latter language focuses on the

---

[104] Marx, *Theories of Surplus Value*, vol. 2, pp. 505, 527.

fact that access to goods in a capitalist market rests not on needs but on the power to command those commodities, typically on the possession of money and therefore on some marketable good or service by means of which to secure that money. That both of these languages appear in Marx's account reflects, not a contradiction in his thought so much as two related aspects of capitalism, conceived of as a system of property relations governed by a purpose or end. Nevertheless, in those pages that Marx dedicates to the study of crises of overproduction, the emphasis is placed squarely on money-backed command over commodities, which is to say that he speaks here primarily in the theoretical idiom of property and entitlement relations.

A contemporary parallel to this analysis, that offered by Amartya Sen, will help us to understand Marx's point better. One central theme of Sen's remarkable study, *Poverty and Famines,* is that in market economies starvation can occur even in the midst of a boom in food production (as in the Bengal famine of 1943). The explanation, in sum, is this: "Market demands are not reflections of biological needs or psychological desires, but choices based on exchange entitlement relations."[105] The ability to avoid starvation is thus a function of a person's relationship to food commodities, where by relationship is meant (a) her ownership bundle and (b) the "exchange entitlement mapping" (E-mapping) she confronts, that is, those bundles of commodities she can acquire in exchange for what she owns. E-mapping is another way of expressing the notion of a socially/legally sanctioned set of legitimate forms of acquisition, possession, and use—that is, of property relations broadly construed. The ownership bundle will depend, Sen states, on the person's position in the economic class structure.[106] "Boom famines" emerge in market economies when (among other possible causes) the person's ownership bundle—goods including labor to be exchanged under the prevailing E-mapping norms—is insufficient to make effective her demand (need) for a sustenance basket. On Sen's analysis, such underconsumption crises in the midst of plentiful food supplies (or of no significant decline in foodstuffs) are evidence of the consequences of one type of E-mapping, that of food as a commodity to which access is secured only through money-backed demand. The capitalist market, operating without distortion and according to the accepted patterns of legitimate exchange, yields results that can quite plausibly be described as normatively objectionable and that are not

[105] Amartya Sen, *Poverty and Famines: An Essay on Entitlement and Deprivation* (Oxford: Clarendon Press, 1981), p. 161.
[106] Sen, *Poverty and Famines,* pp. 1, 3–4, 45–46.

the intention of any actor. The denial of "absolute needs" in the presence of a socially produced scarcity restricts the freedom of its victim, and in that specific sense market-induced phenomena of this type give rise to constraints on just that value, freedom, which the market was expected to promote. On a more general level, this perverse effect reveals again the unintended, "automatic," character of capitalist market operations and thereby points (for Marx) to the gap between the normative inputs of the market (contract, choice, and purposiveness) and its operations and normative outputs (beyond human control, and in some cases intrinsically perverse).

What we have here is another instance of market failure, now not the type of failure that we saw in the case of the colony's labor market (too wide a set of alternatives to the labor market, with the resulting exit from it) but rather a moral one: the failure of the market to satisfy "absolute" (or material) needs, a failure that (we might speculate) runs counter to society's wishes. Once more, as in the preceding instances of market failure, the state is brought in to control against the effects of the unchecked market. Social security and other welfare programs may be seen as constituting so many types of nonmarket entitlements to goods, and together they amount to society's imposing its will, in a sense, on one of its institutional expressions. They are the ways in which society expresses its determination that individuals not starve in the midst of plenty, even though the latter phenomenon may be the result of the legitimate exercise of choice under constraints (ownership and E-mapping) accepted as proper. If one can speak (as I think one can) of autonomy at the level of communities, the community in this scenario imposes its will on, asserts its autonomy against, a process that seems to have become a "self-moving" actor, a purposive chain of events the consequences of which are perverse in our double signification: not willed and contrary to the will of society.

This latter phrasing of "self-moving" processes once more invokes the specter of Marx's reifying metaphors, endowing institutions with wills and purposes. Remolded, however, the point can be better made: the community acts in order to assert its will against the market's unplanned consequences, and in so doing it acts against (constrains) the choices of market individuals. But because both the market and the community in its (democratic) political institutions are composed of the same persons, we might say, with greater precision, that these individuals act so as to constrain themselves from the behaviors and consequences that are an unavoidable (and in a sense compelled) part of markets. The political/social response to market failures of the normative sort, the creation of alternative entitlement patterns, for example, reflects for Marx an assertion (in microcosm) of autonomy at the social level (the substitution of conscious, *ex ante,* decisions for the unregulated workings of the market) and a way of securing the freedom and material well-being of individuals. Marx employs radical market failures of this type not directly because of the intrinsic evils of the consequences he attributes to them, but rather because, by highlighting those unintended and perverse results, he can set out the meaning of contracts and markets, in a phrase of the new location of the economy, in a manner that undermines the classical liberal claim that voluntary bilateral contracts in a private-property market are uniquely freedom-preserving.

8.3.2   Economies of Time

Few modern political philosophers have been as concerned with the problem of time and the economy as was Marx, and that is because (for Marx) no previous economic system was so preoccupied with time (as an economic good) as is capitalism. There is a moral dimension to Marx's reflections on time, one that takes him back to the teachings of the ancients on this subject. I return to that part of his analysis at a later point. For the present I am concerned to explore further the perverse-effects theory begun in the preceding pages. There we examined a single aspect of this theory, the capacity of a market and a pattern of entitlements and ownership for generating undersatisfaction of basic needs in the presence of material abundance. Sen's account develops this market failure as an illustration of the importance of the power to command commodities, with his resulting emphasis on ownership and exchange rules. Marx's version has much the same focus, evident in his discussion of effective demand, but he interweaves the ownership approach with an examination of the purpose of commodity production of the capitalist type: enhanced exchange value rather than the satisfaction of need. In the following remarks on time and capitalism, we will see Marx dealing with the undersatisfaction not of an "absolute" or material need but rather of what has been called a radical need, meaning a need for those things required for human freedom and for the good life, specifically here the need for time free from necessary economic activity.[107] We will also see him largely putting to one side the question of ownership and concentrat-

---

[107] On the idea of radical needs see Agnes Heller, *The Theory of Need in Marx* (New York: St. Martin's Press, 1976), and Adam Przeworski, "Material Interests, Class Compromise, and the Transition to Socialism," in Roemer, ed., *Analytical Marxism.*

ing instead on the subordination of social goods to the valorization process of capital. Once more, the purpose of Marx's argument is to show the specific perverse consequences of capitalism—now in relation to time, but also at a higher level of abstraction—to display the dominance of the unregulated economy in bourgeois society.

The reason for capitalism's concern with time is apparent, Marx says, in an observation from a factory inspector's report: "'Moments are the elements of profit.'"[108] Recast in Marx's vocabulary, we may explain the centrality of time under capitalism as follows. Use-values are not measured by their embodied labor time but exchange-value is, and labor time is also the substance of value. Surplus value is nothing but the ratio of two sorts of time, necessary and surplus, which is to say the ratio of the time required for the reproduction of labor and the excess or surplus time expended in production. The "function specific to capital" is just the production of surplus value which means (embodied) surplus time. I might repeat here that I employ the long-refuted language of value out of exegetical fidelity to Marx; I do suspect, however, that the analysis of leisure and capitalism stands or falls on other grounds than the labor theory of value.

Capital seeks the contraction of necessary time, that required for the worker's reproduction or for the movement of the commodity through its market phase. But it does this, as was intimated in the remark quoted above ("'Moments are the elements of profit'"), in order to expand embodied surplus time (profit). The latter point is key, as we shall see, for in trying to limit the time required for producing the necessities of the subsistence bundle (historically defined) or for bringing commodities from their producers to their end users, capital is interested in the expansion of only one type of unbound time, namely (embodied) surplus labor time. More briefly, we might say that capital frees time in order to appropriate it for itself: capital "usurps" time.[109] I now trace out Marx's analysis of this idea, one of the supreme paradoxes he attributed to capitalism: that an economic formation dedicated to the greatest possible minimization of the constraints on time (i.e., necessary production time) is also a process that more than any other binds the time of human beings.[110] According to Marx, there are two principal ways in which

[108] Marx, *Capital*, vol. 1, p. 352.

[109] Marx, *Capital*, vol. 1, p. 375; Marx, *Capital*, vol. 3, p. 373, and Marx, *MEGA*, II.3.1, pp. 174–75.

[110] For a brilliant analysis of this paradox, and one that in certain respects parallels the argument set out here, see G. A. Cohen, *Karl Marx's Theory of History: A Defense*, pp. 302–7, and the longer version of it in Cohen, "Labor, Leisure, and a Distinctive Contradiction of Advanced Capitalism," in Gerald Dworkin et al., eds., *Markets and Morals*

surplus labor time can be increased: by an extension of the working day toward its physical limits and by technological innovation (and, relatedly, through innovation in the organization of the production process). In the relative absence of the technology and organizational techniques of large-scale production, surplus time can be increased only by the expansion of the number of hours worked. But the working day has natural (and, Marx adds, moral and historical) limits: labor has to reproduce itself and needs rest if it is to reappear the next day as a factor of production. These limits and the social reaction against the extension of the working day are among the incentives for capital to increase the surplus portion of the working day through technology and innovations in technique.

Yet it is also one of the distinguishing features of capitalist production that the labor/time-saving changes it introduces in response to the limits of time physically available for work become themselves powerful impulses to still greater pressures on that time. Indeed, it is the case, Marx writes, that capital's "boundless thirst" for the extension of the working day arose first in those industries undergoing technological revolutions (e.g., the introduction of steam-powered machines) and that the paradoxical convergence of the phenomena of labor-saving technology and of renewed pressure on the working day was not mere coincidence. Rather, the thirst of capital for more labor time, for absolute surplus value, was the consequence of large-scale, mechanized industry.[111] Let us now look briefly at Marx's account of the capitalist introduction and employment of labor-saving technology.

This technological revolution is characterized as one of the transformation of the production process into a large-scale, combined enterprise centered on the use of self-acting machinery, machines whose principal power source is not human effort. It is only with this form of production,

(New York: John Wiley, 1977), pp. 107–36. Cohen's argument diverges from Marx's in its emphasis on the irrational promotion and growth of consumption as a principal factor in the explanation of the paradox of time and capitalism. See also Alan Gilbert, "Marx's Moral Realism," in Terence Ball and James Farr, eds., *After Marx* (Cambridge: Cambridge University Press, 1984), pp. 154–83, especially p. 162, and Moishe Postone, "Necessity, Labor, and Time: A Reinterpretation of the Marxian Critique of Capitalism," *Social Research* 79 (1978): 739–85, and especially pp. 758–59; Maximilien Rubel, *Karl Marx: Essai de biographie intellectuelle* (Paris: Marcel Rivière, 1957), pp. 362–68; Rodney G. Peffer, *Marxism, Morality, and Social Justice* (Princeton: Princeton University Press, 1990), pp. 164–65. See also my "Economies of Time: On the Idea of Time in Marx's Political Economy," *Political Theory* 19 (1991): 7–27.

[111] See Marx, *Capital*, vol. 3, p. 340; vol. 1, pp. 411, 526, 646, and Marx, *MEGA*, II.3.6, p. 2046.

essentially that of the mechanized atelier, that the specifically capitalist production process comes into being.[112] This technological revolution and its accompanying changes in the organization of production are driven by the dominant purpose of capitalism, that is, to expand surplus value/profit. This capitalists help to achieve by contracting necessary labor time or, what amounts to much the same thing, by inducing a fall (absolutely, through an extension of the working day, or, where the length of the working day is given, relatively, through increased productivity) in the value of labor power: "The constant tendency of capital is to force the cost of labour back towards . . . absolute zero." Here we see Marx's overarching theory of technology and time under capital: with improved technology, the worker could in less time produce the same quantity of surplus value for the capitalist.[113] But the valorization circuit, M-C-ΔM, never reaches an equilibrium level of surplus value—at every attained amount it seeks yet another increment, and that is just what is meant by Marx's description of capital's "boundless thirst."

This relationship between time and technology under capitalism is, Marx maintains, nowhere more apparent than in the technological expression of capital, the factory. The "despotic bell" there administers the laws of capitalist production to the world of the factory, compressing or "closing the pores" of time, measuring every action against the clock, and compelling the laborers—"full-" and "half-timers," the "personifications of labor time"—to feel concretely, in the pace of their work, capital's "feverish activity" in pursuit of its "boundless thirst" for surplus time.[114] That grand paradox Marx believed he had seen in the general laws of capital, reduction of necessary labor time coupled with pressure to usurp for itself all surplus time, is here made visible to the eye: social, combined labor and the technology displayed in the factory are the most potent inventions of the human mind for freeing persons from time

---

[112] Marx, *Results of the Immediate Process of Production*, pp. 1024, 1027, 1035; Marx, *Capital*, vol. 1, p. 439.

[113] Marx, *Capital*, vol. 1, p. 748, and see also p. 431 and Marx, *Grundrisse*, p. 334.

[114] Marx, *MEGA*, II.3.6, p. 2023 (quoting Engels, *The Condition of the Working-Class in England*, in *MECW*, vol. 4, p. 467). The "despotic bell" Engels describes is that of the factory calling the workers from their homes. Marx refers to the factory as the technological expression of capital in *MEGA*, II.3.6, pp. 2058–59. For a history of the bell and labor discipline see David S. Landes, *Revolution in Time: Clocks and the Making of the Modern World* (Cambridge: Harvard University Press, 1983), pp. 228–30. E. P. Thompson's "Time, Work-Discipline, and Industrial Capitalism" and Keith Thomas' "Work and Leisure in Pre-Industrial Society," *Past & Present* 29 (1964): 50–66, offer fascinating historical insights into the world of work and time before it was submitted to the command of the despotic bell. See also Marx, *MEGA*, II.3.6, p. 2024, and Marx, *Capital*, vol. 1, p. 353.

bound to the production of the necessities of existence, for permitting them unbound time.[115] In the mechanized atelier, however, these very forces become both the instruments of and one of the incentives to the drive toward the consumption of the person's time up to its outermost limits.

There is yet a further twist to this tale. The attempt to reduce necessary labor time through the increased employment of labor-saving technology is, in the end, labor-displacing. Another way of expressing this idea is to say that the productivity of a machine amounts to the difference between its cost and that of the labor it replaces.[116] While he maintains that there are powerful countervailing tendencies in capitalist production, Marx holds that its basic direction is to reduce the portion of variable capital (wages) as a fraction of overall capital and thereby to reduce the size of the working population, substituting greater intensity of labor for mass. The overall result is that capitalism, through the unfolding of its own laws, must produce a large surplus population. We might say (somewhat loosely) of this process that, in diminishing necessary labor, capital decreases the number of necessary persons and in so doing creates another sort of surplus time, that embodied not in commodities but in redundant human beings, the surplus population. This strange fruit of the (relative) conquest of nature and necessity, the misery of "surplus" humans, reveals the perversity not of capitalists but of a society in which time (and most other qualities) is subordinated to an autonomous economic process, one dedicated to the maximization of surplus labor time.

Under capitalism, time becomes contained within the economic process governing society. Indeed, that process itself is concerned above all with time and its distribution, not between persons but into its necessary and surplus portions. When Marx writes that capital has "usurped" time, he means a number of things, but in the most general sense what he intends by that statement is that time has become economic time, time absorbed into the production of surplus value. This absorption of time by the economic process is evident in the way of conceptualizing time as "necessary" or "surplus." "Necessary" and "surplus" are values attached to units of time in light of their function in the valorization circuit of capital. And it is the tendency of capital to appropriate all time, that is, to transform the free time that it makes possible into surplus time, into time for the production of expanded surplus value. Because persons, on

[115] See Marx, *Capital*, vol. 1, pp. 367, 375, 568, and Marx, *Grundrisse*, pp. 708–9.
[116] Marx, *Capital*, vol. 1, pp. 515, 573.

this view, are seen as potential vehicles for surplus time/surplus value, the hours they spend outside of the production process must be considered either as strictly unproductive, and hence wasted and deplorable, or as recreation, time spent renewing the person so as better to allow for a still more intensive expenditure of his or her productive hours. This subordination of time to production varies in its features according to class, but it is a characteristic of the capitalist economy as such, and it consequently (though in different ways) draws the time of the capitalist as well as that of the worker into its orbit.[117]

Time embedded in this autonomous process, M-C-ΔM, transformed into moments of the drive to create new surplus value, comes to dominate humans: "Time is everything, man is nothing."[118] Time is the measure of human activity, of its value to the production process, and the velocity of time (of the activities which occupy it), governed by the laws of the capital circuit, must incessantly be driven to new heights. Time, that potential forum for human freedom and the development of human faculties, here assumes an imperious voice, expressed in the commanding tocsins of the "despotic bell." In brief, Marx endeavors to show the specific function of time in the capitalist economy (increased amounts of its surplus form), the mechanics by which that overarching determinant is transmitted to individual capitalists (competition as constantly generating downward pressure on necessary labor time), and, last, the manner in which those pressures are translated into innovations in the technologies and techniques (organization) of production intended to extract maximum surplus time from the laboring population. The most developed industry,

---

[117] Marx, *Economic and Philosophical Manuscripts*, p. 316, and Marx, *Results of the Immediate Process of Production*, pp. 990, 1048. The weight of the evidence in Marx's political economic writings strongly indicates that the consumption of surpluses in the form of revenue or leisure rather than in reinvestment was as foreign to Marx's conception of capitalism as it was to Adam Smith's. See Marx, *Theories of Surplus Value*, vol. 2, pp. 503, 528; Marx, *Capital*, vol. 1, pp. 735, 739–40, 769, and vol. 2, p. 521; Marx, *German Ideology*, p. 418n. The texts, however, are not perfectly consistent on this point: cf. Marx, *Capital*, vol. 3, p. 958, and (quoting James Mill) Marx, *MEGA*, II.3.1, p. 188. In one indignant passage from *Capital*, vol. 1, p. 533, Marx compares these different uses of surplus time: to the ancient appropriation of free time, time for the "full human development" of the nonservile population, he contrasts the fruit of the capitalist employment of (embodied) surplus time, e.g., "eminent spinners," "extensive sausage-makers," and "influential shoe-black dealers." In other words, to leisure on the one side is contrasted expanded commerce on the other ("'The master had no time for anything but money the servant no time for anything but labour,'" *MEGA*, II.3.1, p. 201)—a comparison that, for Marx, reveals both the normative superiority of the ancient valuation of time *and* the reason for the stagnant character of its economies.

[118] Marx, *The Poverty of Philosophy*, p. 127.

then, forces the proletarian to work "harder than the savage," that is, harder even than those in societies lacking labor-saving technology.[119]

The anarchy of the market, the absence of conscious control from it together with its establishment of the ruling end of ΔM, is once again claimed by Marx to give birth to systematically perverse effects: "In our days everything seems pregnant with its contrary. Machinery, gifted with the wonderful power of shortening and fructifying human labour, we behold starving and overworking it. . . . All our invention and progress seem to result in endowing material forces with intellectual life, and in stultifying human life into a material force."[120] We have just seen another illustration of this idea in the introduction and employment of labor-saving technology in a capitalist economy. The rapid growth in the invention and use of these devices could in principle, Marx maintains, be put in the service of reducing the number of hours that persons have to devote to drudge labor. But because the goal of capitalist production is the creation of surplus value, and not leisure, those saved hours are "usurped" by capital and made into profit rather than free time, and into a competitive advantage for the innovating firm rather than into a relief of the human estate. Both the pressure to introduce labor-sparing technology and the choice of its employment are profoundly shaped by the need to produce surplus value and thus by the survival requirements imposed by the market. Under those requirements, the rational and efficient use of such inventions is to reduce the cost of production and not to lessen the pressure on labor time.[121] Marx here intertwines two claims, one about the value of time, economic and bound or free, and the other concerning choice—that the employment of these assets is determined by the market and the end it imposes on its actors. The normatively suboptimal use of labor-saving technology is one index, for Marx, of the extent to which persons in a capitalist economy are ruled by forces of their own making but which have escaped their control or, in other words, of the degree to which the creation of greater value is the driving purpose of their society, a purpose enforced by the market mechanism.

Once more, Marx argues, society intervenes against this (moral) failure of the market, limiting the market's operations by erecting barriers against it.[122] Marx contrasts the resulting legally limited working day to the "pompous catalogue of the 'inalienable rights of man.'" He lauds the

[119] Marx, *Grundrisse*, pp. 708–9.
[120] Marx, "Speech at the Anniversary of the People's Paper," in *The Marx-Engels Reader*, 2d ed., ed. Robert C. Tucker (New York: Norton, 1978), p. 578.
[121] Marx, *MEGA*, II.3.1, p. 173.
[122] Marx, *Capital*, vol. 1, p. 416.

Ten Hours' Bill because it is an instance of the subordination of the economy to the purposes of the community rather than to the requirements of the valorization process. The "catalogue of the 'inalienable rights of man,'" Marx seems to suggest, has (to borrow the phrases of *The German Ideology*) freed humans from the "violence of men" only to submit them to the "violence of things," that is, the autonomous economic process. The modest Ten Hours' Bill attempts to reduce that "violence," and it partially returns to the hands of society its power over the market.

8.4   Markets and Firms

I now consider some further reflections of Marx on the consequences of a capitalist market, those arising from the purchase and sale of labor power and the creation of command-type ("despotic") microeconomies out of contract. In the passage from Locke's *Second Treatise* (§85) referred to earlier, we saw that the servant, by contract, enters the master's household and submits himself to "the ordinary Discipline thereof." The entry point of the servant into the family is contractual, a temporary arrangement between juridically equal persons and, contrary to ancient servitude, one unmarked by coercion or status. Once inside the household, however, the servant falls under the "ordinary Discipline" of the family, and discretion over his actions is transferred, for a time, to the master. As we saw, Marx accepts this part too of the liberal construction of the labor contract: a new master/servant relationship is born out of the sale and purchase of labor, a historically unique relationship in the sense that it is mediated by exchange, and therefore established by commodity owners, free as self-owners and equal in their status. But here, as in most other aspects of Marx's genuflections to the liberal tradition, there is a sharply different theoretical use made of the distinction between market/contract and household/discipline, between contractual and non-market authoritarian elements of the economy, and, needless to say, a very different evaluation of both sides of that distinction.

Let us begin with the explanatory side of Marx's analysis. At the most general level, Marx's insight is that while the capitalist economy is virtually boundless in its process of commodification—the drawing of things, persons, and activities into the orbit of the market—the market is not the sole mechanism of coordination in a capitalist economy. Existing alongside the market is a sphere in which the coordinating mechanism is not the impersonal, unintended laws generated *ex post* by a series of exchanges but command, authority, and a priori planning.[123] Marx wants to probe the relation between these two sectors of the economy and specifically to understand why it is that the capitalist market, composed of voluntary, bilateral exchanges, gives rise to the internal command structure of the firm. In sum, he wants to grasp why it is that "anarchy" at the level of the social economy yields something like despotism at the microlevel.[124]

We have already observed one element of Marx's analysis of this process: the existence of persons with no way to secure their livelihood save through the sale of labor power, an idea that combines the historical claim of the dispossession of a segment of the population and a further and related claim about the restricted choices available to those persons. These two propositions are the foundation of Marx's effort to account for the servant's arrival at the master's door or the worker at the factory gates. An additional element to this story, which forms a partial bridge to the internal discipline of the household/firm, is that the producer is a self-owner and hence can alienate his labor or, in fewer words, that labor power has become a commodity. What the purchaser of labor power acquires is, Marx writes, a use-value, and like all owners of use-values she is entitled under the rules of commodity exchange to consume it as she will, subject in the case of human labor to the conditions imposed by the living commodity and by whatever restrictions society may, through its laws, place on the sale of labor. That labor power is a commodity and that commodities are disposed of (within specified limits) at their owner's discretion opens the way for the master to subject the servant to the ordinary discipline of the household, or the factory owner-manager to bring the employee under the command and control functions of the factory/firm.[125]

[123] Marx, *Capital*, vol. 1, pp. 476–77; Ugo Pagano, *Work and Welfare in Economic Theory* (Oxford: Basil Blackwell, 1985), pp. 3, 42. For analyses of the firm as a surrogate market rather than as an authoritarian organization see Michael C. Jensen and William H. Meckling, "Theory of the Firm: Managerial Behavior, Agency Costs, and Ownership Structure," *Journal of Finance Economics* 3 (1976): 310–11; Armen A. Alchian and Harold Demsetz, "Production, Information Costs, and Economic Organization," *American Economic Review* 52 (1972): 777–95, esp. pp. 777, 793, 795. Compare to R. H. Coase, "The Nature of the Firm," in George J. Stigler and Kenneth E. Boulding, eds., *Readings in Price Theory* (Chicago: Richard Irwin, 1952), pp. 332–34, which comes rather closer to Marx's view of the contrast between markets and firms.

[124] Marx, *Results of the Immediate Process of Production*, p. 1002; Marx, *MEGA*, II.3.1, pp. 286, 289–90; Marx, *The Poverty of Philosophy*, p. 185.

[125] For these points, see Marx, *Grundrisse*, p. 282; Marx, *Capital*, vol. 1, pp. 291–92; Coase, "The Nature of the Firm," p. 349; Kenneth J. Arrow, *The Limits of Organization* (New York: John Wiley, 1951), pp. 25, 64.

This part of the explanation of the coexistence of markets and non-market, authoritarian hierarchies is clearly not, by itself, sufficient. It tells us that, as a matter of entitlement, capital becomes, in the person of its owner, an authority over labor. What it does not unpack is why such nonmarket institutions would emerge. Marx ventures two principal and overlapping explanations for the presence of the "despotism" of the factory—"islands of conscious power," to use Ronald Coase's admirable and rather more measured expression (from his "The Nature of the Firm"), in the midst of the anarchy of the market. One, which draws on his (not always observed) theoretical commitment to what G. A. Cohen has called the explanatory primacy of the productive forces, emphasizes the technological revolution that was the "real foundation" of capitalism and the other focuses on market pressures, efficiency, and discipline.

I begin with some observations on the first of these lines of analysis. The core of the modern revolution in the production process consists, as we noted, in the spatio-temporal concentration of production. This concentration, spatial in its bringing of producers into one locale and temporal in its synchronization of labor and in its time-thrift as well, is made possible (and Marx thought, necessary) by a revolution in technology: the employment of a common power source propelling numerous specialized machines. These innovations made team production efficient and provided economies of scale over the putting-out system. The result, in short, was the growth of cities as production centers and, within those centers, the bringing together of workers under a single roof and engaged in interlocking activity. The technological transformation of production gave birth to a new mode of production, including new relations among the workers themselves and between them and the owners of capital. One side of this revolution can be described as the emergence of large-scale production.[126] The cooperation of the workers, made possible by their spatial concentration in the factory, is also decisively shaped in its details by the machines they operate. Those machines perform distinct but interdependent operations, and the persons seeing to their varied operations must be subsumed under the "total process" of mechanized production. Large-scale, interlocking production makes each person dependent on

[126] On the above points see Marx, *Results of the Immediate Process of Production*, pp. 1021–22, 1024; Marx, *MEGA*, II.3.6, pp. 1973, 2002, 2013, 2019; Marx, *Capital*, vol. 1, pp. 602–4; Marx and Engels, *German Ideology*, p. 73; Marx, *Capital*, vol. 3, pp. 172, 731; Alchian and Demsetz, "Production, Information Costs, and Economic Organization," p. 784; North, *Structure and Change in Economic History* (New York: Norton, 1981), p. 41. For a critique of the technological analysis of discipline see David S. Landes, ed., *The Rise of Capitalism* (New York: Macmillan, 1966), p. 14.

her neighbor, and it makes the aggregate of these individual interdependencies subject to the overall functioning of the technology being employed. Like an army or an orchestra, the movements of which in different ways call into being a coordination role, so too in the factory the subordination of the producers to the "uniform motion" of the machines requires orchestration.[127]

Contemporary analyses of the presence of an authoritative element in the firm or factory focus on the costs of contract writing under conditions of uncertainty, the costs of metering input productivity in team production, and the economies of communication/decision making in centralized versus peer-group organizations.[128] Marx tends to cite the need for coordination in a unitary, spatially compressed production process conducted by detached but interdependent agents. This coordination role takes on its more severe disciplinary character because the persons who have contracted their time (not some specified end product) to the employer may have little interest in hard work or economies of material or time, especially if their singular contribution to joint production is not easily monitored. The worker must be constrained to act in the appropriate, economical, manner. The second element of the concentration of the production process is its temporal compression. We saw that this aspect of Marx's argument is grounded in his labor theory of value and in his notion that survival in a competitive market depends on producing at the "socially average" velocity, a velocity the pace of which is set ever steeper by firms innovating technologically or in their techniques. Reducing the labor time necessary to produce a good is therefore key to the enterprise, and one element of this drive is to increase the intensity and/or duration of labor, a task for which discipline and minute supervision are the appropriate means.[129]

[127] Marx, *Grundrisse*, p. 693; Marx, *MEGA*, II.3.6, pp. 1905, 2024; Marx, *Capital*, vol. 1, pp. 448, 549.
[128] See respectively: Oliver E. Williamson, *Markets and Hierarchies: Analysis and Antitrust Implications* (New York: Free Press, 1975), p. 4, and Williamson, "Transaction-cost Economics: The Governance of Contractual Relations," *Journal of Law & Economics* 22 (1979): 233–61, p. 237; Alchian and Demsetz, "Production, Information Costs, and Economic Organization," pp. 778–80; Williamson, *Markets and Hierarchies*, pp. 45–47; Arrow, *The Limits of Organization*, pp. 33–35, 68. Marx suggests something like this at *MEGA*, II.3.1, p. 235.
[129] Marx, *Results of the Immediate Process of Production*, pp. 986–87. See also Marx, *MEGA*, II.3.6, p. 2030, and II.3.1, p. 201; Marx, *Capital*, vol. 3, pp. 178–79; Michael Reich and James Devine, "The Microeconomics of Conflict and Hierarchy in Capitalist Production," *Review of Radical Political Economics* 12 (1981): 27. For related historical material see David S. Landes, ed., *The Rise of Capitalism*, pp. 13–14; Neil McKendrick, "Josiah Wedgwood and Factory Discipline," in Landes, ed., *The Rise of Capitalism*, p. 70; Thompson, "Time, Work-discipline, and Capitalism," pp. 70–71, 78.

The conceptual tie between the technologically determined interdependency (and the resulting coordination function of the modern production process) and the "barrackslike" discipline of the enterprise is provided by the overarching purpose of production in a surplus-driven economy. A basic contention of Marx's is that persons become slaves or wage laborers only within the context of specific economic formations; and likewise with machines—an automatic loom, for example, is only capital, and is only a moment in the valorization process of capital, under certain circumstances. By extension, interdependency and coordination may well be properties of the shift from artisan or yeoman-type-agrarian economies to factory production, but discipline and the "despotism" of capitalism are characteristics the explanation of which demands additional elements. Now, one of those elements (in Marx's account) I have just alluded to: the governing purpose of production—the creation of profit, ΔM—in a market that weeds out inefficient producers and rewards others. Efficiency of a particular sort (very different in purpose from that discussed by Socrates and Ischomachos in Xenophon's *Oeconomicus*), that is, the maximum achievable growth of surplus value (profit), determines the choice of coordination mechanisms, for example, between markets and firms.[130] This standard will guide the enterprise in securing the greatest possible productivity from its inputs, human and inanimate alike. Marx's claim is that where the struggle to generate profits conflicts with the producer's preferences coordination will take the form of discipline. A related assertion is that because the (miniature) community of producers within the factory is brought together under the control of capital and not as a voluntary (horizontally created) association—its members having in common with that community nothing save being subject to the same automaton—discipline will be virtually inevitable, as it is in military organization, and as it has been, in varied ways according to Marx, in all past organizations of production.[131] The sum of these assertions is that the governing end of the economy, an end whose "executor" is the market, acts back as it were upon technologically shaped production relations (interdependency in space and time) and gives them one of their possible forms: the hierarchical, command structure of the firm/factory.

With the above observations, we have the rudiments of Marx's account of the nonmarket sphere of a capitalist economy and of its relationship to

[130] Williamson, *Markets and Hierarchies*, p. 8. Nelson and Winter in *An Evolutionary Theory of Economic Change*, pp. 9, 53, question the exclusive profit motive description but attribute an analogous function to the market.

[131] Marx, *MEGA*, II.3.1, pp. 235–36; Marx, *Capital*, vol. 1, p. 451, and vol. 3, p. 510; Marx, *Grundrisse*, p. 585.

the market and to the large-scale, mechanized production that he maintains was the technological foundation of capitalism. A discussion of Marx's normative assessment of this modern nonmarket economic institution would naturally begin with a remark on his statement that in relation to the "hidden abode" of the production process the market represents a "Garden of Eden" of the rights of man.[132] That passage can easily be read as speaking in a wholly ironic voice. However, as I argued earlier, it is in fact meant to convey the superiority of the market to precapitalist *oikos*-type economic institutions. This superiority resides in the equality, freedom (the field of choice), and in the individuality the market makes possible. And that same cluster of features makes the market superior to the hierarchical and authoritarian internal organization of the factory/firm. In drawing this comparison, it should be noted, I am treating the *oikos,* markets, and the firm as three types of moral economies and I am thus leaving out of the present account the claims developed above (and to which I shall return) concerning the role of markets in generating institutions like the factory/firm.

We saw that Marx maintains that one of the properties of the market relation, the idea of the person as self-owner, is an advance over economies in which living labor is directly and wholly the property of others. The world of the factory contains the (temporary) abolition of that self-ownership inasmuch as labor power is there transformed into a use-value belonging to its purchaser and consumable at his discretion: an indeterminate rather than a specified contract. That such contracts are made because of the greater efficiency of a single open-ended labor contract, leaving it to managers to allocate labor according to the (not entirely predictable) needs of the firm would, for Marx, serve simply to illuminate one of the human costs of an economy dedicated to surplus maximization: the producer ceases to be a self-owner.[133] A second aspect of the market which represents progress over the despotic economy is the freedom of its actors, the range of choices before them, and the absence of coercion and subordination to the will of the master. To be sure, there is the "silent compulsion" of economic laws, but in the market the imperious voice of the antique master has been stilled. The factory is a very different world. To describe it, Marx (revealingly) adopts the language of ancient Greece: the "despotism" of the "factory Lycurgus" who has the power to act like a "private legislator." The literary form here mirrors Marx's normative intent: to point to the re-emergence of the dominating

132 Marx, *Capital*, vol. 1, pp. 279–80.
133 Marx, *MEGA*, II.3.1, pp. 234–35.

will in the nonmarket sectors of the economy—of personal power and of the subordination of one person to another—with the resulting diminution of freedom. Marx's other favored metaphor to describe the "hidden abode" of the production process is as an armylike organization. By this he means to make a number of normative points. The first, and most obvious, is the barrackslike discipline of the factory as a restraint on freedom. The second thought is tied to a view of market society as a promoter of an individuality previously suppressed by the overbearing presence of the community.[134] Self-owners in the market, responsible for themselves and exercising choice based on their own preferences, achieve a hitherto unknown identification of themselves as individuals. The factory, in which each person occupies a functional role determined by the technological requirements of production, "de-individualizes" these agents, making them moments of an objective process.[135]

This is what Marx means when he writes of the "reproduction" of a master/servant relation in capitalism. Elsewhere I underscored the newness of the process by which this relationship is generated (mediated by the market) as well as the distinctive features of the end result, for example, the absence of status. Yet for Marx the nonmarket, authoritarian, and hierarchical organization of factories and firms bears a not unimportant resemblance to the despotic economies that preceded capitalism. A conventional, historically well-known form of unfreedom—ranked powers and direct control over laborers—reappears alongside a world of choice, equality, a world of juridical persons.

If the form of this unfreedom is familiar, the process by which it is produced, from certain properties of a free market, places it among those deep, foundational paradoxes of the coexistence of freedom and compulsion which Marx believed he had seen in capitalism. Marx's theory of market constraints, emphasizing endowments, entitlements, and interdependency, would thus provide him with an answer to the "implicit contract" theorists of hierarchy in the workplace, to those who hold that employees voluntarily submit to the discipline of the firm because such compulsion reduces free-riding, motivates harder work, and therefore promises a healthier enterprise with the expectation of a better salary and a secure job.[136] Marx would, I think, have had little difficulty accepting this as a part of the description of the relation between the labor contract

[134] Marx, *MEGA*, II.3.1, pp. 233, 284–85, 303; Marx, *Capital*, vol. 1, pp. 449–50, 549–50; Marx, *Grundrisse*, pp. 84, 470, 541.

[135] Marx, *MEGA*, II.3.6, p. 2024.

[136] Joseph E. Stiglitz, "Incentives, Risk and Information: Notes towards a Theory of Hierarchy," *Bell Journal of Economics* 6 (1975): 552–79, esp. pp. 571–72.

and the internal organization of the firm. He might have observed, however, that it is the limits of the feasible set (the product of the various market constraints) available to the employees which lead them to submit themselves to the authority of the firm. Within the confines of those boundaries, individuals most certainly have choices, and their preferences among the goods before them may indeed lead them to sacrifice autonomy in the workplace for the sake of higher wages. The normative question that Marx proposes is not whether there is choice in such an economy: "everything touching on the individual . . . leaves him a wide field of choice."[137] Rather, it is *why* those boundaries, if we assume that they are corrigible and that some possible correction of them would allow persons a greater sphere of choice?

We thus have two major nonmarket, authoritarian, and hierarchical models of the economy—alike in the absence of freedom, in their inequality, and dissimilar in that the modern version is purely economic whereas its ancient antecedent was a profoundly political economy. This distinction can be recast in a manner that allows us to understand one further and vital aspect of Marx's theory and evaluation of market and authoritarian economies. Recall that the governing purpose of the *oikos* economy was the master's "organized want satisfaction" (C-M-C or its variants), while the ruling end of a capitalist-type economy, according to Marx, is ΔM. Under the first of these regimes, despotism emerges as the organizational response to the need for leisure and praxis on the part of the master; under the latter order, the authoritative, planned economy of the factory emerges as the most efficient answer to the requirements of the valorization process enforced by the unregulated market institution.[138] For, Marx thought, as long as those requirements prevail as the determinants of economic activity, the economy in all its dimensions—organizational, technological, labor, and so forth—will be subordinated to the production of ever-increasing wealth.

9. The Household Economy Restored

9.1   The Aristotelian Foundations of Marx's Economics

We might say that Marx offers a cluster of market-failure theories. One type consists of the conventionally recognizable sort, that associated with

---

[137] Marx, *Grundrisse*, p. 464.
[138] This distinction is suggested, e.g., in Marx, *MEGA*, II.3.1, p. 84.

the economically suboptimal results of rational market behavior, for example, the falling rate of profit. The second, and more important, subset
of theories was normative. The latter he illustrated using crises of underconsumption in the presence of material sufficiency, the employment of
labor-saving technology (the bourgeois economy of time), and the
market-generated authoritarian microeconomy of the factory. These failures, Marx thought, constitute injuries and wrongs in themselves, and
they also served him as indicators of the capacity of capitalist markets to
deny society control over the use of its economy. The array of perverse
effects Marx sketched was thus one measure of the extent to which the
economy had become autonomous, had supplanted its purposiveness for
that of the community. Said in another manner, the constraints of ownership and entitlement norms on the one side and of the behavior enforced
by market competition on the other continue to restrict both the autonomy of individuals and, in the context of an unregulated economy, the
power of society to determine the use it wishes to make of its material
infrastructure.

Viewed on a broader stage, this argument amounts to a theory of the
modern equivalent of *pleonexia*. In the antique world, it will be remembered, *pleonexia*, the search for ever more things, was considered a malaise of the soul, a corrupt passion that simultaneously rendered its victim
unfree, a slave to wealth, and so unable to lead a good life. The judgment
as to the perversity of such a life may well have rested on the presence (for
some) of other possibilities, of a life devoted for example to citizenship,
philosophy, or to the leisured and virtuous activities of the best of friendships. Wealth, to be sure, was a necessary condition of freedom and the
good life; but, as we saw, the wealth needed for those ends was not
unlimited, and consequently the pursuit of gain beyond these limits was a
choice, and a perverse choice against just those goods that a properly
ordered (contained) economy could offer. For *pleonexia* of that kind,
education and a healing of the soul, a psychiatry, were the remedies, and
that former task is precisely what Xenophon attempted in his
Oeconomicus and Aristotle in his *Nicomachean Ethics* and *Politics*.
Modern *pleonexia*, in Marx's account, is something quite different: a
property (ΔM) of a system, and not an individual malady; a pattern of
behavior induced in market agents by the constraints of the institutions
within which they must act; and, last, a pervasive set of institutions from
which exit is pragmatically impossible. If the mechanisms of *pleonexia* in
the modern world are different, its results are similar—a constrained life,
the diminution of autonomy, and the channeling of goods, time, and
activities into an economically rational direction in the modern sense,

meaning one consistent with the market-enforced purpose of the capitalist economy. In a word, the constraints within which capitalist and worker alike operate are such that they are forced in their actions to adapt to
the requirements of the competitive, surplus-maximizing market.[139] The
consequences of this systemic *pleonexia* for freedom and other fundamental human goods are what Marx was examining in the various normative market failures sketched above.

Much of the conceptual apparatus of Marx's study of this modern
pleonexia comes directly from the economic science that, he thought, sets
out the laws of motion of a capitalist economy. In this sense his economic
theory is, as we observed earlier, firmly rooted in that developed within,
and appropriate to, modernity. So much is clear from Marx's claim that
one of the central discoveries of his economic analysis is the explanation
of the "value form," a concept that, he writes, did not appear in the
ancient world and that indeed is "entirely peculiar" to the modern economy. Marx, then, places the core of his theory of capitalism squarely in
the modern tradition of political economy, a body of thought that, he
argues, first attained the rank of a science with the Physiocrats.[140] He
thereby expresses his allegiance not only to much of the theoretical detail
of classical economics but also to something grander, to its claim to be the
master science of modernity. By contrast, not only had the ancient economists little or no concept of value (other than use-value), but the idea of
an economic science the driving question of which was the increase of
surpluses was not thought of in their world, Marx writes. The issue there
was rather that of how to produce good citizens: an issue indicating the
primacy of noneconomic goods, of citizenship, *ta kala,* or whatever.[141]
The political economy that expresses the laws of a C-M-C economy will
have as its object of investigation the sovereign element in the community,
the household masters or the dominant class, because it is they who rule
over the embedded economy. In such a world, a purely economic science
could hardly exist. At most, it would be a narrow science, the rules of
technē applied to acquisition, in other words, of an art subordinate to
that involved in ruling over the household or city. Modernity, on the other
hand, brings a new political economy and gives that study a different
status. Consider another of Marx's comments on the Physiocrats: "It was
their great merit that they conceived these forms [of production] as phys-

[139] Marx, *Wage Labour and Capital,* in *MECW,* vol. 9, pp. 214–15.

[140] Marx, *Capital,* vol. 1, p. 90; Marx, *Grundrisse,* p. 776; Marx and Engels, *German Ideology,* p. 412.

[141] Marx, *Grundrisse,* p. 487.

iological forms of society: as forms arising from the natural necessity of production itself, forms that are independent of anyone's will or of politics, etc."[142] Economics for the first time becomes a science independent of politics, the study of the autonomous laws of production and exchange and of that force shaping most human affairs. The needs of the dominant community are no longer understood as the determining purpose of wealth-creating activity. Only in modernity does (and can) economics emerge as the independent master science of the social world; prior to capitalism, something like a political science was, in Aristotle's phrase, the master science.[143]

What was missing in that economic science, so much of which Marx himself adopted, was the question of the end or purpose of the economy, or more exactly of a purpose beyond that of the creation of more wealth, of the place of the economy in the universe of human values. The production of wealth, surplus without limits, the efficiency criteria appropriate to that production—these and related ideas marked out the horizon of economic thought and insofar as this system of thought was, according to Marx, the master science of the bourgeois world so too did it trace the outermost limits of that society. To break through that horizon, to open up the possibility of other locations of the economy in the moral architecture of our common household, Marx turned to the ancient tradition, and above all to Aristotle. It is here, as well as in his thinking about freedom and the constraints on it, that Marx's engagement with Aristotle produces the most fertile results, leaving us with, if nothing else, a bequest of questions which enlivens our thinking on these matters and which breaks the deadening hold of our received pieties.[144] Marx's study of the perverse effects of capitalist markets was intended to push to the frontiers of the bourgeois world, to prepare the ground for an Aristotelian understanding of the economy in light of its end: to ask, that is to say, what good was served by the transformation of potential free time into surplus value, by the economically efficient discipline of the factory, or by patterns of entitlement that permitted (more, called into being) the radical undersatisfaction of needs.

---

[142] Marx, *Theories of Surplus Value*, vol. 1, p. 44.

[143] Marx and Engels, *German Ideology*, pp. 409, 412, 414; Marx, *Grundrisse*, p. 104.

[144] Martha C. Nussbaum, *The Fragility of Goodness* (Cambridge: Cambridge University Press, 1986) and her "Nature, Function, and Capability: Aristotle on Political Distribution" (*Oxford Studies in Ancient Philosophy*, suppl. vol., ed. Julia Annas [Oxford: Clarendon Press, 1988], esp. p. 184 n. 47), while not explicitly concerned with this relationship between Marx and Aristotle on external goods, freedom, and the good life, are rich in intimations of it.

He wanted, that is, to bring the horizon of bourgeois society into full view by asking after the use or purpose of its economy. That question he drew from the classical literature on the *oikos*, and its answer virtually called the vast *oikos* back onto the world stage. Recall Marx's excerpt from Xenophon's *Oeconomicus: "The art of household management . . . the science whereby humans are capable of increasing the things of the house . . . the things of the house* [are] *its totality of goods . . . a good is what is useful to each and all . . . useful* [is] *everything which one knows how to use."* Here is another excerpt from the same set (*MEGA*, IV.2) of Marx's notes on the *Oeconomicus: "The same things are goods, for him who knows how to employ them, but not for him who does not understand their use."* What is striking in Marx's selection of passages is the emphasis on the idea of knowing the use of the things in order that they may become goods, that is, things that serve to better the human estate. The Socratic dialogue reported in the *Oeconomicus* sought to draw Kritoboulos and Ischomachos to the question of use, with a view to moving them beyond the desire for acquisition toward an understanding of the relationship between the economy and the good life. We may well imagine that, reading Aristotle and Xenophon, Marx was led to question bourgeois society in a similar way.

That questioning, as we saw, brought Marx to the "cell form" of capitalism, the commodity. In its double aspect of use-value and need satisfaction, on the one side, and of exchange value, of being a vehicle for expanded value, on the other, he saw the heart of the capitalist economy. That heart Marx expressed in the "general formula" of capital, M-C-ΔM, to which he contrasted precapitalist economies, variants of C-M-C. This core of Marx's thought was, as I observed earlier, taken directly from Aristotle's *Politics*, Book 1. I remarked at the beginning of this part of the book that the underlying approach here is clearly Aristotelian: the emphasis on the end or purpose of the economy, on its use. But Marx's indebtedness to that tradition and to Aristotle in particular runs much deeper than to a shared set of questions about the economy. It is rather to be found in the ideal of the contained economy, and correspondingly in the critique of *pleonexia*, in the emphasis on free time as opposed to the economically most productive use of time, in the idea of a community approximating a voluntary and equal association with a freely chosen *philia*, rather than one bound by economic necessity, and finally in a richer understanding of the sources of unfreedom than that allowed within the contractarian discourse.

Consider for a moment the last-mentioned point. Marx writes, in a passage that we examine again in another context, that the Greeks, unlike the moderns, knew of the emancipatory potential of technology.[145] They knew, that is to say, of the relationship between the human metabolism with nature, its impact on their community and through that on the possibility of freedom. Stated negatively, they understood a wide range of sources of constraint and unfreedom. And for that reason they are valuable guides in thinking beyond the confines of the contractarian conceptualizations of freedom and the threats to it. At the same time, Marx, in common with liberalism, placed the emphasis on equal autonomy and thus he rejected the hierarchy and servitude that stood at the center of the classical vision of the good *oikos* economy. Marx, then, turned to Aristotle to find a vantage point from which to discern and judge the nature of the bourgeois world. In order to imagine an economy and society better than the one he saw before him, Marx again took his bearings from the ancient tradition and followed as far as he could the path it marked out.[146]

9.2   The New *Oikos*

Communist society, Marx thought, would be a free association of persons, consciously regulating their production. The foundation of this idea is the critique of capitalism as an economic formation in which the production and circulation of expanded value are independent of and dominant over society and the righting of that condition, namely, the establishment of social control over the economy. Viewed in that light, communism represents the restoration of a needs-driven (*oikos*-type) economy over the surplus-directed model of capitalism, in which needs are not those of a dominant class and where their satisfaction does not entail a corresponding denial of that same satisfaction to a servile population. It is a vision of a society which allows for the satisfaction of radical needs: for the autonomy of individuals and, collectively, of their community. This is a portrait of a society in which the economy, as in the Aristotelian *oikos,* is subject to the governance of the community and in which the economy is governed in order to contain it, to diminish the degree to which its operations determine the lives of persons. As far as is

[145] Marx, *Capital,* vol. 1, pp. 532–33.
[146] This analysis shows how inaccurate Dumont's reading of Marx is, i.e., as the arch modernizer, committed to the primacy of the economic. See Dumont, *From Mandeville to Marx,* pp. 111, 169–70.

possible, the determination of activity by the economy would cease to shape a person's life: "society regulates production and thus makes it possible for me to do one thing today and another tomorrow, to hunt in the morning, fish in the afternoon, rear cattle in the evening, criticize after dinner, just as I have a mind, without ever becoming hunter, fisherman, shepherd or critic." Time will again become the "room for man's development," time free from necessary production.[147] And last, the community will once more take the shape of a voluntary association. Let me now sketch each of these various facets of Marx's picture of communism.

9.2.1   Time

The ancients, Marx writes, "may perhaps have excused the slavery of one person as a means to the full human development of another."[148] This statement, in the context of the passage in which it appears, suggests that in the economies of the classical world, as indeed in all surplus-producing economies (i.e., those above the most primitive technological levels), laborers had to give over not only the time necessary for the production of their own necessities but an extra quantity for their masters. In his discussions of the ancient Greek economy (and of Aristotle as its master character-reader) Marx suggests (a) that the ancients sought the production of free time, or leisure, for the sake of the "human development" of the masters and (b) that, relatedly, in their more utopian moments they envisioned a world without scarcity which would free all persons from necessary labor or, in other words, liberate the time of all from its bound condition.[149] Marx, to be sure, was under no illusions in regard to the requirements of the *oikos* master's leisure—the bound time of his slaves and typically of his wife as well—and he understood the vision of the self-moving shuttle, as did the ancients themselves, as a

[147] Marx and Engels, *German Ideology,* p. 47, and see Marx, *Capital,* vol. 3, p. 959; Marx, *Theories of Surplus Value,* vol. 3, p. 256; Marx, *MEGA,* II.3.6, p. 2027. Michael Walzer's *Spheres of Justice* (New York: Basic Books, 1983), pp.184–96, offers a short account of free time and of Marx's thinking about it.

[148] Marx, *Capital,* vol. 1, p. 533. The single best analysis of the relationship between Marx's and Aristotle's concepts of leisure and servitude is Elisabeth Charlotte Welskopf, *Probleme der Musse im alten Hellas* (Berlin: Rütter & Loening, 1962).

[149] See Marx, *Capital,* vol. 1, pp. 344–45 and 532–33 and context. Of the four passages that Marx (*MEGA,* IV.2, p. 391) excerpted from Xenophon's *Oeconomicus,* the first was on the importance of understanding how to use the things of the economy, the second concerned the fact that manual laborers have "very little free time to care for friends and state" (*Oeconomicus* VI.9). And see Welskopf, *Probleme der Musse,* pp. 278–317.

utopian scheme coexisting with the mundane reality of slavery and other forms of servile labor. Yet it is clear that Marx believed that the ancients had understood something important about the value of time, something that had been lost under capitalism and that, corresponding to this understanding, they had seen (if only in a dream)—the liberating potential of technology. It was less the hierarchy of activities that an Aristotle or Xenophon thought should fill a person's leisure than the connection between the economy, the time it made available, and freedom, a relationship set out with the greatest clarity in *The Politics,* that drew Marx's attention. His emphasis on freedom and time, and his relative neglect of the ancient concern with the hierarchy of best lives to occupy that leisure, were not the result of a misreading of the classical tradition but rather, as I suggest further on, of an appropriation and transformation of that tradition.[150]

These observations are given further detail in Marx's comments on the ancient idea of technology, cited above. Production was subordinate to the goal of leisure, and if, so the Greeks imagined, machines could replace the labor of slaves, then there would be neither master nor slave, because the purposes of production would be fulfilled by machines instead of by humans. Machines (and surplus labor) were seen as instruments for the liberation of time, for the creation of leisure. The ancient idea of technology thus reflected a radically different valuation of time and of the relationship between economy and time. Time was not construed (extrapolating from the analysis I offered in Part One and from Marx's reading) as something to be absorbed as much as possible into the production process. On the contrary, the principal objective, the determining purpose of economic activity, was to provide for time not bound by or absorbed into the process of production and exchange, time to be devoted to citizenship, philosophy or, in general, to noneconomic pursuits. By contrast, modern political economy reflecting the dominance of

---

[150] Sebastian de Grazia in *Of Time, Work, and Leisure* (New York: Twentieth Century Fund, 1962), p. 351, suggests that Marx confused free time and leisure, i.e., misunderstood the ancient distinction between time free from constraining toil and the strenuous tasks of achieving the excellence of leisure. The former is accessible to all; the latter is inherently nondemocratic, being the activity of the well-born. De Grazia underestimates the extent to which the Greeks grasped the connection between time free from the economy and the freedom of the person—that in Aelian's words *argia* is the "sister of freedom," even while building from there a theory of the rank ordering of leisure activities. Equally inaccurate is the charge against Marx, who knew of that hierarchy of ways of living and of its antidemocratic underpinnings and therefore chose to employ another part of the ancient economy of time.

economic value over other types of values or social goods, conceives of time as surplus or necessary, profit or wages, and of time not engaged in production as wasted or, at best, as preparative for still greater productive exertions.[151] Free time will once again become true wealth of individuals and of society, Marx argues; it will be the "space" for human development. This postcapitalist order will be as concerned with the economization of time as is capitalism, but on a profoundly different foundation. Its economization would be a purposeful one directed not to increasing surplus labor time but to the freeing of time from economic constraint. Or, in somewhat different terms, it would be production subordinated to needs, among which the need for unbound time would be central.[152]

Marx's reluctance to set out in any detail the characteristics of communist society does not prevent us from capturing this, one of its principal features. In the contrast between the "despotic bell" of capitalist production and the image (from *The German Ideology*) of hunting in the morning, fishing in the afternoon, and philosophizing in the evening, the different valuation of time is apparent. Under the former regime, time is consumed in the "feverish" search after surplus value; its velocity, measured by the "swinging pendulum," and directed toward the embodiment of ever greater quantities of surplus labor time, dominates humans and appropriates their hours. The new economization of time creates the foundation for a tranquill pace, not frenetic, and in which its value resides in its freedom and in the space for human development it allows. The bell loses its commanding, despotic voice; each is free and can do when and as "he has a mind to." This economy of time aims at a situation in which time need no longer be subject to economic calculation of any sort. It is almost as if, having lost its dictatorial voice in a world where it is no longer "everything," time falls silent. Once it has been freed from its bonds, whether those of the master's whip or of the competitive demands for efficiency in production, time ceases to be a preoccupying object of concern. Free time, we might speculate, becomes freedom from (or better: in the silence of) time, or such at least as can be given to mortal creatures made of flesh and blood. One could say with Marx, then, "Economy of

---

[151] Marx, *Grundrisse*, p. 487, and see Marx and Engels, *The Holy Family*, p. 50.

[152] See Marx, *Grundrisse*, pp. 172–73, 705–6, 708; Marx, *Theories of Surplus Value*, vol. 3, pp. 256–57; Marx and Engels, *The Holy Family*, p. 49; Marx, *MEGA*, II.3.1, p. 168, and II.3.6, pp. 2026–27; Marx, *Capital*, vol. 3, pp. 288–89, 991, and vol. 1, p. 667. For valuable analyses of time and communism see Heller, *The Theory of Need in Marx*, pp. 116–18; Adam Przeworski, "Material Interests, Class Compromise and the Transition to Socialism," in Roemer, ed., *Analytical Marxism*, pp. 181–88, which draws heavily on Heller's account; Cohen, *Karl Marx's Theory of History*, especially chap. 11.

time, to this all economy ultimately reduces itself," but in very different ways.[153]

9.2.2 Community

The idea of the community as a free association signifies, for Marx, that the cooperation of its members is, to the greatest extent possible, something not wholly imposed on them from without: it is not the community as a coercive, external power either in its ancient guise, Eumaios' presence in Odysseus' *oikos*, or in the modern forms exemplified in miniature in the factory community (the "silent compulsion" of economic laws and the despotism of the manager). On a second and related level, the community and its cooperation are not forces that abolish individuality and rob the person of her will. These general features can be derived from Marx's claim that the *summum malum* of capitalism is domination by the valorization circuit, a circuit that is autonomous in relation to the will of the community it controls, and from his critique of the premodern community. The future society is a "free association" in the sense that it sets its own ends, rather than being governed by ΔM. And it is also free inasmuch as its members are not "assigned" (through class position) their cooperative situation, nor are they related to one another as bearers of functional moments in the production/market processes. The cement binding this community would not be the cash "nexus," the strictly economic need of the members of one class for the members of another class. The interactions of its members would not be determined by the sorts of (corrigible) constraints that shape their choices in the market, constraints that direct their behaviors and their combination toward the production of expanded value. Certainly, material interdependency (the social economy) would remain a defining property of this world, as it had been for the citizens of the communities discussed by Aristotle in Book 5 of the *Nicomachean Ethics*. But it would now be regulated so as to allow a higher form of sociability, one that flourishes in freedom, away from the economy, and that consists of a chosen bond with others. Such a community resembles nothing so much as the better association of friends described in Aristotle's *Nicomachean Ethics*, a partnership not in production but in a shared *philia;* an association in which persons choose to spend their days together, doing whatever it is that they love best in life.

This rather thin account is given more color in the hunting, fishing, and

---

[153] Marx, *Grundrisse*, p. 173.

philosophizing passage from *The German Ideology*. The (postcapitalist) world of those who hunt in the morning and fish in the afternoon is a classless society. We can discern this classlessness in the fact that neither the individual nor his activities are determined by a production/exchange process. He is not, as individuals in bourgeois society are, in a "situation of being assigned." Rather, he does what "he has a mind to" and not what the "representative" of capital or labor power must do according to his role in the metamorphosis of value. His activities are under the dominion neither of another person nor of the laws of the market, and hence they are not bound down by some purpose or goal other than that set by the person himself. The result, then, of the abolition of classes (understood as the abolition of the allocation of functional roles by the market) is, according to Marx, individualization in the sense of self-determination.

Observe also that only a single individual is mentioned. Moreover, all of his activities—fishing, hunting, and philosophizing—are, given the circumstances in which he conducts them, potentially solitary (unlike, for example, fishing for profit or primitive food hunting, in which cooperation is mandated by the requirements of efficiency, as in the first case, or by necessity as in the latter). But Marx's hunters, fishermen, and philosophers may also do "what they love best of everything" in each other's company, if they so choose; they have a "free association" because their bonds are not those imposed by capital but adopted by them. The preceding is, however, rather too playful an interpretation, even of this fantastical, partly tongue-in-cheek passage. For they cannot choose against being social creatures (that is their unchangeable inheritance, a result of their lack of complete self-sufficiency and, in a good society, the foundation of their freedom and individuality) any more than, according to Aristotle, humans might elect not to be political animals. But it is open to them to determine some large element of the *philia* (though not the residue of the necessity of production) which unites them, and to dispose over their free time as they have a mind to. As was the case for the friends portrayed in the *Nicomachean Ethics,* this community and its freedom are possible only on the condition of a contained economy. Friends like Socrates and Ischomachos may spend time in conversation, in each other's company, because they have the leisure to attend to those affairs of friends and city—because, in brief, the economy is for them contained, its impact on them reduced to the smallest possible compass.

Thus far I have skirted one of the most vexing aspects of Marx's theory of the postcapitalist community: the apparent rejection of the language and institutions of justice and rights. It is as if his thinking about the community stopped with Aristotle's discussion of friendship ("if men are friends, there is no need of justice between them," *Nicomachean Ethics* 1155a25ff.). Perhaps, as others have suggested, Marx actually had a theory of justice, *malgré lui;* perhaps his historicism prevented him from using ideas of justice for critical purposes, or his aspiration to a scientific critique led him to shun the normative propositions of his socialist ancestors. These debates, best set out in the exchanges between Ziyad I. Husami and Allen W. Wood, are not my concern here.[154] Rather, what interests me is the issue of whether he holds that such norms and institutions will be necessary or desirable in some future society. It could be, for example, that he assumes that with the advent of a postscarcity society the material circumstances (scarcity) calling justice into being would no longer be present. This expectation may, in fact, be part of the explanation for Marx's confidence in the transcending of justice, though I shall attempt below to make a case more sympathetic to Marx inasmuch as it does not rely on the implausible premise of superabundance.[155] If the less charitable version adumbrated here is accurate, so much the worse for Marx, not only because of the implausibility of the postscarcity postulate but, relatedly, for failing to grasp the many nonmaterial goods that, as Fred Hirsch has shown, can become scarce, generate conflict, and mandate rules of justice.[156]

We shall come back to this question later, but before turning to other issues permit me to offer this last speculation on Marx's theoretical motivation in rejecting the institutions of justice. Marx, like some of the classical liberals and their libertarian adherents in this century, considers the state to be an essentially coercive institution. The more active, the more centralized the state, the more it cramps individuals and their freedoms: in almost Tocqueville-like terms, Marx criticizes the centralization of political power, calling it a "boa constrictor" and a "deadening in-

[154] Ziyad I. Husami, "Marx on Distributive Justice," *Philosophy and Public Affairs* 8 (1978): 27–64; Allen W. Wood, "The Marxian Critique of Justice," *Philosophy and Public Affairs* 1 (1972): 244–82; Wood, "Marx on Right and Justice: A Reply to Husami," *Philosophy and Public Affairs* 8 (1979): 267–95.

[155] Kymlicka makes this connection between Marx's rejection of justice and a condition of postscarcity in *Liberalism, Community, and Culture*, pp. 113, 119. See also Peffer, *Marxism, Morality, and Social Justice*, pp. 318, 330–31.

[156] See Fred Hirsch, *Social Limits to Growth* (Cambridge: Harvard University Press, 1978), esp. p. 168.

cubus."[157] Preferable to the employment of state power were the free actions of individuals in voluntary associations. For one branch of liberalism this meant, and means, giving the widest possible scope to the market and allowing for state interference only in the case of its most dramatic failures or in those rare instances where the state is a more efficient manager. The now familiar structure of Marx's critical response reappears here: he shares the liberal desideratum, the substitution of the sphere of the voluntary for that of state force, but claims that the market is anything but a forum in which freedom flourishes. A better society would indeed be one in which the state is reduced to a minimum (or to nonexistence). Assuming that what is sought is an increase of freedom, rather than of capital, the expansion of the market domain is not the solution. I said earlier that Marx could be read as thinking about capitalism as a normative market failure on a massive scale—a failure, that is, to deliver on its promise of freedom—and that he saw such measures as the Ten Hours' Bill as the first tentative steps of society's exerting its control, and thus its autonomy, over the market. His reflections on communism, justice, and the state strongly suggest that he did not mean to propose, via this market-failure analysis, that the state was to be brought back in with a vengeance, à la russe. Once again, however, we are presented with the refrain of the dilemma of Marx's thought: the rejection of the market as the locus of voluntary actions, the rejection of the state (in the best of worlds) as a substitute for markets, and the belief that a good society would minimize or do away altogether with it (both in the name of the liberal desideratum of autonomy), coupled with the failure to provide an alternative mechanism.

9.2.3   Freedom

The new household economy differs from its Aristotelian predecessor in these respects among others: it is nondespotic and the end to which it is subordinate is in the first instance (equal) freedom. The case for this interpretation has to be advanced on the basis of Marx's scarce and thin texts on communism, and, as well, on the fact that its emphasis on freedom runs counter to a widely accepted and formidably argued read-

---

[157] In Marx's first draft of *The Civil War in France,* in Furet, *Marx and the French Revolution,* p. 227. This partial similarity between Marx and right libertarians has been observed by Philippe Van Parijs, "Nozick and Marxism [sic] Socialist Responses to the Libertarian Challenge," *Revue internationale de philosophie* 146 (1983): 337–62, especially p. 337.

ing of Marx, one that discerns in his writings a quasi-Aristotelian perfectionist concern with the good life.[158] I suggest that, on the contrary, what
is striking in Marx's works is precisely the virtual absence of a discussion
of the good life. Still more remarkable is the fact that he hardly seems to
have thought it necessary to so much as raise the question. Marx does, of
course, write in a manner suggestive of a background theory of the good
life, and such a theory is by no means necessarily incompatible with a
commitment to freedom. Indeed, some would argue that the latter commitment makes sense only if the freedom it cherishes is in the service of
the pursuit of a good life, and Marx does point to such a relationship.
"The associated producers," he writes, "govern the human metabolism
with nature in a rational way, bringing it under their collective control
instead of being dominated by it as a blind power."[159] This conscious
control of the economy, the greatest achievable human autonomy in the
productive interaction between man and nature, creates the foundation of
the "true realm of freedom, the development of human powers as an end
in itself." But overwhelmingly, Marx's emphasis is, like that of liberalism,
on what we might (borrowing from Amartya Sen) call liberty as control,
the freedom to determine for oneself and within as broad a circumference
as possible one's own plans and activity, the use of one's time, and so
forth; to determine oneself against the "preponderance of force" (the
traditional liberal objects of fear: coercion and paternalism), as well as
against the "violence of things" (the marxist picture of capitalism and
especially of its central institution, the market). The normative perplexity
standing behind the idea of liberty as control is captured in this question
from Marx's notes to *The German Ideology:* "How does it happen that
[human] relations assume an independent existence over against them?
and that the forces of their own life become superior to them?"[160] Communism, Marx thought, would be the righting of this loss of self-
legislation: "men once more gain control of exchange, production and

[158] Jon Elster, "Self-realization in Work and Politics: The Marxist Conception of the
Good Life," *Social Philosophy & Policy* 3 (1986): 97–126, and Elster, *Making Sense of
Marx,* p. 521; Alan Gilbert, "Marx's Moral Realism," in Ball and Farr, eds., *After Marx;*
Richard W. Miller, *Analyzing Marx: Morality, Power and History* (Princeton: Princeton
University Press, 1984); Frederick G. Whelan, "Marx and Revolutionary Virtue," in J. Ro-
land Pennock and John W. Chapman, eds., *Nomos 26: Marxism* (New York: New York
University Press, 1983). Recent questioning of that reading of Marx's relationship to Aristot-
le includes Kymlicka, *Liberalism, Community, and Culture,* p. 126, and Peffer, *Marxism,
Morality, and Social Justice,* pp. 100–114.

[159] Marx, *Capital,* vol. 3, p. 959.

[160] Marx and Engels, *German Ideology,* p. 93.

the way they behave to one another." The desideratum Marx focuses on here is an extension of autonomy, of self-rule beyond the limits set by the liberal agenda of freedom from coercion, to freedom from the independent laws of the economy.[161]

Serge-Christophe Kolm has accurately (and provocatively) identified this core concern: "The fundamental Marxist reference point [is] . . . the ethic of liberty. . . . Exactly as in liberalism . . . [it] is the hypothesis that the person has the right to the free disposition of herself."[162] Consider once more the celebrated banderole from *The German Ideology:* "In communist society . . . society regulates production and thus makes it possible for me to do one thing today and another tomorrow, to hunt in the morning, fish in the afternoon, rear cattle in the evening, criticize after dinner, just as I have a mind (to)." I referred earlier to the affinity of the idea of community expressed in this passage with that of Aristotle's analysis of friendship in the *Nicomachean Ethics.* So great is this affinity that Marx's sentence reads almost as if it were a direct play on Aristotle's account of friendship and leisure: "some friends drink or throw dice together, others practice gymnastics and hunt or philosophize together; each sort spending their time together in the activity they love best of everything in life."[163] What I underscore now is not their affinity but the distance between them. Here is one profound and telling difference: unlike Aristotle, who embeds his examination of friendship in a work devoted to the good life, Marx does not raise the question of whether, for example, philosophy is to be preferred to hunting or, in general, of what the good life is. What is necessary for Marx, as for liberal political philosophy, is that one can do what one "has a mind to," that the individual

---

[161] Marx and Engels, *German Ideology,* p. 48. Though Marx was savagely critical of Kant (see *German Ideology,* pp. 193, 195), there is a Kantian resonance in his idea of autonomy. Contrasting analyses (one from a Kantian perspective, the other from Marx's) of this aspect of Marx's thought are to be found in my *Interpreting the World: Kant's Philosophy of History and Politics* (Toronto: University of Toronto Press, 1986), pp. ix–xiii, 58–61, and "The Limits of Autonomy: Karl Marx's Kant Critique," in R. S. Beiner and W. J. Booth, eds., *The Starry Heavens and the Moral Law: Kant's Legacy for Political Philosophy* (New Haven: Yale University Press, forthcoming). Kymlicka has also remarked on this aspect of Marx's thought in *Liberalism, Community, and Culture,* p. 126.

[162] Kolm, *Le libéralisme moderne,* p. 92; my translation. On related topics see George G. Brenkert, *Marx's Ethics of Freedom* (London: Routledge and Kegan Paul, 1983), pp. 87–88; Allen W. Wood, *Karl Marx* (London: Routledge and Kegan Paul, 1981), pp. 50–51; Kymlicka's section on Marx in *Liberalism, Community, and Culture,* especially pp. 100–131, and Peffer, *Marxism, Morality, and Social Justice,* pp. 123–37.

[163] Aristotle, *Nicomachean Ethics* 1172a23–5. And so too Marx's picture of the constrained community of capitalist society is very close to Aristotle's account of an association formed under the compulsion of need in, for example, *Politics* 1256b5ff.

be free of constraint. It may well be that Marx had a notion of what ought to be done with that freedom, as most surely did Locke, Kant, and other classical liberals. But the first goal was to secure freedom or to see its circumference widened: for that is an indispensable precondition of all the goods of life, a condition without which a person's actions, however much they might accord with some conception or other of the good life, would be rendered near to valueless. It is this freedom that also shelters the person from the invasion of others, even if she should fail to attain what we consider the good life or not even attempt to lead a good life of any sort.

Marx places his emphasis on freedom rather than on the Aristotelian perfectionist idea of a hierarchy of ways of living, and correspondingly he rejects the notion of the despotic organization of the household, the latter being a reflection of and a means for the preservation of that hierarchy. Marx was fully aware that the *oikos* economy, while regulated by human intention and not by the anarchic market, was at its core a despotic community inasmuch as its purposiveness resided in the master and his needs. In relation to those ends, the other members of the household were the objects of exploitation, from the wife down to the slave, who was a thing, not a person.[164] And finally, that same rejection of *pleonexia* in favor of an economy subordinated to praxis, the pursuit of the good life, meant that the instruments for emancipating human beings (as far as is possible) from absorption in the requirements imposed by their material needs were not nurtured within the world of the *oikos*. For in that society, with its idea of a ceiling on the things needed for a good life and with noneconomic activity as the goal, there was, as we observed above, little incentive for technological innovation. Accordingly, while the Greeks knew of the liberating potential of technology, they had neither economic nor (in view of their acceptance of hierarchy and unfreedom) moral imperatives to seek it out.

The despotism of the ancient *oikos* economy was understood by Marx to have been a consequence, not of the search for ever greater productivity or surpluses (as in the factory or firm), but rather of the emancipation of some from the grim world of the provisioning of humankind under conditions of scarcity and primitive technology. An admirer of the Aristotelian vision of the embedded and contained economy, Marx nevertheless could not accept the radical inequality and unfreedom that were intimately

---

[164] Marx, *Results of the Immediate Process of Production*, p. 1083; Marx, *Capital*, vol. 1, pp. 620–21, and vol. 3, p. 731.

bound up with that vision. The destruction of C-M-C type economies and their replacement by one of the capitalist sort were the material prerequisites to the solution of the scarcity problem insofar as that destruction was necessary to "whip forward" the growth of labor-replacing technology. Just that growth of technology, with its accompanying potential for liberation, was for him the "historical justification" of capitalism.[165] The dissolution of status- and gender-based distinctions between persons which was to accompany the emergence of the pervasive market society was also the moral precondition of what Marx holds would be a higher form of community, one in which the economy would again be embedded and contained, only now in a nondespotic form. Marx, in criticizing the nonmarket economy of the patriarchal household and in attacking the "despotic" nonmarket economy of the modern firm and industrial enterprise, suggests that the nonmarket organization of the postcapitalist economy must not be a despotic or a command economy of any sort. The same reasons that led Marx to reject what Kolm has called the planning function of *pater familias* in the patriarchal household also would have led him to reject its analogues at the social level.

10. Marx, Markets, and Household Economies

The critical point toward which the preceding reflections drive is unequivocal: arguing from an essentially liberal ethic of freedom as autonomy—as the power of a person to dispose over herself—Marx maintains that individual autonomy, the free association of the new community, and the free time of persons were thinkable only on the foundation of an embedded and contained economy. Therefore in tracing the outlines of that new household, Marx could not accept as his model the known forms of command economy, whether directed to the freedom and excellence of a few, as in the case of the *oikos*, or to the creation of profit in the case of the modern firm. The market, taken as an abstract, ideal-type institution and with considerations of its antecedent constraints and perverse consequences left to one side, was thought by Marx to be normatively superior to either major type of nonmarket economy. That is the

---

[165] Marx, *Theories of Surplus Value*, vol. 2, p. 405; Marx, *Grundrisse*, p. 325; Marx, *MEGA*, II.3.1, p. 327.

fairly straightforward part of the story. Much more thorny, however, is a related set of problems: how to imagine a more or less nonmarket social (interdependent) economy that would not reproduce the evils Marx attributes to the antique and capitalist varieties. In the following pages, I summarize Marx's thoughts on markets and discuss candidate accounts of his theory of socialism.

A first step in exploring these issues would be to ask how all-embracing his rejection of the market was, keeping in mind that Marx accepted certain central normative claims of liberal political and economic thought both in its rejection of the patriarchal model and in its advocacy of a market/contract alternative. Clearly the unequal initial endowments of market agents—reducible for Marx to those who dispose over capital on the one side and over their own labor power on the other, a distribution that mediated through the market constantly reproduces (via its constrained option set) the essential capital/labor relation—places severe limitations on the claim that freedom is secured in the market. But the market here is the medium that preserves an initial endowment pattern, itself often (in Marx's account) the result of nonmarket forces. Indeed, in Marx's own illustration of an opened option set and a withdrawal of persons from the labor market (*Capital,* vol. 1, chap. 33), he implies that they are enabled to withdraw by a market stocked with cheap land. We must, then, look elsewhere for the heart of Marx's objection to markets.

One part of that core is his critique of the labor market. While its premise of self-ownership is plainly superior to an arrangement in which persons, rather than some limited quantity of their time and effort, are sold, it is in large measure responsible for producing anew the master/servant relationship. The basis of this claim is, as we have seen, that one unique quality of labor power as a commodity is that it is inseparable from the person who sells it, from her will, activity, and time.[166] To give disposition over this commodity to another person, a feature of all commodity exchanges, is to transfer (within limits) the agent herself to her purchaser—and that produces a relationship having a partial resemblance to slavery, as Marx and before him Aristotle had argued. Marx finds unsatisfactory the legitimation through contract of this new master/servant relation for two reasons: (1) the antecedent conditions that bring the partners to the market and the hidden compulsion (endowments, entitlements, markets) standing behind their exchange, and

[166] Marx, *MEGA,* II.3.1, pp. 93–94.

(2) the fact that their exchange gives rise to a despotic relation (that of the firm's microeconomy) which might be avoidable on the basis of another feasible economy.

A second part of the core of Marx's objection to markets and one that leads him directly to the idea of a re-embedded economy is his critique of the "anarchy" of the market. We said that Marx does not mean by this that market society is without order or laws of any kind. What he intends is rather that markets execute the laws of capital and not those of a conscious, a priori (*ex ante*), and overarching human purposiveness. These laws prescribe behaviors to agents in the market, weed out mal-adapted strategies, and promote decisions that are rational as "judged" by the market, its end, and its selection mechanisms. The anarchy of the market, the absence of conscious control from it together with its estab-lishment of the ruling end of ΔM, is an important part of why it must, according to Marx, give birth to the sorts of perverse effects sketched above.

So much for those aspects that Marx most clearly seems to have re-jected. In the preceding paragraphs, I have written in the manner custom-ary in discussions of Marx's critique of the market, as if that latter were a single form of economic institution; occasionally I have been somewhat more specific and have written of markets "of the capitalist type" but without further elaboration. That language is, however, too coarse-grained for, as we intimated earlier, Marx's distinction between C-M-C and M-C-ΔM economies suggests that there are a number of types of markets, some capitalist and others not. These market mechanisms, like the overarching processes of which they are a part, are shaped by the ends they serve, consumption (broadly construed) or the growth of capital, C or ΔM.[167] An illustration of markets of the first type is provided by Xenophon in his *Ways and Means:* with Athenian military power in decline, Xenophon proposed a trade policy for Athens which would make it a more hospitable place for commerce. He put forward these measures in order "that every Athenian may receive sufficient mainte-nance at the expense of the community." This was to be a market subor-dinated to the (noneconomic) ends of the community. The capitalist mar-ket, on the other hand, in the words of the encomium to capitalism of the *Communist Manifesto,* had "in scarce one hundred years . . . created more massive and more colossal productive forces than have all preceding generations together." The explosive dynamism of the capitalist market

---

[167] Marx, *Contribution to the Critique of Political Economy,* p. 50.

indicates that it is of a very different type than that envisioned by Xenophon, and the locus of this difference is to be found in its peculiar driving purpose.

A careful examination of the perverse consequences Marx attributes to capitalism will reveal that, in his analysis, their specific content can be traced to the pursuit of efficiency in the service of the maximization of surplus value. To be sure, that drive is enforced by the market, but it is no more an eternal, transhistorical property of markets than is the creation of profit the forever ordained end of productive technology. The market appears as a villain in this version of Marx's story because, unembedded and left to itself, it denies the community the possibility of reappropriating the directing purpose of its own economic activity. This way of phrasing his core critique of markets points us to the argument (broached above) that the object of social control of the economy is not for the public to invade the space of individual choices but to weaken the power of the invisible hand to compel certain choices.[168] The liberal desiderata—autonomy (disposition over oneself), equality and voluntary associations—are not asked to yield their pride of place. Quite the contrary, Marx accepts their primacy and grounds his critique of ancient despotic and modern capitalist economies on them. He wants rather to make the argument that these goods are not achievable (or not as achievable as they might be) without a re-embedding of the economy in institutions governed by the social determination of the ends to which the economy is to be subordinated.

With this, we are brought full circle and back from the exegetical openings that suggest something less than a wholesale rejection of markets to the essential Marx: "men once more gain control of exchange, production"—"once more," meaning to restore something like the *oikos*

[168] Cf. Serge-Christophe Kolm, who argues that Marx rejects markets entirely: "Introduction à la réciprocité générale," *Information sur les sciences sociales* 22 (1983): 569–621, especially p. 571. See also Allen Buchanan, "The Marxist Conceptual Framework and the Origins of Totalitarian Socialism," in E. F. Paul et al., eds., *Marxism and Liberalism* (Oxford: Basil Blackwell, 1986), p. 135. The question of marxism and market socialism is, for obvious reasons, a thorny one. See Hervé Moulin and John E. Roemer, "Public Ownership of the External World and Private Ownership of the Self," *Journal of Political Economy* 97 (1989): 347–67, and John E. Roemer, "Public Ownership and Private Property Externalities," in Jon Elster and Karl Ove Moene, eds., *Alternatives to Capitalism* (Cambridge: Cambridge University Press, 1989). For contemporary arguments that market socialism and freedom are incompatible see John Gray, "Contractarian Method, Private Property, and the Market Economy," and Narveson, "The Justice of the Market," both in John W. Chapman and J. Roland Pennock, eds., *Nomos 31: Markets and Justice* (New York: New York University Press, 1989).

economy, with its production subordinated to human needs and above all the need for freedom from the world of production, only now not on a foundation of servitude and despotism—hence a new household economy. The *oikos* aspect of this economy strongly suggests, contrary to the evidence presented above, that it was to be nonmarket: as in the family where "no *commodity* is produced, [where there is] no exchange and still less a self-expanding series of exchanges mediated by money and in two opposed phases [M-C/C-ΔM]."[169] How to make sense of the idea of a nondespotic but embedded/contained economy in the context of complexity and interdependency is no simple task. Statements such as Marx's that socialism will resemble Robinson Crusoe's world, only now in a "social" form, restate both the central attributes of the future economy as he saw it and the ambiguities (if not the ultimate incoherence) inherent in that vision.[170] In Marx's version of the tale, Crusoe plans and allocates his time and materials according to his needs, and not for the sake of the creation of surpluses. The constraints on Crusoe are those of nature, of the elements and the materials at hand. Neither the power of another class nor the "silent" forces of the market exercise any sway over him. Crusoe's world is a use-value, C-driven, economy that carries with it, in its single actor form, the idea of autonomy.

It is a fairly simple matter to see how, in one way, the "free association" will mirror Crusoe's economy: the social control of the economy, the plan, will be the multiple actor analogue of Crusoe's control over his own affairs. It is, however, just this point that raises the question of autonomy in a many-person economy. Liberal theorists draw from this same story the lesson that the market is the coordination mechanism most capable of reproducing at the level of the interpersonal economy something like the freedom of Crusoe on his island.[171] We have examined Marx's grounds for disputing that specification of institutions, and we have also noted the shared desideratum. To see this latter point, compare the following expression of the (liberal) normative center of the Crusoe story (quoted from David Gauthier) to the above-cited (at note 162) quotation from Kolm on the "fundamental" marxian ethical reference point: "Crusoe is free to use her capacities in whatever way will best fulfil her preferences

---

[169] See Marx, *Ökonomische Manuskripte, 1863–1867*, in *MEGA*, II.4.1, pp. 220–21; my translation. The language of restoration is also to be found in Engels' account of socialism, as in, e.g., the concluding quote from Morgan in Engels, *The Origin of the Family*, p. 276 (*Wiederbelebung* in the phrase italicized by Engels), and in Engels, *Über die Assoziation der Zukunft*, in *Karl Marx. Friedrich Engels Werke*, vol. 21, p. 391.

[170] Marx, *Capital*, vol. 1, p. 171.

[171] See Gauthier, *Morals by Agreement*, pp. 90–91.

given the external circumstances in which she finds herself."[172] The coexistence of autonomy and *ex ante* control poses no problem in a single-member economy, and indeed the second property might be seen as analytically derivable from the first. The historical illustrations Marx provides of (many-agent) use-value economies between the Crusoe myth and the "free association" are also unproblematic because they do not even seek to combine autonomy and control, being on the contrary openly despotic. Socialism was meant to incorporate the use-value orientation of these noncapitalist economies, actual and mythical, and to marry that property to the autonomy of Crusoe in his economy, now in a social form. Beyond that statement, Marx is a poor guide.

I do not intend to attempt to fill in this canvas, which Marx himself left mostly in the white, but only to sketch some conclusions that can fairly be drawn on the basis of what little he did say. I begin by rejecting two candidate accounts of Marx's idea of the new household economy. The first I consider to be manifestly implausible on the basis of the evidence already provided in these pages, and so I shall not rehearse its details. This we might call the dictatorial reading. According to that view, when Marx writes that the opponents of socialism object to it because of features already present in their own factories, he means precisely that socialism would have an economy run in the manner of a factory, that is, a "single-firm" economy (to borrow Ugo Pagano's phrase). On this argument an authoritative command-type economy, *à la russe,* with a state agency taking the place both of the invisible hand of the market and the more evident hand of the "factory Lycurgus" was not the unforeseen consequence of Marx's critique of capitalism but the happily envisioned alternative to the market.[173] The contrary evidence consists of Marx's oft-repeated criticisms of the despotic economy, ancient (*oikos*) and modern (the factory). It is not credible, in the light of the testimony, to assert that somehow the substitution of the force of the state over society for that of the despot over his household or of the capitalist over his employees was seen by Marx as a corrective. In comparing socialism and the factory, what Marx did intend, I think, was to point to one specific shared attribute: human sovereignty, expressed in the mechanism of an *ex ante* plan in juxtaposition to the *ex post* (beyond social control) regulation by the market.

[172] Gauthier, *Morals by Agreement,* p. 91.

[173] There is a long and unfortunate background to this conceptualization of the socialist economy along the lines of an army or a factory. See V. I. Lenin, "One Step Forward, Two Steps Back," in Lenin, *Selected Works in Three Volumes* (New York: International Pub-

The second candidate reading of this "new household economy" is the virtual mirror-image of the preceding one. Here Marx emerges as the starry-gazed visionary, a utopian who imagined a world of superabundance in which none of the choices generated by scarcity would have to be made and in which there would be no need for authority, or justice, of any kind.[174] I said above that I would attempt a sympathetic response to this charge. Here is that defense. There are, to be sure, elements in Marx of the prophet announcing a society in which the "springs of common wealth flow more abundantly."[175] But Marx's more apocalyptic pronouncements notwithstanding, we do not necessarily have to attribute to him the thought of a radical rupture: a world of superabundance and anarchical freedom on the one side and a world of artificial scarcity and compulsion on the other. We also have a more sober Marx who saw the limits of the feasible: the author who wrote of the continued necessity of labor, of the scarcity-driven interchange with nature. And there is too the Marx who maintains that the scale and interdependencies of modern production give rise to a directing function, independently of the particular economic formation.[176] This Marx is capable of a more measured approach: praising, for example, the legislatively enacted ten-hour day as a desirable move to reduce the economy's autonomous capacity to "usurp" the time set free by its technology and writing admiringly of cooperative factories as the herald of a different form of coordination at

lishers, 1967), pp. 412, 417, 419, and for a critique from the marxist left see Rosa Luxemburg, "Organizational Questions of Russian Social Democracy," in *Selected Political Writings of Rosa Luxemburg,* ed. Dick Howard (New York: Monthly Review Press, 1971), p. 291. The military image of a socialist economy predates Lenin. For some illustrations from the French Revolution see François-Noel (Gracchus) Babeuf, "The Defense of Gracchus Babeuf," and Sylvain Maréchal, "Manifeste des égaux," both in John A. Scott, ed. and trans., *The Defense of Gracchus Babeuf* (Amherst: University of Massachusetts Press, 1967), pp. 57, 76, 95. De Tocqueville, in *L'ancien régime et la révolution* (Paris: Flammarion, 1988), pp. 254–55, points to the centralizing, statist tendencies of the socialism of revolutionary France.

174 See Alec Nove, *The Economics of Feasible Socialism* (London: George Allen & Unwin, 1983), p. 15; Gauthier, *Morals by Agreement,* pp. 333–35; Kymlicka, *Liberalism, Community, and Culture,* pp. 109, 112–13, 119. In *Making Sense of Marx,* p. 527, Elster notes the high utopian nature of the postscarcity postulate and maintains that it has little textual foundation in Marx's writings.

175 Marx, *Critique of the Gotha Programme,* in MECW, vol. 24, p. 87; Marx, *Capital,* vol. 3, p. 958.

176 Marx, *Capital,* vol. 3, p. 511, and vol. 1, pp. 448–49. For a different reading see Stephen A. Marglin, "What Do Bosses Do? The Origins and Functions of Hierarchy in Capitalist Production," in André Gorz, ed., *The Division of Labour* (Atlantic Highlands, N.J.: Humanities Press, 1976), pp. 13–14.

the microlevel of the economy. This sobriety stems from a sense of the limits of the feasible, but from something more as well: from his Aristotelian theory of the contained economy. Communism is in considerable measure a vision of a return to a C-M-C type of economy, a form that was, on Marx's own account, inherently less dynamic than capitalism. And that in turn would also appear to imply a certain asceticism and a restriction on the flourishing of needs. There would thus be something fundamentally conservative about socialism insofar as it shared with pre-capitalist economies the properties of being governed by existing needs and of being without a spur to the creation of new needs.

Is there not an anomaly here, though? For Marx is critical of ascetic socialism and praises capitalism for its generation of expanded needs while, at the same time, arguing that it transforms those needs into a source of power over persons.[177] On one reading, then, we see a Spartan Marx imagining a society of pinched needs; on the second reading, we might think him to be espousing a society of virtually unlimited abundance. Such, Carl Menger argues, were the only two conditions under which a communism of property would be possible: the overcoming of scarcity either through the suppression of need or through a material superabundance.[178] Now, it is true that there is a quiet, nonfrenetic current running through Marx's portrait of communism, in for example the bucolic picture from *The German Ideology* of hunting, fishing, and philosophizing—a current that stands in sharp contrast to the portrayal of the "feverish" pace of capitalism, with its "revolutionary thrust" driving the economy in its unceasing expansion. Marx's socialism would indeed lack that thrust which "whips" humans forward to ever more effort and more profitable production. That image is not necessarily one of asceticism, though, or at least not in the sense of a negative valuation of wealth itself as corrupting and evil. To see this point, consider this part of the Crusoe fable, one that must have appealed to Marx, just as for very different reasons the rational economizing under scarcity facets of the tale appeal to those who see in him an exemplar of the universality of *homo oeconomicus*. Here the castaway declaims against acquisition beyond need: "In a Word, The Nature and Experience of Things dictated to me upon just Reflection, That all the good Things of this World, are no farther good to us, than they are for our Use. . . . I possess'd infinitely

---

[177] Marx, *Grundrisse*, p. 287; Marx, *Economic and Philosophical Manuscripts*, pp. 304, 306. See Miller, *Market, State, and Community*, pp. 209, 213.

[178] See Carl Menger, *Principles of Economics*, trans. James Dingwall and Bert F. Hoselitz (New York: New York University Press, 1976), p. 97.

more than I knew what to do with. . . . I had, as I hinted before, a Parcel of Money, as well Gold as Silver. . . . Alas! There the nasty sorry useless Stuff lay; . . . and if I had had the Drawer full of Diamonds, it had been the same case; and they had been of no manner of Value to me, because of no Use."[179]

Of what use, then, is wealth? Marx, like Aristotle, recognized the material prerequisites of freedom and the good life and for that reason he was an unashamed admirer of wealth. But again like Aristotle, Marx distinguishes between material and radical needs. The former he considers the requirements of life; they are bound up with the latter, the things of freedom and of a good life, and they are directly involved in making that life possible. The first were thought to have limits, the second to be virtually unlimited. The idea of communism as a use-value-governed economy contains within it the notion of a threshold beyond which the further production of things would be judged irrational, and in that sense it is, in comparison to capitalism, a conservative regime. It is not a vision of communism as the Elysian fields, overflowing with abundance, of a "feverish city" (to use Plato's description from the *Republic*, 372E), consuming at will. It is rather a community that has inherited from capitalism the means to provision itself in the necessities of life and in the things of the good life, freedom in the first instance, insofar as those have a material foundation. No more than did Aristotle's portrait of a group of friends demand a theory of unlimited wealth does Marx's notion of communism require a world of superabundance. What was most necessary was that the *oikos* master, or the members of the "free association," institute a use-value economy, one subordinated to the satisfaction of their needs, and above all their radical needs for freedom, leisure, and so forth. Marx would also argue though that as far as radical needs are concerned—those associated with "full human development," for example, the need for free time and autonomy—this is an expansionary and

[179] Daniel Defoe, *Robinson Crusoe*, ed. by Michael Shinagel (New York: Norton, 1975), p. 102. For the modern *homo oeconomicus* reading of Crusoe the rational economizer see Paul Veyne's brief remarks, which draw on Menger, in "Débat sur l'oeuvre de Karl Polanyi," *Annales: Economies, Sociétés, Civilisations* 29 (1974): 1375–80, and, on the economizing activities of solitary individuals, see Menger, *Principles of Economics*, pp. 96, 101. Ian Watt's essay, "*Robinson Crusoe* as a Myth," in Shinagel, ed., *Robinson Crusoe*, makes clear that Defoe's own understanding of Crusoe is closer to bourgeois man than to the premodern economic actor ventured here. Marx himself, of course, did not miss this facet of the castaway, calling him "a good Englishman, [a keeper of] a set of books" even while mocking Ricardo's anachronistic bourgeoisification of Crusoe. See Marx, *Capital*, vol. 1, pp. 170 and 169.

revolutionary order. That is the best sense that can be made, I think, of Marx's picture of communism if the postscarcity postulate is dropped. I confess without hesitation that it suffers from the exegetical difficulty of being a highly speculative gloss on Marx. It suffers too from this second, and more damaging, problem, that the acknowledgment of a condition of scarcity calls for a theory of justice and its institutions, a theory of distributive justice, rights, limits on public and private power, and so forth. And we have noted that Marx, at least in his discussion of communism, does not heed this call.

This project (whether of superabundance or not) entailed, Marx argued, the reappropriation by society of the purposiveness of the economy. Now, that objective itself raises what is perhaps among the most telling rejoinders to marxist socialism: the argument that there is a "centralizing logic" inherent in the idea of a marketless, use-value economy, one in which use-value is determined by the "prior control" of society.[180] I do not consider it possible to give a full response to this claim on the basis of Marx's texts, but in reflecting on the force of this argument we would do well to keep before us the following elements of his analysis. These elements, I must insist, do not disarm the charge of the centralizing logic of a use-value conception of the economy, but they do raise further complexities in understanding how that charge might apply to Marx's variant of it. First, we need to remind ourselves of Marx's design in putting forward the idea of a new household economy. The core of his objection to the regulation of the economy by ΔM was that, in the institutional context of the unregulated market, it tends to subordinate all human goods (including those most prized by liberalism) to the goal of wealth creation. We may infer from this that Marx's concept of a use-value-directed economy does not speak to the issue of the usefulness of goods, of whether brown or black shoes should be made, for instance, or radios rather than cars. His concern is at a rather different level of end or purpose: whether the absorption of human time and activity into the process of the reproduction and increase of capital is the best use of the economy.

This point (that about the level of use-value which concerned Marx) hints at the possibility that Marx did not foresee a micromanaged socialist economy, one in which the plan would substitute for the market (and so for individual choice) down to the level of, for example, personal consumption goods. His repeated emphasis on *ex ante* control was in-

<hr />

[180] See Nove, *The Economics of Feasible Socialism*, pp. 29–30, 50, 59; Kolm, "Introduction à la réciprocité générale," p. 577; Dumont, *From Mandeville to Marx*, pp. 106–7.

tended rather to point to the claim that the commanding purpose of economic activity needed to be recaptured and subordinated to the freely willed ends of society and not to the ends imposed by the valorization process of the capitalist market. The "wide field of choice" of capitalism would, no doubt, be diminished though, as was mentioned earlier, he also held that many choices under capitalism are induced by the array of incentives and punishments which the market applies to actors. Viewed in that manner, suppressing ΔM must have seemed to Marx as a way of freeing persons to make choices previously unavailable to them. These thoughts on the purpose of re-embedding the economy suggest that Marx did not see the idea of "conscious control" as a foundation for the intrusion of the community into the fine-grain of economic decisions or as the means for regulating (repressing) needs, Spartan fashion, for the sake of an ascetic society. The earlier remarks on his rejection of socialism as the "feverish city" add another dimension: that the purpose of social control of the economy is not to produce more, to exchange the discipline of the market for that of the community in order to drive the production of things to still greater heights, in short, to create through this new discipline an unfree but materially satiated world.

What we are left with, in the end, are the fragments of an argument. And it is far from obvious what coherent whole can be constructed out of these theoretical shards. Here in summary form is what one can say, with greater or lesser confidence, of Marx's arguments concerning markets and socialism. (1) Marx knew of, and criticized, two distinct nonmarket and despotic economies, the *oikos* and the factory, each characterized by a measure of *ex ante* control. (2) He considered the liberal market to be preferable to both because of the freedom, independence, and equality that typified it. (3a) He thought that these admirable qualities of the market were in reality severely affected by the background (historical) antecedents of the modern market and by its consequences. (3b) Marx's attention focused on the consequences of the market: its perverse effects including (centrally) a diminution of freedom. (4) He argued that the solution was "once again" to control the economy, to restore the needs-driven economy of the *oikos,* and he believed that this could be done without reproducing the freedom-denying features of earlier economic formations. (5) Marx saw the needs to be satisfied in such an economy principally as radical needs, those that form the core of what he called "full human development," with freedom as self-determination being central among them.

By returning to the narrower-gauge horizon of the issue of time and its allocation, we can better see the conundrum in which this involves Marx. He praises the ancients for their valuation of time away from the economy, and he is critical of that world for the despotic assignment of bound time to the servile population—as in (1) and (2) above. Liberalism transforms laborers into juridical persons who are self-owners and who therefore can alienate their time in a labor-market contract. As such, liberalism, expressed in markets, succeeds in its way in removing the control of the *oikos* despot and in putting time under the control of the individual. In the same moment, however, time is usurped by capital, subordinated to the market-enforced laws of growth and reabsorbed into the realm of the necessary: it is (liberally) juridically free and substantively bound—as in (3b). The restoration of an *oikos*-model economy, absent its historically conditioned despotic form, is the solution to the encroachments of capital on time. Now, markets, on Marx's own account, allow individuals a measure of choice, if a limited one, over the use of their time for leisure, income, and so forth. How their time could be allocated noncoercively (respecting their autonomy) in the absence of markets is a microlevel illustration of the overarching and central problem mirrored in Marx's ambiguous relation to the traditions he engaged: the embedded despotic economy of the ancient world, the autonomy of the contractarian person of liberalism, and the freedom of the individual in the new household economy of socialism.

The disparate fragments displayed here leave so many questions unanswered that one has to resort to a rather amorphous level of reflection in an effort to get hold of the heart of their meaning. Marx writes that humankind had "long dreamed" of something that it could now realize in practice. He did not tell us directly what that dream was, but he did allude to it when he wrote that the task of modernity is to replace the "domination" of circumstances over persons by the dominion of individuals over their world. That task is to achieve a condition in which the "impact of the world . . . is under the control of the individuals themselves."[181] In bourgeois society, what is required for such a control on the "impact of the world" is a reappropriation by society of the end ruling the (now) social economy, and that is the background condition of the rustic and dreamy passage on hunting, fishing, and philosophizing. I wish finally to say two things about that passage. The first is to observe its familiarity,

---

[181] Marx and Engels, *German Ideology*, p. 292. Marx's "long dreamed" phrase can be found in *Letters from Deutsch-Französische Jahrbücher*, in *MECW*, vol. 3, p. 144; translation slightly modified.

indeed its almost evocative quality; reading it calls to mind encountering Aristotle's words on friendship or, more distantly still, Achilles' shield, the activities and pastimes portrayed on its folds and the households that made them possible. Like those earlier passages, it calls up an image of a community and of the place of the economy embedded in its relations and directed to the satisfaction of its needs. However far removed these communities may be from us, in time and ethically as well, we have little difficulty recognizing the seductive power of the *oikos* idea and its modern variants. The attractive pull of that world, especially in contrast to the society of the cash nexus, is likely a part of the explanation for the influence of its most forceful modern proponent, marxism.

The second and last observation I wish to make is that however much these images of a non- (or subordinated) market economy may awaken a certain recognition, the one major attempt in the modern period to think through the meaning of a reinstitution of the household economy at the social level was not a theoretical (or, needless to say, a political or economic) success. Indeed, what emerges from these pages and from the writings they explore are the conceptual difficulties (or perhaps impossibilities) in this attempt to combine the values of autonomy, equality, and individuality (which Marx took over in a transformed fashion from classical liberalism) with a complex and interdependent social-household economy in which the market plays no or only a very subordinate role. Like most great thinkers, Marx, even if he was not able to cement these theoretical potsherds into a cohesive vessel, nevertheless showed us (to change metaphors) the puzzle and its parts. Perhaps, as Roemer has suggested in another context, we stand in the same relation to a theoretical grasp of what such a moral economy would look like as did, for example, the medieval economist in relation to the full-blown industrial capitalist world.[182] Or perhaps it is not possible after all to compose those varied elements into a coherent whole, in which case they might still serve us as markers (made more modest by the recognition of their inability to offer a feasible and better counter to the existing order), tracing the outermost normative boundaries of this economy as well as showing its virtues. What we can say, I think, is that the question of the proper use of wealth, so central to classical Greek reflection on the economy and so clearly developed to show the limits of markets and the chrematistic life, drew Marx onto a path that those ancient thinkers had marked so that

[182] John E. Roemer, "On Public Ownership," Working Paper Series, no. 317 (Department of Economics, University of California, Davis, 1988), pp. 1–2, 4.

we might be brought back to the *oikos*. Marx thought that he could remake the moral architecture of that household, yet still preserve it as an *oikos*. And in that he was wrong. The failure of this century's experiment in advanced nonmarket economies gives us occasion once again to consider the meaning of this long-enduring part of our intellectual inheritance.

CONCLUSION

" THIS HOUSEHOLD IS
WHAT IS COMMON
TO US "

In a poem dedicated to one of the great Marx commentators of the postwar world, Octavio Paz wrote that "man is his visions."[1] Few visions have captured the human imagination so powerfully as did Karl Marx's, something itself worthy of investigation. Yet as this century draws to a close, so too does one variant of the debate to which Marx dedicated his life and which has dominated much of our theoretical inquiry and political practice, that concerning market society. We can now state with certainty that Marx, this most forceful and coherent of the critics of capitalism, was unable to provide the materials on which to found a feasible and superior alternative to the society he rejected. Or it may be, as we suggested at the end of Part Three, that it was not Marx's failure at all; perhaps it is the case that whatever the limitations of the economic institutions he so criticized, there is no feasible alternative that satisfies the desiderata he set out. The difficulties evident in analyses that seek to retain the autonomy requirement together with some version of marxian socialism (usually a variant of the idea of common ownership of the world together with its corollary of joint and *ex ante* decision making

---

[1] Octavio Paz, "Kostas Papaioannou," in *The Collected Poems of Octavio Paz, 1957–1987*, trans. Eliot Weinberger (New York: New Directions, 1987), p. 543.

over the economy, that is, the plan in one guise or another) drive to the conclusion that this failure cannot be laid at Marx's feet alone and that it is rather entailed by the central concepts themselves. I use these pages to reflect one final time on the family of theories to which Marx belonged, theories of the household as a counter to the world of the emporium and to market society generally. This Conclusion is therefore a coda to Part Three, recapitulating its principal themes. And as such it begins with Marx, his failures and the residual value of elements of his system; but it uses Marx as an anteroom to thinking about the grand household that is the economy and its place in the moral architecture of our communities.

Let me begin by adapting an argument presented by G. A. Cohen on self-ownership and socialism. Cohen wants to preserve what he finds intuitively attractive in the classical liberal argument (here represented by Nozick)—that is, the idea of self-ownership as a way of expressing freedom—without following the Nozickean/Lockean road to (private) ownership of the external world. The alternative he explores is thus a world in which individuals retain the personal freedom of liberalism but in a jointly owned external environment. Cohen's question is whether there is substantive freedom in such a world or merely the socialist analogue to the "formal" freedom of bourgeois society? The question virtually invites this answer: insofar as substantive freedom must also involve control over external goods, and insofar as that control is exercised (in this jointly owned world) through, let us say, a democratic decision-making procedure, it is the case, he concludes, that substantive freedom is limited here, and in fact amounts to little more than the formal, liberal type of freedom, so roundly condemned by marxists. That is, the power to do "as one has a mind to" is conditioned by the activities and decisions of others, the capitalist in the one instance, the democratic body in the other, with the familiar freedom-threatening problems inherent in the latter.[2] On the one side, this argument suggests that since Nozick's rather emaciated theory of self-ownership/autonomy allows as free the sale of labor in a capitalist labor market, it ought also to be untroubled by the types of interdependencies found in socialism thus defined. But what it

[2] See Gerald A. Cohen, "Self-ownership, World-ownership, and Equality" (Part I), in Frank S. Lucash, ed., *Justice and Equality Here and Now* (Ithaca: Cornell University Press, 1986), and "Self-ownership, World-ownership, and Equality: Part II," in E. F. Paul et al., eds., *Marxism and Liberalism* (Oxford: Basil Blackwell, 1986). Other critiques in a similar vein include Jeffrey Reiman, "Exploitation, Force, and the Moral Assessment of Capitalism: Thoughts on Roemer and Cohen," especially pp. 40–41, and Allen E. Buchanan, "The Marxist Conceptual Framework and the Origins of Totalitarian Socialism," in Paul et al., eds., *Marxism and Liberalism*.

also shows, Cohen writes, is that marxists must give up the (absolute) idea of self-ownership if they are to retain the notion of a jointly owned world, conceding thereby the incoherence of two central marxian desiderata: individual freedom with a socialized or jointly owned and governed external world as its precondition. For that reason, among others, the promise that stands at the center of Marx's project, that in the words of the *Journal* of the Communist League "in no social order will personal freedom be so assured as in a society based upon communal property," has been shown to be unredeemable.[3]

In a practical mirror of these theoretical failures, attempts in our century to institutionalize "communal property" in the form of a planned economy have been, without exception, accompanied by high levels of restraint and unfreedom.[4] Undoubtedly some major part of this outcome is best explained by factors specific to the countries, parties, and individuals involved. My interest, however, is (by moving into a larger conceptual compass than the one that circumscribes the Cohen argument) to think about the sources of that failure of marxism (and the wellspring of its achievements as well); in other words to consider more sweepingly the conceptual family of which that doctrine is but one moment. As we attempt to trace those sources, we are at once confronted with the theoretically disappointing fact that Marx himself was a poor guide in showing why we should accept his claim that the desiderata he set out could be put in motion in some feasible world. What is striking is that he does not appear even to have seen the need to think through the problem of a nonmarket, nondespotic, and complex, interdependent society. It is difficult, exceedingly difficult in fact, to account for this momentous silence. It is certainly not the result of a romantic antiquarianism: Marx knew that Robinsonades were children's fairy tales, that the individual (household) economies of the precapitalist world had given way to the "social" economy, and that that development could not be reversed (and that such a reversal, if it were possible, would be undesirable). More telling still, Marx, in his observations on the microeconomy of capitalist production, saw that in the absence of the "silent compulsion" of markets (which nevertheless allowed, relatively speaking, a "wide field" of choice), other mechanisms would fill the vacuum, in order to coordinate production, collect information, prevent free-riding, and induce work of sufficient

---

[3] Quoted in Arthur Lipow, *Authoritarian Socialism in America* (Berkeley: University of California Press, 1982), p. 1.

[4] See Serge-Christophe Kolm, "Introduction à la réciprocité générale," *Information sur les sciences sociales* 22 (1983): 576–77.

intensity and duration. This recognition ought to have (at least) suggested to him one of the central problems of the society he foresaw replacing capitalism, that is, a nonmarket, noncoercive coordination of complex, interdependent activities.

If Marx was not an antiquarian in the sense of imagining a return to some gilded precapitalist past, he was, as we have said, profoundly indebted to the past, and above all to the Aristotelian critique of markets and to its conception of the *oikos* economy. Modern revolutions, Marx wrote, must "draw their poetry from the future"; yet his own project is deeply rooted in a way of thinking about the economy, about labor, time, and community, which predated modernity. That idea of the economy embedded in the noneconomic institutions of the community, subordinated to its purposes, and relieving persons from the unfreedom of the economic realm, and its contrast with an autonomous, surplus-driven market economy, clearly captured Marx's imagination and informed his theorizing about capitalism and socialism. I have discussed the details of the relationship between Marx's and Aristotelian economic thought in the preceding pages. Here I want to observe that it was precisely this neo-Aristotelianism that determined, in its broad outlines, the conundrum at the heart of his life's project. In Aristotle, Marx found not only a framework for thinking about economic formations according to their governing end, not only the conceptual elements for challenging and going beyond classical liberalism in reflecting on freedom and the economy. Marx also discovered there, he thought, a solution to the dominant type of unfreedom which he attributed to the capitalist economy. Counterintuitive as his appropriation may be at first blush, because it involved a return to the idea of the despotic-household model, this aspect of Aristotelian economics provided Marx with an alternative conception of an "embedded" and contained economy. Marx thus considered that he had uncovered, in these ancient texts, an answer to a very modern concern: the problem of freedom. He knew, though, that the Aristotelian household economy answered the problem of freedom in a way deeply at odds with some of the most dearly held commitments of modernity, his own among them. In place of the "silent" discipline of the market, it offered the commands of the *oikos* despot; for the preferences of all, the governing preferences of the free household members or of the master; and for the impersonality (equality) of market actors, the hierarchical, status-derived order of the household. In that sense, its viability as a moral and economic unit rested, unashamedly, on the denial of freedom and the good life for many of its members. Marx thought that unfreedom in the *oikos* was driven in large measure by scarcity, by the need to allocate limited goods, time perhaps the most important of all, in a manner that secured the greatest possible freedom for some. That being the case, a (relative) solution to the problem of scarcity, such as was made feasible by the technological revolutions of capitalism, promised a new household economy, now social in scale and without domination. This is, in sum, Marx's neo-Aristotelianism: the attempt to graft the most ancient model of nonmarket economies onto the core liberal values of autonomy—indeed, to assert that the former is the precondition for the full realization of the latter.

So far I have traced and recapitulated the central difficulties in this marriage of two traditions, the ancient Greek and the marxist ones. These are the cramped definition of scarcity, the too great faith in technology, and, most important, the failure to point to a mechanism that could coordinate the nonmarket economy without itself reproducing the despotic features of the *oikos*. These failures, and above all the last-mentioned one, are not to be counted Marx's alone. They represent rather the difficulty or impossibility of wedding the Aristotelian model of the nonmarket economy subordinated to the (noneconomic) needs of its members with the idea of a "free association" in which "the free development of each is the condition for the free development of all."[5] But we should temper our zeal in concluding from this that classical liberalism and its expression in market society have decisively won the day. For the questions that Marx, and through him Aristotle, have placed on the agenda are not so readily dismissed, even if, as is now fully apparent, the major attempts in this century to establish a more or less completely nonmarket society have collapsed both conceptually and practically. These questions can be grouped under three headings: (a) meta-economic, setting an ethical framework in which to embed thinking about the economy, (b) freedom and the economy, exploring the possibilities of freedom and constraints on it, beyond the contractarian approach, and (c) the critique of market society. In the pages that follow, I sketch the issues raised under each of these headings.

(a) The meta-economic approach at the theoretical core of this neo-Aristotelianism seeks to embed the study of the economy in a higher-order framework, one that has a conception of the good and its enabling conditions at its center. The argument here is that the reduction of eco-

---

[5] Marx, *Communist Manifesto*, in *Karl Marx and Frederick Engels: Collected Works* (New York: International Publishers, 1975–), vol. 6, p. 506.

nomic science to the study of efficiency, of how to produce more with less, of revealed preferences, and of a thin rationality employed in the pursuit of those preferences detaches that study from the most important questions put before us by our existence as *homo oeconomicus*. The fact that the economy is a constellation of institutions through which are transacted not only things but human activity and time; that it is one central element of the means by which humans seek to secure whatever noneconomic ends they may set for themselves; and that, finally, it is the forum in which much of the human interchange with nature is conducted—these properties, which combine to yield a picture of relations internal to the economy (relations of production and distribution), of the location of the economy in relation to other goods and of the human intercourse with nature, compel us to reflect on the economy from a higher vantage point, one that transcends the customary horizons of economic theories as well as those of theories of distributive justice. And that vantage point must allow us to set the economy in an overarching moral/political context, in which the provisioning of human beings is subordinated not only to the principles of the distribution of things, but also to the end(s) the economy ought to serve.

That modern economic science has lost sight of the (noneconomic) context of the object it studies is, for Marx, both its limitation and a reflection of the peculiar shift in the location of the economy that gave birth to it. The move from *oikonomikē,* from the study of the ordering of the members of the household, their aims and the material and human means for securing them, to modern economics is, in Marx's account, the move from a theory of freedom and the good life, with economics as one of its elements—and correspondingly from a needs-driven economy to an all-embracing theory of the creation of surplus and to an economy "indifferent," except in an indirect (via its determining purpose, profit) and limited (by effective demand) way, to the satisfaction of human need. The autonomy or separation of economic theory from a conception of the good mirrors, in Marx's view, the freedom from human control of economic phenomena under capitalism. The call for a moral economic science of this new yet still very ancient kind is, conversely, a call for an "embedded" economy; thus the contribution, and the danger.

(b) I have argued that Marx, unlike the ancients, sought the good to be secured by the economy not in some notion of the activities of a good life, but in autonomy, in the power of disposition over oneself. That is true, but it is also the case that in seeking to understand freedom and its relationship to the economy, Marx again turned to Aristotle and, once more, the neo-Aristotelian economics that emerged from this encounter left a fertile set of ideas and questions. At the heart of this aspect of Marx's thought is the idea that fundamentally molding the scope of freedom is the human interchange with nature: that humans must produce and reproduce the conditions of their existence. And that process involves them in the "grim poverty" of toil, which is, among other things, a poverty of freedom. The expansion of freedom is accordingly won in a struggle with nature, a struggle for time away from necessary production and in which the principal weapons are technology. "Economy of time, to this all economy ultimately reduces itself": control over one's own time and therefore activity is thus simultaneously a way of speaking about wresting ourselves from nature's grip and redistributing freedom (understood here as the allocation of leisure among persons). Poverty, then, is constraining in a twofold sense: in the labor to which it forces the person and in the subordination, even via contract, to another. In sum, the notion that it is the (malleable) restrictions on freedom as autonomy, whatever their provenance, that matters and that the economy, both as interchange with nature and among humans themselves, is a principal locus of unfreedom—these ideas stand at the center of Marx's turn from the traditional political philosophical concern with justice to his critique of political economy. In so doing, Marx pressed our understanding of the moral significance of the economy beyond the limits of the contractarian approach and, relatedly, raised questions about the limits of the liberal understanding of freedom.

(c) Marx's critique of capitalism moves along many lines, and here I have selected just one, which, however, I take to be the dominant and most interesting avenue. This critique, which focuses on the ways in which freedom is diminished in a capitalist economy, shows clearly the intellectual juncture occupied by Marx. Committed to a fundamentally liberal ethic of autonomy, he develops a neo-Aristotelian critique of the unregulated, growth-oriented economy and of its claim to embody a rich freedom in its economic institutions. From this critical engagement emerges Marx's theory of communism as the new household economy.

To liberalism (in its Lockean form), Marx concedes the achievement of having erected barriers to direct coercion, of transforming humans into self-owners among whom relations of authority or power can be established only through consent or contract. He then sets out to demonstrate that the institutional context in which liberal self-ownership is located substantially diminishes this achievement. Marx's strategy is, in the first instance, to extend our understanding of the sources of constraint beyond those that occupied the founding liberals—that is, direct, especially governmental, coercion—to structural constraints said to inhere in pervasive markets of the capitalist type. These constraints are, broadly speaking, the consequence of competition-imposed survival/expansion requirements for both firms and individuals. Overall, they substitute a systemically induced purposiveness, economic expansion (ΔM), for the purposiveness of individuals or communities. That characteristic, as we have seen, is for Marx the source alike of capitalism's revolutionary dynamism and of its indifference to human needs, and especially those radical needs the satisfaction of which it itself makes possible for the first time. Phrased negatively, unfreedom in a pervasive market society takes the form (particularly in the labor market) of a reduced choice set, one that effectively excludes the non-sale of labor for one segment of the population and counteradaptive (nongrowth) behavior for others. The pervasiveness of contract in this society masks these constraints until (as in *Capital*, vol. 1, chap. 33) an alternative baseline is offered. That is one facet of Marx's analysis of freedom. A second variant is cast at the level of the community: here the claim is that the aggregate consequence of individual decisions is the setting in motion of natural lawlike forces that rob the community of the power to control its destiny. The anarchy of the market, which is one way of unpacking the emancipation of individual economic activity, yields unfreedom, a perverse consequence most dramatically displayed for Marx in economic crises.

The force of Marx's questioning of the liberal concept of freedom resides not in a denial of its importance, but just the opposite: in his adoption of one of its core desiderata, autonomy or disposition over oneself, followed by his critique of the limited liberal definition of it and then, last, in his argument that the dominant liberal economic institution, the market, works against autonomy. The "disembedding" of the economy, that central element of the liberal project, the transferring of its decisions to individual self/external world owners with contract as their nexus, is thus accepted as a major transformation, normatively and positively, in the human economy—a watershed especially evident when that economy is contrasted to antecedent formations. Marx, at his best, traces the limits of the freedom secured in this process of "disembedding." These limits are revealed, as I have just said, in the perverse consequences of the market, in the constraints imposed by pervasive markets, entitlements, and a certain pattern of asset distribution and, at the microlevel, in the market-generated hierarchies within the firm/factory. After Marx, and after the questions he placed on the philosophical/political agenda, it is difficult to cling to the classical contractarian account of autonomy, unfolded into economic liberalism. For the definition of direct coercion as the only (morally interesting?) source of unfreedom now seems artificially constrained and counterintuitive, whether in the original Lockean (see the *Venditio* manuscript) account or in Nozick's "moralized" historical justification.[6] And the Kantian emphasis on autonomy, in its intentional foundation of action with its virtual disregard of natural and other constraints on the power to choose, may be exhilarating in its Stoic sublimity, but it also seems too thin after Marx. In these versions of liberalism, the near-complete dismissal of consequentialist arguments, foremost among them that argument which works the enhancement or diminution of freedom into the consequences to be employed in the normative evaluation of economic regimes, rests ill with the claimed centrality of autonomy.

In other respects, too, Marx's challenges retain their power. His picture of an unrestrained growth economy, driven to ignore the nonprofit-yielding needs of human society and nature, and the resulting imperative to subordinate the market to political regulation, is now a widely accepted part of our ethos, and that across political lines. In measures such as the Ten Hours' Bill, Marx saw society responding against the market, and he read from those developments the heralding of a future in which the market would be completely dissolved as an autonomous institution. Where that future arrived, it did so in a form that recreated and magnified the evils of the despotic household economy: a "vast *oikos*" indeed, but of a type having more in common with the patrimonial/patriarchal regimes of the tzars—in which the country, its persons, and wealth were extensions of the ruling household—than with anything Marx may have imagined. In the democratic world, parts of that future came into being as issues of social justice, and concerns for the environment and quality of life called into play increased political interventions against the market. Marx's intuition that in the Ten Hours' Bill he heard the herald of a new, nonmarket world was thus not entirely off the mark: incompletely, in piecemeal fashion, and in uncomfortable coexistence with markets, elements of the response he foresaw did materialize. In short, the idea that markets would fail normatively, that is, would produce consequences antithetical to the human good, and that these failures would draw the community "once more" to control its economy by conscious,

[6] I take the term "moralized" from G. A. Cohen, "The Structure of Proletarian Unfreedom," *Philosophy and Public Affairs* 12 (1983): 4.

ex ante deliberation—this thought, so basic to Marx's enterprise, has resonated, theoretically and practically, throughout this century in ways that make the proponents of fully free markets appear to be the true utopians.

It is these questions and arguments that will continue to call us back to Marx, long after those regimes that carried his name have one and all passed from the face of this earth. Three intertwined clusters of ideas are the parts of Marx which, in the silence of the political passions made possible by developments in the (former) Soviet Union, in Eastern Europe, and elsewhere, we can assess for their conceptual worth alone: (1) his attempt to embed the study of the economy in a wider normative and historical context (in, for example, his claim that the focus on labor and time as commodities gives a warping and excessively narrow, economic definition to them); (2) his efforts to push the idea of autonomy beyond the contractarian confines and to see constraints emerging from the two pillars of classical liberal economic theory, self-ownership and ownership of the external world; and (3) his analysis of the perverse consequences of an economic system driven to unlimited growth. It will, however, be clear to the reader that the above catalogue is a selective list of what may be of enduring value in Marx's bequeathment. What is missing from that survey is the other dimension of the impact of its background, the one that provided the conceptual link to the future such as Marx imagined it would be. That background is again the theory of the *oikos*, now grasped as a world in which need (use-value) and therefore the community predominates, in which the economy is both "embedded" and contained. What I wish to expand on here is the claim that this ancestry, while it helped to prepare the ground for much of what is best in Marx, also contributed powerfully to the conceptual collapse of his system, and thus to the failure of the neo-Aristotelian project in the economic sphere.

Marx's pronouncements, for example that humans have "long dreamed" of a society in which they "once more gain control of exchange, production and the way they behave to one another," intimate as we saw in Part Three the power that the idea of the household economy had over him. We have also traced the more explicit impact of that tradition on Marx's thinking—in his admiration for their reflections on use-value, time, and technology. More generally, we can see in his overarching critique of capitalism and in his portrait of communism the scaffolding that surrounds, simultaneously sustaining and limiting, the critical conceptual core. In the idea of the household economy, Marx discovered a picture of a community not bound together by the cash "nexus," a community controlling the economy and subordinating it to its (non-economic) purposes. In short, he found there a picture of a nonmarket community, one whose very name, the *oikos,* evokes the unity of economy and community with the latter presiding—a community in which its purposes, the character of relations between persons, and the allocation of goods and persons were not determined by market forces. He well understood, as I observed earlier, that standing in for those market forces as the source of coordination was the household master. What is more, Marx knew that the problem of this coordinating mechanism without markets posed no great ethical issues for an Aristotle or a Xenophon: the acceptability of servitude, from slaves, wives, and others, was sufficiently well established that the despotic or command-type character of household administration was not jarring, and it therefore did not generate a theory of a nondespotic *oikos.* Marx ought to have understood that the latter option was not available to him, that wedded as he was to the liberal ethic of individual self-determination, indiscriminately distributed, the problem of how to coordinate economic activity in a manner consistent with that desideratum but without the market vehicle for individual choice and (in the labor market) disposition over oneself was *the* central problem, if there was to be a feasible and superior alternative to capitalism. That this problem is hardly posed in Marx's writings is silent testimony to the thralldom in which he stood to the *oikos* ideal. At times, he seems to come to the edge of the problem, only then to retreat from it. Consider, for example, Marx's comment (discussed above and in the preceding section) that socialism would resemble Robinson Crusoe's world, only in a social form. He means by this that it would be use-value oriented and nonmarket. Marx, in those same pages, also offers a historical illustration of such economic formations, yet when he reached for an analogue to socialism he chose the fantastic one, the target here and elsewhere of his scorn. The reason for this improbable selection, I would speculate, is that because it was a single-actor economy, Crusoe's world allowed Marx to sidestep the issue of noncoercive coordination in an interdependent, nonmarket society. Had he selected another of his precapitalist economies, the patriarchal household for example, he would have been confronted immediately and unavoidably with the question of how socialism would coordinate many persons without a hierarchical, command function and in the absence of a market.

A second, and (perhaps) more generous, reading of Marx is that he assumed that the contained economy of communism would so restrict the domain over which coordination and principles of distributive justice would need to operate that the issues raised by autonomy and coordination in an expansive economic sphere would hardly appear. In that sense, we might see Marx as proceeding from the celebrated passage of Aristotle's *Politics* in which, in a world where shuttles moved themselves, there would be no master or slave, or scarcely a need (we might add) for a coordinating mechanism or principles of distributive justice. The issue of freedom and (economic) interdependence would thus be provided with a technical solution: the shrinking of direct human involvement in the economic domain. To be sure, there would be a residue of necessary engagement in the economy and so, therefore, of direction, compulsion, and so forth, but within dramatically smaller confines. Marx, at times, writes in that manner, and I have discussed these reflections and some of their attendant difficulties in Part Three. It is, I think, clear how unsatisfactory a solution this is. Where it is not utopian in its expectations, it is radically incomplete as a specification of the range of choices that must be made in an economy, even one in which (in this wildly improbable assumption) direct labor actually has been rendered unnecessary (or very nearly so) by labor-replacing technology. As such, it tends to minimize the coordination problems (and their profound normative implications) that would remain, even granting the feasibility of the conditions needed for a contained economy of this type.

One suspects that the overwhelming simplicity and directness of ancient Greek reflection on the household, and the seductiveness of the idea of the economy subordinated to the good life, so deeply entranced Marx that he either did not see that a teaching that had despotism at its center would need radical rethinking if it were to be married to a liberal ethic of autonomy. From the classical Greek conceptual core of use-value, the "embedded" and contained economy, the human interchange with nature, and free time and the economy, Marx managed to extract criticisms of market society that will endure. That same framework fostered a mirage, an illusory solution to the limitations Marx thought he had discovered in capitalism. The failed attempt, at so tremendous a cost, to found an advanced nonmarket society is the denouement of Marx's project, and with it of Aristotle's, at least insofar as Marx carried forward into modernity central elements of the Aristotelian theory of the proper location of the economy. This failure, it is vital to underscore, is most certainly not to say that capitalism emerges unscathed from its encounter with Marx. His voice, and Aristotle's behind it, have captured something—a picture, I suppose, for want of a better word—in which we see a different sort of boundary to market society. I refer here not to the specific critiques of the limits of freedom under capitalism: critiques in which Marx engaged liberalism on its own normative terrain, while invoking in that battle the assistance of ancient economic thought. Those issues I have addressed in some detail above and in Part Three. Rather, what I am speaking of now is a loosely woven collection of ideas, a moral background if you will; some of this background finds expression in Marx's concept of a communist society, other elements of it in classical Greek texts, and still others in a variety of contemporary rejoinders to market society. Together, these ideas may be said to compose a picture of the household as an alternative to markets.

The household: the idea, in our civilization, is of great antiquity, at least as old as its first magnificent literary expression in Homer's *Odyssey*. It is, as we noted, an intensely personal world, colored by the individuals who populate it. The relations between those persons are not determined by economic position but by the "human" aspect of the home: their appropriate positions in the household, their relation to the public world, and to the gods. These relations are anything but impersonal (or neutral, or egalitarian), and contract, with its suggestion of the mutual pursuit of self-interest, is completely alien to the fabric of that society. It is a community bound by affection, the relations of which are characterized, in part, by reciprocity and altruism and in which it is the overarching institution and its values that shape the elements. There is justice here, but no bureaucracy or state to enforce it; distribution, but no market mechanism; human bonds, but no contract; gifts, but no commodities; fairness, but not impersonality. The first explicit contrast between the market and the household is to be found in Aristotle's *Politics*, Book 1. Cleansed of its inegalitarian underpinnings, these passages express the idea of a community and its economy, the echoes of which resonate still. In thinking about this, I have focused principally on Marx, on his theory of communism unfolded as a "vast *oikos*"—of an "embedded" and contained economy dedicated to the satisfaction of noneconomic ("radical") needs. Marx, in other words, set out to imagine an (egalitarian) *oikos*-type economy—nonmarket, *ex ante* control, need-oriented—at the level of social institutions, and for that reason his project, set walking through the world, has echoed perhaps the most loudly. But in other theoretical locales we also hear of the household (or its analogues) as a counter to the market.

The "substantivist" school in economic anthropology is, in an important sense, centered on just that distinction between householding (broadly defined) and market economies, and there is no mistaking the transformational/critical agenda attached to it. Here again the argument is pitched on a macrolevel: the "embedded" economy as against the controlling "market juggernaut," with the emphasis on end-setting (control over the economy) and the negative character of market-induced motivations. The prescriptive side of this current of thought thus comes close to Marx's, though vaguely and in a manner often critical of Marx.[7] More recently, and partially in response to the influence of *homo oeconomicus,* in his market guise, on the study of politics (and especially in response to the use of rational choice/game theoretic models), other aspects of the household ideal have been taken up. Kolm has developed an alternative to both markets and plans in an economy of "general reciprocity," and he has located in the intrafamilial economy a tangible microlevel illustration of the "nœud de réciprocitiés"[8] that would be the heart of the new but nonmarxist household economy. Here it is not the planning function of the household which attracts attention but rather the element of nonmarket exchange, of gift giving and reciprocity. The attractiveness of this idea is also to be seen in Richard Titmuss' remarkable study *The Gift Relationship,* in which the possibility of an altruistic gift economy is extended beyond the intimate society of family or friends to a large-scale anonymous community of persons, for example, blood donors and recipients. That altruism among strangers, and in the absence of face-to-face encounters, is not only possible but that it also produces a more efficient system (than, as Titmuss explains, do commercially driven blood collection systems) for the delivery of needed things may be read as a suggestion of the feasibility of a noncoercive, noncommercial household-type economy at the social level.

If the two currents just mentioned are concerned with a controlled ("embedded") economy as against the autonomous market and with gift/reciprocity-based distribution mechanisms, a third current picks up another strand of the household vision, a strand found in some contemporary feminist literature.[9] Here the emphasis is on the intimacy and affective ties of the household, in which the bonds of obligation are not

[7] The clearest statement of this critical agenda is to be found in Karl Polanyi's "Our Obsolete Market Mentality," in Polanyi, *Primitive, Archaic, and Modern Economies: Essays of Karl Polanyi,* ed. George Dalton (Garden City, N.Y.: Doubleday, 1968), pp. 59–77.

[8] Serge-Christophe Kolm, *La bonne économie: La réciprocité générale* (Paris: Presses Universitaires de France, 1984), p. 58.

[9] See Virginia Held, "Mothering versus Contract," in Jane J. Mansbridge, ed., *Beyond Self-Interest* (Chicago: University of Chicago Press, 1990); Jean Bethke Elshtain, "Feminism, Family, and Community," *Dissent* 30 (1983): 442–49, and Nancy J. Hirschmann, "Freedom, Recognition and Obligation: A Feminist Approach to Political Theory," *Ameri-*

mediated through contract and which leads to a sharply different conception of human motivation and of the cement of society from that of contractarianism. This approach does not concentrate on the planning or control function within the household, the role of the *kurios,* as did the traditional literature from Homer through to Marx. Indeed, it distinguishes itself from that literature, in part, by rejecting the patriarchal household (and the theory that drew from it a model of society) and by looking instead at the mothering relationship as an alternative to contract. And that relationship it contrasts to the market view of social relations (impersonal, nontuistic, egoistic) and to the analogues of the latter in the political sphere: liberal concepts of rights, social-contract theory, notions of political power, and so on. Here, in place of an agenda in which the household is reconceptualized through the use of the language of markets, rights, and contracts, we are confronted with a rejection of that language which readily finds elements of its dominant (antiliberal) discourse in the household and which invites us, again, to extend the relations of that community into the broader one. It is also not difficult to discern traces of this discourse in the communitarian argument, with its critique of markets, atomism, and isolated monads as the malaise of modernity and its longing for "thick" community.

Two of these theoretical paths, that associated with Kolm's theory of general reciprocity and the feminist effort to recover the (nonpatriarchal) household as a critical device, can be read as (in some substantial measure) varied responses to the failures of marxism: to its practical failure (for Kolm) to provide the liberty it promised, to its relative neglect of gender in the second case. In these pages I do not discuss the many differences between those approaches. Rather, in considering them as members of one cluster of theories, I have sought to draw out the centrality of the household idea in the critique of liberalism and of its market expression. In the face of the failure of the experiment with Marx's new household economy, it is difficult to see what route lies before those who would remake the larger community in the image of the household. What is not difficult to discern is the resilience of the idea and the accompanying hostility to markets and, a fortiori, to market society.

I have spoken thus far of the echoes of this *oikos* ideal across a range of

---

can Political Science Review 83 (1989): 1227–44. A more mixed approach can be found in Susan Moller Okin's "Reason and Feeling in Thinking about Justice," *Ethics* 99 (January 1989): 229–49, and in Mary G. Dietz, "Citizenship with a Feminist Face: The Problem with Maternal Thinking," *Political Theory* 13 (1985): 19–37. Will Kymlicka, "Rethinking the Family," *Philosophy and Public Affairs* 20 (1991): 77–97, provides a valuable overview, as well as a critical account of Okin's most recent work on the family.

theoretical/critical enterprises. In my discussion of Marx, I noted another way in which the idea meshes with our perceptions, that is, in the very fact of its familiarity. We know directly of communities without markets, bound by unspoken obligations in which altruism and reciprocity appear to govern and in which cohesion is maintained without coercion. These are our families. And they make so familiar to us some of the principles at work in the *oikos* ideal of society that it is jarring to read the classical liberal authors (Hobbes particularly) bringing the idiom of contract into the household. Still more disconcerting is when the full-blooded econom-ic approach is brought to bear on relations within the household, as for example in Gary Becker's *Economic Approach to Human Behavior.* The disorienting, counterintuitive quality of these analyses produces the-oretically fertile results, for it positively invites us to reflect on the limits of the economic-behavior model applied outside of its obvious do-mains.[10] It is also normatively fertile, for it reminds us of an alternative to market society, and in the same moment it indicates that much of our lives, even we who live in a pervasive market society, is spent in associa-tions governed by very different principles.[11] More than that, the recogni-tion of those principles may also awaken in us admiration, and so corre-spondingly a negative appreciation of markets. The language of gifts, altruism, of the intimacy of the household and of its freedom, both in setting its ends and in the absence of coercion in its relations (at least in the stylized, nonpatriarchal version) is tempting, and all the more so when contrasted with the egotism, the commodification of persons and things, the indifference (neutrality) and coldness of the contrac-tarian/market view of the world. Having yielded to this temptation, it is not a great step to thinking of the grander *oikos,* to attempting to concep-tualize a society ordered according to one or more of the strands that compose the idea of the household.

We begin to understand the limits of liberalism (including its economic regime) by reflecting on households—our own, and those passed down to us in literature and in the tradition of political philosophy. From this contrast between household and market, we learn to question, at the explanatory level, the more universal claims of *homo oeconomicus.* We

---

[10] Gary Becker, *The Economic Approach to Human Behavior* (Chicago: University of Chicago Press, 1976). For very different perspectives see Amartya Sen, "Rational Fools," in Jane J. Mansbridge, ed., *Beyond Self-Interest;* Sen, "Economics and the Family," in Sen, *Resources, Values, and Development* (Oxford: Basil Blackwell, 1984); Jon Elster, *Solomonic Judgements* (Cambridge: Cambridge University Press, 1989) and Elster, *The Cement of Society* (Cambridge: Cambridge University Press, 1989).

[11] See Held, "Mothering versus Contract," p. 304.

also come to doubt the liberal confidence that asserts for its core values and institutions an unchallengeable primacy. Households, we might say, are a part of us: of our experience, of our history and theory, and a part irreducible to the market and its explanatory and normative discourses. From Homer to Aristotle, from Aristotle to Marx and, most recently, feminist theory—all, in their ways, call our attention to this experience, and in their reminders we find an important part of their value. These theoretical acts warning us against a liberal hubris are all the more valuable as the great efforts of modernity to erect the long-held dream of a vast *oikos* on the world stage collapse in ruin.

All the more valuable perhaps, but the temptation to try it again, in some new form, is surely also great; and so too are the stakes high. Little, either in political practice or in the theoretical literature, offers a clear way of marrying the vast household with the crucial good of freedom. In light of the failure of marxism, the burden of proof must surely now be on those who would recreate at the level of the entire community the norms and institutions internal to households. In that sense liberalism is resilient. We understand its outermost boundaries more clearly by thinking through the counterworld of the *oikos*. And after reading Marx we also grasp more fully some of its specific limitations, especially those involving its ideas and institutions of freedom. Yet much as we may recoil from the motivations that markets induce, from the coldness of a regime that celebrates nontuism as one of its cornerstones, and from the (often barely visible) restrictions the market places on autonomy, the market arguably remains a robust institution for securing disposition over oneself. Even when we acknowledge its limits in that latter regard, it is difficult if not impossible to conceive of a superior, feasible alternative to the market. The defender of markets can support her position by reference to more than the impossibility of an autonomy-preserving alternative to markets. For she would argue that hers too is a moral economy, just as "embedded" as the *oikos* variant, but in a different architecture, one that specifies (in its dominant contractarian discourse) the foundation and limits of relations of power between persons and that aims at preserving autonomy against one historically important (and by no means finally banished) form of coercion. Applied to that economic institution which has for so long been the locus of normative concern—that is, the mechanism for appropriating the labor of others—her moral economy specifies a consensual basis, in the interests of all parties, not tainted by status and with an exit option available. She may quite well accept that the labor market is more constraining for its occupants than was (at least for males) the labor-allocation mechanism of the more or less self-sufficient yeoman household or, on an imaginary level, that found on Crusoe's island. She might also concede that a principal source of these constraints, especially of the imperative to sell labor in the first place, is unequal ownership of (control over) the means of production. But because the option put before her in the "new household economy" model is not a return to the yeoman's or Crusoe's world but to a nonmarket social economy, she might ask whether joint ownership of the means of production would not, in fact, merely transfer the source of compulsion (from owners of greater assets to whoever "consciously controls" the economy) rather than eliminate constraints altogether. She could add to this argument that there is a larger issue than simply exchanging one source of compulsion for another: the labor market offers an exit option, if a limited one. Where, she would ask, is an exit option from the sources of "conscious control" if the external world is jointly owned?[12] And finally, in rejoinder to the charge of creating a cold society, motivated by self-interest and indifferent to others, she might respond in the following two ways: (1) That in relations between persons, often strangers in a mass society, and in relation to government, the coldness and impersonality of the market model, its "blindness" in relation to the attributes, beliefs, and so forth of individuals is the key to its neutrality and as well to its nonintrusive nature. (2) That, as even its critics allow, the market and its public analogues do not exhaust the possible or actual forms of human association or motivation. In some domains, they encourage (via reward or punishment) certain types of actions and motivations, but they do not force these on us; in other areas, the family for example, we are free to act in a different manner, from altruism and in a mesh of relationships the underpinning of which is not the interest-generated contract. For that reason, markets are choice-expanding, and objections to them as a threat—to altruism, for example—may amount to covert attacks on the choices that people do make when given options or, as in the case of Titmuss' study, his not very concealed distaste for the consequences of free choice.[13]

[12] The dangers inherent in the absence of a labor market under socialism are discussed in Ugo Pagano, "Single-Firm and Anti-Firm Communism: Contradictions and Evolution in the Marxian Alternatives to Capitalism," in Bernard Chavance, ed., Marx en perspective (Paris: Editions de l'Ecole des Hautes Etudes en Sciences Sociales, 1985), pp. 114–15. See also Claus Offe, Disorganized Capitalism (Cambridge: MIT Press, 1985), p. 64, and Philippe Van Parijs, "Nozick and Marxism [sic] Socialist Responses to the Libertarian Challenge," Revue internationale de philosophie 146 (1983): 356.

[13] See Richard M. Titmuss, The Gift Relationship: From Human Blood to Social Policy (New York: Random House, 1971), especially chap. 14 and p. 242. Kenneth J. Arrow

In the pages of this book, I have sought to show both the power of the arguments just sketched and, in bracketing them with two variants of the *oikos* alternative, to mark out their limits. Some of those limits can be discerned within the horizon of liberal values themselves—and that is part of Marx's project in working through his critique of freedom in market society. Others are visible only when the foundations of market society are seen in the light of another formation, represented here in the idea of the household. At the end of the twentieth century, it hardly needs to be stressed that the outer boundaries of the new household economy are fully apparent when we attempt to see its defining elements writ large and made consistent with freedom. I do not intend this recognition to be an exercise in intellectual evenhandedness. The point is rather that each language captures, in its way, central and not wholly commensurable values. Like Odysseus' Eumaios, some may want, in a sense, to return home: to subordinate the economy to our (*ex ante*) collective will; to live in a society bound not by the cash nexus but by deeper affective bonds; to be part of a community whose members are not transformed into commodities and in which the praxis of the good life triumphs over unbridled growth and profit. It is just that very familiar world that we understand ourselves to have lost, at least in central moments of our existence, and recapturing it stands at the heart of the dream that, as Marx writes, humans have "long possessed." We also know what we have gained in the liberal, contractarian household: not profound, intimate ties, not altruism or the (*oikos*-type) community but a sort of freedom, economic and political, and with that a sort of new community as well. We are in a sense citizens of both these worlds: members of nonmarket, household communities and of larger, more impersonal, and less altruistic associations; members of communities in which reciprocity (and status/gender) largely determines the distribution of goods and tasks and in which the ends of the household's occupants direct the internal economy, and of those where the market allocates these things and aggregates our actions into outcomes not under our control or foresight. We are also theoretical citizens, so to speak, of the household and the market, understanding in turn the normative parameters of the latter through the use of the idea of the household, as well as the horizons of the former in the illumination of

---

develops a similar challenge in his "Gifts and Exchange," *Philosophy and Public Affairs* 1 (1972): 343–62, especially pp. 360–61. For a defense of Titmuss see Peter Singer, "Altruism and Commerce: A Defense of Titmuss against Arrow," *Philosophy and Public Affairs* 2 (1973): 312–20.

the market. Neither of these domains rests easily with the other, neither in theory nor in the world. Resistance to conceptualizing the household in the language of markets and contracts, despite the voluntaristic and anti-status underpinnings of that discourse, and the inability (impossibility?) to think through the extension of the household's institutions and motivations into the public realm without loss of liberalism's (arguably) attractive features—these intimate the radical incommensurability of the two worlds we occupy in thought as well as in our lives. Marx's attempt to unite them, the most profound and thorough such attempt yet ventured, is, in its failure, a salutary warning against optimism in this regard. We can, however, predict that the exhaustion of the one major effort of modernity to assert the household over the market has not forever ended the contest. Nor can it, I imagine, be ended. For perhaps our home must necessarily count among its members Homer, Aristotle, and their modern descendants as well as Locke and his: the world of the *oikos* and of the market.

INDEX